WATCHING BRITISH DRAGONFLIES

Watching British Dragonflies

Steve Dudley,
Caroline Dudley
and
Andrew Mackay

SUBBUTEO NATURAL HISTORY BOOKS

A DIVISION OF CJ WILDBIRD FOODS LTD

www.wildlifebooks.com

Subbuteo Natural History Books
A Division of CJ Wildbird Foods Ltd
The Rea, Upton Magna, Shrewsbury SY4 4UR

CONTENTS

ACKNOWLEDGEMENTS

We embarked on this book (and its forthcoming sister volume *Watching British Butterflies* [in prep.]) in the early 1990s. At first it was no more than an idea between ourselves and our friends, Tim and Margaret Benton. Between us we started to gather detailed site information for dragonflies and butterflies. Realising the resource we were collecting, and also realising how much a modern field guide to the dragonflies of Britain was needed, we set out on the road to write this book. Tim and Margaret, whilst not wanting to share the burden and responsibility of being authors, continued to support our work by feeding us with new site information throughout the project.

At an early stage it was obvious that we needed an artist, and we were relieved when our first choice, Andy Mackay, agreed to join the project. Andy was already an accomplished bird artist, and we knew that his style would be suited to the detail needed to accurately illustrate both dragonflies and butterflies. Andy has provided a stunning set of illustrations which rival any insect illustrations in print.

Our many years of site visits and data collection have been largely spent alone, or on trips with Tim and Margaret Benton. On the way we met and befriended many other dragonfly and butterfly watchers and thank them for their time and company and for the information which they freely shared with us; they have assisted the production of this book greatly.

We would like to pay particular thanks to Eric and Lesley McCabe and to Ian Rippey. Eric and Lesley joined us in the field on a number of occasions, and also provided invaluable assistance with Scottish localities, as well as many constructive comments when the book was in draft form. Ian undertook a similar role for Northern Ireland. Without Eric, Lesley and Ian's input, the Scotland and Northern Ireland site sections would not be as detailed or as comprehensive as they are.

Steve Hall managed to translate Steve's original site maps into the impressive and detailed maps used throughout the site section.

We would also like to thank Mark Tunmore, Paul Hill and Tim and Margaret Benton for providing comments on earlier drafts.

Andy would also like to pay particular thanks to Tim Benton, David Dell, Steve Dudley, Jeff Higgott and Eric McCabe for the loan of slides and photographs during the preparation of the colour plates specially commissioned for this book.

Steve Dudley, Caroline Dudley and Andrew Mackay
June 2007

INTRODUCTION

This book is concerned solely with the flying adult stage of the dragonfly. Other guides, for example *The Dragonflies of Great Britain and Ireland* (Hammond, Harley Books, 1985) and *Field Guide to the Dragonflies and Damselflies of Great Britain and Ireland* (Brooks, British Wildlife Publishing, 1997), provide information on larval stage of the life cycle and identification of dragonfly larvae.

In this book, we refer to damselflies and the larger, true dragonflies collectively as 'dragonflies'.

Watching British dragonflies

Watching dragonflies in Britain is an easy and enjoyable pastime, the sheer spectacle and their theatrical behaviour of these often brightly coloured, jewel-like insects can be completely absorbing.

Little specialist equipment is required other than a pair of binoculars (preferably close-focusing), a good field guide and waterproof footwear. Most species found in Britain are approachable with care, and all can be identified without needing to be caught and examined in the hand (this should in any case be undertaken only by experienced people and usually only for confirming of the presence of a difficult-to-identity species at a site).

Few people live far from a good dragonfly site. Indeed, streams, ponds, canals, lakes, rivers, and other water bodies and courses will hold some species. The commoner species are readily seen at such sites, but many species have more specific habitat requirements, are found in certain parts of Britain or at only a handful of sites. So the ability to travel is really the only other requirement you need if you wish to see species which do not occur in your area.

Your first glance through a dragonfly field guide can be daunting – there may seem to be little difference between one species and another. But there are fewer than 50 species, including vagrants, to contend with (the birdwatcher has over 500!), and while at first many species may appear similar, careful observation of the relevant features of any dragonfly should ensure the correct identification.

As with any new wildlife hobby, read up on the common species first, and get to know them. Visits to local nature reserves and walks along suitable stretches of waterway – streams, canals or rivers – will introduce you to the species of your local area. Spend time observing their different field characteristics – colour, flight, habitat preference, and so on. All these are clearly detailed in the species accounts of this book. The best places to go initially are small ponds or lakes where you can get to the water's edge easily, without trampling vegetation. Some reserves have raised walkways through the best areas.

Dragonflies are least active during the cooler parts of the day – early morning and evening – and they are then easier to approach, and, if disturbed, should fly only a short distance before settling. Even on a warm summer's day, it will still take many species until around 10am to get sufficiently warm to go about their daily rituals of breeding and feeding. In the evening, many species will become much less active after 6pm. Getting close to the insect is the key to successful identification, study and photography.

During the heat of the day, dragonflies are at their busiest, and the males of some species will then rarely perch. Water bodies, bankside habitats and nearby sheltered spots are alive with feeding and breeding insects. A pool that was largely deserted during the morning can be alive by noon, with swarms of damselflies dancing over the water surface and battling darters and chasers over the open water and along the water's edge, while the odd emperor or hawker might steam through much like a Lancaster Bomber. On the hottest summer days, however, activity can be greatly reduced as the insects must avoid overheating. Some species, such as the darters, will also combat overheating by standing on tip-toe and pointing their abdomen tips vertically towards the sky (known as the 'obelisk' position). This reduces the surface area exposed to the sun and so prevents the insect from overheating.

The ability to closely approach a settled insect will depend on several factors, but will improve with experience. Clothing, equipment and technique all play a part. Wear light, comfortable clothing of natural colours – greens and browns – so that you don't stand out too much. A peaked or brimmed hat is essential to keep the heat of the sun off your head (neck and shoulders) and the sun's glare out of your eyes – particularly useful when using binoculars or a camera.

As your interest advances, the following equipment will also be useful:

- Telescope – a 60mm spotting scope with 20x or 30x (wide-angle) eyepiece is very useful for watching insects perched in trees or for viewing water bodies which you cannot get close to.
- Thin stick or pea cane – several species will readily perch on sticks placed in suitable positions for easy viewing or photographic opportunities.
- Camera – the advent of digital photography has made it easier than ever to record all aspects of the hobby, from habitats to individual insects – all with the same compact digital camera. You can even combine some compact digital cameras with a good spotting scope (with wide-angle eyepiece) to 'digiscope', which allows you to photograph more unapproachable species, insects sat high up in bushes and trees or perched on reeds in water.
- OS map of the area.
- Compass.

- Hand-held Global Positioning System (GPS) unit.
- Insect repellent – vital at some sites.
- Sleeveless activity vest (multi-pocketed) – a great way of carrying all those small items such as sunglasses, camera, etc.
- Notebook and pencil.
- Sun cream (keep it topped up), sunglasses and sunhat.

Dragonflies

As long ago as the Carboniferous period, dragonflies graced the skies of our planet, including the largest dragonfly ever known, which had a wingspan of over 70cm. Three hundred million years later, over 5000 species are found throughout the world, including the current giants in South America, with an 18cm wingspan. Most species live in the warm tropical regions, but Europe hosts around 120 species, of which 40 regularly breed in Britain and Ireland.

The two distinct types of dragonflies – damselflies (Zygoptera) and the true dragonflies (Anisoptera) – form the insect order known as Odonata.

Damselflies are relatively small, thin, delicate-looking insects with four similarly shaped wings (which have different venation from that of the true dragonflies). They generally have a fluttery flight low over the water surface and tend not to wander too far from the breeding areas, preferring to keep close to waterside vegetation. Their eyes are widely spaced on either side of the head and at rest they fold all four wings back along the length of the abdomen (or at an angle just off the abdomen).

The true dragonflies are made up of the medium-sized and large species such as darters and hawkers. Their abdomens are robust, sometimes quite broad or flattened and they are stronger fliers than damselflies. Darters, chasers and skimmers perch in sunny locations on a twig, plant stem or similar vantage point (or on open ground) from where they undertake rapid dashes to catch their prey or defend their territory. Hawkers are large, powerful dragonflies with long abdomens and are noted for their tireless patrolling in search of prey or a mate. The hindwings of dragonflies are broader than the forewings and both pairs are held at right angles to the body in what people think of as the true dragonfly shape. The eyes usually meet at some point in the middle.

It is not surprising for a family of insects that has seen little structural change in 300 million years that their flight technique is relatively primitive compared to that of other insects. Dragonfly wings work independently of each other and rarely reach 30 beats per second. Many other insects have a faster wingbeat (bees' wings reach up to 300 beats per second). Yet dragonflies are extremely agile fliers, managing complex manoeuvres to catch their prey on the wing, some species reach speeds of up to 20 miles per hour.

The life cycle of dragonflies

This book is dedicated to the final stage of the life cycle of dragonflies. Much of a dragonfly's life is spent underwater where, once hatched from the egg, the larval form matures and increases in size, before finally pulling itself clear of the water to emerge as the flying insect.

Where and how eggs are laid varies among species. Eggs can be laid singly or in groups, inserted into soft plant tissue (dead or alive), onto floating vegetation, scattered freely over the water surface or laid directly into mud or other soft substrate. Eggs come in two shapes: cylindrical and spherical. Cylindrical eggs are are usually laid directly into plant tissue; spherical eggs are usually scattered (often in strings) onto the water surface. The time between egg-laying and hatching varies among species, some eggs hatch within three weeks, some take three months, whilst others remain virtually undeveloped over the winter and internal changes commence only with the onset of spring. Eventually, a prolarva emerges from each egg. For species which lay their eggs below the water surface, this worm-like nymph stage lasts only minutes, as once it is free from the egg case and the plant or soil matter in which the egg was laid, it begins to moult into the more familiar larva. For species which lay their eggs above the water surface, the prolarva wriggles to the water on hatching and moults within a few hours. This second stage may last only a few days, and the larva may not even feed. This is the first of a series of moults which takes place as the insect increases in size and matures.

As the underwater larva matures, it will shed its skin up to 15 times before it is ready to emerge as an adult. The amount of time it takes a larva to mature depends on the species, food availability and on water temperature – individuals of the same species will take longer to develop in northern latitudes than in the south. Some species, such as Emerald Damselfly, overwinter at the egg stage and the larvae take only three months to mature, whereas Golden-ringed Dragonfly larvae take between two and five years to mature depending on food availability and water temperature.

Dragonfly larvae are formidable predators, killing and eating anything of suitable size that ventures close enough – some of the large dragonfly larvae regularly take small fish. Species which live in the sediment at the bottom of the water body or watercourse are well concealed and catch their prey using the element of surprise. Species that live amongst the underwater aquatic vegetation, on the other hand, actively stalk their prey. Dragonfly larvae have specially adapted mouthparts which allow the lower jaw to be 'spat out', rather like a spear, at their prey.

When it is time to transform into a flying adult insect, the larva must first pull itself clear of the water. Most species will climb up plant stems or onto the bank.

Some, such as Downy Emerald, will climb waterside trees, and emerge several metres up in outer branches overhanging the larval pool. Emergence usually takes place in the early morning, but some species emerge throughout the day, and others (such as hawkers) emerge at night. Most species emerge vertically but those that emerge on the bankside, on rocks or floating leaves emerge horizontally.

Once the outer skin has dried out, the body of the larva begins to split behind the head and the adult starts to emerge, head first. As it wriggles free of the dead skin, the adult falls backwards and hangs vulnerably upside down, with the lower part of the abdomen still within the dead skin. From this position, the emerging insect must gather the energy to raise its head, body and upper abdomen so that its strengthening legs can take hold of the same stem that the larva climbed. Once upright, and maintaining a firm grip, the newly emerged adult dragonfly must dry off, and pump fluid through the veins in its wings to expand them to their full size. The emergence process takes between one (damselflies) and three (larger dragonflies) hours to complete. This is a very vulnerable time as the defenceless insect is open to predation from other insects and birds. The empty larval case left clinging to the plant stem is called an exuvia, most of which can be identified to species with practice.

The first flight of the young adult dragonfly is on shimmering, unsteady wings. Many fly a short distance away from the emergence pool to a nearby sheltered area – a stand of tall grass, a hedgerow or bushes. Some species, however, head straight for the skies to disperse on air currents, sometimes covering many miles. This dispersal is vital for species that breed in static pools and ponds which are prone to drying out or, in modern times, to prevent losses when aquatic habitats are damaged or destroyed by human activities.

The dragonfly is now in its 'teneral' stage, during which it gains full coloration and matures sexually. During the early part of this stage, immature of both sexes resemble adult females. The amount of time it takes to attain mature adult colours and become sexually active depends on the species, the weather and food availability, but on average takes around a week.

For the first few days the flight remains weak and unsteady and the wings are clearly shiny and more reflective than those of the mature adult (this is caused by the fluid used to pump up the wings to full size remaining between the upper and lower wing membranes). The teneral stage is spent away from water, in the shelter of trees, bushes or long grass, and both sexes feed and roost together wothout showing any territorial or sexual behaviour.

Once sexually mature, the fully coloured adults return to water. Males usually return first as they mature more quickly. From this time on, the breeding cycle recommences. The breeding behaviour of different species varies considerably. The males of some species vigorously defend a territory – a stretch of water or bank – from males of the same species, while other species show no such territorial behaviour.

The mature adult insect must now find a mate, breed and, in the case of the female, lay eggs. Most species of damselflies and dragonflies live for a maximum of three to six weeks – some individuals have been known to live for longer, such as Emperor Dragonflies, which may live for up to 12 weeks. Many adult damselflies die within a week of sexual maturity (two weeks old).

The mating behaviour of species is also varied, but common to all is the 'wheel' (or 'heart') position which the male and female adopt so that the transfer of sperm can take place. The male transfers a packet of sperm from his genitalia near the tip of his abdomen to accessory genitalia at the base of his abdomen which the female then collect with her abdomen tip during the 'wheel' position. Mating takes just seconds in some species but can last several hours in others. Once paired and mated, females begin to lay eggs, in some species guarded by the male. This guarding may take the form of the 'tandem' flight, in which the male's anal appendages remain attached to the back of the female's head and to prevent another male from pairing with her, or he may hover nearby and chases other suitors away.

This is a simplified account of what is a complex subject. More detailed accounts of dragonfly life cycles can be found in other titles.

Behaviour

A feature common to all dragonflies is their ability to catch prey on the wing, although the method of hunting varies. Some species, such as darters and chasers, hunt from a perch, whilst others, such as hawkers, patrol in search of prey. Once a prey item has been selected, the method of capture is the same. As the dragonfly draws up to the prey, it forms a 'basket' with its six legs, the front legs being held wide and the rear legs almost together. The prey item is 'scooped' up in this basket and transferred to the mouth.

Larger dragonflies, such as hawkers, eat their prey in flight, but most species of smaller dragonflies, including damselflies, eat whilst perched. Damselflies take small flying insects, whilst larger dragonflies take butterflies, moths, flies, damselflies and even teneral dragonflies. Feeding for many species takes place away from the water and the breeding areas and, in the case of males, is often undertaken during the afternoon, after they have spent the morning defending a breeding territory and mating.

At the end of the day, a dragonfly must find a safe roost site. For some species, this is away from water in tall grasses, bushes and trees; others take refuge in dense waterside vegetation such as reeds and rushes.

Migration and colonisation

Many dragonflies remain to breed at the waters where they developed as larvae but some species regularly undertake extensive movements, occasionally in large numbers. These migrations are not the outward and return migrations we associate with migrant bird species, but one-way flights away from the larval area. Several medium-sized dragonflies are well known for migrating in large numbers, particularly Four-spotted Chaser and the darters. The largest of these migrations occurred in 1862: around 2400 million Four-spotted Chasers were seen in Germany heading west.

More modest migrations have occurred in modern times. In 1995, more than 1000 Yellow-winged Darters arrived in Britain. With them were much lower numbers of Common, Ruddy, Black and Red-veined Darters and the first Vagrant Darters to be recorded in Britain since 1946. Subsequent summers saw small breeding colonies of Yellow-winged Darters in England, but none became self-sustaining suggesting that our climate is not (yet) suitable for colonisation.

Red-veined Darter is an annual migrant to the south and east coasts of England, and the occasional site records breeding activity. These annual immigrations vary but over time appear to be getting stronger. The exceptionally hot summer of 2006 saw the largest-ever recorded influx with over 800 individuals throughout England, the Scottish borders (the first since the only previous record in 1911) and into Ireland; locally bred, second-generation emergence was recorded at many sites, and for the first time away from southern counties, as far north as Lancashire and Yorkshire (Parr, A. 2007. *Atropos* 30: 26–35). Despite the emergence of what would have been thousands of insects (some single sites recorded hundreds of emerging insects), very few mature adults were noted during the autumn. It appears that recent emergents disperse before reaching sexual maturity (the same dispersal technique that brought so many insects to Britain in the first place and which allows breeding to occur within the same summer), but where they go we simply don't know. This unprecedented breeding may have been due to the exceptional weather, but it may yet prove to be the step this species needs to establish itself as a resident breeding species. Time will tell whether it will still have to depend on the annual arrivals from the Continent in order to sustain its population.

Vagrant Emperor also occasionally reaches Britain, from North Africa and southern Europe, and is the only species of dragonfly to have been recorded from Iceland. Its close relative, Lesser Emperor, was recorded in Britain for the first time as recently as 1996. Within three years, over 22 records (of 25 individuals) had been recorded, including the first confirmed breeding. It now occurs and breeds annually in increasing numbers, as far north as Yorkshire. At least 90 individuals were recorded in 2006, and this species spent only ten years as a national rarity reportable to the Odonata Records Committee. It is now probably best considered as semi-established. We do not yet know, however, how dependent this embryonic population will be on fresh arrivals from Europe.

Another species recently discovered breeding in Britain is Small Red-eyed Damselfly, in 1999. Amazingly this species had never even been recorded here before but, after the publication of an article in the popular insect journal *Atropos*, a small breeding population was found at several coastal sites in Essex. Whilst numbers at most sites were low, the population at one site suggested that colonisation had occurred the year before, or even earlier. A year later, it was found at other Essex localities (including inland sites) and at several sites on the Isle of Wight and by 2006, individuals had reached the River Severn and west Dorset in the west and the north shores of the Humber estuary in the north. This annual range extension indeed suggests that Small Red-eyed Damselfly is a recent colonist. Time will tell just how widespread the species will become throughout Britain and how well established it is as a breeding species. The biggest question regarding its occurrence and spread is, why? Is it in response to changing climate? Or has the species simply undergone an opportunistic range extension, after favourable winds allowed it to cross the North Sea barrier from the Continent, the subsequent colonisation and spread throughout Britain being both natural and straightforward?

Although rare migrant or vagrant species often take the headlines, the range expansion of a now more common British species is also worthy of mention. Migrant Hawker was until relatively recently an uncommon visitor from southern Europe with records known only from extreme south-east England. By the 1940s, however, it occurred throughout counties between the River Severn and The Wash. From the 1970s, the species began to spread slowly west and north, breeding being confirmed in Cornwall in 1991 and in Cheshire in 1993. Migrant Hawker is now relatively common throughout most of south-east England, and not uncommon in England in western counties north to Cheshire and Yorkshire. It is also found along the southern coast of Wales. It can still be classed as a vagrant to the far north of England and to Scotland, and was recorded for the first time in Ireland during 2000 and from Northern Ireland in 2006. The breeding population increases in late summer, boosted by influxes from the Continent, which while varied can number thousands of individuals. In 1982, over 1000 insects were seen in a single coastal woodland in Sussex.

Distribution

At the end of the last ice age, around 14,000 years ago, there were no dragonflies in Britain. As the ice sheet retreated northwards, dragonflies slowly colonised Britain via the land bridge connecting south-east England to continental Europe. It is plausible to suggest that the first to colonise were those species which are now restricted to northern regions, and the most recent to colonise are those now confined to south-east England.

Today, 40 species of dragonfly regularly breed in Britain (plus Irish Damselfly, which breeds in Ireland). Most species have restricted ranges and two things largely influence this: climate and available habitat.

Species such as Black-tailed Skimmer are restricted to southern England, and seem unable to tolerate the cooler conditions of northern England and Scotland. Others, such as Golden-ringed Dragonfly, are concentrated mainly along the south and west coasts of Britain, preferring the milder winters and wetter summers there. Species such as Azure Hawker are found only in Scotland, and, although the exact reason for this is not yet known, it is thought that they are unable to compete against the greater number of species in the south and have developed to survive the harsher climate of northern areas and so maintain an ecological niche.

Most species of dragonfly require specific habitats for breeding and this plays an important role in their distribution. Closely related species, such as Banded Demoiselle and Beautiful Demoiselle, may occur in very different habitats. Banded prefers slow-flowing rivers and canals, while Beautiful breeds in fast-flowing streams and rivers. Banded Demoiselle occurs throughout much of England, Wales and Ireland, but is absent from the higher, wetter, deeper valleyed, faster-flowing river areas, whilst Beautiful Demoiselle shows a bias to the predominantly fast-flowing river areas of south-west England, Wales, southern Ireland and isolated pockets in north-west England and western Scotland. Interestingly, the restricted range in Scotland shows that there is a climatic control on this species' distribution. It is able to breed in the milder western regions, but unable to tolerate the cooler summer conditions of central and northern Scotland, which otherwise hold plenty of suitable habitat. Some species, such as Emerald Damselfly, occur throughout the whole of Britain, and can obviously tolerate a range of temperatures, while Common Blue Damselfly can tolerate a wide range of temperatures and occurs in a wide range of habitats.

The rarest dragonfly species that breed in the British Isles have highly specific climate and habitat requirements. They are at the edge of their breeding range here and are more numerous (often common) in continental Europe. Norfolk Hawker is a classic example. This species occurs throughout much of southern and central Europe, where it breeds in a range of water habitats and shows no strong affinity with any aquatic plant species. It is rare in northern Europe and in Britain it is restricted to the Broadland area of East Anglia, where it breeds only in unpolluted ditches containing Water Soldier, a partially submerged aquatic plant, itself largely confined to East Anglia.

Dragonfly extinctions in Britain

The northwards spread of species such as Migrant Hawker, and more recently Lesser Emperor, could be a direct result of climate change. But regardless of climatic changes, a species is unable to survive, let alone spread, if there are not sufficient suitable water areas in which to breed. Many species have seen their British breeding ranges contract during the last century through loss of available sites (due to drainage or infilling, so that the land can be used for agriculture or development) and habitat degradation (due to pollution, turbidity and bank erosion caused by boating, over-stocking with fish, removal of aquatic vegetation, and eutrophication and algal blooms) and three species, which occurred at only a handful of sites, have been lost entirely. Dainty Damselfly (last recorded in 1952) was lost when its breeding sites were flooded by the sea; Norfolk Damselfly (last seen in 1957) disappeared when its favoured sites dried out; and Orange-spotted Emerald (last seen in 1963) was lost owing to pollution. Dainty and Norfolk Damselflies could be the subjects of reintroduction programmes in the future.

Dragonfly conservation in Britain

The recent colonisation and spread of some species during the last couple of decades coincides with an improvement in the water quality of many of our river systems and other waterways, as well as an increased interest from wildlife groups. Protected areas have long been managed for the benefit of many rare and declining bird species, but this was sometimes at the cost of other, commoner species of bird and other forms of wildlife. The increased public interest in general wildlife has either led to or coincided with better protection of non-bird species – plants, mammals, amphibians, butterflies, moths, dragonflies – and these have benefited through improved management of key sites. The last two decades have seen a huge shift in environmental attitudes and wildlife organisations have received greater public and governmental support, with increases in both membership and funding (from their members as well as from government). During the 1990s, Britain's Wildlife Trust network saw an increase in membership of more than 20%, and the Royal Society for the Protection of Birds (RSPB) saw an increase of over 10%, taking its membership over the one-million mark.

The Wildlife Trusts manage around 2300 nature reserves across Britain and Northern Ireland, and the RSPB manages a further 150 reserves, covering over 250,000 acres. Many other sites are also protected for wildlife and plantlife – National Nature Reserves (managed by Natural England (formerly English Nature), Scottish Natural Heritage, Countryside Council for Wales and the Environment and Heritage Service in Northern Ireland), National Trust sites, Local Nature Reserves (managed by local and/or regional governmental authorities), Wildfowl & Wetlands Trust reserves, Forestry Commission sites, plus many privately owned or managed sites. The number of protected sites, and total area covered by then, is ever increasing – from a small stretch of stream looked after by local residents, to the vastness of an open highland moorland owned and managed by a national conservation body.

Designation of a site as protected is not on its own enough to conserve Britain's wildlife. The correct management regime must be put into practice for a diverse wildlife habitat to thrive. Gone are the days of single-species management, which often saw the exclusion, and sometimes loss, of other animals along the way. The relationships among different species and wildlife groups are now better known and understood. This improved knowledge has been used well and Britain's dragonfly populations have benefited enormously.

The individual can also play an important role in dragonfly conservation. Gardens which hold a pond, large or small, will nearly always attract dragonflies, many of which will breed if conditions are right. A good dragonfly pond should grade from deep water to marginal shallows to well-vegetated shores (for details of how to create and care for a wildlife pond see *Dig a Pond for Dragonflies*, British Dragonfly Society – see p. 335 for address). Your back garden pond might hold only a single pair of breeding dragonflies and several pairs of damselflies, but add all the nation's ponds together, and the garden pond becomes an important national nature resource.

Dragonflies have become more popular with the wildlife-watching public. They are attractive and relatively easy to watch and have long been known as the 'birdwatchers' insect'. Many birdwatchers watch sites which include water, so dragonflies more than any other group take their eye. Indeed, it was through their interest in birds that the authors of this book became interested in dragonflies, butterflies, moths and wildlife in general.

Dragonfly books

Interest in any wildlife group can be maintained only if sufficient literature, in particular field guides, exists. Until relatively recently, dragonflies were served by a handful of largely out-of-date books. For many years *The Dragonflies of Great Britain and Ireland* (Hammond, 1977, Harley Books) was the best guide on offer. This large-format guide, although superb for its day, and the standard reference for nearly 20 years, now looks clumsy and out-dated compared to the greatly improved guides to birds. For many people, the lack of good books prevented them from extending their wildlife-watching hobby. Although several well-produced photographic titles helped, it was not until 1997, with the publication of the groundbreaking *Field Guide to the Dragonflies and Damselflies of Great Britain and Ireland* (Brooks & Lewington, British Wildlife Publishing), that saw dragonfly illustration and field guides matched the high standard already reached by those for birds (and by now butterflies). This title was hotly followed in 1999 by *A Guide to the Dragonflies of Great Britain* (Powell, Arlequin Press) and by a revised edition of *Field Guide to the Dragonflies and Damselflies of Great Britain and Ireland*. These two new titles quenched the immediate thirst for modern guides to dragonfly identification. In 2006, a sister volume to *Field Guide to the Dragonflies and Damselflies of Great Britain and Ireland* was published, and the *Field Guide to the Dragonflies of Britain and Europe* (Dijkstra & Lewington, British Wildlife Publishing) will be the standard European guide for many years to come.

While birdwatchers had books dedicated to where to go and see birds, insect watchers had none, relying almost entirely on word of mouth and articles in wildlife magazines. In 1996 the first insect site guide arrived in the form of *Butterflies and Dragonflies: a site guide* (Hill & Twist, Arlequin Press). Predictably, this small guide proved immediately popular; an updated version covering more sites was published in 1998, but was soon out of print.

Watching British Dragonflies (and the sister volume *Watching British Butterflies* [Dudley, Dudley & Mackay, in prep.]) brings together for the first time the field guide and the site guide. The two projects (dragonflies and butterflies) began in 1994, and over a decade of planning, fieldwork, writing and painting have produced what is hoped will be the two 'ultimate' single 'field books' dedicated to finding, identifying and watching the flying adults of both insect groups.

Your dragonfly records

You can provide important information on dragonfly numbers, distribution and activity by submitting your sightings to the relevant recorders. The British Dragonfly Society (BDS) maintains a national network of dragonfly recorders (see p. 339 for details). On a local basis, you can directly supply details to individual site managers or owners with the information or send details to your local Biological Records Centre. Your records will help to build up a better understanding of individual species' needs in Britain, will help to record a change in distribution (expansion and contraction) and generally help conservation agencies to better manage their sites for dragonflies.

When submitting records, include the species' name, numbers present and activity – including any breeding behaviour such as pairs in tandem, pairs copulating, egg-laying females, emerging adults, exuviae or larvae found (the last three are important in proving successful breeding at any site).

Caring for the countryside

Whenever any of us visits the countryside, we have a direct impact upon it and our presence can put considerable strain on the immediate environment. Some of these pressures, such as trampling of vegetation, leaving litter and damaging fences and walls, are caused by sheer thoughtlessness.

Wherever you are, you should always adhere strictly to the Country Code:

- Enjoy the countryside and respect its life and work
- Guard against all risk of fire
- Fasten all gates
- Keep your dogs under close control
- Keep to public paths across farmland
- Use gates and stiles to cross fences, hedges and walls
- Leave livestock, crops and machinery alone
- Take your litter home
- Help to keep all water clean
- Protect wildlife, plants and trees
- Take special care on the country roads
- Make no unnecessary noise

Birdwatchers have had their own code of conduct for many years. Additions that are appropriate for other wildlife groups are included within square brackets:

- The welfare of the bird [plant, animal or insect] must always come first
- Habitats must be protected
- Disturbance to birds [plants, animals or insects] and their habitats should be kept to a minimum
- If you find a rare bird [plant, animal or insect], think carefully about who you should tell
- Do not harass migrants and rare vagrants
- Abide by the bird [wildlife] protection laws at all times
- Respect the rights of landowners
- Respect the rights of other people using the countryside
- Make your records available to the local and national records committees
- Behave abroad as you would at home

In addition, whilst out dragonfly-watching:

- Do not trample vegetation to reach the waterside or to take photographs
- Take care not to unduly flush any insect (at times, though, flushing is impossible to avoid)
- Do not attempt to catch any insect (unless absolutely necessary for identification and any relevant permissions have been obtained; teneral dragonflies should certainly not be caught as they are particularly easily damaged at this important development stage)
- Be aware of your own safety around water and in boggy habitats

As authors of a book which actively encourages others to go out into the countryside and enjoy our native wildlife, we acknowledge the impact that increased observer interest may have on some sites and the insects at individual sites. Our aim in publishing a book of this nature is to promote a wider and better understanding of our countryside and the wildlife within it. We cannot in any way be held responsible for the actions of others at any of the sites covered in this book and obviously condemn any acts that may cause damage to a site, habitat or insect. It is the responsibility of the individual to ensure that they do not damage the habitat they are in and the wildlife they encounter.

HOW TO USE THIS BOOK

With this book, we have for the first time combined an identification guide with a site guide. This will enable you to decide where you want to go to see dragonflies, what to expect when you get there and how to identify them when you do.

Geographical coverage

This is clearly a guide to British dragonflies. Only one regularly occurring species in the British Isles does not occur in Britain – Irish Damselfly. For completeness, we have therefore included Irish Damselfly in the species accounts and some Northern Ireland sites within the gazetteer section of this guide. The whole of Ireland has also been included on the distribution maps for each species.

Identification Guide

The first of the main sections of the book, the *Identification Guide*, is dedicated to identification of the flying adult stage of each species of dragonfly and damselfly found in Britain. This section is split into two parts.

The first part of the Identification Guide, the **Quick ID Reference Guide** (p. 23), depicts the mature adults (male and female) of each species alongside other members of their group or family. This enables similar species to be compared side by side and should therefore assist identification.

The second part, the **Species Accounts** (p. 39), details the main characteristics of each species, how to separate confusion species, behaviour, habitat and distribution. These accounts appear opposite the specially commissioned colour illustrations. The plates illustrate most forms including age, sex, colour forms, variations, etc. that you are likely to encounter regularly in Britain.

For each resident species, we have included a distribution map. These are based on the maps from the *Atlas of the Dragonflies of Britain and Ireland* (Merritt *et al*, 1996, HMSO) but, where necessary (particularly for species with expanding ranges such as Small Red-eyed Damselfly, which colonised Britain after the *Atlas* was published), we have updated distributions after reviewing periodical literature (e.g. *Atropos*), gathering information from websites (e.g. British Dragonfly Society, county dragonfly sites such as Cheshire Dragonflies and Damselflies – www.brocross.com/dfly/dfly.htm, NBN Gateway – www.searchnbn.net), corresponding with others and using personal knowledge. Small, thumbnail maps cannot be totally accurate and can provide only a representation of the known range of any species.

Site Guide and Site Gazetteer

The remainder of the book is divided into two sections dedicated to sites where you can go and see dragonflies. *Watching British Dragonflies* obviously concentrates on sites around Britain. For completeness, however, we have included Irish Damselfly, so Northern Ireland is included in the gazetteer section.

The first of these sections, the **Site Guide** (p. 134), is a selection of some of the best sites in Britain for dragonflies (at either a regional or national level). All sites in this section are covered by at least a single page, while some larger sites/areas have two pages. Information given includes:

- Site name, county and site owner/manager
- OS Landranger map number
- Six-figure grid reference
- List of species to look for (key species in **bold** type)
- Habitat
- A map of either the location or the site itself
- Detailed description on how to get to the site by car
- Access details, including any specific areas to search
- Timing – when it would be the best time to visit the site
- Other significant wildlife interest or site details

We have attempted to be as accurate with our directions as possible. This has involved extensive fieldwork over many years, visiting sites not only to look at the dragonflies but also to ensure that routes to the sites and locations within the sites were familiar to us so that we could accurately describe them. During our visits, key grid references have been checked using a hand-held Global Positioning System (GPS) unit. This handy device enabled us to pinpoint locations on site. In particular, it allowed us to take references of remote locations that may have been difficult to accurately locate on a map. Each site mentioned includes the relevant OS Landranger map number (or Discoverer Series for Northern Ireland sites) on which to locate it.

The final section, the *Site Gazetteer* (p. 239), details sites by county, and includes not only those known for their local or national dragonfly interest, but those which are good for commoner species. Many of these sites are nature reserves and more information will be available on site. Others are simply water bodies that have public access or public rights of way running by or around them. It is important that you abide by any on-site instructions and visitor arrangements. There are many more sites than can be included in a guide of this nature. Any water body or watercourse with public access is a potential site for you to explore for dragonflies and other wildlife. Try checking out the streams, rivers, canals, ponds and lakes near to where you live and discover what lies on your own doorstep.

When visiting any site (and not just those covered within this guide), please keep strictly to paths and other areas of permitted access. In 'open access' areas (such as moorland), please bear in mind what impact your actions can have on a site and take care not to damage habitats (see pp. 19–20).

We have tried to include information on accessibility for wheelchair users and the quality of paths. Many sites do not have facilities for disabled visitors, but many organisations are now trying to provide at least some sites with paths suitable for wheelchairs and toilets for the disabled.

We have included, where known, information on any charges (admission or parking) and facilities such as visitor centres, cafés and toilets (the last now nearly always cater for disabled visitors).

Please also note that many nature reserves do not allow dogs (even on leads). Some country parks are more tolerant.

If a particular facility is important for your visit, we strongly advise that you contact the site owner/manager (names given for all sites) before your visit for up-to-date information.

The inclusion of any site does not denote right of access to all parts of the site. Please follow any on-site instructions, keep to paths and trails and behave responsibly.

QUICK REFERENCE GUIDE
Your at-a-glance guide to dragonfly topography, flight periods and
side-by-side comparisons of Britain's damselflies and dragonflies

Quick Guide

Quick Guide

FLIGHT PERIODS

	May	Jun	Jul	Aug	Sep	Oct
Demoiselles						
Beautiful Demoiselle		■	■	■		
Banded Demoiselle		■	■	■		
Damselflies						
Emerald Damselfly			■	■	■	
Scarce Emerald Damselfly		■	■	■		
White-legged Damselfly		■	■	■		
Large Red Damselfly	■	■	■	■		
Small Red Damselfly		■	■	■		
Large Red-eyed Damselfly		■	■	■		
Small Red-eyed Damselfly			■	■	■	
Southern Damselfly		■	■	■		
Northern Damselfly		■	■	■		
Irish Damselfly		■	■			
Azure Damselfly	■	■	■	■		
Variable Damselfly		■	■	■		
Common Blue Damselfly	■	■	■	■	■	
Scarce Blue-tailed Damselfly		■	■	■		
Blue-tailed Damselfly	■	■	■	■		
Norfolk Damselfly[1]		■	■			
Dainty Damselfly[1]	■	■	■	■		
Hairy Dragonfly	■	■	■			
Hawker dragonflies						
Azure Hawker		■	■	■		
Migrant Hawker			■	■	■	■
Common Hawker		■	■	■	■	
Southern Hawker		■	■	■	■	■
Brown Hawker		■	■	■	■	■
Norfolk Hawker	■	■	■			
Emperor dragonflies						
Emperor Dragonfly		■	■	■		
Lesser Emperor Dragonfly[2]	■	■	■	■	■	
Green Darner[2]					■	■
Vagrant Emperor Dragonfly[2]	■					■
	May	Jun	Jul	Aug	Sep	Oct

Quick Guide

	May	Jun	Jul	Aug	Sep	Oct
Club-tailed Dragonfly	■	■				
Golden-ringed Dragonfly		■	■	■	■	
Emerald dragonflies						
Downy Emerald	■	■	■			
Brilliant Emerald		■	■	■		
Northern Emerald		■	■			
Chaser dragonflies						
Four-spotted Chaser	■	■	■	■		
Scarce Chaser	■	■	■			
Broad-bodied Chaser	■	■	■			
Skimmer dragonflies						
Black-tailed Skimmer	■	■	■	■		
Keeled Skimmer		■	■	■	■	
Darter dragonflies						
Common Darter			■	■	■	■
Highland Darter			■	■	■	
Ruddy Darter			■	■	■	■
Red-veined Darter[3]		■	■	■	■	
Yellow-winged Darter[2]			■	■		
Vagrant Darter[2]			■	■	■	
Black Darter			■	■	■	
White-faced Darter	■	■				
Banded Darter[2]			■	■	■	
Scarlet Darter[2]	■	■	■	■		
	May	Jun	Jul	Aug	Sep	Oct

Notes (see individual species accounts)

[1] Extinct in Britain but may be candidate for reintroduction programme.

[2] Vagrant or migrant species – the flight period indicated covers known British records and/or the species' flight period for its normal range.

[3] Semi-resident species with small breeding population(s) supplemented by annual immigrations from the Continent.

TOPOGRAPHY OF A DRAGONFLY

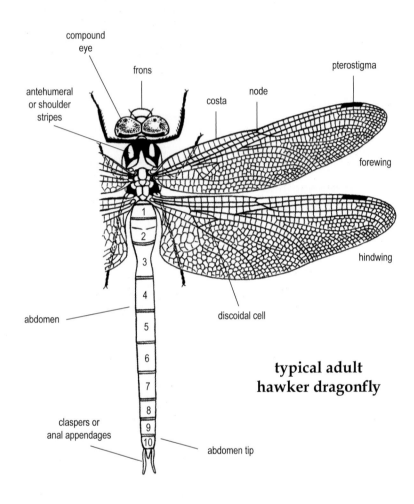

**typical adult
hawker dragonfly**

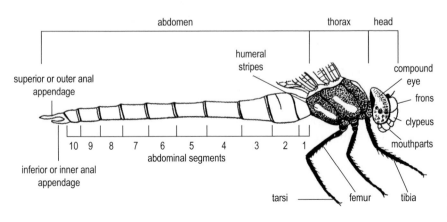

SPECIES AT A GLANCE

Demoiselles
Actual size

Beautiful Demoiselle
p. 40

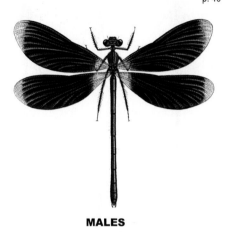 

MALES   **FEMALES**

Banded Demoiselle
p. 42

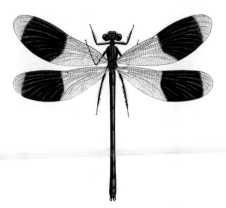 

Emerald, White-legged and Red Damselflies
Normal individuals. For variations see individual species accounts.
x2

| Emerald
p. 44 | Scarce
Emerald
p. 46 | White-legged
p. 48 | Large
Red
p. 50 | Small
Red
p. 52 |

MALES

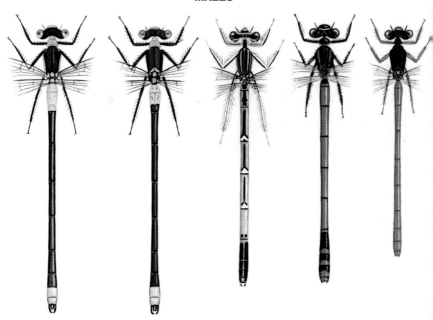

FEMALES

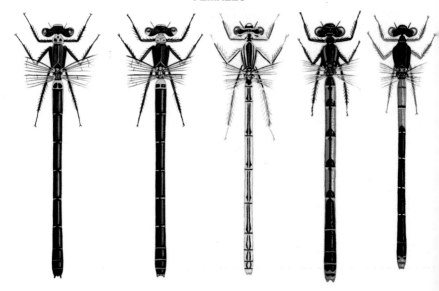

Blue Damselflies
Normal individuals. For variations see individual species accounts.

x2

Southern	Northern	Irish	Azure	Variable	Common
p. 58	p. 60	p. 62	p. 64	p. 66	**Blue**
					p. 68

MALES

detail of of typical segment 2 of males

FEMALES

Quick Guide

Red-eyed and Blue-tailed Damselflies

Normal individuals. For variations see individual species accounts.

x2

| Large Red-eyed p. 54 | Small Red-eyed p. 56 | Scarce Blue-tailed p. 70 | Blue-tailed p. 72 |

MALES

FEMALES

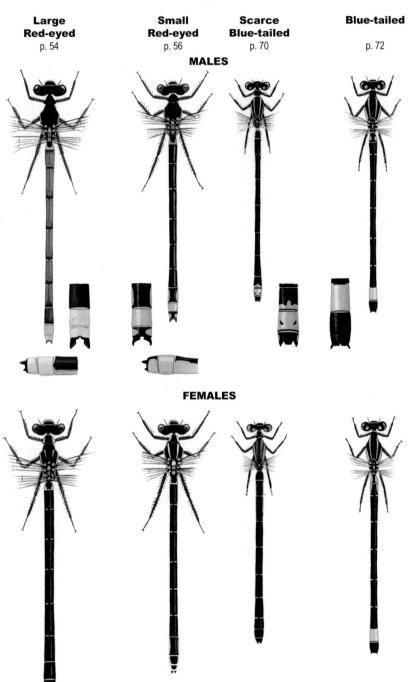

Hairy Dragonfly and Hawker Dragonflies
Normal individuals. For variations see individual species accounts.
Actual size

| Hairy
Dragonfly
p. 76 | Azure
Hawker
p. 78 | Migrant
Hawker
p. 80 | Common
Hawker
p. 82 | Southern
Hawker
p. 84 |

MALES

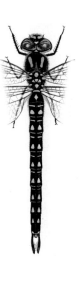

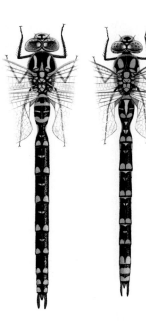

FEMALES

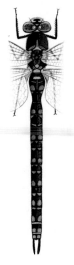

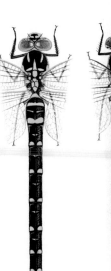

Brown and Norfolk Hawkers
Club-tailed and Golden-ringed Dragonflies
Normal individuals. For variations see individual species accounts.
Actual size

| Brown Hawker p. 86 | Norfolk Hawker p. 88 | Club-tailed Dragonfly p. 98 | Golden-ringed Dragonfly p. 100 |

MALES

FEMALES

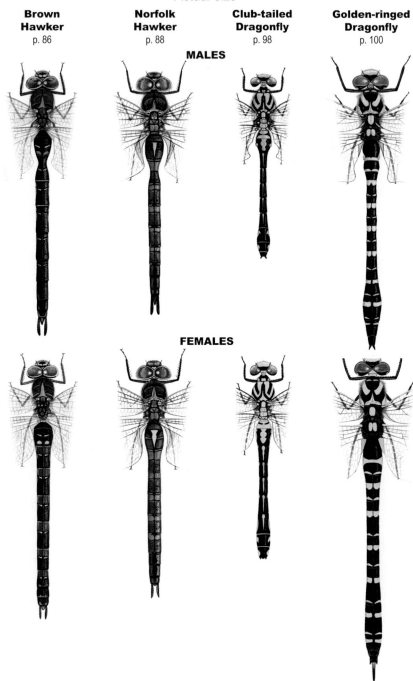

Emperor Dragonflies

Normal individuals. For variations see individual species accounts.
Actual size

Emperor	Green Darner	Lesser Emperor	Vagrant Emperor
p. 90	p. 94	p. 92	p. 96

MALES

FEMALES

Emeralds
Actual size

Downy	Brilliant	Northern
p. 102	p. 104	p. 106

MALES

FEMALES

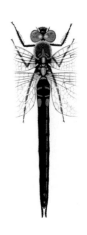

faces
(not actual size)

Chasers and Skimmers

Normal individuals. For variations see individual species accounts.
Actual size

Four-spotted Chaser p. 108	Scarce Chaser p. 110	Broad-bodied Chaser p. 112	Black-tailed Skimmer p. 114	Keeled Skimmer p. 116

MALES

FEMALES

Red Darters

Normal individuals. For variations see individual species accounts.
Actual size

Common	Highland	Ruddy	Vagrant	Red-veined	Yellow-winged
p. 118	p. 120	p. 122	p. 128	p. 124	p. 126

MALES

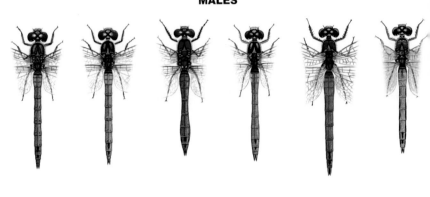

heads
(not actual size)

FEMALES

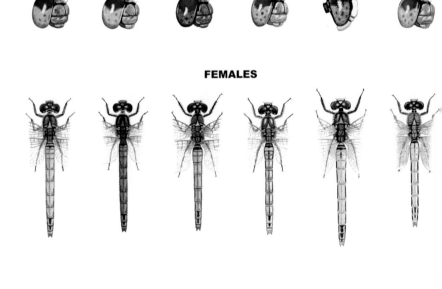

Black and White-faced Darters

Normal individuals. For variations see individual species accounts.
Actual size

Black
p.130

White-faced
p.132

MALES

face
(not actual size)

FEMALES

SPECIES ACCOUNTS
Your comprehensive guide to Britain's dragonflies

Species

Species not included in this guide :
Southern Emerald Damselfly *Lestes barbarus* (Europe: immigrant and potential colonist; suspected breeding in Norfolk and Kent 2003-2004)
Southern Migrant Hawker *Aeshna affinis* (S Europe: vagrant - three records: Kent 1952, and Sussex and Hampshire 2006)
Orange-spotted Emerald *Oxygastra curtisii* (W Europe: former resident but now extinct in Britain)

In species accounts the size ranges for total length (L) and wingspan (WS) are given under 'Description'.

Beautiful Demoiselle   *Calopteryx virgo*

A species of fast-flowing, stony- or sandy-bottomed streams, the Beautiful Demoiselle is the most exotic-looking British dragonfly.

Species

Flight period
Late May to late August.

Description   L 45–49mm, WS 58–63mm
The largest British damselfly (along with Banded Demoiselle).
Male Unmistakable, with entirely metallic blue-and-green head, thorax and abdomen. Broad wings are almost completely deep blue-black – pale at wing-tip and base – with purple and green iridescence. Younger individuals have browner wings and pale wing-tips and bases. Dark red eyes.
Female Very similar to Banded Demoiselle, with metallic bronze-green head, thorax and abdomen. Abdomen tip bronze-coloured with a fine pale brown line running down the centre of the upperside of segments 8–10. Translucent, golden-brown wings with white false (pseudo-) pterostigma (larger on forewing than on hindwing). Fine pinkish-coloured wing veins.

Similar species (p. 27)
Male is unmistakable but the female can be easily confused with female Banded Demoiselle.

Banded Demoiselle (p. 42)
Male Banded Demoiselle has less extensively coloured wings, as the blue is confined to a patch on the outer half of the wing. The blacker wing color-ation of Beautiful can extend along the total length of the wings in mature males but often falls short at the wing-tip and base (the browner-winged immatures have more extensive clear areas at wing-tip and base).
Female Banded Demoiselle has narrower, green- not brown-coloured wings with coarser, green veins.
Habitat Banded prefers slow-running, muddy-bottomed waterways to the faster-flowing, stony-bottomed waters favoured by Beautiful Demoiselle.

Behaviour
Graceful, butterfly-like flight characteristic of the demoiselle family. Like other demoiselles, males are territorial, but will gather in 'dancing' groups, when they increase the speed of their wingbeats in order to attract a female. Females are usually seen at water only when ready to breed, spending most of their time in nearby meadows or along sheltered hedgerows. Young males also mature in these areas and adult males will also feed along nearby field margins. The female oviposits into submerged plants, guarded by the male, who perches or hovers close by.

Habitat
A species of clean, fast-moving stony- or sandy-bottomed streams and rivers, mainly in heathland and moorland areas, but also in farmland and woodland. It will tolerate shade much more readily than Banded Demoiselle and is frequently found along tree-lined river stretches.

Distribution
Beautiful Demoiselle has a wide but scattered distribution. It is most abundant in south-west England, Wales and southern Ireland, but there are small, local populations in south-east England, North Yorkshire, the Lake District and western Scotland (including the Inner Hebrides).

Site Guide pages
154, 160, 166, 168, 179, 191, 192, 204, 205, 206, 207, 211, 212, 213, 217, 218, 226, 229, 232.

Beautiful Demoiselle

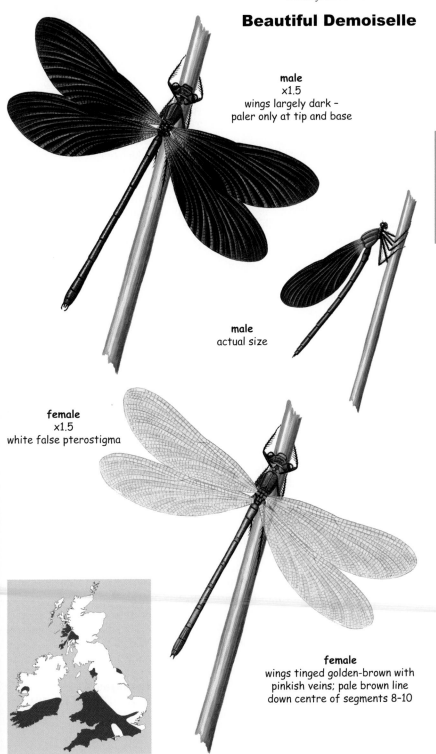

male
×1.5
wings largely dark –
paler only at tip and base

Species

male
actual size

female
×1.5
white false pterostigma

female
wings tinged golden-brown with
pinkish veins; pale brown line
down centre of segments 8–10

Banded Demoiselle   *Calopteryx splendens*

A startlingly bright, colourful and exotic-looking insect with iridescent body and unusual butterfly-like flight.

Species

Flight period
Late May to late August.

Description   L 45–48mm, WS 61–65mm
Along with Beautiful Demoiselle (the only likely confusion species, particularly in the case of females) this is the largest British damselfly.
Male Unmistakable. Head, thorax and abdomen are brilliant metallic green-blue (bluest along central segments of abdomen). Broad wings with distinctive deep-blue wing-patches (brown in immatures) on outer half of wings. Deep red eyes.
Female Metallic bronze-green head, thorax and abdomen. Abdomen reddish-bronze at tip with a fine pale line down the centre of the upperside of segments 8–10. Translucent, green-tinged wings with white false (pseudo-) pterostigma (longer on forewing than on hindwing). Wing veins green.

Similar species (p. 27)
The male is unmistakable but the female can be easily confused with female Beautiful Demoiselle.

Beautiful Demoiselle (p. 40)
Male Beautiful Demoiselle has much more extensively dark-coloured wings – only the extreme wing-tip and base are pale. Finer wing venation. Wing colour is deep blue on Banded but almost black, with purple, green and blue iridescence, on Beautiful. **Female** Beautiful Demoiselle has brown- not green-coloured wings and the wing veins are pinkish (green on Banded) and finer than on Banded. **Habitat** Beautiful prefers fast-flowing, stony-bottomed waters rather than the slower-moving, muddy-bottomed waterways favoured by Banded Demoiselle.

Behaviour
The Banded Demoiselle's butterfly-like flight is characteristic of the demoiselle family (of which only one other species, Beautiful Demoiselle, occurs in Britain). The flight is slow, languid and very graceful. Although aggressive and territorial, males can occur at high densities. They perch in open, sunny positions over or near the water's edge, opening and shutting their wings to display their deep-blue wing-patches as other males approach. The male's elaborate courtship flight is one of the great dragonfly spectacles. They perform an aerial dance in front of the perched female, moving their wings alternately, not together as in normal flight. Females spend most of their time away from water, which they visit only to breed. Nearby field margins and hedgerows are used for feeding by both sexes and immature insects. The female lays her eggs into floating vegetation. The male guards her by hovering or perching close by.

Habitat
Favours wide, slow-running, mud-bottomed streams, rivers and canals with open banks with lush, tall vegetation and waterside meadows. Also breeds on lakes adjacent to such areas.

Distribution
This is a widely distributed species throughout lowland areas of much of England, Wales and Ireland (absent from Scotland).

Site Guide pages
140, 162, 165, 177, 178, 186, 193, 194, 196, 205, 218, 222, 233.

Banded Demoiselle

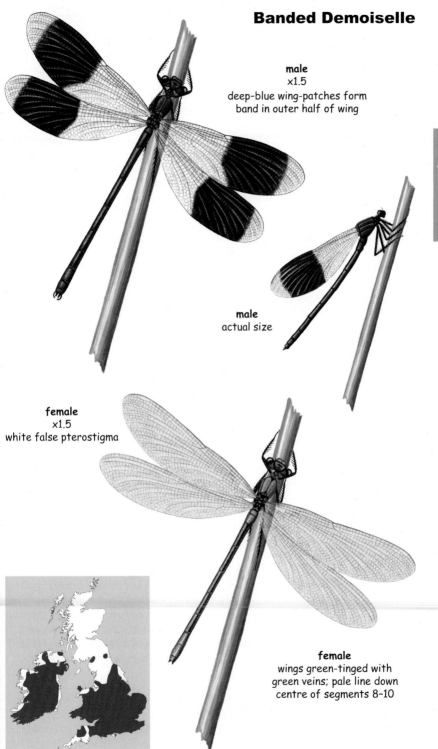

male
x1.5
deep-blue wing-patches form
band in outer half of wing

male
actual size

female
x1.5
white false pterostigma

female
wings green-tinged with
green veins; pale line down
centre of segments 8–10

Species

Emerald Damselfly   *Lestes sponsa*

A large and not uncommon damselfly found throughout most of Britain and Ireland. Characteristically holds its wings half open when at rest.

Flight period
Early July to mid-August.

Description   L 36–39mm, WS 42–45mm
This is a large damselfly with brilliant-green body parts.

Male A long, slender, delicate-looking insect with brilliant metallic-green head, thorax and abdomen; powder-blue pruinescence to eyes, sides of thorax, base of abdomen (segments 1–2) and abdo-men tip (segments 9–10). Blue areas buffish-pink in immatures, gradually turning blue with maturity, the blue coloration wearing off with age, particularly on the abdomem. Bronze sheen to thorax and abdomen (segments 6–8). Abdomen tip (segments 8–10) slightly swollen. Long dark pterostigma. Inner (inferior) anal appendages at end of male's abdomen are narrow and straight and easily visible between the outer (superior) appendages, which curve inwards (see illustration).

Female Shorter in length than male, but much more robust having a thicker abdomen. Metallic green slightly duller than on male, with cream-coloured area at base of wings. Within this area, note the two green, rounded/triangular spots on segment 2. Immatures have pink sides to thorax and abdomen, which turn green a few days after emergence.

Similar species (p. 28)
Both sexes are similar to Scarce Emerald Damselfly. Female demoiselles have green bodies, but also have broader, brown- or green-coloured wings and a white pseudo-pterostigma.

Scarce Emerald Damselfly (p. 46)
Male The blue pruinescence on segment 2 is less extensive on Scarce, and ends about two-thirds the way down the segment rather than covering the whole segment. But beware, this pruinescence wears off with age in both species. Scarce is also more robust, with a distinctly thicker abdo-men, especially the tip, which also appears to have a larger blue area (segments 9–10 are larger on Scarce Emerald). Scarce's pterostigma is also slightly shorter, broader and squarer than Emerald's. Inner anal appendages are broad and curve inwards (mirroring the outer appendages) and are often almost impossible to see, unlike Emerald's narrower, straight inner appendages.

Female Scarce clearly more robust with abdomen almost twice as thick as Emerald's. Note the two green spots (surrounded by cream) on segment 2, which are square-shaped on Scarce and more rounded/triangular on Emerald. Scarce's ovipositor protrudes beyond tip of segment 10; Emerald's falls level with tip.

Behaviour
Rarely found far from water, both sexes spend most of their time sat up in tall, dense vegetation, fluttering rather weakly from stem to stem. During cool periods (inc. mornings and evenings), insects perch with their wings closed but, as they warm up, they open them to about 45 degrees in a half-open position. Males territorial but will occur in densities of around one insect per metre of water's edge. Ovipositing takes place in tandem, and the eggs are inserted into plant stems under the water surface (the female often becoming completely submerged for lengthy periods).

Habitat
Prefers shallow static or near-still water bodies including small ponds, ditches, lakes, canals and bogs with tall emergent vegetation.

Emerald Damselfly

male
x2
powder-blue colour covers
whole of segments 1–2

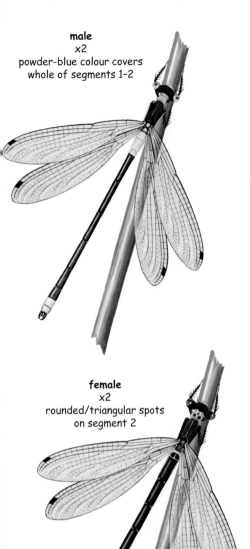

male
actual size

male
abdomen tip showing narrow,
fairly straight
inner anal appendages

female
x2
rounded/triangular spots
on segment 2

pterostigma
quite long and thin

female
side view of abdomen tip
showing short ovipositor

Distribution
One of the most widespread species in
Britain and Ireland.

Site Guide pages
145, 155, 166, 167, 169, 187, 198, 200, 201,
210, 216, 221, 231, 237.

Scarce Emerald Damselfly *Lestes dryas*

This large and robust damselfly is also one of our rarest, found at only a handful of sites in Norfolk, around the Thames Estuary and the Irish Midlands.

Flight period

Mid-June to mid-August.

Description L 34–39mm, WS 45–47mm

A large, robust metallic-green damselfly.

Male Brilliant metallic green with long, slender abdomen and a powder-blue pruinescence on the eyes, sides of thorax, base of abdomen (segments 1–2) and abdomen tip (segments 9–10). Blue areas buffish-pink in immatures and turn blue with maturity, but blue pruinescence wears off with age, particularly on the abdomen. Blue colour on segment 2 covers only upper two-thirds of the segment, and the lower third is green. Abdomen tip (segments 8–10) distinctly swollen. Wings clear with quite broad, more square-shaped, dark pterostigma. Inner (inferior) appendages are broad and curve inwards and are difficult to see between the outer (superior) appendages, which also curve inwards (see illustration).

Female Very similar to, but clearly more robust than Emerald Damselfly. Shorter in length than male, but has a broader abdomen. Metallic green as male, with off-white (cream) area at base of wings. Within this area, note the two square spots on segment 2. Immatures have pink sides to thorax and abdomen, which turn green with maturity.

Similar species (p. 28)

Very similar to Emerald Damselfly. Female demoiselles also have green bodies but have broader, brown- or green-coloured wings and a white pseudo-pterostigma.

Emerald Damselfly (p. 44)

Both sexes Emerald clearly less robust than Scarce Emerald (male Emeralds, especially, look very delicate) and has a longer, slightly narrower pterostigma. **Male** The blue pruinescence on segment 2 is more extensive on Emerald, and covers the whole segment. But note that this blue coloration wears off with age and older Emerald Damselflies can often res-emble Scarce Emerald. Inner anal appendages narrow and straight in Emerald (broad and curved in Scarce Emerald). **Female** Emerald clearly thinner with abdomen almost half the width of Scarce Emerald's. Note the two green spots (surrounded by cream) on segment 2, which are clearly rounded/triangular on Emerald and square-shaped on Scarce Emerald. Emerald's ovipositor falls level with tip of segment 10; Scarce's protrudes beyond tip.

Behaviour

Usually found within a few metres of water. Both sexes best looked for sat up in tall, dense vegetation, where they flutter from stem to stem. As Emerald Damselfly, holds its wings half open at 45 degrees when warmed up, but holds them along its abdomen in more typical damselfly fashion in cool conditions. Although territorial, males can occur in quite high densities. The female lays her eggs into plant stems above the water surface whilst in tandem. She will sometimes oviposit into plants in pools which have temporarily dried out for the summer.

Habitat

Prefers shallow ponds and ditches with tall emergent vegetation. Will tolerate brackish conditions (coastal marshes) and some shade (woodland pools).

Distribution

One of our rarest dragonflies, found at only a handful of sites in Essex, Kent, Lincolnshire, Norfolk and Ireland.

Scarce Emerald Damselfly

male
x2
powder-blue reduced to
segment 1 and upper half to
two-thirds of segment 2;
abdomen tip clearly swollen

male
actual size

male
abdomen tip showing broad,
curved inner appendages

female
x2
thick, robust
abdomen; square-shaped
spots on segment 2

pterostigma
quite short and broad

female
side view of abdomen tip
showing long ovipositor

Site Guide pages
221, 231.

White-legged Damselfly   *Platycnemis pennipes*

Superficially resembles the blue-coloured damselflies, but this is the only species found in Britain with swollen white legs and a 'skeleton-like' appearance.

Flight period
Late May to mid-August.

Description   L 35–37mm, WS 43–46mm
A pale insect with broad white legs.
Male Similar to a blue damselfly in general size and appearance, but blue coloration more pastel and washed-out. Powder-blue shoulder stripes on thorax (can be tinged green) and abdomen. Broad black stripe along centre of abdomen, thickest on segment 2 and tapering to a thin line on segment 5. Segment 6 blue with two black spots. Segments 8–10 black with thin blue central line. Anal appendages (claspers) blue with black tips. Pale brown pterostigma. 'Swollen' green-white (or off-white) legs with central black stripe (very narrow on tibia) and long bristles (feather-like).
Female Very pale and 'skeleton-like' in appearance. Mature females have black thorax with greenish-white shoulder stripes. Green-white abdomen has broad black dorsal stripe with a thin off-white line running down its centre. Immature females are largely creamy or off-white, with black on abdomen reduced to spots at the base of each of the segments 2–6, although segments 8–10 are as mature female's. Pale brown pterostigma.
Side view Male illustrated. Note the 'swollen' green-white (or off-white), feather-like legs. Sides of thorax appear heavily striped white and black with green tinge.

Similar species
Although superficially similar to the blue damselflies, the combination of powder-blue or white coloration, 'swollen' white

legs, and black-and-whitish-striped sides of thorax easily separate from even the palest blue damselflies (including pale immature forms of Common Blue Damselfly).

Behaviour
Non-territorial and can therefore be found in high numbers in suitable habitats. Males dangle their swollen white legs during courtship (this is the only non-demoiselle species to under-take a courtship display) and as a threat display against other males. Often best looked for resting up in tall bankside (or nearby) vegetation, particularly nettlebeds. Ovipositing occurs in tandem, with the female laying her eggs into floating leaves and stems.

Habitat
Slow-moving, muddy streams, rivers and canals with abundant, lush, dense bankside (or nearby) vegetation. Can be found on ponds and lakes near favoured river sites.

Distribution
A local species with a scattered distribution throughout central and southern England. Absent from northern England, Scotland, Ireland and most of Wales. White-legged Damselfly is very susceptible to pollution and is a good indicator of water quality.

Site Guide pages
143, 154, 160, 168, 171, 181, 193, 196, 203, 205, 206, 211, 213.

White-legged Damselfly

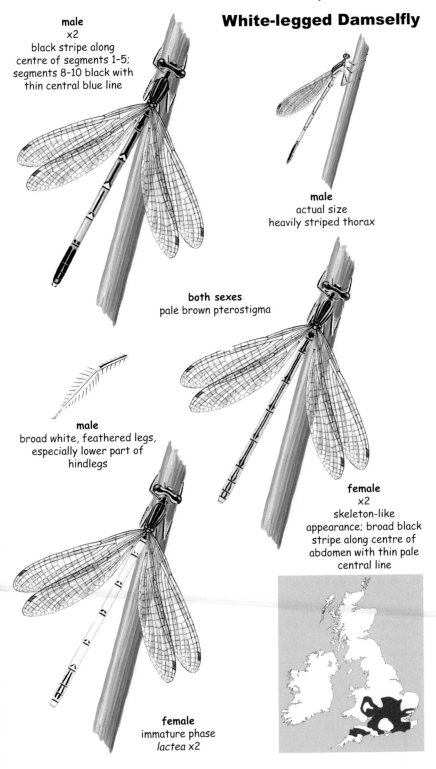

male
x2
black stripe along
centre of segments 1-5;
segments 8-10 black with
thin central blue line

male
actual size
heavily striped thorax

both sexes
pale brown pterostigma

male
broad white, feathered legs,
especially lower part of
hindlegs

female
x2
skeleton-like
appearance; broad black
stripe along centre of
abdomen with thin pale
central line

female
immature phase
lactea x2

Large Red Damselfly

Pyrrhosoma nymphula

This large, robust damselfly is one of the most widespread and common of all British dragonflies and usually the first species on the wing in spring.

Flight period
Late April to mid-August.

Description L 34–36mm, WS 44–48mm
A large red-and-black damselfly. Holds its wings slightly off its body (not flat along the abdomen like most other damselflies).
Male Black head with red eyes. Thorax bronze-black with red shoulder stripes. Long abdomen largely red with bronze-black on segments 7–9. Blackish pterostigma.
Female Normal form, *typica,* similar to male but red coloration not quite as bright. Abdomen clearly thicker and more robust-looking than that of male. The first five segments of the abdomen have a fine black central stripe ending in a black 'bell-shaped' mark. Segments 6–9 largely black. Two other forms occur – a second red form, *fulvipes* (illustrated), is similar to the normal red female form but has reduced amount of black on the abdomen; the black form, *melanotum* (illustrated), has a largely black abdomen with red restricted to the sides with paired yellow spots above and yellow (not red) shoulder stripes.
Immature Immatures of both sexes have yellow shoulder stripes.
Side view Male illustrated. Note black legs and yellow underside of thorax.

Similar species (p. 28)
The only other red species of damselfly in Britain is the much rarer Small Red Damselfly (which is not found in Ireland).

Small Red Damselfly (p. 52)
Both sexes Small Red Damselfly is clearly smaller than Large Red. Small Red also has blood-red (or yellowish) legs (black in Large Red) and red pterostigma (black in Large Red). **Male** Small Red Damselfly is 'totally' blood-red in colour, including eyes, legs and pterostigma. Small Red lacks the black abdominal markings and broad red shoulder stripes of Large Red Damselfly. Small Red looks yellow on sides of the thorax and has black half-stripes rather than a single, complete one. **Female** Small Red Damselfly is clearly smaller than Large Red. Small Red lacks or has greatly reduced shoulder stripes.

Behaviour
An aggressive and territorial species unlikely to be found in high densities at any single site (highest density around 30 adults per 100 metres of water's edge). Both sexes hold wings slightly off their body, at around 30 degrees (not quite the half-open posture of the emerald damselflies). Eggs are laid whilst in tandem and are inserted into floating leaves of plants such as pondweed.

Habitat
Occurs in a variety of habitats throughout Britain and Ireland – ponds, lakes, dykes, canals, streams, rivers and bogs (including acid bogs). Can tolerate slightly polluted waterways.

Distribution
Widely distributed and common throughout most of Britain and Ireland including many offshore islands (though not Shetland).

Site Guide pages
138, 155, 167, 170, 176, 183, 188, 194, 196, 208, 210, 211, 222, 224, 226, 231, 237.

Large Red Damselfly

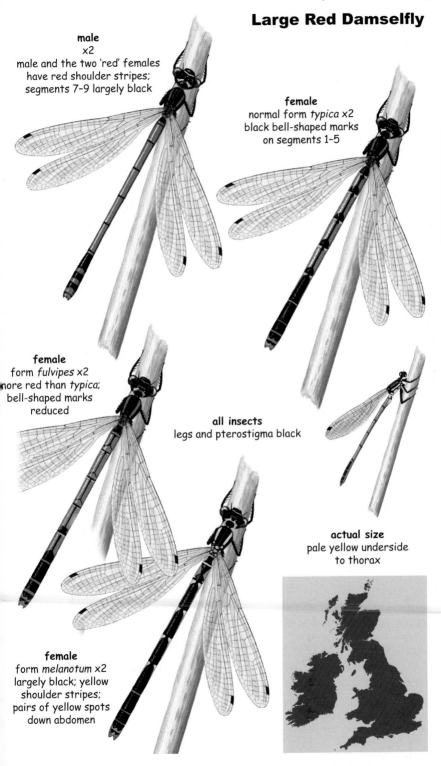

male
x2
male and the two 'red' females
have red shoulder stripes;
segments 7–9 largely black

female
normal form *typica* x2
black bell-shaped marks
on segments 1–5

female
form *fulvipes* x2
more red than *typica*;
bell-shaped marks
reduced

all insects
legs and pterostigma black

actual size
pale yellow underside
to thorax

female
form *melanotum* x2
largely black; yellow
shoulder stripes;
pairs of yellow spots
down abdomen

Small Red Damselfly   *Ceriagrion tenellum*

A small, bright, blood-red damselfly of bogs and lowland heaths.

Flight period
Late May to early September.

Description   L 27–35mm, WS 34–40mm
Male Blood-red eyes, abdomen, legs and pterostigma unique amongst British damselflies. Bronze-black thorax with very narrow (red or yellow) or no shoulder stripes.
Female Three forms occur. The normal form, *typica* (illustrated), has red eyes (duller than those of male), bronze-black thorax with very thin, or no shoulder stripes and a black abdomen with red on segments 1–3 and 9–10. The red form, *erythrogastrum* (illustrated), differs by having a wholly red abdomen and is more likely to have thin red shoulder stripes on its greeny-black thorax. The all-black form, *melanogastrum* (illustrated), is black apart from pale red or brownish eyes, yellowish-brown on thorax at the wing joints and a tiny amount of red around the joints of segments 8–10. All forms have red legs and red pterostigma.
Side view Male illustrated. Note red legs, completely red (no black) abdomen and pinkish-white (or cream) sides to thorax with two black half-stripes.

Similar species (p. 28)
The only other red species of damselfly occurring in Britain is the much commoner Large Red Damselfly.

Large Red Damselfly (p. 50)
Both sexes Large Red is clearly larger than Small Red. Large Red has black legs and pterostigma (Small Red has red (or yellowish) legs and red pterostigma), and obvious red shoulder stripes (shoulder stripes very thin or absent on Small Red). **Male** Segments 7–9 are marked with black on Large Red (Small Red's abdomen is totally blood-red), and the sides of the thorax are yellow with a complete black stripe (cream with two half-stripes on Small Red). **Female** Large Red has obvious red or yellow shoulder stripes.

Behaviour
Both sexes have very weak flight and rarely wander far from the water's edge. Can occur in unusually high densities for a territorial species – around 150 adults per 100 metres of water margin. Eggs are inserted into *Sphagnum* moss (and other plants) whilst in tandem.

Habitat
This is primarily a lowland heath species, preferring small pools and seepages in *Sphagnum* moss-rich areas. It is also found along ditches, on tiny pools and seepages of peat bogs, old clay pits and calcareous valley mires. Although the most favoured sites are still water, it can tolerate very slow-moving waterways.

Distribution
Small Red Damselfly has a patchy and scattered distribution, the main areas being the lowland heaths of southern England from Surrey to Cornwall. In Wales it is scattered along the western seaboard from Pembrokeshire in the south to Ynys Môn (Anglesey) in the north. A single site remains in East Anglia. It is absent from all other areas of Britain and Ireland.

Site Guide pages
140, 141, 165, 168, 194, 196, 202, 218, 222.

Species

Small Red Damselfly

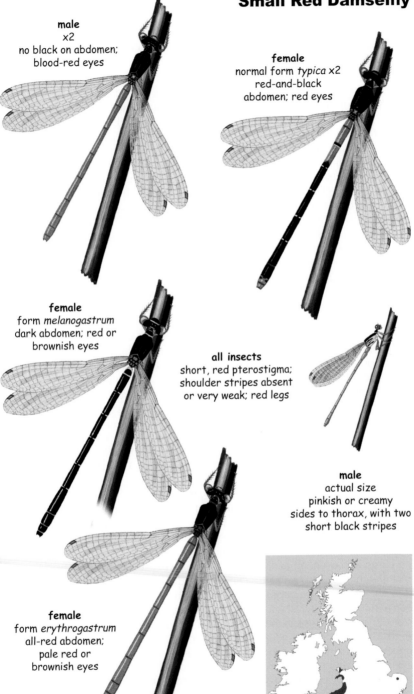

male
x2
no black on abdomen;
blood-red eyes

female
normal form *typica* x2
red-and-black
abdomen; red eyes

female
form *melanogastrum*
dark abdomen; red or
brownish eyes

all insects
short, red pterostigma;
shoulder stripes absent
or very weak; red legs

male
actual size
pinkish or creamy
sides to thorax, with two
short black stripes

female
form *erythrogastrum*
all-red abdomen;
pale red or
brownish eyes

Species

Large Red-eyed Damselfly *Erythromma najas*

A locally common insect of southern and eastern England that has a distinct preference for still or slow-flowing waterways with an abundance of floating aquatic vegetation such as water-lilies.

Flight period

Late May to mid-August.

Description L 33–37mm, WS 41–48mm

Male A robust, largely dark insect, with large, bright ruby-red eyes. Top of thorax dark bronze and lacks shoulder stripes. Segment 1 of abdomen blue with black central square. Blue abdomen tip (segments 9–10). Rest of abdomen black above with grey-blue pruinescence. Pale blue along underside of abdomen. Legs blackish. Pterostigma pale brown with obvious black sides.
Female Largely black with dull yellow markings (green on older females) on sides of thorax and at joints of abdomen segments (but joints are blue towards abdomen tip). Short yellow shoulder stripes on thorax. Eyes dull red-brown. Legs blackish. Pterostigma as male.
Immatures Immature male and female similar to mature female but with more extensive and brighter yellow markings. Eyes yellow-green.

Similar species (p. 30)

Small Red-eyed Damselfly (p. 56)

Both sexes Small Red-eyed is smaller and less robust with weaker black lines through blue sides (yellow in female) of thorax. **Male** Eyes brighter ruby-red, more bulbous and more conspicuous on Large Red-eyed. Note difference in blue abdomen tips: from above, segment 8 is wholly black on Large Red-eyed but Small Red-eyed shows blue on sides; also black cross-shaped mark on segment 10 on Small Red-eyed. Anal appendages more pointed on Small Red-eyed. **Female** Lone females should be separated with care. Small Red-eyed has stronger/complete shoulder stripes and blue sides to segment 10 are visible from above (not visible on Large Red-eyed).

Blue-tailed Damselfly (p. 72)

Both sexes Blue-tailed is smaller and less robust and black lines on side of thorax weaker. **Male** Blue-tailed has blue-and-black eyes, blue on segment 8 only and complete blue shoulder stripes. **Female** Shoulder stripes complete on Blue-tailed (short on Large Red-eyed). Upperside of segment 8 entirely blue or brown on Blue-tailed; just the segment joint is blue on Large Red-eyed.

Behaviour

A distinctive insect with a strong, direct flight low over the water. Males prefer to rest on the floating leaves of water-lilies and other floating plants. Males make short dashing territorial flights before returning to the same leaf. Males will rest amongst nearby vegetation if floating vegetation is scarce. Females spend most of their time away from water in nearby fields, along tree lines, bushes, etc., returning to water only to breed. Egg-laying usually takes place in tandem with both sexes often submerging. Often flies backwards.

Habitat

Large lakes, ponds, canals and other still or slow-moving watercourses with an abundance of floating vegetation.

Distribution

Widely distributed but rather localised south of a line from Flamborough Head (East Yorkshire) to the Mersey estuary. Largely absent from Wales and south-west England (known from only a handful of sites in south Devon).

Site Guide pages

143, 160, 171, 179, 181, 182, 185, 193, 194, 199, 206, 212, 213, 217, 220, 224, 226, 229, 232, 236.

Large Red-eyed Damselfly

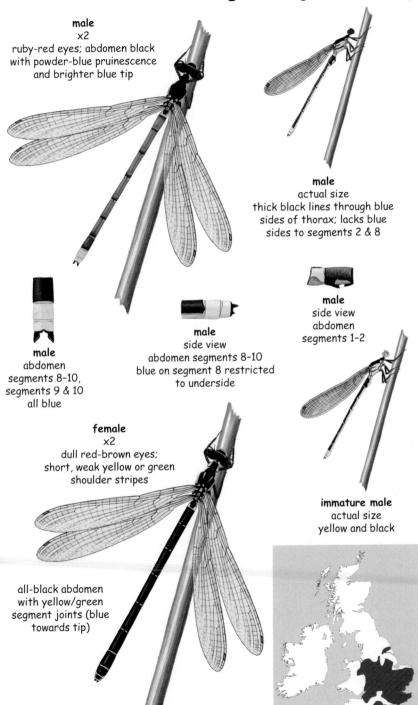

male
x2
ruby-red eyes; abdomen black
with powder-blue pruinescence
and brighter blue tip

male
actual size
thick black lines through blue
sides of thorax; lacks blue
sides to segments 2 & 8

male
abdomen
segments 8–10,
segments 9 & 10
all blue

male
side view
abdomen segments 8–10
blue on segment 8 restricted
to underside

male
side view
abdomen
segments 1–2

female
x2
dull red-brown eyes;
short, weak yellow or green
shoulder stripes

immature male
actual size
yellow and black

all-black abdomen
with yellow/green
segment joints (blue
towards tip)

Species

Small Red-eyed Damselfly   *Erythromma viridulum*

This species was discovered in Britain in 1999 and breeding was confirmed in 2002. It is similar to, although less conspicuous than Large Red-eyed Damselfly.

Flight period
July to mid-September.

Description   L 26–32mm, WS 36–42mm
Male A slender black damselfly with 'tomato'-red eyes (green on underside). From the side, blue markings on thorax extend onto segments 1–2 of the abdomen. Abdomen – blue markings at tip clearly visible on sides of segments 8–10 and from above on the sides of segment 8 and the whole of segment 9. Segment 10 from above is blue with a distinct black cross. Lacks shoulder stripes. Pointed anal appendages.
Female   Two forms, both with black upper surface, complete yellowish shoulder stripes, reddish-brown eyes with green underside, and black legs. *Green form* has all-green underside and segment joints. The scarcer *blue form* has blue sides to the thorax, blue on the underside of segments 1–3, blue upper segment joints of segments 1–2, 2–3 and 9–10 (can also have some blue on sides and underside of segments 9–10), and green on the underside of all other segments and upperside segment joints.

Similar species (p. 28)
Large Red-eyed Damselfly (p. 54)
Both sexes Large Red-eyed is larger and more robust than Small Red-eyed Damselfly. Flight is also stronger and more direct than Small Red-eyed's. **Male** Note the difference in the blue markings on segments 2 and 8–10 – no blue on sides of segments 2 and 8 on Large Red-eyed Damselfly. Anal appendages clearly less pointed on Large Red-eyed. Large Red-eyed's eyes are more ruby-red than the orange- or tomato-red of Small Red-eyed, and are also more bulbous and conspicuous. **Female** From green form of Small Red-eyed: Large Red-eyed has reduced shoulder stripes.

Blue-tailed Damselfly (p. 72)
Because of its size, Small Red-eyed looks superficially more like this species than it does Large Red-eyed. **Male** Blue-tailed Damsefly lacks orange-red eyes and only segment 8 (rather than segment 9) is wholly blue. **Female** Blue-tailed very variable but segment 8 always either entirely blue or yellow/brown.

Behaviour
Like Large Red-eyed Damselfly, males habitually rest on floating vegetation such as water-lilies and pondweed, but unlike Large Red-eyed, characteristically curve the abdomen tip upwards when at rest. Less conspicuous than Large Red-eyed, particularly in flight, because of its much smaller size and slightly weaker, slower, less direct flight; this gives it a noticeably different jizz – looks more like Blue-tailed than Large Red-eyed Damselfly. Males are more active than Large Red-eyed males, actively patrolling the water body for females. Females spend most of their time away from water in nearby fields (or similar), returning to the water body only to breed. Egg-laying takes place in tandem and the eggs are inserted into floating plant matter such as pondweed. Both sexes often submerge for long periods.

Habitat
Preferred sites are relatively sheltered (with nearby mature trees and bushes) enclosed pits (old sand workings, etc.) with an abundance of floating plant matter (waterweed, etc.). In The Netherlands, sites appear to be much as for Large Red-eyed Damselfly, but Small Red-eyed possibly prefers smaller, slightly more sheltered waterways with an abundance of floating vegetation, such as lakes, ponds and canals.

Small Red-eyed Damselfly

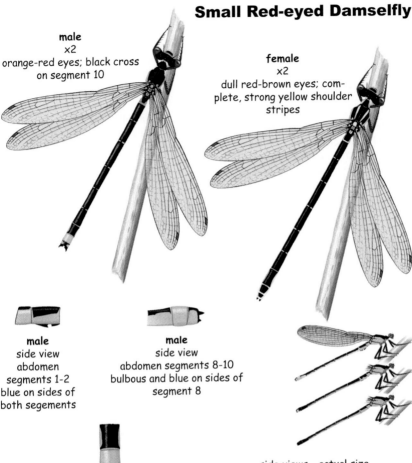

male
×2
orange-red eyes; black cross
on segment 10

female
×2
dull red-brown eyes; com-
plete, strong yellow shoulder
stripes

Species

male
side view
abdomen
segments 1-2
blue on sides of
both segements

male
side view
abdomen segments 8-10
bulbous and blue on sides of
segment 8

male
abdomen segments 8-10
blue sides of segment 8 visible
from above

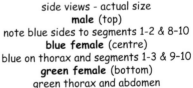

side views - actual size
male (top)
note blue sides to segments 1-2 & 8-10
blue female (centre)
blue on thorax and segments 1-3 & 9-10
green female (bottom)
green thorax and abdomen

Distribution

Discovered in Essex in 1999. By 2006
present, albeit patchily, over much of
southern England (see map), and is
certainly overlooked elsewhere. Further
expansion is expected annually. Fresh
immigrations occur from continental
Europe, for example in 2004 (Parr, A.
2004. *Atropos* 24: 31–35) and 2006 (Parr,
A. 2006. *Atropos* 29: 45–47).

Site Guide pages

145, 195, 219, 221, 222, 232.

Southern Damselfly
Coenagrion mercuriale

The smallest of the blue-and-black damselflies. Its restricted range, small size and weak flight should easily separate it from other species.

Flight period
Late May to early August.

Description   L 27–31mm, WS 33–37mm
Male Deeper blue than other species. Black 'mercury' mark at the top of the abdomen (segment 2) variable (see illustration). Also has black 'cigar'-shaped mark on segment 3 (sometimes also on segments 4–5). Segment 8 is all blue, usually with a pair of black spots. Segment 9 is largely black with blue band along top edge. Abdomen looks equally blue and black from above. Thin blue shoulder stripes. Note straight rear edge of pronotum (see detail) with only a short central projection. Short pterostigma dark in centre.
Female Two forms, green (illustrated) and blue (see side view); blue form has a greenish tinge to underside of the thorax. Both forms largely black with green/blue segment joints. Note pale bar between rear of eyes. Pterostigma as male.
Side view Female blue form illustrated. Side of thorax has a distinct green tinge and is broken by two black lines; a half-line above and a full line below.

Similar species (p. 29)
Southern Damselfly sites are within the ranges of Common Blue, Azure and Variable Damselflies, although it is unlikely to be found alongside these species because of its different habitat preference.

Common Blue Damselfly (p. 68)
Both sexes Common Blue larger with stronger flight; broad shoulder stripes; one, complete stripe on side of thorax; no point in centre of pronotum. **Male** Common Blue has 'lollipop' mark on segment 2; segment 9 all blue. **Female** Segment 8 – Common Blue has 'lantern/ star' mark on top and spine below.

Azure Damselfly (p. 64)
Both sexes Azure – clearly larger with stronger flight, lacks an obvious blue/green bar between the eye spots, and the rear edge of the pronotum more scalloped. **Male** Azure has 'U'-shaped mark on segment 2 and a 'crown' mark on segment 9. **Female** Azure – all-dark pterostigma.

Variable Damselfly (p. 66)
Both sexes Variable is clearly larger with stronger flight; pronotum has three clear lobes on rear edge; grey pterostigma. **Male** Shoulder stripes incomplete in Variable; black 'wineglass' mark on segment 2. **Female** see above.

Behaviour
Non-territorial and usually found in relatively small numbers. Often on the wing during early morning (before other species) and also during overcast conditions (when other species have taken to cover). Flies slowly and weakly low down through emergent vegetation or low over the water surface. Egg-laying takes place in tandem and eggs are laid into floating aquatic vegetation.

Habitat
Prefers slow-flowing, gravel- or marl-bottomed runnels and streams on heathland, but in Wales is also found in calcareous ditches alongside water-meadows or in valley mires.

Distribution
Restricted to a handful of sites in England between Hampshire and Devon (preferring the pebble-bed heaths in this region), south and south-west Wales and Ynys Môn (Anglesey).

Southern Damselfly

male
variation in segment 2

male
x2
mercury mark on seg-
ment 2; 'cigar' mark on
segment 3; short, dark
pterostigma

female
blue form - actual size

female
head and thorax
rear edge of pronotum with
slight central point

female
side view of abdomen
segments 7-10; no spine below segment 8; green bar between eye spots
(blue in male)

female
green form x2
both forms are largely
dark

Species

Note
This is one of only three species of
British dragonfly protected under the
British Wildlife and Countryside Act
1981, and a permit is required to catch
this species.

Site Guide pages
140, 142, 157, 165, 196, 215.

Northern Damselfly

Coenagrion hastulatum

A delicate blue-and-black damselfly restricted to a handful of sites in Scotland.

Flight period
Late May to early August.

Description   L 30–33mm, WS 37–43mm
Male Blue not as vivid as on other blue-and-black damselflies and thorax tinged with green. Note the black 'arrowhead' mark at the top of the abdomen (segment 2) with a small black line above it on either side, and the 'fir tree' mark on segment 3. As in all of the blue damselflies, the markings can be variable, and the two side markings on segment 2 sometimes join the base of the spearhead forming a 'W' or a 'U' (similar to Azure marking) if the tip of the spearhead is reduced (see plate). Note also the blue bar between the rear half of the eyes. Segments 8–9 blue apart from two black dots on segment 9. Two short, black lines on sides of thorax. Short dark pterostigma (both sexes).
Female 'Pea-green' and black (older females darker). Extensively marked green down sides of abdomen; from above, black centre of each segment edged green. Note the thin green bar between the eyes (see plate). Rear edge of pronotum curves to a point in the middle (both sexes, female illustrated).
Side view Male illustrated. Sides of thorax broken by two short black lines.

Similar species (p. 29)
Only likely to be found alongside Common Blue Damselfly, which occurs at most of this species' Scottish sites. Azure Damselfly has been reported from a single Northern Damselfly site, in Tayside.

Common Blue Damselfly (p. 68)
Both sexes Common Blue has stronger flight; just one, complete black line on the side of the thorax; and a straight rear edge to the pronotum. **Male** Common Blue has black 'lollipop' mark on segment 2 and lacks vertical lines either side of it. **Female** Common Blue has a 'lantern' mark on top of segment 8 (black on Northern covers most of segment) and spine under segment 8. Green form of Common Blue not as deep green as Northern.

Azure Damselfly (p. 64)
This species is expanding northwards.
Both sexes Azure – larger with stronger flight; lacks the coloured bar between the eyes; has one half-line and one complete line on sides of thorax; rear edge of pronotum tri-lobed (pointed in Northern).   **Male** Azure lacks stalk on segment 2 marking and has 'crown' mark on segment 9. **Female** Azure more lime-green . Abdomen of Azure largely black with joints of segments 8–10 blue.

Behaviour
A rather inconspicuous, non-territorial species with a rather weak flight. Flies low down amongst waterside vege-tation, settling frequently, and rarely straying from the water's edge. Immatures of both sexes typically found away from water along sheltered spots such as nearby woodland glades. It is the only blue damselfly to perch with wings held half-open. Egg-laying takes place in tandem, and eggs are laid into plants such as Bog Pondweed and Water Horsetail.

Habitat
Prefers shallow, sheltered woodland pools and boggy lochans but can be found along sheltered margins of small to medium-sized lochs. Can survive the temporary drying out of its habitat.

Distribution
Confined to three areas of central-northern Scotland, occurring in Speyside, Deeside and Tayside.

Northern Damselfly

male
variation in segment 2 markings – the black vertical side lines are always present but vary in length

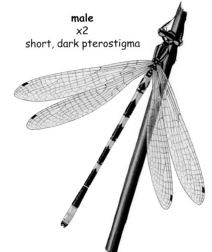

male
x2
short, dark pterostigma

male
actual size
two short black lines on sides of thorax

female
side view of abdomen segments 7–10; no spine below segment 8

female
head and thorax
rear edge of pronotum curves gently outwards to a point in centre

female
x2
'pea-green' colour; extensive green markings down sides of abdomen either side of broad black central stripe

Site Guide pages
138, 146.

Species

Irish Damselfly   *Coenagrion lunulatum*

A typical blue-and-black damselfly found only in Ireland.

Species

Flight period
Late May to mid-July.

Description   L 30–33mm, WS 37–43mm
Male Appears largely black with the blue restricted to semi-circles or bands of decreasing width between the joints of segments 3–7. Segments 8–9 entirely blue giving a distinctive 'blue-tailed' appearance. Black 'chevron' mark on segment 2 has a small black line in front of it on either side.

Female Largely black with yellow or yellow-green shoulder stripes and head markings (see plate), and blue bands on segments 8–9. The black mark on segment 8 is characteristically dome-shaped with a central 'spike' that projects into the blue band above it. The rear edge of the pronotum is wavy and forms three lobes, the central one being raised up in the middle (both sexes).

Side view   Male illustrated. Note the green underside to the eyes, thorax and abdomen. Sides of thorax broken by two black lines.

Similar species (p. 29)
Occurs alongside Common Blue, Azure and Variable Damselflies but both sexes of Irish Damselfly are darker and shorter than these species.

Common Blue Damselfly (p. 68)
Both sexes Common Blue largely blue while Irish looks very black. Common Blue has just one long black line on sides of thorax (rather than a short line and a long line). **Male** Common Blue has black 'lollipop' mark on segment 2, and blue, rather than green underside to eyes and abdomen. **Female** Common Blue has less extensive black markings and the green female form has green, not yellow, shoulder stripes. Female Common Blue has black 'lantern' mark on segment 8 (rather than dome-shaped mark with central spike). Blue female Common Blue has blue on all abdominal segments from above (just segments 8–9 have blue on Irish).

Azure Damselfly (p. 64)
Male Azure largely blue while Irish looks very black. Azure has black 'U'-shaped mark on segment 2, and black 'crown' mark on segment 9. **Female** Azure has blue or green, not yellow, shoulder stripes and lacks a coloured bar between the eye spots.

Variable Damselfly (p. 66)
Male Variable has black 'wineglass' mark on segment 2 and black mark on segment 9. **Female** Green form of Variable has green eye spots and shoulder stripes, not yellow, but marking on segment 8 has central spike similar to that of Irish.

Behaviour
A non-territorial species which swarms over open water. Males like to settle on floating vegetation, but insects usually stay within the shelter of waterside vegetation. The females lay their eggs whilst in tandem.

Habitat
Prefers slightly alkaline waters – shallow ponds, lakes and fen areas but also found on some acidic peat-bog pools.

Distribution
Although this species occurs throughout northern Europe east to Siberia, in the British Isles it is, strangely, found only in the north of Ireland, where it was discovered as recently as 1981. There is a remote possibility that it has yet to be discovered in Wales, north-west England or south-west Scotland.

Site Gazetteer pages
317, 319.

Irish Damselfly

male
x2
'blue-tailed'; 'chevron' and side
lines on segment 2

male
actual size
green underside to eyes
and abdomen

male
segment 2

female
side view of abdomen
segments 7–10 – no spine
below segment 8

female
abdomen segments 7–10
– segments 8–9 pale blue

female
x2

female
head and thorax
- note the yellow eye spots on the rear
of the eyes (turn blue with age) and the
yellow bar between them

Azure Damselfly   *Coenagrion puella*

A common damselfly found throughout much of Britain and Ireland.

Flight period
Mid-May to late August.

Description   L 32–35mm, WS 38–44mm
Male Similar to other blue-and-black damselflies, but careful study allows separation from other species in the field. Note the black 'U'-shaped mark at the top of the abdomen (segment 2) and black markings on segments 3–5 which superficially resemble the marking on segment 2. Segment 8 blue with two black dots and segment 9 has black 'crown'-shaped mark – this combination is not found on any other species. Thin blue shoulder stripes. The rear edge of the pronotum curves downwards in the middle. Black pterostigma.
Female Predominantly black with either green (typical) or blue markings. The green form has a mainly black abdomen with green segment joints. The blue form may show fairly large blue semi-ellipse shapes on the top edge of segments 3–6. Both forms have a black thistle-head mark on segment 2. Neither sex has a coloured bar between the eye spots.
Side view Male illustrated. When seen from side, blue colour on thorax broken by one short and one long black line.

Similar species (p. 29)
Five other blue-and-black damselflies occur in Britain and Ireland. Azure Damselfly is unlikely to occur alongside Irish and Southern Damselflies, so main concern is separating from Common Blue and Variable Damselflies.

Common Blue Damselfly (p. 68)
Both sexes Common Blue has broader shoulder stripes and only a single complete black stripe on side of thorax (it lacks the short black line of Azure), and the rear edge of the pronotum looks virtually straight. **Male** Common Blue has 'lollipop' mark on segment 2 and segments 8 and 9 are all blue (lacks black 'crown' segment 9). **Female** Common Blue has 'holly leaf' mark on segment 8, a prominent spine projecting from below segment 8 (see p. 69), and a coloured bar between the eye spots.

Variable Damselfly (p. 66)
Both sexes Pterostigma grey in Variable (black in Azure). Rear edge of pronotum has three lobes in Variable. **Male** Variable – 'wineglass' mark on segment 2; shoulder stripes incomplete; segment 9 largely black with blue top edge. **Female** Variable – blue/green bar between rear of eyes (lacking in Azure).

Northern Damselfly (p. 58)
Azure Damselfly recorded from only one Northern Damselfly site so confusion unlikely. See Northern Damselfly account.

Behaviour
A non-territorial species often found in large numbers. Males typically fly low over the water surface and are best looked for patrolling around the vegetated water margins. Males frequently settle on floating vegetation or perch on top of waterside vegetation. Often found feeding along nearby hedgerows and field margins. The females lay their eggs into floating or submerged plants whilst in tandem.

Habitat
Found in a variety of habitats – ponds (including in gardens), lakes, streams, rivers, canals, ditches and peaty pools.

Distribution
Widespread throughout England, Wales and Ireland. Occurs in central and southern Scottish lowlands (expanding north). Absent from some upland areas including Snowdonia and the Pennines.

Azure Damselfly

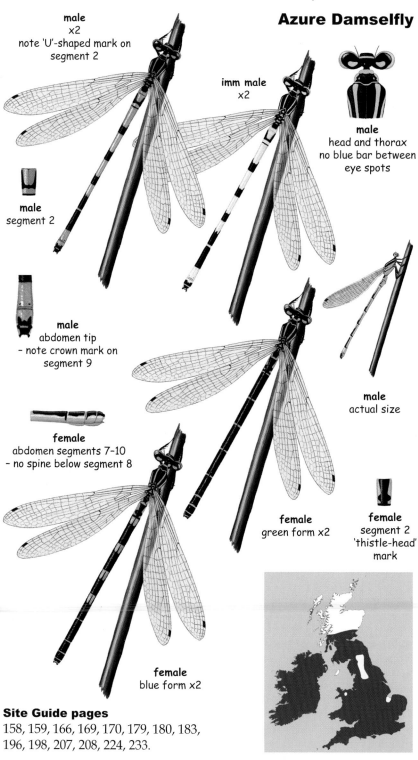

male
x2
note 'U'-shaped mark on
segment 2

imm male
x2

male
head and thorax
no blue bar between
eye spots

male
segment 2

male
abdomen tip
– note crown mark on
segment 9

female
abdomen segments 7–10
– no spine below segment 8

male
actual size

female
green form x2

female
segment 2
'thistle-head'
mark

female
blue form x2

Site Guide pages
158, 159, 166, 169, 170, 179, 180, 183,
196, 198, 207, 208, 224, 233.

Variable Damselfly

Coenagrion pulchellum

A widely scattered, but uncommon, blue-and-black damselfly.

Flight period
Mid-May to early August.

Description   L 31–35mm, WS 39–45mm
Male The black 'wineglass' marking at the top of the abdomen (segment 2) is very variable and occasionally lacks the 'stalk' so that it resembles Azure Damselfly's 'U'-shaped mark. Abdomen appears more black than blue and this species looks distinctly more 'blue-tailed' than other blue damselflies (apart from Irish); segment 8 is blue with two black dots and segment 9 contains a black square with a wavy top and blue band above. Shoulder stripes thin and incomplete, broken or occasionally absent. Note the obviously wavy rear edge of the pronotum forming three distinct lobes. Grey pterostigma.
Female Blue form largely black. 'Mercury'-type mark on segment 2 (similar to male Southern) and blue semi-ellipse marks on top edge of segments 3–7. The less common green form has 'thistle'-shaped mark (like female Azure and Common Blue) on segment 2 and an almost entirely black abdomen. Both forms have unbroken/complete shoulder stripes. Grey pterostigma.
Side view Male illustrated. Blue side of thorax broken by two short black lines.

Similar species (p. 29)
Confusion most likely with Common Blue and Azure Damselflies.

Azure Damselfly (p. 64)
Both sexes Pterostigma black (not grey). **Male** Azure has 'U'-shaped mark (no stalk) on segment 2; complete shoulder stripes; black 'crown' mark on segment 9; does not look blue-tailed. **Female** Azure's 'thistle-head' mark on segment 2 distinguishes it from blue form of Variable, but green form also has 'thistle-head', not 'mercury' mark. Azure lacks a coloured bar between the eye spots.

Common Blue Damselfly (p. 68)
Both sexes Common Blue is more robust with broader shoulder stripes and a single, complete black line on sides of thorax. **Male** Common Blue has 'lollipop' mark on segment 2 and segments 8–9 are all blue; does not look as blue-tailed. **Female** Segment 8 – Common Blue has 'lantern' mark and spine below.

Southern Damselfly (p. 56)
Irish Damselfly (p. 60)
Restricted ranges of Southern and Irish Damselflies means confusion unlikely. See these species' accounts.

Behaviour
Another non-territorial species. Both sexes mature away from water along densely vegetated, sheltered hedgerows and field margins. Mature males swarm over open water during sunny spells. Females oviposit in tandem and insert eggs into plants such as pondweeds, as well as other floating plant matter.

Habitat
Prefers fen-type habitats and found along well-vegetated ditches, dykes and pools. Appears to prefer sites with more emergent vegetation than other species.

Distribution
Although widely distributed through-out England, Wales and Ireland, nowhere is it really common (other than at a handful of areas in Ireland). In England and Wales, the species has a patchy, near-coastal distribution, and isolated inland populations. It is known from only a couple of sites in western Scotland.

Site Guide pages
152, 164, 210, 213, 224, 227, 232, 236.

Variable Damselfly

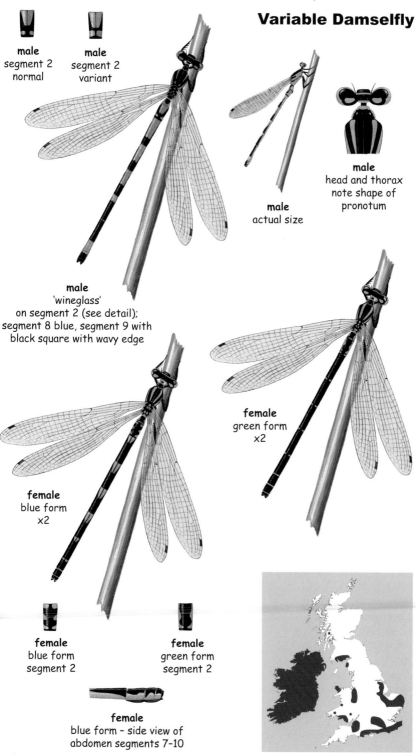

male
segment 2
normal

male
segment 2
variant

male
actual size

male
head and thorax
note shape of
pronotum

male
'wineglass'
on segment 2 (see detail);
segment 8 blue, segment 9 with
black square with wavy edge

female
green form
x2

female
blue form
x2

female
blue form
segment 2

female
green form
segment 2

female
blue form – side view of
abdomen segments 7-10

Common Blue Damselfly   *Enallagma cyathigerum*

The most widespread and abundant of all British dragonflies. It is one of a group of blue-and-black damselflies which needs to be separated with care.

Flight period
Late May to early September.

Description L 29–35mm, WS 35–41mm
Male The bluest of the blue-and-black damselflies. It is best separated from other blue-and-black damselflies by the black 'lollipop' mark at the top of the abdomen (segment 2) and the black markings on segments 3–5, which look like broad, pointed versions of this 'lollipop' mark. Segments 8–9 are entirely blue from above. Broad blue shoulder stripes. Rear edge of pronotum virtually straight (both sexes). Immature (teneral) males are lilac and black.
Female Heavily marked black on a straw, green, lilac, brown or blue background. Broad shoulder stripes as male. Note the 'thistle-head' mark on segment 2 and the pronounced spine below segment 8 (see plate), which is absent in all other female blue damselflies. Black 'lantern'-shaped mark on segment 8.
Side view Male illustrated. In both sexes the sides of the thorax are blue with just a single weak black line visible (Common Blue lacks the short, half-line present on the side of the thorax of the other blue-and-black damselflies).

Similar species (p. 29, pp. 58–66)
Five other blue-and-black damselflies occur in Britain and Ireland. Common Blue is often found alongside Azure Damselfly but can occur alongside any of the blue damselflies.

All other blue damselfly species
Both sexes Can be separated at all times from all other blue-and-black damselflies by the presence of only a single weak black line on the side of the thorax; the short black half-line of

the other species is absent. Northern, Southern and Irish all have noticeably weaker flight. **Males** Note difference in the blue and black markings on the abdomen, in particular on segments 2 and 9. **Females** Separated from all other species by the black 'lantern'-shaped mark on segment 8 and the spine below segment 8.

Behaviour
A robust species with a strong, fast flight low over the water. Often forms frantic swarms close to the water surface, often far from the water's edge. Frequently settles on surface vegetation. Males can often be found some distance from water, especially in dull weather when they will roost in tall grass or bushes. Egg-laying usually takes place in tandem, when the eggs are inserted into floating vegetation. The male will, however, uncouple from the female if she submerges to insert her eggs into plant stems below the water surface.

Habitat
A species of still or slow-moving water and found in moderately sized ponds, lakes, rivers and canals. Will even tolerate brackish conditions.

Distribution
The most widespread and abundant dragonfly in Britain and the only species to breed in Shetland. Found in large numbers both in lowland areas and at altitude, where it will outnumber both Azure and Blue-tailed Damselflies. In Scotland, it can be the only dragonfly species found at a site.

Site Guide pages
138, 143, 167, 170, 173, 187, 188, 194, 196, 198, 200, 201, 208, 216, 233

Common Blue Damselfly

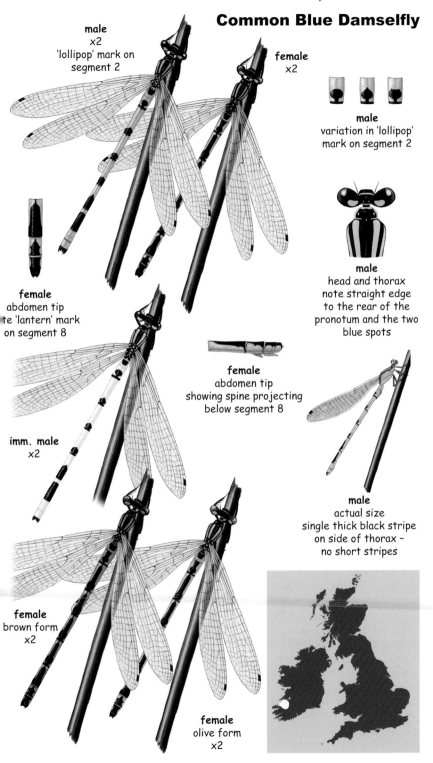

male
x2
'lollipop' mark on
segment 2

female
x2

male
variation in 'lollipop'
mark on segment 2

male
head and thorax
note straight edge
to the rear of the
pronotum and the two
blue spots

female
abdomen tip
te 'lantern' mark
on segment 8

female
abdomen tip
showing spine projecting
below segment 8

imm. male
x2

male
actual size
single thick black stripe
on side of thorax –
no short stripes

female
brown form
x2

female
olive form
x2

Species

Scarce Blue-tailed Damselfly   *Ischnura pumilio*

A small, dark, secretive damselfly confined to a handful of areas in southern England (mainly south-west), southern Wales and Ireland.

Species (side tab)

Flight period
Late May to early August.

Description   L 27–31mm, WS 30–36mm
Male Largely black with rich-blue markings on eyes, thorax and at tip of abdomen (segments 8–9). Younger males have green or turquoise thorax markings. Note the extent and exact position of the blue on the abdomen, covering the lower edge of segment 8 and the whole of segment 9 (see plate). Short wings with rounded bicoloured pterostigma that appears blob-like.
Female Females begin life as orange immatures (*aurantiaca* phase), when their eyes, body, upper abdomen and abdomen tip are extensively marked with vivid orange (see plate). As they mature, they acquire the final brown-green coloration to the eyes, thorax and sides of the abdomen. The upperside of the abdomen becomes all black apart from some green at the segment joints. Maturing females can appear dual-coloured having a combination of green and orange markings. Pterostigma browner and less bicoloured than male's.
Side view Immature male illustrated. Note the extent of blue at the abdomen tip. Green or blue sides of thorax.

Similar species (p. 30)
Only ever likely to be confused with the much commoner Blue-tailed Damselfly.

Blue-tailed Damselfly (p. 72)
Both sexes Blue-tailed is larger with much stronger flight; bicoloured pterostigma is longer than Scarce Blue-tailed's; central 'peg' on rear edge of the pronotum. **Male** Blue-tailed – blue band at abdomen tip confined to segment 8 and segments 9–10 are black; the blue band is further from the abdomen tip

than on Scarce Blue-tailed. **Female** Blue-tailed Damselfly has a coloured band at the abdomen tip (either blue or brown) in all colour morphs; abdominal segments on adult Scarce Blue-tailed are all black.

Behaviour
A highly secretive species which keeps low and close to emergent and waterside vegetation. Has a very characteristic, weak, jerky flight, rarely flying far and usually just from one plant stem to another. It is, however, capable of long-distance movements on favourable air currents as part of its dispersal from emergence sites. The female lays her eggs alone into the stems of emergent vegetation.

Habitat
This species can tolerate both acid and alkaline waterways. It prefers areas with shallow, sparsely vegetated, mineral-rich, boggy seepages, runnels and streams and is often associated with heathland. In 1987 it was discovered in a Bedfordshire chalk pit, and has since been found at several other similar sites in southern England, some of which had been created only a short time before colonisation occurred.

Distribution
In southern England and Wales, it occurs on boggy heathland in Hampshire, Dorset, Devon, Cornwall, South Wales and on the Llyn Peninsula and Ynys Môn (Anglesey) in North Wales. In central-southern and west England it occurs more frequently on man-made sites (e.g. chalk pits, quarries). Widespread but patchy distribution in Ireland, where it occurs in both habitat types. Recently discovered at new localities, this species is possibly still overlooked elsewhere.

Scarce Blue-tailed Damselfly

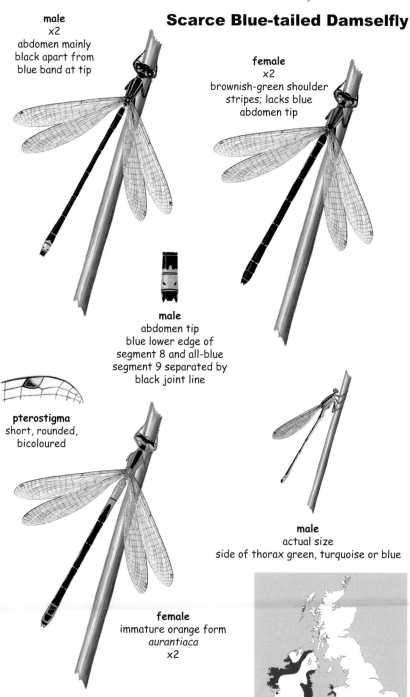

male
x2
abdomen mainly
black apart from
blue band at tip

female
x2
brownish-green shoulder
stripes; lacks blue
abdomen tip

male
abdomen tip
blue lower edge of
segment 8 and all-blue
segment 9 separated by
black joint line

pterostigma
short, rounded,
bicoloured

male
actual size
side of thorax green, turquoise or blue

female
immature orange form
aurantiaca
x2

Site Guide pages
140, 151, 163, 165, 186, 194, 196, 202,
218, 233, 238.

Blue-tailed Damselfly   *Ischnura elegans*

A common and widespread damselfly occurring on still or slow-moving waterways throughout much of Britain and Ireland.

Flight period
Mid-May to early September.

Description   L 29–33mm, WS 34–40mm
Male Largely black with blue markings on eyes, thorax and at the abdomen tip. Note the extent and position of the blue on abdomen tip – whole of segment 8 is blue with segments 9–10 black. Pterostigma long, bicoloured and diamond-shaped. Immature males have green thorax and pinkish markings at abdomen tip and on thorax.

Female Abdomen is thicker than the male's and largely black above. Two distinct immature forms and three mature forms (see plate). Immatures begin life as either a violet form (*violacea*) with a violet-coloured thorax and a blue abdomen tip, or as a reddish/pink form (*rufescens*) with a pink or reddish body and blue abdomen tip. After around eight days, both of these forms begin to acquire mature female characteristics. The violet females can mature into either the normal female form (*typica*), with a male-like pattern and coloration, or into a brown form (*infuscans*), which has brownish markings and abdomen tip. The reddish/pink individuals turn into a yellow-brown form (*infuscans-obsoleta*), with yellowish body and brown abdomen tip. Pterostigma browner and less bicoloured than male's.

Similar species (p. 30)
Scarce Blue-tailed Damselfly (p. 70)
Both sexes Scarce Blue-tailed is smaller and more delicate-looking; has weak, jerky flight; pterostigma is shorter and rounder than Blue-tailed's; lacks prominent 'peg' on rear of pronotum.
Male Pay particular attention to the blue abdomen tip, the extent and position of the blue is important – the base of segment 8 and the whole of segment 9 is blue on Scarce Blue-tailed (whole of segment 8 is blue on Blue-tailed) – the blue band is therefore nearer the abdomen tip on Scarce Blue-tailed.
Female Upperside of segment 8 is black on Scarce Blue-tailed (always blue or brown on Blue-tailed).

Large Red-eyed Damselfly (p. 54)
Both sexes Large Red-eyed clearly larger and more robust with all-black legs. **Male** Large Red-eyed has red eyes and lacks shoulder stripes; segments 9–10 blue. **Female** Large Red-eyed has short shoulder stripes and segment 8 is black; Blue-tailed shows either blue or yellow/brown on segment 8. Egg-lays in tandem (Blue-tailed oviposits alone).

Small Red-eyed Damselfly (p. 56)
Male Small Red-eyed has orange-red eyes and blue on segments 8–10. **Female** Small Red-eyed – segment 8 black above (not blue or brown). Egg-lays in tandem.

Behaviour
One of the few damselflies to be found on the wing in cool conditions. Both sexes keep low down among waterside vegetation. Can be found some distance from water. The female oviposits alone, inserting eggs into emergent plant stems.

Habitat
Occurs in a wide variety of still or slow-moving water bodies (ponds, lakes, streams, canals, rivers) and can tolerate both slightly polluted or brackish waters. An early coloniser of recently created ponds or pools.

Distribution
Widely distributed throughout most of Britain and Ireland. Absent from some areas of central and northern Scotland. Present on Orkney but not on Shetland.

Blue-tailed Damselfly

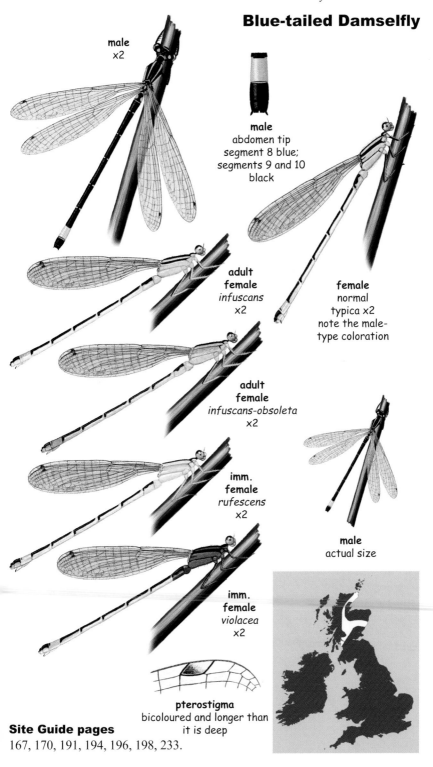

male
x2

male
abdomen tip
segment 8 blue;
segments 9 and 10
black

**adult
female**
infuscans
x2

female
normal
typica x2
note the male-
type coloration

**adult
female**
infuscans-obsoleta
x2

**imm.
female**
rufescens
x2

male
actual size

**imm.
female**
violacea
x2

pterostigma
bicoloured and longer than
it is deep

Site Guide pages
167, 170, 191, 194, 196, 198, 233.

Species

Dainty Damselfly   *Coenagrion scitulum*

A small blue-and-black damselfly which formerly occurred in southern East Anglia and may be the subject of a reintroduction scheme.

Flight period
Late May to late July.

Description   L 30–34mm, WS 36–42mm
Male Very similar to other blue-and-black damselflies. 'Wineglass' ('U' on a stalk) marking on segment 2 of abdomen but, as with other species, this can be variable. Segments 6–7 are all black. Segment 8 is all blue and segment 9 is mainly blue with a black 'bow tie'-shaped mark of variable size (sometimes absent). Pterostigma diagnostic, being nearly twice as long as it is deep, pale brown and edged in black.
Female Pterostigma diagnostic (see illustration).
Side view Male illustrated. Underside of the eyes, thorax and abdomen lemon-yellow. Female also lemon-yellow from below.

Similar species (p. 29, pp. 58–68)
Azure (p. 62), Common Blue (p. 66) and Variable (p. 64) Damselflies occur across this species' restricted former British range. Dainty's pterostigma is diagnostic, as is the lemon-yellow underside of the thorax of both sexes.

Behaviour
Typical of the family, this species is non-territorial. Eggs are laid into floating vegetation whilst in tandem, with the male leaning forwards more than other species, which typically have an upright posture when in tandem.

Habitat
Its former Essex sites were well-vegetated, stagnant ditches, some of which were brackish, in coastal grazing marsh.

Distribution
First found in 1946 near Benfleet, Essex and known only from this area until 1953, when much of the East Anglian

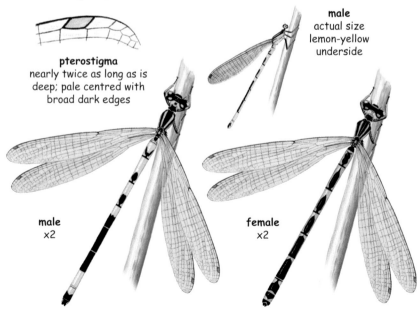

pterostigma
nearly twice as long as is deep; pale centred with broad dark edges

male
actual size
lemon-yellow
underside

male
×2

female
×2

Species

Norfolk Damselfly

Coenagrion armatum

A delicate insect now extinct in Britain.

Flight period
Late May to late July.

Description   L 30–34mm, WS 38–44mm
Male A slender insect which looks more like Blue-tailed Damselfly than the other blue-and-black species. A bronze-black damselfly with a clear blue 'saddle' at the top of the abdomen and distinctly 'blue-tailed'. No shoulder stripes. Sides of thorax blue. Long anal appendages are clearly visible and unusual in damselflies.
Female Bronze-black; lime-green shoulder stripes and sides of thorax, greenish-blue saddle and abdomen tip.

Similar species (pp. 30, 54, 56, 72)
Within its former East Anglian range, only Blue-tailed and Large Red-eyed Damselflies bear any resemblance, but both of these species lack the blue saddle of Norfolk Damselfly and are more robust insects. The recently discovered Small Red-eyed Damselfly is superficially similar but this too lacks the blue saddle.

Behaviour
A non-territorial species which swarms over open water. Males like to settle on floating vegetation.

Habitat
Prefers moderately nutrient-rich ditches, slow-moving rivers and ponds with extensive aquatic vegetation, reed and sedge beds.

Distribution
Discovered in Britain in 1902 in Broadland Norfolk; last recorded there in 1957. When surveyed in the 1970s, the species' former Broadland sites were found to be overgrown and dry. It is possible that a reintroduction scheme may be attempted to try to re-establish the species within its former East Anglian range. Rediscovered in The Netherlands in 1999.

Species

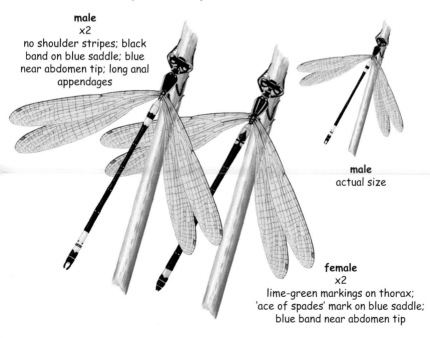

male
x2
no shoulder stripes; black band on blue saddle; blue near abdomen tip; long anal appendages

male
actual size

female
x2
lime-green markings on thorax; 'ace of spades' mark on blue saddle; blue band near abdomen tip

Hairy Dragonfly   *Brachytron pratense*

The smallest hawker-type dragonfly. The female is the hairiest British dragonfly; the
fine pale hairs on the thorax and abdomen are clearly visible with close views.

Flight period
Early May to early July.

Description   L 53–62mm, WS 69–75mm
Male A dark insect with pairs of pale,
tear-drop-shaped blue spots on each
segment of a black abdomen, separated
by pairs of narrow yellow triangles.
Note the yellow-green spot at the top
of the abdomen (centre of segment 1).
The abdomen is most hairy at the base.
Hairy brown thorax with green shoulder
stripes and sides. Blue eyes. Note the
long, narrow, yellow-brown pterostigma. Long, hairy anal appendages.
Female Abdomen as for male but paired
spots are yellow and covering of fine
hairs more extensive. Hairy, brown
thorax has reduced (or lacks) yellow
shoulder stripes. Wing-bases suffused
with saffron. Pterostigma as on male.
Very long anal appendages.
Side view Female illustrated. Yellow or
greenish markings extend down the side
of the abdomen forming a broad line.
The sides of the male's abdomen have
more broken, blue-green spots and the
sides of the thorax are green.

Similar species (p. 31)
Has been confused with the larger
Common and Southern Hawkers, but
a small, hairy hawker with a long,
narrow, pale brown pterostigma early
in the season cannot be any other
species. Migrant Hawker has narrower
hindwings and flies from mid-July.

Common Hawker (p. 82)
Flight periods overlap slightly. **Male**
Common has longer yellow, not green,
shoulder stripes; blue-and-green stripes
on the sides of the thorax (green on
Hairy); and lacks Hairy's central yellow-
green spot on segment 1. Long central
anal appendage (short on Hairy). **Female**

Common Hawker has brown (not black)
abdomen with larger yellow spots.

Southern Hawker (p. 84)
Flight periods do not normally overlap
but a late-flying Hairy could be seen
alongside an early-flying Southern.
Southern has a yellow triangle on segment one (yellow spot on Hairy). **Male**
Southern has large green spots and broad
shoulder stripes and only the markings
at the abdomen tip are blue, those on
segments 9–10 forming bands. **Female**
Southern has green, not yellow, markings including broad shoulder stripes.

Behaviour
Both sexes are frequently found feeding
some distance from water in woodland,
along tree lines, hedgerows or well-
vegetated field edges. Males patrol
stretches of canals, dykes or wet ditches,
moving swiftly in and out of marginal
vegetation. Frequent clashes occur with
neighbouring territorial males. Females
are found at water only during pairing
and egg-laying. Insects soon settle amidst
emergent vegetation or in trees and bushes
during dull conditions. Copulation is long
and is followed by the female laying eggs
alone into floating vegetation.

Habitat
Canals, dykes, drainage channels and,
occasionally, slow-moving streams and
rivers; requires tall, lush marginal vegetation
and abundant floating vegetation.

Distribution
Hairy Dragonfly has a very scattered
but widespread distribution in southern
England, Wales, western Scotland and
Ireland. Nowhere is it common, al-
though it is an easily overlooked species.
Recent warm summers have allowed it
to expand its range.

Hairy Dragonfly

both sexes
hairy thorax; long, thin, pale pterostigma; saffron-coloured costa

male
x1.5
thick green shoulder stripes; thick abdomen (not waisted) with pairs of blue spots and yellow streaks; yellow-green spot on segment 1

female
right and below - actual size
yellow shoulder stripes reduced or lacking; broad yellow or greenish markings down side of hairy thorax and hairy abdomen; saffron wing-bases

Species

Site Guide pages
142, 152, 153, 164, 165, 171, 177, 184, 186, 203, 207, 212, 215, 218, 219, 221, 224, 226, 231, 232, 236, 239

Azure Hawker   *Aeshna caerulea*

One of the smaller hawkers. The blue-and-black male is unmistakable. Restricted to the Highlands of Scotland and central Galloway.

Flight period
Early June to mid-August.

Description   L 55–65mm, WS 76–84mm
Male Dark brown thorax with thin, short blue shoulder stripes. Blackish abdomen with pairs of brilliant sky-blue spots. The colour of the markings varies with temperature and on cool days can appear greyish-blue or violet rather than blue. Golden-brown costa (leading edge of wing); long, blackish pterostigma. The bright blue eyes touch slightly in the middle.
Female Two colour forms – blue and brown. Both have a dark brown base colour with smaller pairs of spots on the abdomen than the male. Blue females have greyish-blue spots and brown females have golden-brown spots. The square-shaped spots on segment 9 are distinctive. Neither form has shoulder stripes. Pterostigma and eyes dark brown.
Side view Male illustrated. Sides of thorax have two narrow stripes, each with a blue upper half and a whitish lower half.

Similar species (p. 31)
Common Hawker (p. 82)
Common Hawker is the only blue hawker that shares the same habitat and flight period. It is a much larger insect. In both sexes the eyes are joined more in the middle than they are on Azure. **Male** Common is a large, dark insect whereas Azure has more extensive and more brilliant blue markings on the abdomen, which from a distance make it look entirely blue. Common has yellow and blue markings on the abdomen (Azure never shows any yellow); broader, yellow shoulder stripes (blue on Azure); broader, blue-and-green stripes on the side of the thorax (blue and white on

Azure); and a bright yellow costa (duller golden-brown on Azure). **Female** Both species have a dark brown base colour, but female Common has bright yellow spots on the abdomen (Azure's spots are duller, golden-brown or greyish-blue). Common Hawker may have reduced shoulder stripes (Azure always lacks shoulder stripes); and the spots on segment 9 are dome-shaped on Common (square-shaped on Azure). Common has green eyes (Azure's are brown).

Behaviour
During the warmer, middle part of the day, males patrol the *Sphagnum* breeding pools in search of females. They are then very active and wary of humans. Both sexes feed and bask along sunny woodland glades and wood edges and it is here that they may be more easily approached and observed. Before the heat of the day, and in cooler conditions, look for them basking on pale tree trunks, boulders and grass tussocks; when disturbed, they often return to the same spot. The female lays her eggs alone into *Sphagnum* moss or directly into soft mud. Egg-laying takes place only in sunny conditions and lasts around three minutes at any one place.

Habitat
This species breeds in extensive *Sphagnum* bog areas which are usually devoid of trees and shrubs. Nearby birch-rich woodland is important for non-breeding insects, providing sheltered areas to mature and for immature and adult insects to feed.

Distribution
A scarce insect which is difficult to see. Found only in Scotland where it occurs throughout the Highlands and in central Galloway.

Azure Hawker

male
actual size
looks largely blue; greatly
reduced shoulder stripes;
abdomen markings can be
blue-grey or violet in cool
conditions (see right)

Species

both sexes
eyes touch only at rear;
abdomen lacks bright
yellow markings

female
brown form - actual size
looks largely brown; shoulder
stripes absent; spots on segment
9 square-shaped; blue females
have blue-grey abdomen markings

Site Guide pages
144, 146, 174, 175, 188, 214.

male
actual size
two narrow stripes on side of dark
thorax are blue above and whitish below

Migrant Hawker   *Aeshna mixta*

One of the smallest British hawkers. It is slowly extending its range northwards and westwards and becoming more abundant in southern and central England whilst many other species are becoming increasingly scarce.

Species

Flight period
Mid-July to late October.

Description   L 55–65mm, WS 81–89mm
Male A brown insect with pairs of pale blue, dome-shaped spots and narrow cream triangles down the abdomen. Note the yellow, downward-pointing triangle above the blue saddle at the base of the abdomen (between the hindwings). Shoulder stripes reduced to yellow spots. Eyes blue and brown.
Female As male but with smaller, dull yellowish-green replacing the blue markings down a browner abdomen. Yellow, downward-pointing triangle at base of abdomen as on male but yellow spots replace the blue saddle. Greenish-brown eyes. Has the longest anal appendages of any British hawker. The markings (and eyes) of immatures of both sexes, and of some adults in very cool weather, are pale lilac.
Side view Male illustrated. Yellow (or greenish) stripes on side of thorax tinged blue at wing-bases.

Similar species (p. 31)
Can be confused with Common and Southern Hawkers, but is much smaller and not as brightly coloured as either of these two species. The two larger hawkers do not occur in groups.

Common Hawker (p. 82)
Both sexes Common Hawker has bright golden-yellow costa on forewing (brown on Migrant) and lacks the yellow triangle at base of abdomen.

Southern Hawker (p. 84)
Both sexes Southern Hawker has broad green shoulder stripes and coloured bands (not spots) on segments 9–10 .

Behaviour
Most often seen away from water, along woodland rides, hedgerows and other sunny, warm, sheltered spots (including gardens), where groups can be encountered hawking several metres above the ground. Individuals in large feeding groups (sometimes numbering hundreds) show little or no aggression to one another. In flight, abdomen held slightly arched giving a drooped-tip appearance. Males patrol low over the water and along vegetated margins in search of females. Pairing takes place amongst waterside vegetation. The female oviposits alone, inserting eggs into emergent plants such as bulrush and occasionally into soft mud. A wary dragonfly and easily disturbed when perched, but flying individuals can approach very close.

Habitat
Prefers well-vegetated, still or slow-moving water bodies such as lakes, ponds, canals, ditches and streams.

Distribution
Once an uncommon migrant from southern Europe, this is now a species easily seen throughout much of central and southern England. Although obviously expanding its range north and west, it remains scarce in south-west England and Wales and is absent from much of Wales and northern England. The first Irish records occurred in 2000 and the first record for Scotland was in 2004. The population is boosted annually by migrants from the Continent.

Site Guide pages
141, 145, 153, 158, 159, 160, 163, 169, 171, 173, 179, 180, 183, 185, 198, 201, 208, 210, 216, 217, 234.

Migrant Hawker

male
actual size
yellow triangle points to a thin
blue saddle at base of abdomen;
blue eyes

Species

female
actual size
brown and yellow;
very long anal
appendages; greenish-
brown eyes

both sexes
downward-pointing yellow
triangle on segment 2; shoulder
stripes reduced to yellow spots

male
actual size
two broad yellow stripes tinged
blue at wing-bases on thorax

Common Hawker
Aeshna juncea

A large and powerful dragonfly. The male's black-and-blue coloration and large size distinguish it from the other bright hawkers.

Species

Flight period
Mid-June to October.

Description L 66–80mm, WS 90–100mm
Male A blackish-and-blue insect with yellow markings on the thorax and abdomen. From above, always appears dark with blue markings , never green. Last two segments of abdomen (9–10) have paired blue spots (not bands). Narrow yellow shoulder stripes. Note the bright golden-yellow costa (leading edge) of the forewing.
Female A brown insect with bright yellow markings on the abdomen, which can be either greenish or bluish in some older individuals. Shoulder stripes much reduced or absent. Costa bright golden-yellow as male. There is also a rare blue form, which resembles the male (found mainly in Scotland).
Side view Male illustrated. Stripes on sides of thorax have blue upper half and yellow-green lower half.

Similar species (pp. 31–32)
In Scotland can be confused with the smaller and brighter Azure Hawker, but in England and Wales confusion possible with Migrant and Southern Hawkers. Females have been mistaken for Golden-ringed Dragonfly.

Southern Hawker (p. 84)
Both sexes Southern has a clear yellow triangle at the top of the abdomen (between the hindwings), brown rather than golden-yellow costa, and much broader, green shoulder stripes and the sides of the thorax are largely green (formed by two very broad stripes). **Male** Southern – blue on abdomen restricted to the last two segments (9–10) and forms two bands (paired spots on Common). **Female** Stripes on thorax and spots down abdomen green on Southern (yellow or blue on Common).

Azure Hawker (p. 78)
Occurs only in Scotland. Clearly smaller. Leading edge of forewing is not as yellow as Common's. Azure lacks yellow markings. **Male** Azure is brighter blue and looks all blue at a distance (Common looks dark). **Female** Azure duller, with greyish-blue or golden-brown spots and square, not rounded, spots on segment 9.

Migrant Hawker (p. 80)
Much smaller than Common. Both sexes have yellow triangle at top of abdomen.

Golden-ringed Dragonfly (p. 100)
Female Golden-ringed is black and yellow (not brown and yellow) and has broad yellow shoulder stripes. Note also shape of anal appendages.

Behaviour
A relentless flyer. Occurs in woodland rides, moorland, upland streams and lowland heaths and bogs. It is often on the wing on cool days but takes cover in heather, bracken or low bushes during rain. Does not investigate humans as some other hawkers do. Females oviposit alone, inserting eggs into submerged plant stems or soft mud.

Habitat
Prefers acidic conditions on heaths and moorland, where it breeds in bog pools and around margins of ponds and lakes. In Ireland it uses peaty fenland areas. Both sexes can often be found some distance from water, feeding over heather, or more commonly in forest rides.

Distribution
Found in heath and moorland areas of south-western, western and northern Britain and much of Ireland. Only isolated populations in south-eastern England, East Anglia and east Midlands.

Common Hawker

male
actual size
largely black abdomen with pairs of large
blue, dome-shaped spots and thin yellow
triangles; narrow yellow shoulder stripes

Species

both sexes
golden-yellow costa

male
actual size
two broad blue-and-yellowish-green
stripes on side of thorax

female
actual size
abdomen spots usually yellow or yellow-
green, but occasionally blue; shoulder
stripes either reduced (as above) or
completely absent

Site Guide pages
138, 144, 146, 147, 148, 149, 153, 155, 164,
173, 174, 176, 183, 188, 190, 191, 199, 200,
210, 214, 217, 230.

Southern Hawker   *Aeshna cyanea*

A large, familiar species of southern England and Wales, often found alongside other species such as Brown Hawker and Emperor Dragonfly.

Flight period
End of June to early October.

Description   L 65–75mm, WS 94–106mm
Male The dark brown thorax and abdomen are heavily marked with bright green, blue and yellow. Broad yellow-green shoulder stripes. Abdomen with pairs of dome-shaped green spots and blue tip – segment 8 with two large blue spots joined at base and segments 9–10 with two complete blue bands. Downward-pointing yellow triangle on segment 2 at the top of the abdomen (between the hindwings). 'Hour-glass' waist at base of abdomen. **Female** Similarly marked to male but has green abdomen tip. Markings on segments 9–10 also bands (not spots). 'Hour-glass' waist not as pronounced. **Side view** Male illustrated. Shows combination of green above and blue below along the sides of the abdomen and largely green sides to the thorax.

Similar species (p. 31)
Common Hawker (p. 82)
Both sexes Common has spots, not bands, at abdomen tip (segments 9–10), narrower, yellow shoulder stripes and a bright yellow costa (leading edge of wings). Common also lacks the downward-pointing yellow triangle on segment 2 and has longer pterostigma. **Male** Abdomen markings green with two blue bands at the tip in Southern – Common has blue markings ending in two pairs of spots at abdomen tip. Common appears an altogether darker dragonfly. **Female** Southern green and brown – Common is bright yellow and brown.

Migrant Hawker (p. 80)
Both sexes Migrant is clearly smaller and has spots, not bands, at the abdomen tip (segments 9–10). Migrant has small yellow spots on thorax (not green stripes); stripes on side of thorax are yellow (tinged blue in males). **Male** Yellow triangle on segment 2 of Migrant points to a blue saddle (points to two green spots on Southern). **Female** Migrant is predominantly yellow and brown (Southern green and brown) and has much longer anal appendages.

Behaviour
A territorial insect which is highly inquisitive and will often approach the observer to within a few feet. Several males can share a pool or pond, but each individual visits it at different times of the day. One of the few dragonflies that flies in dull or damp conditions – even into the night. May settle for long periods and often easy to approach. Copulation is lengthy (up to two hours) and takes place away from water. The female lays her eggs alone into vegetation, dead wood and mud around the water's edge.

Habitat
This species occurs in a wide variety of habitats, including open water bodies, canals, slow-moving streams and rivers, ponds, pools and even water tanks. Often found feeding along woodland rides, hedgerows and tree lines.

Distribution
A common dragonfly of southern England south of the Mersey Estuary–Humber Estuary divide. Largely absent from much of north Wales, northern England and Scotland, and not recorded from Northern Ireland.

Site Guide pages
149, 155, 158, 159, 170, 171, 173, 185, 191, 193, 198, 200, 208, 215, 216, 217, 224, 231, 233, 234, 238.

Southern Hawker

Species

male
actual size
broad green shoulder stripes;
blue on segments 8-10,
forming bands on 9 & 10

female
actual size
thick green shoulder
stripes; green spots down
abdomen form bands on
segments 9 & 10

both sexes
yellow, downward-
pointing triangle at top
of abdomen

male
actual size
sides of thorax largely green
in both sexes; markings on
underside of abdomen blue

Brown Hawker   *Aeshna grandis*

A large, unmistakable and familiar insect of summer throughout much of England and Ireland. It is one of only two large brown British dragonflies and the only species with completely amber-brown wings.

Flight period
Early July to mid-October.

Description   L 69–77mm, WS 96–108mm
Male A large brown insect with noticeably amber-brown, or saffron-coloured wings (both venation and membrane) even in flight. Males are marked with blue – on the top of the eyes, two spots on segment 2 (at base of the abdomen), a spot at each wing-base, and a row of marks along each side of the abdomen. Thorax lacks shoulder stripes. Differs from the female in having a thin waist at base of the abdomen. Pterostigma long and orange-brown.
Female Very similar to male, but is decidedly more robust and lacks the thin waist and blue markings. The two spots on segment 2 are violet or greyish in colour. Wings amber as male.
Side view Female illustrated. Male and female both have brown legs and diagonal yellow stripes on sides of the thorax. Males have blue markings along the sides of the abdomen.

Similar species (p. 32)
Norfolk Hawker (p. 88)
Norfolk Hawker is the only other large brown dragonfly in Britain. Confusion, however, is unlikely as Norfolk Hawker has clear, not amber, wings, green eyes, a yellow triangle on segment 2 and lacks any blue markings. Norfolk Hawker also has an earlier flight period (end of May to end of July). Note also the restricted British distribution of Norfolk Hawker.

Behaviour
Most often seen hawking singly high over grassland, along hedgerows and wood edges, as well as over open water, where it prefers the central, deeper areas. A strong and tireless flyer which is difficult to approach. Males are highly territorial, even defending territories away from water in the feeding areas. Will stay on the wing to near dusk and is a typical sight on warm summer evenings within its range. After a lengthy copulation, the female lays her eggs unattended. Eggs are inserted into plants and dead wood on or below the water surface.

Habitat
Brown Hawker prefers well-vegetated, medium to large, open water bodies and slow-flowing rivers, ditches and canals. Favours less acidic waters than many of the other hawkers. Will often venture into gardens.

Distribution
Widely distributed throughout central and southern England south of Cumbria and North Yorkshire. Absent from Scotland, northern England, most of Wales and south-west England. Present through much of Ireland except in the extreme south-west and extreme north-east.

Site Guide pages
145, 153, 158, 159, 160, 166, 169, 170, 171, 179, 183, 185, 198, 203, 208, 210, 224, 226, 232, 234, 236, 237, 238.

Brown Hawker

male
actual size
blue on top of eyes;
pair of blue spots on
segment 2; thin waist

female
actual size
no blue on brown
eyes and the spots on
segment 2 are violet
or greyish

both sexes
wholly amber wings;
no shoulder stripes

female
actual size
both sexes have two yellow
stripes on side of thorax

Norfolk Hawker   *Aeshna isosceles*

One of the smallest and earliest-flying hawkers, with an unmistakable combination of reddish-brown body, clear wings, bright green eyes and orange face. Note the restricted British range.

Flight period
End of May to end of July.

Description   L 64–68mm, WS 89–97mm
Male Reddish-brown thorax and abdomen, with a narrow but clear downward-pointing yellow triangle or 'arrowhead' between the hindwings on segment 2. Wings are clear with black veins and amber suffusion at the extreme base of the hindwings and long, orange-brown pterostigma. Eyes bright green. Shoulder stripes faint or absent.
Female As male but slightly duller with more conspicuous yellow 'arrowhead' on segment 2.
Face Both sexes have bright green eyes and orange face.
Side view Male and female have brown legs and two yellow stripes on sides of thorax. No blue or yellow markings on sides of abdomen.

Similar species (p. 32)
Brown Hawker (p. 86)
Both sexes The larger Brown Hawker has a darker brown thorax and abdomen and amber-brown wings, and lacks the yellow arrowhead at the top of the abdomen. Eyes brown (with blue spots on male), not green.

Behaviour
Males patrol sections of well-vegetated dykes, flying slowly back and forth about 3–4 feet above the water surface, stopping to make frequent and lengthy hovers, often in the same spot, from which they suddenly dash off in pursuit of prey. Females are usually seen around water only during mating and egg-laying. Both sexes can also be found hawking around bushes and trees, but never far from a broad or dyke. Males can occur at quite high densities and mid-air clashes are frequent. Copulation is brief, and afterwards the female lays her eggs alone into floating or submerged plants, usually Water Soldier. When egg-laying on Water Soldier, the female often holds onto the white flower and inserts her eggs into the leaves just below the water surface. Emergence usually also takes place on this plant, and the distinctive near-black larvae (or later the exuviae) can be easily picked out on the pale green leaves.

Habitat
Occurs in fenland and grazing marsh along unpolluted, well-vegetated dykes with nearby bushes and trees. Within its restricted British range of Broadland East Anglia, breeding appears to be totally dependent on dykes containing the aquatic plant Water Soldier. This strange plant is an excellent indicator of good water quality.

Distribution
In the UK, this species is confined to the Norfolk/Suffolk Broads. However, there have been several reports of what is almost certainly this species on the Fens/Breckland border. It is thought that larvae may have been transported on plants from the Broads as part of a Fenland restoration project.

Note
Norfolk Hawker is one of only three species (with Southern Damselfly and White-faced Darter) which are specifically protected under British law. The species is listed on Schedule 1 of the Wildlife and Countryside Act 1981, and a permit is required to catch this species.

Site Guide pages
152, 153, 207, 219, 224.

Norfolk Hawker

male
actual size

both sexes
green eyes; downward-pointing
yellow triangle on segment 2;
clear wings with tiny patch of
amber at base of hindwings and
orange-brown pterostigma;
no blue markings

Species

face
both sexes have
green eyes and
orange facial disc

female
actual size

male
actual size
both sexes with weak yellow
stripes on side of thorax;
no blue markings

Emperor Dragonfly

Anax imperator

In terms of wingspan, the Emperor Dragonfly is Britain's largest dragonfly species (and only the female Golden-ringed Dragonfly has a longer body). The aggressive, brightly coloured male is a tireless flyer of open water and a common sight in southern and central England.

Species

Flight period
Early June to early September.

Description L68–86mm, WS 100–110mm
Male The unmistakable combination of deep-green head and thorax, bright blue abdomen and large size is unique amongst resident British dragonflies. Note the black central line down the full length of the bright blue abdomen and thick hairy anal appendages (claspers).
Female Size and pale green colour with dark stripe down the centre of the abdomen make this an unmistakable insect. Note that the eyes can appear brown. Some females acquire some blue or turquoise coloration to the abdomen when older or during warmer conditions. Anal appendages more delicate than the male's.
Side view Male illustrated. From the side, males show a vivid green body, and blue-and-black abdomen. Note complete absence of any stripes on the sides of the thorax, unlike the brightly coloured hawkers.

Similar species (p. 33)
Only really confusable with the rare Lesser Emperor, a recent colonist, and Green Darner, an extremely rare vagrant from North America (see p. 94).

Lesser Emperor Dragonfly (p. 92)
Female Lesser superficially resembles male Emperor but note Emperor's more uniformly blue abdomen and green thorax.

Behaviour
Males are tireless flyers and patrol over ponds, lakes and canals, vigorously defending their territory. In flight, the end of the abdomen is clearly drooped.

They tend to settle only in dull weather or when eating a large prey item, either on the outer edges of a reedbed or high up in waterside trees and bushes. In moorland areas they will settle in heather if no taller vegetation is available. Females are seen much less frequently than males, and spend much of their time away from the attentions of patrolling males (which are rarely found away from water). Copulation takes place away from water, often in trees and bushes, and lasts around 10 minutes. The female egg-lays alone, inserting her eggs into floating and submerged aquatic plants.

Habitat
Well-vegetated ponds, lakes, canals and slow-running rivers.

Distribution
Emperor is widely distributed through-out southern England and south Wales, although it is absent from upland areas of south-west England and from some of the chalk downlands of southern England. Absent from north Wales, much of northern England (north of the Mersey–Humber divide) and Scotland, although numbers are increasing in the north of its range. Recorded from Ireland for the first time in 2000 (Parr, A. 2001. *Atropos* 12: 16–19) and now regular along the south-east coast.

Site Guide pages
142, 143, 145, 151, 155, 157, 158, 159, 160, 165, 170, 171, 173, 177, 178, 179, 183, 184, 185, 193, 194, 196, 199, 201, 208, 210, 211, 218, 221, 222, 228, 230, 231, 232, 233, 234, 236, 238.

Emperor Dragonfly

male
actual size
green head and thorax; vivid blue
abdomen (although segment 1
green) with black central stripe

female
actual size
largely green with thick
black central stripe
down abdomen

male
actual size
wholly green
sides to thorax

Lesser Emperor Dragonfly   *Anax parthenope*

First recorded in Britain in 1996, this species was found breeding in 1999. This is one of two rare emperor dragonflies which visit Britain from the Continent. The males of both species have a distinctive blue saddle.

Flight period
May to September.

Description L 63–75mm, WS 93–107mm
Male Smaller than Emperor with a very obvious powder-blue or violet-coloured 'saddle' at the waist, which is clearly constricted (segments 2–3). Note also the broad yellow band at the top of the blue 'saddle'. The rest of the abdomen is greenish-brown with a broad, black central stripe. The thorax is entirely dull brown apart from a pale or yellowish central stripe (joint) on the upper surface. Green eyes with blue edges towards rear. Can show a light saffron suffusion across much of wings.
Female Female usually similar to male but lacks a waist, the brown areas are paler, and the eyes are more yellow-green. Some females acquire blue abdomen with dark central stripe, but abdomen tip is always paler.

Similar species (p. 33)
A rare dragonfly which is likely to be confused only with other emperor dragonflies and Green Darner.

Vagrant Emperor Dragonfly (p. 92)
Males should be confused only with Vagrant Emperor, but note that male Vagrant has a more restricted, purple-blue saddle and lacks the pronounced 'waist' of Lesser. Female Vagrant has a violet saddle. Both species have pale spots at the abdomen tip. Both sexes have brown rather than green-and-blue eyes.

Emperor Dragonfly (p. 90)
Brighter, blue-bodied female Lesser superficially resembles male Emperor but note Emperor's green thorax and more uniform and brighter blue abdomen. Emperor also lacks the yellow band on segment 1 that both male and female Lesser Emperor show.

Green Darner (p. 94)
Blue-bodied female Lesser Emperor also resembles male Green Darner but note Green Darner has brown eyes, green thorax and lacks the yellow band on segment 1 of the abdomen.

Behaviour
Habits similar to those of Emperor although in flight the abdomen is held straight and not curved. The species is unusual among hawkers in that egg-laying occurs in tandem.

Habitat
In Europe this species uses ponds and lakes for breeding. UK records have all been associated with large ponds, small lakes and flooded pits.

Distribution
Occurs throughout much of southern Europe but nowhere abundant. First recorded in Britain in 1996; at least 11 insects seen in 1998 and up to 16 in 2000 including the first records from northern England, Scotland and Ireland (Parr, A. 2001. *Atropos* 12: 16–19). Breeding was confirmed in south-west England in 1999 (Pellow, K. 2000. *Atropos* 9: 28–29). Increased numbers are found annually, including a record 90+ in 2006 (leading to its removal from the Odonata Records Committee 'rare species list') (Parr, A. 2007. *Atropos* 30: 26–35), including breeding has occurred at sites as far north as West Yorkshire. It seems to be establishing at least a toe-hold in Britain.

Site Gazetteer pages
235.

Lesser Emperor Dragonfly

male
actual size
blue saddle; constricted waist

Species

female
actual size
bright blue usually only at base
of abdomen but some females
acquire blue sides to the
abdomen, but always with paler,
violet-grey tip

both sexes
green eyes with blue rear edge;
yellow saddle stripe; slight saffron
suffusion to wings; brown thorax with
upward-pointing pale yellow triangle

Green Darner   *Anax junius*

A very rare vagrant from North America which closely resembles our native Emperor Dragonfly. The first European records (the first of any American dragonfly) were found in south-west England during the autumn of 1998.

Flight period
Vagrants likely to occur again in September–October after suitable transatlantic weather conditions.

Description   L 67–81mm, WS 95–115mm
Male Blue abdomen is brightest at base and fades to pale blue or grey at tip. Blue is variable, depending on temperature, and in cool conditions turns purple or violet. Black stripe down centre of abdomen from segment 3 is broadest at tip. Note spikes on anal appendages – visible only when perched. Bright green thorax. Eyes brown. Note the 'bull's-eye' marking on top of the frons.
Female Abdomen is a green version of male's with brown central stripe. Extent of green on top and sides of abdomen variable – some individuals from above look completely brown. Head and thorax as male. Note the 'bull's-eye' marking on top of the frons.

Similar species (p. 33)
Emperor Dragonfly (p. 90)
The most likely confusion species. In both sexes, green coloration is brighter on Emperor than on Green Darner, and there is much less contrast between thorax and abdomen on Green Darner. Emperor lacks the 'bull's-eye' marking on the frons. Emperor has green not brown eyes. **Male** Note the difference in markings on segments 1–2 – the horizontal black lines are broader on Emperor than on Green Darner. Segment 2 – Emperor has black central line with thick 'moustache' on either side – no central line and much weaker 'moustaches' on Green Darner. Note also the difference in markings at the top of segment 1 – the two spots are clearly blacker and more triangular than the brown, rounded spots on Green Darner. Emperor also has two blue triangular markings on top of thorax; Green Darner has all-green thorax. In cool conditions, Green Darner's abdomen clearly purplish in colour with blue saddle, similar to Lesser Emperor. Emperor lacks spikes on anal appendages. **Female** As on male, note the different patterns on segments 1–2 – Emperor has two black triangles in the centre of the top edge of segment 1, whereas Green Darner has rounded spots at the wing-bases. Both species have a Y-shaped mark with a broad vertical stem on segment 2 but the upper 'V' is broad on Emperor and narrow on Green Darner.

Lesser Emperor Dragonfly (p. 92)
Female Lesser Emperor resembles male Green Darner but Lesser Emperor has green eyes, brown thorax and a yellow band on segment 1 of the abdomen.

Behaviour
Green Darner's flight is faster and swifter than Emperor's and includes frequent sharp changes in direction, often vertically. Abdomen drooped in flight as in Emperor. Male highly territorial.

Distribution
This is the commonest dragonfly species in North America and regularly migrates down the eastern seaboard of the USA. The only British records concern at least eight individuals found in September 1998. The first record was a male found at Penlee Nature Reserve, Cornwall (where a second male and a female were later found). Subsequent records were from a second Cornish site and from the Isles of Scilly (Pellow, K. 1999. *Atropos* 6: 3–7; Parr, A. 2001. *Atropos* 12: 28–29). It is likely to occur again in south-west, England or possibly north-

Species

Green Darner

male
actual size
left, far left and bottom
green thorax and blue abdomen;
abdomen paler or violet when
cold (see far left)

female
actual size
entirely green
and brown

both sexes
chestnut eyes; bull's-eye on
top of frons between front of
eyes; green thorax – no blue;
thick dark stripe down the
centre of abdomen

west Scotland, when weather conditions
(such as a hurricane along the eastern
seaboard of the USA) displace insects
which are then blown across the North
Atlantic by fast-moving weather fronts
(Davey, P. 1999. *Atropos* 6: 8–11).

Vagrant Emperor Dragonfly   *Hemianax ephippiger*

A medium-sized dragonfly which has been recorded on fewer than 20 occasions from the British Isles. The much rarer of the two migrant 'blue-saddled' emperor dragonflies which visit Britain.

Flight period
Recorded in June, July (5), August, October (4), November (3), January and February.

Description   L 60–70mm, WS 90–100mm
Both sexes Brown thorax and abdomen. Eyes chestnut-brown.
Male Note the rather small, bright purple-blue 'saddle' at the top of the abdomen, which is restricted to segment 2. Rest of the abdomen is quite a bright golden-brown with a dark central stripe and clear yellowish spots at tip (segments 9–10). Hindwings are suffused with a variable amount of yellow.
Female Similar to male but with a broken pale violet-tinged brown saddle or no saddle at all and the dark central stripe continuing up the abdomen onto segment 2. Colour of abdomen ranges from golden-brown to dull brown. Pairs of bright spots on segments 8–10 make the abdomen distinctly paler at the tip.

Similar species (pp. 32–33)
Lesser Emperor Dragonfly (p. 92)
Males should be confused only with Lesser Emperor but note the difference in colour and pattern of saddle, no pale spots at tip of abdomen in Lesser, very constricted waist of Lesser and difference in eye colour – brown in Vagrant, green and blue in Lesser. Female Lesser Emperor's abdomen tip also paler than the rest of the abdomen, but base of abdomen always bright blue (not violet as on Vagrant Emperor) and sides of abdomen grey-blue to blue.

Norfolk Hawker (p. 88)
Female Vagrant Emperor superficially resembles this species. Norfolk Hawker has green eyes, a downward-pointing yellow triangle on segment 2 and lacks a broad dark stripe along the length of the abdomen.

Brown Hawker (p.84)
In flight, female Vagrant Emperor could also resemble this species, but note that Vagrant lacks the totally amber-coloured wings of Brown Hawker and has a much narrower abdomen with a broad dark central stripe. Vagrant overall paler than Brown Hawker.

Behaviour
Habits similar to those of Emperor but males are not territorial. Disperses over long distances in search of new breeding sites. Just as likely to be found in late autumn and winter as in mid-summer. Although most records have been since 1980, this species is still not recorded annually in the UK.

Habitat
Vagrants could be recorded from anywhere, including dry sites.

Distribution
This is a species of North Africa east to Asia which breeds occasionally in southern and central Europe. British records have been scattered across southern England with additional records from southern Ireland and the Isle of Man. It is the only dragonfly species to have been recorded from Iceland.

Vagrant Emperor Dragonfly

male
actual size
purple-blue saddle
on segment 2

female
actual size
robust; thin, pale yellowish
band bordered with black
above the violet-tinged saddle
on segment 2

both sexes
chestnut-brown eyes: abdomen pale
brown with thick black central stripe
and pairs of pale spots at tip

Club-tailed Dragonfly

Gomphus vulgatissimus

An early flying, medium-sized dragonfly with a 'skeleton-like' appearance. It is restricted to only a handful river systems in southern Wales, western and southern England. Unlikely to be confused with any other British species.

Flight period
Mid-May to early July.

Description   L 46–52mm, WS 60–70mm
Male Mature males are jet-black with lime-green markings on head, thorax and down the centre and sides of the narrow abdomen. Note in particular the widely spaced eyes and the prominent swollen club-tailed appearance of the abdomen tip. Legs black. Immature males are yellow and black (as females) and become progressively lime-green with age. Note the angular inner edge of the hindwings. Tiny anal appendages.

Female More robust-looking than male with a thicker abdomen and a less noticeably clubbed abdomen tip. Markings bright yellow and more extensive than on the male. Legs black. Hindwings rounded, which helps to separate from immature males. Tiny anal appendages.

Side view Female illustrated. Both sexes are heavily marked in yellow or lime-green (depending on age and sex) on the sides of the thorax and down the sides of the abdomen. Black legs have yellow bases.

Similar species (p. 32)
Golden-ringed Dragonfly (p. 100)
The only other black-and-yellow dragonfly in Britain. However, Golden-ringed frequents faster-flowing streams and rivers, and although there is a small overlap in flight periods (from mid-June), Golden-ringed is usually on the wing much later in the year, is clearly larger, has a black thorax with yellow stripes (rather than a lime-green/yellow thorax with black stripes) and its eyes join in the middle.

Behaviour
Mature males hold territory with slow-flying patrols along still stretches of river edged with tall bushes and trees. Females visit the river only to mate and oviposit. Both sexes have a rather weak, fluttery flight when hawking. Hovers frequently and likes to settle on riverside vegetation, from where it is often disturbed. Will also settle on stones, when their cryptic appearance can make them almost invisible. Immatures feed and mature in woodland clearings and can be found considerable distances from their natal river area. Often found alongside White-legged Damselfly and Banded Demoiselle. Copulation takes place away from water, after which the unaccompanied female flies low over the water surface and, in flight, or whilst stopping briefly, dips her abdomen tip into the water surface.

Habitat
Club-tailed Dragonfly occurs on unpolluted, silt-bottomed stretches of slow-flowing rivers. Areas with lush bankside vegetation and trees and nearby woodland are preferred.

Distribution
In Britain, this species is restricted to eight river systems of southern Wales, western and southern England. The strongest populations are found on the rivers and tributaries of the Severn, Thames and Arun. It also occurs on the rivers Dee, Lugg, Teifi, Tywi and Wye. Absent from the rest of England, Scotland and Ireland.

Site Guide pages
154, 192, 193, 204, 206, 211, 213.

Club-tailed Dragonfly

Species

all insects
skeletal appearance; spots on
sides of segments 8 & 9 (the club)
are always yellow (even on mature
males)

male
x1.5
lime-green and black;
pointed inner hindwing

both sexes
eyes dull green and widely spaced;
club-tailed (male especially so); short
anal appendages

female
actual size
below and right
yellow and black; rounded
inner hindwing

Golden-ringed Dragonfly   *Cordulegaster boltonii*

A striking black-and-yellow dragonfly of fast-flowing rivers and streams of upland areas and lowland heaths. The female is the longest-bodied of all British dragonflies.

Flight period
Early June to mid-September.

Description L(m) 73–79mm, (f) 81–87mm WS 96–106mm
Male A long black insect with bold yellow rings down the length of the abdomen and yellow shoulder stripes. Note constricted abdomen (segments 3–6) with swollen tip (segments 7–9). Hindwings angular next to body. Grass-green eyes (brown in immatures) just touch in the middle.
Female The longest of all British dragonflies due to its uniquely shaped, long ovipositor. The long abdomen is broader and more parallel-sided than on the male, and the tip is less swollen. Yellow markings larger and bolder than on the male. Hindwings rounded next to body. Grass-green eyes.
Side view Female illustrated. Both sexes are completely yellow and black apart from green eyes. Black legs.

Similar species (pp. 31–32)
The female is so large that it is unlikely to be confused with any other species. Males have been confused with Club-tailed Dragonfly and Common and Southern Hawkers.

Club-tailed Dragonfly (p. 98)
Males have been confused with this species, but the restricted range of Club-tailed and the central yellow stripe rather than yellow bands on the abdomen distinguish the two species.

Common Hawker (p. 82) and
Southern Hawker (p. 84)
Confusion has occurred with immature and female Common and Southern Hawkers, but neither of these species is entirely yellow and black. Careful observation of the markings (hawkers have coloured dome-shaped spots rather than bands on the abdomen), the shape of the anal appendages (very different on male and female Golden-ringed from those of any hawker) and the extent to which the eyes are joined should easily rule out either of these two species.

Behaviour
Males patrol stretches of streams and rivers flying fast, direct and low over the water surface. They are aggressive but not territorial. These patrols are very predictable and are seldom disturbed. Both sexes are frequently found away from water, hawking woodland rides, forest edges or heather moorland. Will rest on grasses, reeds, heather, bushes and boulders, where they can be readily approached. The lengthy copulation takes place away from water. The female inserts her eggs directly into the substrate along the stream margins by thrusting her abdomen vertically downwards in a stabbing fashion.

Habitat
Found along acidic, moderate to fast-running peat-, silt-, gravel- or stony-bottomed streams and rivers of upland areas and lowland heaths.

Distribution
A widespread species found across southern and south-west England, Wales and western Scotland. It is thinly distributed in eastern Scotland and northern England and almost entirely absent from central and eastern England. Does not occur in Ireland.

Site Guide pages
138, 140, 142, 146, 147, 148, 150, 151, 156, 157, 162, 163, 165, 167, 172, 174, 176, 178, 187, 189, 193, 196, 203, 214, 222, 228, 233, 234, 238.

Golden-ringed Dragonfly

male
actual size
hindwings angular near body;
anal appendages short and pointed

both sexes
yellow and black;
bright green eyes meet
at a point in the middle;
yellow markings on
abdomen form obvious
rings alternating broad
and narrow; swollen
abdomen base and tip

female
actual size
right and far right
long ovipositor projecting
from end of abdomen; black
and yellow stripes on sides of
thorax; hindwings
rounded near body

Downy Emerald   *Cordulia aenea*

This is the most widespread of the three emerald species found in Britain. It appears all dark and unremarkable unless seen well.

Flight period
Mid-May to late August.

Description L 46–54mm, WS 64–72mm
Male A short, compact insect with a constricted waist and swollen-ended, bronze-green abdomen. The two yellow dashes on top of segment 2 are virtually impossible to see in the field. Brilliant green eyes (brown in immatures) and bronze-green, down-covered thorax. Wings suffused yellow at base. Note the angular inner edge of the hindwings. Dark pterostigma. Short, open, outward-pointing anal appendages.
Female More robust than male with thicker, more parallel-sided abdomen. The thin yellow line on segment 2 is virtually impossible to see unless extremely close. Colour as male but with more suffusion to wing-bases (can cover all of wings on older females). Hindwings rounded on inner edge. Short, weak anal appendages.
Side view Female illustrated. Unmarked thorax. Green eyes. No protruding vulvar scale on underside of abdomen tip. Male lacks yellow and white patches on underside. Legs black.
Face Note face pattern and compare yellow markings with those of Northern and Brilliant Emeralds (see pp. 34, 107).

Similar species (p. 34)
Brilliant Emerald (p. 104) and
Northern Emerald (p. 106)
Confusable with the other two British emerald species. All three species occur in several areas of Scotland. **Both sexes** Dark pterostigma separates from Brilliant only (brown pterostigma). Compare face patterns (illustrated). **Males** Outer anal appendages angular with long, pointed central appendage in Brilliant; inward-curving in Northern; outward-curving in Downy. The widest point of the abdomen on Downy is nearer the tip than for the other two species. **Females** Brilliant has a long, pointed vulvar scale below segment 9 – lacking in Downy. Note the shape and colour of the abdomen, including any discernible markings on segments 2–3 – brownish lines and spots on Northern; yellow lines and spots on Brilliant; yellow dashes or line on Downy.

Behaviour
In southern areas this is a dragonfly of warm, sunny days, disappearing into waterside bushes and trees as soon as the sun disappears. In Scotland it can be found on the wing during much cooler, duller conditions. Males are very aggressive and territorial. They fly at great speed, rarely more than 1m above the water's surface, frequently stopping to hover between stands of marginal vegetation as they patrol the water's edge. In flight, the abdomen is held above the horizontal so that the tip is higher than the base, giving a distinctive profile. Females are seen more often away from water, in woodland rides and glades. Copulation takes place in bushes and trees close to the water body. The female lays her eggs alone, hovering above the water and repeatedly dipping the tip of her abdomen into the water.

Habitat
Well-vegetated ponds, lakes and canals with sheltered bays and overhanging bushes and deciduous trees. In Scotland and Ireland found in more open, peaty moorland with nearby woodland.

Distribution
This species has a very scattered distribution. The bulk of the population is in south-central England and it is not uncommon in Surrey, Hampshire

Downy Emerald

face
both sexes -
jaws yellow with pale
band above

Species

male
x1.5
constricted waist;
swollen abdomen
tip; short, outward-
pointing anal
appendages

note
all emerald species
have a hairy thorax

both sexes
bright green eyes;
down-covered thorax;
dark pterostigma;
wings clear with yellow
at base

female
actual size - left and above
no vulvar scale visible below abdomen tip;
yellow and white markings on underside

and Dorset. Scattered sites occupied in Devon, Gloucestershire and south Wales, and up the west coast of England to Scotland. Occurs at a single site in East Anglia. In Ireland it is found only in the extreme south-west.

Site Guide pages
141, 150, 156, 163, 168, 174, 175, 186, 199, 203, 213, 215, 220, 222, 229, 238.

Brilliant Emerald   *Somatochlora metallica*

This is the largest and brightest of the three emerald dragonflies found in Britain.

Flight period
Mid-June to mid-August.

Description L 49–57mm, WS 74–82mm
Male Brilliant-green eyes, thorax and abdomen. The eyes in particular are dazzling when the sun catches them. The paired orange-yellow marks on segments 2–3 are extremely difficult to see in the field. Note the constricted waist and swollen lower two-thirds of the abdomen, and the long, angular outer anal appendages and pointed, elongated central appendage. Wings tinged with saffron. Inner edge of hindwings sharply angled.
Female As with the other emeralds, the female is much more robust, has a more parallel-sided abdomen and is longer than the male. Saffron wing-suffusion more obvious than on male, particularly at the bases and on fresh individuals. The orange-yellow markings on segments 1–3 are difficult to see unless insects are perched at close quarters. Note the long, straight anal appendages. Hindwings rounded at base.
Side view Female illustrated. Both sexes green with brilliant-green eyes. Note the female's pickaxe-like appearance to the abdomen created by the dagger-like vulvar scale, which protrudes from near the abdomen tip at a right-angle. Long anal appendages. Males lack the white and yellow markings of the female's underside. Legs black.
Face As Downy Emerald's but with the addition of a flattened yellow 'U' on the upper half (see pp. 34, 107).

Similar species (p. 34)
Downy Emerald (p. 102) and
Northern Emerald (p. 106)
Can be confused with our other two emerald species; several Scottish areas hold all three species. **Both sexes** Pterostigma – brown on Brilliant; black

(or very dark) on Downy and Northern. Note face patterns (see illustrations). **Males** Anal appendages – curving outwards in Downy; inwards in Northern; and angular with long sharp central appendage in Brilliant. **Females** Note the vulvar scale protruding under segment 9 of the abdomen on Brilliant – inconspicuous on Downy and Northern. Also note the shape and colour of the abdomen, including any discernible markings on segments 2–3 – thin yellow lines or dashes on Downy; brownish lines and spots on Northern; yellow lines and spots on Brilliant.

Behaviour
Typical of the group, this species is usually seen only during warm, sunny weather, immediately disappearing into the treetops as soon as the sun is lost. Patrolling males behave similarly to Downy Emerald, but prefer to fly under overhanging trees, slightly further from the bank and hover less frequently. Both sexes mature and feed in nearby woodland. Copulation takes place in bushes and trees away from water. The unaccompanied female lays her eggs whilst hovering, repeatedly dipping the end of her abdomen into shallow water, wet *Sphagnum* moss or wet peat.

Habitat
Well-vegetated, wooded canals, ponds and lakes in England and small peaty lochans with nearby woodland (usually containing some pine) in Scotland.

Distribution
There are two very separate populations in Britain: in southern England around the Weald of Sussex, Kent, and the Surrey, Hampshire and Berkshire heaths, and in the Scottish Highlands centred on Glen Mor and Glen Affric.

Brilliant Emerald

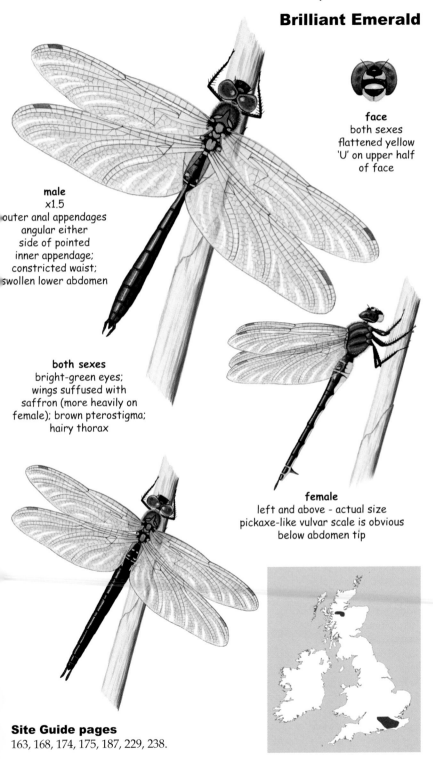

face
both sexes
flattened yellow
'U' on upper half
of face

male
x1.5
outer anal appendages
angular either
side of pointed
inner appendage;
constricted waist;
swollen lower abdomen

both sexes
bright-green eyes;
wings suffused with
saffron (more heavily on
female); brown pterostigma;
hairy thorax

female
left and above - actual size
pickaxe-like vulvar scale is obvious
below abdomen tip

Site Guide pages
163, 168, 174, 175, 187, 229, 238.

Northern Emerald   *Somatochlora arctica*

This dark, fast-flying dragonfly is the rarest of the three emeralds found in Britain, and care should be taken during identification to exclude both Brilliant and Downy Emeralds, which can occur at several of this species' Scottish sites.

Flight period
End of May to early August.

Description L 44–52mm, WS 64–72mm
Male Dull, dark green (almost black) abdomen is darker than on other emeralds. Bright metallic-green eyes and thorax similar to the two other species. The extremely narrow waist is the narrowest of the three species, and is very noticeable, particularly when seen from below. The 'earwig-like' anal appendages differ from those of Downy and Brilliant Emeralds. Amber sheen to whole of the wings is noticeable in flight when seen from above. Hindwings sharply angled near body.
Female Orange-brown spots (not yellow as in other species) on the sides of the upper abdomen (segments 1–3) are diagnostic but difficult to see in all but the closest of perched views. Apart from the swollen base and tapering tip, the abdomen is fairly parallel-sided. Wings tinged amber only at base. Note the long, pinched-in anal appendages. Hindwings rounded near body.
Side view Female illustrated. The vulvar scale under segment 9 protrudes slightly and is short and blunt. Male lacks yellowish marks on underside.
Face Note face pattern and compare yellow markings with those of Brilliant and Downy Emeralds (see opposite).

Similar species (p. 34)
Downy Emerald (p. 102) and
Brilliant Emerald (p. 104)
Both Downy and Brilliant Emeralds occur at several of this species' Scottish sites. **Both sexes** Pterostigma – pale brown on Brilliant; black (or very dark) on Downy and Northern. Face pattern (see opposite). **Males** Outer anal appendages – curving outwards on Downy; angular with long, pointed central appendage on Brilliant; and curving inwards on Northern. **Females** Vulvar scale below segment 9 separates from Brilliant only (which has a noticeably long, pointed scale held at 90 degrees to the abdomen). Also note the shape and colour of the abdomen, including markings on segments 2–3 – thin yellow dashes or lines on Downy; yellow lines and spots on Brilliant; brownish lines and patches on Northern.

Behaviour
Warm days with regular sunny intervals are needed to see this species. Males patrol suitable *Sphagnum* pools, typically about 1m above the water and hovering periodically, and make regular visits to margin areas and frequently move between pools. A unique char-acteristic of this species is the sweeping 'figure of eight' motion high over open pools. When seen low over open water and when hovering, the bronze sheen of the wings is very noticeable. Luck is needed to see this species perched, which can be either high in trees or amongst heather. Copulation takes place in heather or bushes away from water and lasts over an hour. The unaccompanied female lays her eggs in flight by dipping the end of her abdomen directly into water or wet mud.

Habitat
Sphagnum bogs with shallow open pools within areas of pine and birch woodland, particularly within the remnant areas of Caledonian pine forest.

Distribution
Found only in north-west Scotland (restricted to the remnant areas of Caledonian pine forest) and south-west Ireland.

Northern Emerald

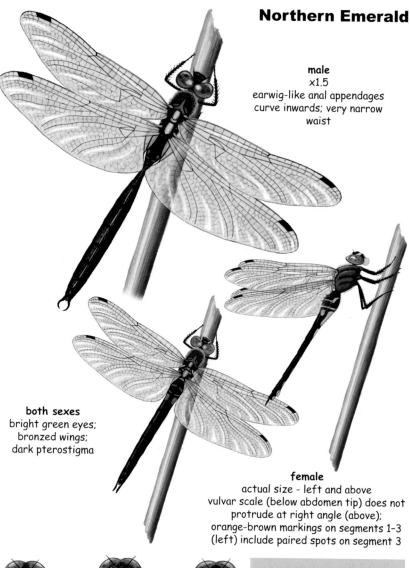

male
x1.5
earwig-like anal appendages
curve inwards; very narrow
waist

both sexes
bright green eyes;
bronzed wings;
dark pterostigma

female
actual size - left and above
vulvar scale (below abdomen tip) does not
protrude at right angle (above);
orange-brown markings on segments 1–3
(left) include paired spots on segment 3

Northern   Downy   Brilliant

faces of the three emerald species
note extent and distribution of black and
yellow markings on the frons (upper half of
face) - Northern has two yellow spots, Downy is
entirely black, Brilliant has a yellow band

Site Guide pages
138, 142, 146, 174, 175, 188.

Four-spotted Chaser   *Libellula quadrimaculata*

A common and widespread species found over much of Britain and Ireland. Known commonly as 'Quad'.

Flight period
Mid-May to mid-August.

Description L 39–47mm, WS 72–82mm
Male   A striking insect when seen well. Mature males show a two-tone, tapering abdomen, the upper half to two-thirds being grey-brown and the tip black. The upper half darkens with age. Elongated yellow spots along the side of the abdomen are visible from above. Thorax plain brown. The wing markings are distinctive. Each wing has two black spots along the leading edge – one halfway along (at the node) and the other (the pterostigma) near the wing-tip. There are therefore eight spots in total, four spots on each pair of wings, hence the species' name. Besides the black spots, the leading edge of each wing is suffused saffron. Also note the obvious dark patches at the base of the hindwings common to chasers.
Female   Very similar to male and best separated by the straight anal appendages (the tips of the appendages curve outwards on the male). Some old individuals can show little or no yellow down the sides of the abdomen.
Immatures Not illustrated. Abdomen orange-brown with dark tip.
Side view   Male illustrated. Note the yellow markings down the side of the heavily tapered abdomen, and yellow on lower sides of thorax. Legs black in both sexes. Whitish or yellowish face darkens with age.
Form *praenubila* Note that the black spots at the node and pterostigma form elongated black smudges. This form is not uncommon.

Similar species (p. 35)
Although similar in colour and appearance to the other female chasers, Four-spotted Chaser is the only species with distinctive wing spots halfway along the leading edge of each wing.

Behaviour
Territorial males guard their chosen sites fiercely by hovering and dashing to and fro at speed. Battles with rival males are just as likely to be heard as seen, as the two insects noisily clash wings. Regular visits are made to favoured perches overlooking their territory. If you disturb one from its perch, wait for its return and you should get a close view. Males will chase anything that intrudes into their territory, but will tolerate other dragonfly species which stick to different levels for feeding. Females spend very little time at the water. Mating occurs on the wing and lasts only seconds. Females scatter their eggs in flight directly onto the water surface, usually above submerged vegetation. Occurs at high densities in heathland and is a favourite prey item of Hobby. Although largely sedentary in Britain, individuals will wander and can be found some distance from breeding sites.

Habitat
A still-water species which occurs in a wide variety of habitats including ponds, lakes, canals, coastal dykes, heathland bogs and pools and mountain lakes and lochans.

Distribution
Because of its ability to take advantage of many different habitats, this is a very widespread and abundant species throughout much of Britain and Ireland, including many of the Scottish islands (such as the Outer Hebrides). However, it is unusually absent from many suitable areas of England (see map opposite).

Four-spotted Chaser

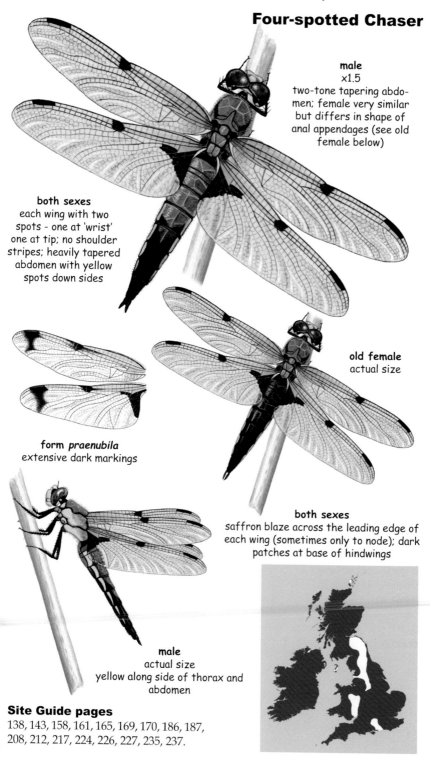

Species

male
x1.5
two-tone tapering abdomen; female very similar but differs in shape of anal appendages (see old female below)

both sexes
each wing with two spots - one at 'wrist' one at tip; no shoulder stripes; heavily tapered abdomen with yellow spots down sides

old female
actual size

form *praenubila*
extensive dark markings

both sexes
saffron blaze across the leading edge of each wing (sometimes only to node); dark patches at base of hindwings

male
actual size
yellow along side of thorax and abdomen

Site Guide pages
138, 143, 158, 161, 165, 169, 170, 186, 187, 208, 212, 217, 224, 226, 227, 235, 237.

Scarce Chaser

Libellula fulva

A very distinctive and beautifully marked medium-sized dragonfly that occurs on only a handful of well-vegetated river systems in southern England.

Flight period
End May to end July.

Description L 42–46mm, WS 70–78mm
Male Powder-blue abdomen with black base and neat black tip (segments 8–10) the black coming to a point on segment 8. Older males show black patches halfway down the abdomen where the females' legs have rubbed away the blue pruinescence during mating. The thorax is dark brown (almost black) and lacks any stripes. Eyes blue-grey. Broad brown patch at base of hindwing; dark brown stripe at the base of forewing. Small, faint brown smudge at wing-tip beyond dark pterostigma.
Female Abdomen broader than male's, a distinctive ochre-brown with a stripe of black bell-shapes along its centre when viewed from above. The brown thorax lacks stripes. Eyes also brown. Yellow suffusion from wing-base along leading edge of each wing. Brown patch at base of each wing. Dark smudge at wing-tip, beyond dark pterostigma, more extensive than on male.
Mature female Old females become very dark and may acquire some blue coloration to the abdomen and eyes.
Immature Similar to female but head and body mainly bright orange.

Similar species (p. 35)
Broad-bodied Chaser (p. 112)
Both sexes Broad-bodied has pale blue shoulder stripes, yellow markings down the side of the abdomen, more extensive brown base to forewings and lacks 'smudge' at wing-tip. **Male** Broad-bodied has only small black tip to abdomen and brown eyes (bluish on Scarce Chaser). **Female** Broad-bodied is browner and black line down centre of abdomen is very narrow.

Black-tailed Skimmer (p. 114)
Both sexes Black-tailed lacks brown wing-bases and smudge at wing-tip. **Male** Black-tailed has orange-yellow marks down side of abdomen.

Keeled Skimmer (p. 116)
Both sexes Keeled Skimmer has a clearly narrower abdomen, lacks brown wing-bases, has creamy shoulder stripes and a pale pterostigma. **Male** Keeled Skimmer lacks Scarce Chaser's extensive black tip to abdomen.

Behaviour
Males perch in open on waterside plants from where they defend their territories. When perched, the male has the peculiar habit of placing its forelegs behind its head to allow greater freedom of movement of the head to search for prey, rival males and females. Females spend much of their time perched in nearby herbaceous areas such as nettlebeds. Insects mature, roost and feed in nearby woodland and scrub. Pairing takes place in waterside vegetation and lasts over 15 minutes. The male attends the ovipositing female, who lays her eggs by dipping the tip of her abdomen into the water between hovers.

Habitat
Prefers slow-moving, muddy rivers and streams, such as floodplain basins with extensive backwaters and drainage ditches, with lush waterside vegetation and nearby bushes.

Distribution
The rarest of the chasers, it is confined to a handful of river systems in East Anglia and the southern counties.

Site Guide pages
152, 181, 203, 207, 239.

Scarce Chaser

male
x1.5
powder-blue abdomen
with dark base and tip;
blue-grey eyes;
dark thorax; faint dark
smudge at wing-tip

all insects
saffron blaze along
leading edge of
each wing (less
extensive on males);
smudge-mark at tip
of wings; no
shoulder stripes;
no yellow markings
on side of abdomen;
dark brown
pterostigma

female
actual size
pale orange
abdomen with dark
central stripe

immature male
actual size
rich orange colour extends to
head and thorax

old female
actual size
very dark insect

Broad-bodied Chaser   *Libellula depressa*

A distinctive medium-sized 'dumpy' dragonfly of shallow sunny pools.

Flight period
Mid-May to early August.

Description L 40–46mm, WS 42–50mm
Male Has a broad, flattened, stumpy-looking powder-blue abdomen with yellow spots down the sides. Only the very tip of the abdomen (segment 10 and anal appendages) is black. Thorax mid-brown with pale blue shoulder stripes. Extensive brown patches at base of all wings and dark pterostigma. Eyes brown.
Female Flattened, yellow-brown abdomen is even shorter and broader than male's and more extensive yellow spots form stripes down sides. Brown thorax with short bluish-white shoulder stripes. Eyes brown. Extensive brown patches at wing-bases.
Immature Bright ochre abdomen with thin black dorsal stripe. Eyes and centre of thorax initially pale brown. Pale shoulder stripes less obvious.
Mature female Older females can acquire blue-grey tinge on abdomen.
Side view Male illustrated. From side, flattened abdomen clearly curves upwards at the tip. Brown thorax and underside of abdomen.

Similar species (p. 35)
No other species has such a broad flattened abdomen or such extensive dark patches at the wing-bases.

Scarce Chaser (p. 110)
Both sexes Scarce Chaser lacks shoulder stripes, yellow markings on abdomen and brown patches at wing-bases are smaller. Scarce Chaser usually shows dark smudge at wing-tip, especially females. **Male** Scarce Chaser has extensive black tip to abdomen and bluish eyes. **Female** Scarce Chaser has orange abdomen with a broad black stripe down centre.

Black-tailed Skimmer (p. 114) and Keeled Skimmer (p. 116)
Both sexes Both of these species have narrower abdomens and lack brown wing-bases.

Four-spotted Chaser (p.108)
No problem separating males. **Female** Four-spotted has a distinctive spot halfway along the leading edge of each wing and golden-yellow suffusion to wing-bases and leading edge; lower half of narrower abdomen blackish; no dark patch at base of forewing and thorax lacks shoulder stripes.

Behaviour
Males perch for long periods in the open on tall vegetation in sunny spots. Males defend territories aggressively during the middle of the day. They will defend a site for several days, often using the same perches, before resorting to wandering in search of females. Females spend most of their time sat up in vegetation close to breeding areas. Pairing occurs in flight and last just seconds. The female flies low between marginal vegetation flicking her abdomen tip to deposit eggs directly into the water. Males occasionally hover close to egg-laying females, but egg-laying is usually undertaken alone.

Habitat
This species is often one of the first to colonise suitable new pools such as those in gardens. It prefers small, well-vegetated lakes, pools and ditches in sheltered, sunny locations.

Distribution
Widely distributed throughout Wales and southern England south of a line drawn between the Ribble and Humber estuaries but is expanding northwards.

Broad-bodied Chaser

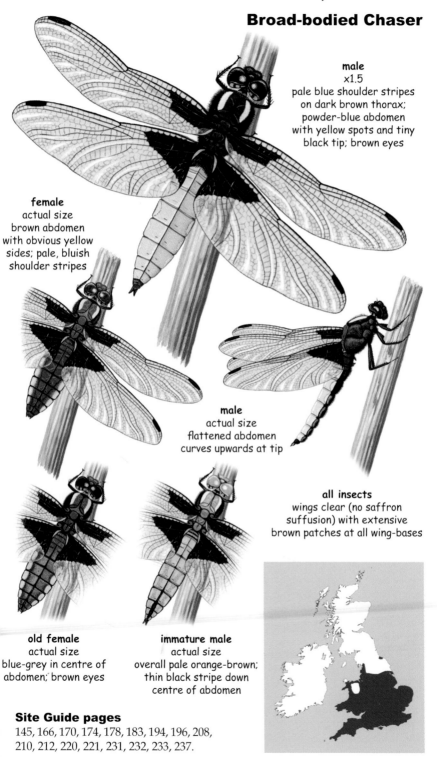

male
x1.5
pale blue shoulder stripes
on dark brown thorax;
powder-blue abdomen
with yellow spots and tiny
black tip; brown eyes

Species

female
actual size
brown abdomen
with obvious yellow
sides; pale, bluish
shoulder stripes

male
actual size
flattened abdomen
curves upwards at tip

all insects
wings clear (no saffron
suffusion) with extensive
brown patches at all wing-bases

old female
actual size
blue-grey in centre of
abdomen; brown eyes

immature male
actual size
overall pale orange-brown;
thin black stripe down
centre of abdomen

Site Guide pages

145, 166, 170, 174, 178, 183, 194, 196, 208,
210, 212, 220, 221, 231, 232, 233, 237.

Black-tailed Skimmer *Orthetrum cancellatum*

A very active medium-sized dragonfly typically found around water bodies surrounded by lots of bare ground, such as gravel pits, reservoirs, canals and rivers.

Flight period
Mid-May to early August.

Description L 44–52mm, WS 73–81mm
Male Slim, powder-blue tapering abdomen has orange-yellow spots down the sides (gradually turn blue with age) and blackish tip (segments 7–10). Olive-brown thorax. Eyes greeny-blue. Wings have yellowish leading edge (costa) but otherwise lack any colour. Black pterostigma. Immature males as female but with paler eyes from above.
Female A striking insect with golden-yellow thorax and abdomen. Two thick black, crescent-like markings on each segment of abdomen form continuous lines either side of the centre. Eyes brown. Older females can have blue-grey pruinescence.
Side view Female illustrated. Sides of thorax bright yellow. Thick black line down length of abdomen.

Similar species (p. 35)
Keeled Skimmer (p. 116)
Both sexes Keeled Skimmer has creamy-yellow shoulder stripes and pale, yellowish pterostigma.

Broad-bodied Chaser (p. 112)
Both sexes Broad-bodied Chaser is clearly shorter and broader, and both sexes have dark brown patches at the wing-bases (clear in Black-tailed) and pale bluish shoulder stripes.

Scarce Chaser (p.110)
Both sexes Scarce Chaser has brown wing-bases (clear on Black-tailed Skimmer) and usually shows dark smudge at wing-tips (more extensive on females). **Female** Scarce Chaser has orange rather than yellow abdomen with a single thick black line down the centre.

Behaviour
Males bask, with wings held forward, on pale bare ground such as dry mud, shingle and rocks. They often fly up at the observer's feet before alighting some distance away on another patch of bare ground. When hot, insects rest on a prominent low perch. Males are highly aggressive to other males; they patrol and defend a bankside territory up to 50m in length. In flight they skim low over the water surface. Females feed in nearby fields, reedbeds or along hedgerows and treelines, returning to the water's edge only to mate, when they are quickly seized by a male. Mating takes place in the air, on the ground or on a perch and lasts between 30 seconds and 15 minutes. Males guard egg-laying females as they dip the end of their abdomen into the water whilst flying low over the surface.

Habitat
Occurs in a variety of lowland habitats with plenty of bare ground, including reservoirs, gravel pits, quarries, lakes, ponds, dykes, slow-running rivers, canals. Can tolerate brackish conditions. It is often one of the first dragonflies to colonise newly created water bodies such as reservoirs and gravel pits.

Distribution
Widely distributed and not uncommon throughout England south of a line between the Severn and Humber estuaries, and along the coastal strip of south Wales. Isolated pockets occur in coastal mid-Wales, Lancashire, Shropshire and Co. Durham. In Ireland it is found in the midlands and west.

Site Guide pages
143, 168, 170, 171, 173, 183, 194, 208, 220, 224, 231, 235.

Black-tailed Skimmer

male
x1.5
long powder-blue abdomen
with extensive black tip
and orange-yellow sides;
eyes greeny-blue

Species

all insects
clear wings with
yellow costa and
black pterostigma

female
right and upper right
actual size
two bold, wavy black
stripes down yellow
abdomen; sides of
thorax bright yellow;
eyes dark brown above

old female
actual size
steel-grey abdomen

Keeled Skimmer · *Orthetrum coerulescens*

A small, darter-like dragonfly of wet heaths and moorland areas of southern and western Britain.

Flight period
End May to end August.

Description L 38–46mm, WS 57–63mm
Male A slender insect with a wholly powder-blue, tapering abdomen, dark brown thorax (turns blue with age), short creamy shoulder stripes (fade with age) and dark blue eyes. Blue pruinescence on the upper abdomen wears away to form a dark saddle where the female holds on with her legs during mating. Anal appendages black. Wings clear with long, thin pale brown (or yellowish) pterostigma and pale yellow costa. Legs black. Young (teneral) males similar to female but with pale eyes, thick black markings down sides of abdomen and across the segment joints.
Female Golden-brown, parallel-sided abdomen (shorter than male's) with thin black line down centre crossed by short horizontal lines above segment joints. Brown thorax with yellowish shoulder stripes. Saffron blaze along inner half of leading edge of all wings. Old females have dull grey-brown abdomens. Eyes brown with hint of blue-grey.
Side view Female illustrated. Pale golden-brown along abdomen. Sides of thorax flesh-coloured to yellowish.

Similar species (p. 35)
Black-tailed Skimmer (p. 114)
Both sexes Black-tailed Skimmer lacks pale yellowish shoulder stripes and has blackish pterostigma. **Male** Has extensive black tip to abdomen and yellow spots on sides. **Female** Has broader, tapering, abdomen with two broad black stripes along its length.

Broad-bodied Chaser (p. 112)
Both sexes Broad-bodied Chaser has broader abdomen and both sexes have dark brown wing-bases.

Scarce Chaser (p. 108)
Both sexes Scarce Chaser has broader abdomen, brown wing-bases, dark pterostigma, a dark smudge at wing-tips and lacks shoulder stripes.

Behaviour
Males rest low down on the ground or on a low perch, with wings often held downwards and forwards. They are easily disturbed, but with patience can be approached. When disturbed, they fly fast and erratically, skimming low over the water (usually along the water's edge) or ground. Although not very territorial, males will fly up to investigate other insects intruding into their area. Females spend much of their time settled in vegetation, often quite close to water. Mating takes place low down in vegetation and may last for over half an hour. The female egg-lays by dipping her abdomen in the water whilst in flight, guarded by the male.

Habitat
A species of open heath and peaty moorland, where it breeds in the boggy margins of small streams, runnels and open bog pools with an abundance of bog-loving plants.

Distribution
Widely distributed, but never common, across the southern counties of England, in western Wales, north-west England and western Scotland. Isolated populations outside these areas along the English–Welsh border, in North Yorkshire and Norfolk. Scattered distribution in Ireland.

Site Guide pages
140, 141, 155, 161, 163, 172, 180, 184, 186, 194, 196, 218, 228, 238 .

Species

Keeled Skimmer

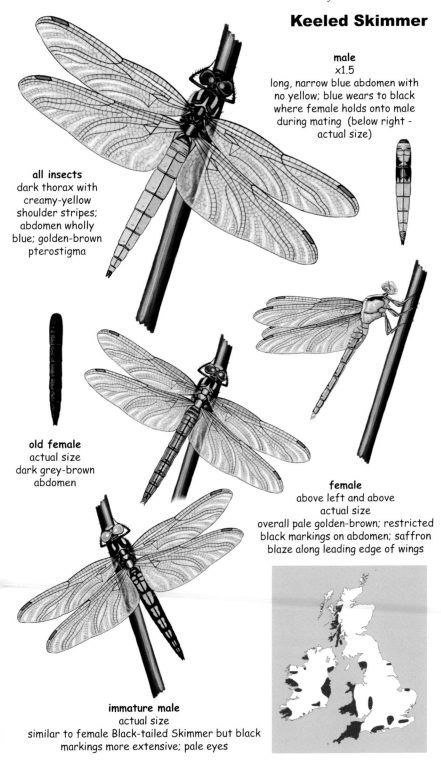

male
x1.5
long, narrow blue abdomen with
no yellow; blue wears to black
where female holds onto male
during mating (below right -
actual size)

all insects
dark thorax with
creamy-yellow
shoulder stripes;
abdomen wholly
blue; golden-brown
pterostigma

Species

old female
actual size
dark grey-brown
abdomen

female
above left and above
actual size
overall pale golden-brown; restricted
black markings on abdomen; saffron
blaze along leading edge of wings

immature male
actual size
similar to female Black-tailed Skimmer but black
markings more extensive; pale eyes

Common Darter   *Sympetrum striolatum*

A small dragonfly and the commonest and most widespread of the red darters. It is found in a variety of habitats, often in large concentrations.

Flight period
End of June to end of October.

Description L 34–42mm, WS 55–62mm
Male Orange-red abdomen with a slightly swollen tip. Dull yellow-brown spots on the sides of segments 2–3 and short, vertical black marks on segments 8–9. Brown thorax can show pale shoulder stripes. Eyes chestnut-brown. Wings clear (although dull brown-grey on older insects) apart from small patch of saffron at base. Pterostigma yellow- or reddish-brown. Legs black with yellow stripe along whole length.
Female Abdomen yellow-brown and eyes mid-brown above. Other markings similar to those of male. Abdomen of mature females turns greyish and may be marked with red.
Immature (not illustrated) As female but has yellow-brown eyes and thorax and sides of abdomen entirely yellow. Young males have a red stripe running down the centre of the yellow abdomen
Side view Female illustrated. Both sexes have two broad greenish-yellow diagonal stripes on sides of the thorax separated by a brown (female) or red (male) stripe. Vulvar scale starts midway down the underside of segment 8, onto segment 9, and protrudes at an angle of 45 degrees (see detail).
Face Male illustrated. In both sexes, note that the thin black line running across the top of the facial disc (frons) does not extend down the sides of the face. The male's eyes are chestnut above and yellow-brown or green below. Face becomes redder with age, but never as deep red as Ruddy Darter's (see also p. 36).

Similar species (pp. 36–37)
Ruddy Darter (p. 122)
Both sexes Ruddy has entirely black

legs (black and yellow on Common).
Male Ruddy's reddish thorax lacks yellow stripes on sides; abdomen clearly brighter red, obviously constricted with clubbed tip and lacks yellow spots at base. **Female** Sides of thorax on Ruddy are plain yellow and lack brown centre of Common (beware – immature Common has plain yellow sides also). Vulvar scale inconspicuous on Ruddy.

Highland Darter (p. 120)
Both sexes Highland has more extensive black markings on the thorax and underside of abdomen.

Black Darter (p. 130)
Black Darter has a black pterostigma. **Female** Black Darter has a dark triangle on the top of the thorax (lacking in all other darters) and wholly black legs.

Behaviour
Males are territorial, perching in prominent positions from which they dart after intruders, often returning to the same spot. Both sexes like to settle on pale surfaces (bare ground, stones, branches, etc.). Copulation occurs around water and egg-laying takes place in tandem, with the male pushing the female downwards so that her abdomen breaks the water surface. Can be approached to within inches with patience, when minor details such as facial markings and the female's vulvar scale can be seen.

Habitat
Occurs in a wide range of water areas including ponds, lakes, ditches and slow-moving streams. Both sexes can be found well away from water and are frequently found in woodland, often in large concentrations.

Common Darter

all insects
brown thorax; tiny amount of
saffron at wing-bases; pterostigma
yellow-brown or reddish-brown;
black legs with yellow stripe

male
x1.5
orange-red
abdomen

female
note vulvar scale below
segments 8–9

female
left and above right
actual size
straw-yellow abdomen;
greenish-yellow stripes separated by
darker panel (brown on female, red on
male) on sides of thorax

face
note that black mark
across the top of the
frons does not extend
down the sides

Distribution

Widespread and abundant throughout much of England, Wales and Ireland, although absent from much of the upland areas of northern England and northern Wales. Spreading northwards through southern Scotland. Migrants from the Continent probably arrive most years.

Site Guide pages

143, 158, 169, 173, 179, 183, 191, 198, 201, 208, 214, 216, 234, 235.

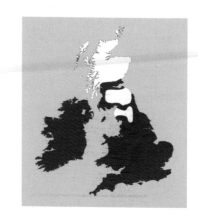

Highland Darter   *Sympetrum nigrescens*

A scarce species restricted to the northern and western areas of the Highlands of Scotland, where it replaces Common Darter. Although some authorities consider this to be a smaller, darker subspecies of Common Darter, subtle differences in the genitalia provide some evidence for it being treated as a distinct species.

Flight period
End of June to early October.

Description L 31–37mm, WS 52–58mm
Male From above, almost indistin-guishable from Common Darter but the black bands at the base of the abdomen (segment 1) are broader. See side view for further differences.
Female Very similar to female Common Darter when seen from above but has more black at top of abdomen (segment 1) and black on sides of first few and last few segments visible from above. Darkened individual illustrated.
Immature (not illustrated) Similar to female.
Side view Male illustrated. Both sexes have extensive black markings around the yellow-green diagonal stripes on the sides of the thorax; these two yellow stripes are separated by a black panel containing three reddish (male) or yellowish (female) spots. Highland Darter also has more extensive black markings than Common Darter on the sides and underside of the abdomen. Both sexes have black-and-yellow legs, but the yellow is restricted to a stripe on the tibia (lower leg).
Face Male illustrated. In both sexes, note that the black line running across the top of the facial disc (frons) is broader than that on Common Darter and extends down the sides of the face slightly.

Similar species (p. 36–37)
Common Darter (p. 118)
Both sexes See above for main differences. In the few areas that Highland and Common Darters both occur, individuals showing intermediate characteristics can be found.

Black Darter (p. 130)
Both sexes Black Darter has black pterostigma. **Female** Black Darter has a dark triangle on top of the thorax and wholly black legs.

Behaviour
Habits are as Common Darter but generally less active. Shows a strong preference for pale-coloured objects on which to perch. Breeding behaviour also as Common, with copulation taking place around water, and oviposition in tandem with the male controlling the downward dipping motion that allows the female's abdomen to break the water surface.

Habitat
Found around many water types including bog pools, lochs, lochans and slow-moving streams, especially those near the coast. Away from water, both sexes can be found in woodland clearings and rides, on heather moorland and sand dunes.

Distribution
Found in the north-west of Scotland. Believed to also occur in western Ireland and the Isle of Man.

Site Guide pages
146, 174, 175, 176, 187, 188, 189.

Highland Darter

male
x1.5
black bands at top of
segment 1 broader than
on Common Darter

all insects
yellow-brown or
red-brown
pterostigma

older female
actual size
overall quite dark; dull straw-yellow
abdomen; black markings on segment 1
broader than on Common Darter

male
actual size
extensive black markings to sides of
thorax and underside of abdomen; legs
black with yellow stripe on tibia only

Highland

Common

faces of Highland and Common Darters
note that the broader black mark at the top of
the face on Highland Darter extends slightly
down the sides

Ruddy Darter   *Sympetrum sanguineum*

This small dragonfly is superficially similar to Common Darter, but the abdomen of a mature male Ruddy Darter is deep, blood-red rather than orange-red.

Flight period
End of June to mid-October.

Description   L 32–38mm, WS 52–58mm
Male One of the smallest of the red darters. The mature male is best told from other red darters by its blood-red abdomen, which is clearly constricted at the waist (segments 3–5) giving a very heavy, club-ended appearance, with prominent black marks in the centre of segments 8–9. Red-brown thorax lacks shoulder stripes. Note also the red pterostigma and the small patch of saffron at the wing-bases. Immature male similar to female, but with reddish tinge to eyes, thorax and centre of abdomen.
Female Very similar to female Common Darter. Yellow-brown abdomen narrow below swollen base. Thorax brown without shoulder stripes. Ptero-stigma red-brown. Wings obtain yellow cast with age. Older females acquire red coloration.
Side view Female illustrated. Note that both sexes have entirely black legs (black-and-yellow in other red darters). Eyes brown above, yellow below. Sides of thorax entirely yellow (entirely red-brown on male).
Face Male illustrated. Note the eyes are brownish-red above, dark green below. The facial disc is blood-red and the black line above the frons (upper half of facial disc) extends down the sides of the face.

Similar species (pp. 36–37)
Common Darter (p. 118)
Both sexes All ages and sexes of Common have black-and-yellow legs (black in Ruddy). Mature Common have yellow stripes on the sides of the thorax separated by a brown panel (unstriped in Ruddy) and are less heavily marked with black on the sides of the abdomen than Ruddy. **Male** Common has paler, orange-red abdomen with straight sides (no narrow waist) and yellow-brown spots on sides of segments 2–3. **Female** Common has prominent vulvar scale (inconspicuous on Ruddy).

Black Darter (p. 130)
Immatures and females Ruddy lacks the black triangle on the upper thorax of Black Darter, but both species have black legs. Note also the extensive black sides to the abdomen, black central panel on side of thorax, and black pterostigma of Black Darter.

Behaviour
A quick darter, although when disturbed does not usually fly far before settling. Flight not as direct as that of Common Darter, appearing more 'skippy', and also hovers more often. Sits on open perches like other darters and also enjoys basking on pale-coloured surfaces, such as bare ground or a log. Males will defend a small area around favoured perches, but are not as territorial as Common Darter. Copulation takes place in waterside vegetation, after which egg-laying occurs in tandem, with the female's abdomen tip breaking the water surface in a swinging motion.

Habitat
Prefers lushly vegetated ponds, ditches, lakes and canals and can tolerate quite brackish conditions. Woodland is usually close by for feeding.

Distribution
A localised species throughout its stronghold of south-eastern England but has recently expanded its range northwards and westwards in England, Wales and Ireland. Small influxes from the Continent probably occur most years.

Ruddy Darter

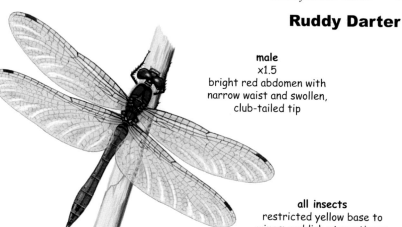

male
x1.5
bright red abdomen with
narrow waist and swollen,
club-tailed tip

Species

all insects
restricted yellow base to
wings; reddish pterostigma;
black legs - no yellow; thorax
lacks shoulder stripes;
abdominal segments 8 & 9
with prominent black dashes
from above

female
actual size
bright yellow-straw abdomen; all-yellow sides to thorax - no stripes;
vulvar scale below segments 8 & 9 does not protrude noticeably

Ruddy
eyes chestnut on top
and dark green below;
red face

Common
eyes chestnut on top
and pale green below;
pale face

faces of Ruddy and Common Darters
note difference in colour of face and the extent
of the black mark across the top and sides of the
frons (upper half of face)

Site Guide pages
145, 158, 159, 171, 179, 180, 183, 184, 186,
198, 201, 210, 212, 221, 224, 230, 235,
236, 239.

Red-veined Darter   *Sympetrum fonscolombii*

A bright darter found annually as an immigrant in varying numbers in southern England, with small numbers breeding. Males have bright red veins (yellowish on females) in the wings, from which the species gets its English name.

Species

Flight period
Arrives in Britain from early June onwards, but usually seen during July and August. Immigrations associated with southerly or south-easterly winds. Flight period in southern Europe is from June to October.

Description L 34–42mm, WS 57–63mm
Male Larger and more robust than other red darters. All wings with obvious bright red veins in the inner half of each wing and along the front edge (including the costa) as far as the pterostigma. The pterostigma is distinctive (both sexes), with the pale brown centre contrasting sharply with the thick black veins above and below it. Bright pinkish-scarlet, parallel-sided abdomen. The short, vertical black markings in the centre of segments 8–9 are thicker than on other red darters. Brown thorax lacks shoulder stripes.

Female Although similar to other female darters, Red-veined always appears more uniformly yellow (including the thorax) with fewer, but clearer, black markings, including larger markings on segments 8–9 (as male). Some older females can have reddish coloration, especially along abdominal joints. Wing venation yellow at bases and along leading edge. Less yellow than male at wing-bases.

Side view Female illustrated. Note the blue-green sides of the thorax and distinctive blue lower half of the eyes (same in male) with brown above (more reddish-brown on male). Legs largely black with thin yellow stripe along their length. Female has whitish face (male reddish) with black line along the top and extending down sides of frons (upper half of facial disc).

Similar species (p. 36)
Both sexes are generally quite similar to all of the other red darters, but the red/yellow wing venation, pale brown pterostigma edged with thick black veins, and blue lower half of the eyes are characteristic. See also individual species accounts, pp. 118–129, 134–5.

Behaviour
Like other members of the genus, prefers to perch on vegetation out in the open or on bare ground. Males are aggressive in defence of their territories. Males have a rapid zig-zagging flight interspersed with regular, often prolonged, hovering. Egg-laying females repeatedly dip their abdomen tips into the water, often when still in tandem. Strongly migratory.

Habitat
In the UK, Red-veined Darter is usually found on small to medium, well-vegetated, shallow ponds, lakes and ditches, including coastal brackish waters.

Distribution
Small numbers are recorded annually, usually from the south-east and south-west of England, and in particular the southern tip of Cornwall. Several sites in Kent, Dorset and Cornwall regularly hold small numbers of breeding individuals. The record influx of 2006 saw over 800 insects arrive across England and into Ireland and breeding confirmed from inland areas such as Cambridgeshire and as far north as Lancashire and Yorkshire. The influx also saw only the second-ever record for Scotland (see p. 13).

Red-veined Darter

male
x1.5
extensive red veins along leading
edges of wings and in inner half of
wings (some not as well marked as
illustrated); thick, black vertical
dashes on segments 8 & 9

all insects
pale brown pterostigma bordered by
broad black veins; yellow patches at
wing-bases more extensive than on
Common and Ruddy Darters

female
above and right - actual size
wings with extensive yellow veins; bright
yellow abdomen with clean black markings -
these include short vertical dashes on segments
2 & 3 and thicker dashes on segments 8 & 9;
blue-green sides to thorax

female head
characteristic blue lower eyes; frons
white or off-white (reddish on male)

Yellow-winged Darter   *Sympetrum flaveolum*

A rare but near annual migrant from the Continent, easily distinguished from other red darters by the extensive saffron-yellow colouring on all wings.

Species

Flight period
Mid-July to mid-September.

Description L 31–37mm, WS 52–58mm
Male Saffron-yellow wing markings typically occupy the inner third of the wing and appear brighter and more obvious on the hindwing. The wing veins are orange and yellow within these coloured areas but black throughout the rest of the wings. The wing-patches and veins are usually brighter and more extensive on males than females. Abdomen orange-red with extensive black markings down sides; parallel-sided below swollen base. Thorax reddish-brown without shoulder stripes. Yellow-brown pterostigma with obvious dark lines above and below.
Female Extensive colour to wings as male, but many females also have a second patch around the wrist (node). Yellow patches fade with age. Straw-coloured abdomen is similar to that of other female darters from above, but sides more heavily marked with black.
Side view Female illustrated. Abdomen with thick black line down side and very pale blue-grey along the length of the underside. Sides of thorax are yellowish (both sexes). Legs are black with a yellowish stripe along their length. Eyes chestnut above and yellowish below (more brown below on male).
Face Male illustrated. Both sexes have an orange facial disc with the black line across the top extending part-way down the sides of the face.

Similar species (p. 36)
Yellow-winged should not be confused with other red darters as no other species has such extensive saffron wing-patches – Common (p. 118) and Ruddy (p. 122) show a very limited amount of yellow at wing-bases; Red-veined (p. 124) has

more extensive yellow wing-bases than these two species but the male has red wing veins and both sexes have bluish lower halves to the eyes and thick black veins surrounding the pterostigma.

Behaviour
This species has the most fluttery flight of the red darters, and frequently settles low down in sheltered vegetation. Tends to hover just before landing. Shows a preference for pool margins. Females oviposit in tandem among aquatic vegetation at the water's edge.

Habitat
Breeding sites are typically lushly vegetated shallow pools, ponds and small lakes. Although breeding was previously suspected (and almost certainly overlooked), it wasn't confirmed until 1996 and 1997 after the massive 1995 immigration (see below).

Distribution
Widespread over much of western, central and eastern Europe, with near annual immigrations to Britain – mainly in the east. Most British records come from coastal areas (or not far inland), but in exceptional immigrations (e.g. 1995) insects move across Britain and may appear on the west coast and breeding has then been recorded. Coastal records are just as likely from dry habitats as from wet habitats, and obviously denote point of arrival in many cases, e.g. Great Yarmouth Cemetery, Norfolk, in 1995, when several hundred insects arrived en masse. From these arrival locations, numbers soon disperse, but in the event of large numbers this can take several days.

Site Guide pages
163, 171, 221.

Yellow-winged Darter

male
x1.5
extensive yellow wing-patches;
black down sides of abdomen
visible from above

female
left and right - actual size
straw-coloured abdomen; underside of abdomen
powder-blue with obvious paired black lines (female)
or single, broader black line (male) along the side;
sides of thorax yellowish – no stripes

all insects
extensive yellow wing-patches with
orange and yellow veins; yellow-brown
or pale-red pterostigma with dark
borders; strong black markings down
sides of abdomen

male
some males have more
yellow on wings

face
eyes chestnut on top, pale below; note
extent and shape of black across top
and down sides of frons (face)

Vagrant Darter

Sympetrum vulgatum

An extremely rare vagrant that has probably been (and continues to be) overlooked owing to its similarity to Common Darter.

Flight period
In Britain, recent records have all been in August and September and are certainly of Continental origin, where it is on the wing from July to September.

Description L 33–39mm, WS 57–63mm
This species lies between Common and Ruddy Darter in appearance. It is easiest to describe it by direct comparison with Common Darter and other darters.
Male a) abdomen slightly brighter red with more obvious constriction between segments 3–5 and more bulbous tip than Common (but shape not as pronounced as Ruddy); **b)** two yellowish spots on either side of segments 2–3 at the top of the abdomen (three in Common); **c)** short, black 'dagger-tip' marks on segments 8–9 – longer but blunter on Common; **d)** thorax sides uniformly coloured (as Ruddy) the same shade of brown as the upper thorax and lack the distinct yellow-green stripes of Common; **e)** face – the black line across the top of the face extends part-way down sides of face – does not extend down sides on Common ; **f)** legs – yellow with black stripe (black with yellow stripe on Common); **g)** wings – red veins on forewings and pterostigma pale reddish-brown with more contrasting black veins than Common's; **h)** paired black spots on upperside of segments 3–8 ringed in orange-yellow (barely notice-able on Common).
Female Compared to Common Darter the main differences are: **a)** sides of thorax are poorly marked brown or yellow and lack the central 'dark' panel of Common; **b)** note that the vulvar scale protrudes at 90 degrees to abdomen and is entirely below segment 9, whereas in Common it protrudes at 45 degrees, is much less prominent and extends from segment 8 onto segment 9; **c)** facial pattern as male; **d)** wings (with yellow veins on forewings) and legs as male.

Similar species (p. 36)
Vagrant Darter has been recorded only from eastern and southern England and is likely to be confused only with Common Darter. As many as possible of the 'suite' of features listed above should be noted when confronted with a possible Vagrant Darter. When seen well, Vagrant Darter is not a difficult species to identify. See also individual species accounts, pp. 118–126, 134–5.

Behaviour
A typical darter, perching in the open, with a preference for pale objects.

Records
This is a common and widespread species in central and north-eastern Europe. In the UK, it has been found during mass immigrations of other Continental species such as Yellow-winged Darter. Finding localities have been largely coastal, including pools and lagoons as well as parkland-type habitats (denoting point of arrival). Most of the eight pre-1946 records came from the London area, with others from the Sussex coast and the Humber area of Yorkshire. In 1995, the first of that year's influx of 25 individuals (and the first since 1946) were identified in Great Yarmouth Cemetery, Norfolk (S. P. Dudley, C. Dudley, T. J. & M. Benton, P. J. Milford *et al*; Heath, P. 1996. *Atropos* 1: 12–17) during a mass immigration of Yellow-winged Darters. Four (three males and a single female) were found on 2nd August, and at least ten individuals were present the following day. Several other sites in southern England recorded small numbers during the same period, incl. Dungeness, Kent, from 3rd to 9th August.

Vagrant Darter

male
x1.5
two pairs of yellowish spots on segments
2 & 3 below black-banded abdomen base;
segments 3 to 5 constricted; clean,
dagger-like black marks on segments 8 &
9: reddish veins in forewings

Species

female
actual size
yellowish veins in forewings; sides
of thorax usually poorly marked and
plain brown or yellow and always lack
darker central panel

female
note vulvar scale protruding at 90
degrees below segment 9

all insects
pale reddish-brown pterostigma with
black borders; short pale shoulder
stripes (sometimes absent); yellow legs
with black stripe

Vagrant

Common

Highland

Ruddy

**Yellow-
winged**

Black

faces of different male darter species
note colour of face and the extent of the black mark across the top
and sides of the frons (face)

Black Darter
Sympetrum danae

The smallest British darter. The mature male Black Darter is the only member of the group with a largely black abdomen. A widespread species of acid heaths.

Species

Flight period
Early July to early October.

Description L 33–40mm, WS 50–56mm
Male Mainly black from above. Thorax lacks shoulder stripes. Yellow spots on sides of segments 1–5 and pairs of yellow spots on top of segments 8–9 darken with age to dull orange. Note also the totally clear wings with black ptero-stigma. Abdomen constricted between segments 3–5. Immatures are very similar to adult females, and have the dark downward-pointing triangle on top of the thorax (see below), but the eyes are pale and the pterostigma is yellow or brown.
Female Eyes dark brown. Thorax and abdomen largely golden-yellow (becoming browner with age). Note the dark, downward-pointing triangle on the top of the thorax, which is unique in British dragonflies. Abdomen gently tapered from swollen base and segments 8–9 have distinctive inverted black 'T'-shaped markings. Black pterostigma. Small amount of saffron at wing-bases. Females darken with age and long-lived insects are largely grey.
Side view *All ages* – two yellow stripes on the sides of the thorax separated by a black panel with three yellow spots; abdomen black along lower sides and on underside; legs all-black at all stages in both sexes. *Female* (illustrated) – much black on sides of abdomen and thin black lines along segment joints; note the prominent vulvar scale below segment 9 held at 90 degrees to the abdomen. *Maturing male* (illustrated) – abdomen golden-yellow on emergence but turns progressively black with age.
Face Mature male illustrated. Yellow face darkens with age but usually retains some yellow around the sides. Eyes blackish (brown on female).

Similar species (pp. 36–37)
White-faced Darter (p. 132)
Flight periods overlap in July. White-faced Darter has white face, obvious shoulder stripes (red on male, yellow on female and immatures), and dark patches at wing-bases. Female and immature White-faced Darter are predominantly black with line of yellow spots down centre of abdomen.

Other darters (pp. 118–135)
Immature males and females Black Darter can be separated from all other immature and female darters by its dark downward-pointing triangle on the upper thorax. All-black legs separate from all but Ruddy Darter.

Emerald dragonflies (pp. 102–106)
The three emerald dragonfly species may be confused with male Black Darter as they are uniformly dark and share its habitat, but they are larger and obviously green when seen well. Note also different behaviour.

Behaviour
From a low perch, males dart low over the boggy areas of breeding ponds, frequently hovering before returning to the same or another favoured perch. Flight is 'skippy' and similar to that of Ruddy Darter. Females hide in heather or grass and wait for a male to find them. Egg-laying usually occurs in tandem, the male dipping the female down to the water and up again in flight. Can occur in high densities.

Habitat
Acid bogs, shallow pools, lake margins and ditches in upland moorland bogs and lowland heaths. The best sites contain much *Sphagnum* with sheltered fringe vegetation.

Black Darter

male
x1.5
mainly black from above with yellow spots
(darkening with age) on sides of segments 1-5
and pairs of yellow spots on top of segments
8-9; constricted waist and swollen abdomen tip

face of male
eyes blackish on
top, paler below;
yellow face
darkens with age

all insects
black pterostigma;
black legs

female
above left and right
actual size
thorax - dark, downward-pointing triangle
above and three yellow spots in black panel
between yellow stripes on sides; abdomen
- yellow above with inverted 'T' marks on top
of segments 8 & 9 and (from side) vulvar scale
under tip held at 90 degrees; small saffron
patches at wing-bases

maturing male
actual size
yellow on top of abdomen broken
by black extending up from sides

Distribution
A widespread but localised species
due to its habitat preference of lowland
heaths and upland moorland, but more
widespread in the uplands of the north
and west. Late-summer immigration
from the near Continent also noted.

Site Guide pages
138, 141, 144, 146, 147, 149, 156, 164,
167, 172, 174, 182, 187, 189, 190, 199,
210, 218, 230.

White-faced Darter

Leucorrhinia dubia

This rare, aptly named, striking dragonfly is black with yellow (immatures and females) or deep red (males) markings.

Flight period
Mid-May to end of July.

Description L 31–37mm, WS 50–58mm
Male This is the only British dragonfly which is predominantly black with red markings. Thorax black with red shoulder stripes and red spots between the wing-bases. Abdomen is narrow and slightly constricted; red at base and red spots in centre of segments 4–7 darken with age. Dark brown patches at wing-bases (larger on hindwings) and wings have a smoky-blue sheen in the sun. Pterostigma dark brown. Legs black. White face is clearly visible from above.
Female Similar to male but markings are yellow and more extensive on segments 1–7. The markings darken to ochre with age. Note that the dark brown wing-bases are edged with saffron.
Side view Male illustrated. Appears largely dark from the side, with the red restricted to stripes on the sides of the thorax and to patches at the base of the abdomen. White patch below segments 3–4. Legs black.
Face All insects have a brilliant-white face. Four-spotted Chaser has a whitish or yellowish face, but this is usually greyer and darkens with age (and the abdomen and wings of the two species are obviously very different).

Similar species (p. 37)
Black Darter (p. 130)
Males unmistakable, but females can be confused with male Black Darter. Black Darter occurs at many of this species' sites but note that flight periods overlap only in July. In addition, male Black Darter lacks shoulder stripes and has two broad yellow stripes separated by a black panel on the side of the thorax, clear wing-bases, and black-and-yellow rather than white face.

Behaviour
An energetic species which will quickly disappear when disturbed. Flight very bouncy. Territorial males patrol low over the water, frequently hovering, and will suddenly speed off to catch a prey item or take up aerial combat with a rival. Frequently settle low down close to the margins of bog pools on vegetation, bare ground, logs or stones. Copulation takes place low down amongst vegetation, bushes or heather. The female usually lays her eggs alone (although the male is often not far away), dipping her abdomen tip into areas of wet moss and between other swamped vegetation.

Habitat
Sheltered lowland *Sphagnum* bogs with fairly deep pools which contain no fish (the larvae feed by day and so are susceptible to predation). Scrub and woodland used for maturing, feeding and roosting.

Distribution
A rare species in Britain with isolated populations in Staffordshire, the English–Welsh border, Cumbria and Scotland. Scotland is the stronghold, and it is an easy species to see around Speyside and the West Highlands. Recent extinctions in Surrey and Cheshire. Colonies have also been lost in some areas of Scotland and this species is now one of only three species (with Southern Damselfly and Norfolk Hawker) protected under Schedule 1 of the Wildlife and Countryside Act 1981, and a permit is required to catch this species.

Site Guide pages
138, 144, 146, 156, 174.

White-faced Darter

male
x1.5
unique black-and-red markings; much red at base of abdomen and red spots on top of segments 4-7 (latter darken and become less obvious with age)

all insects
white face; shoulder stripes - red on male, yellow on female and immatures; wing-bases brown - most obvious on hindwings: short dark pterostigma; black legs

female
actual size
black-and-yellow markings give 'skeletal' appearance

face
bright white face visible from most angles

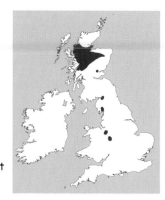

male
actual size
red stripes on sides of thorax; abdomen with red at base and white patch below segments 3-4

Banded Darter   *Sympetrum pedemontanum*

This small darter is distinctive but is an extremely rare vagrant to Britain.

Flight period
On the Continent, July to October.

Description L 30–36mm, WS 50–56mm
Male Unmistakable. Brown bands across each wing; bright red pterostigma. The bright red abdomen superficially resembles that of Ruddy Darter, but is slightly broader and less constricted. Eyes and thorax reddish-brown. Legs black.
Female Unmistakable. Wings as the male but yellow-brown pterostigma. Abdomen like a female red darter's.

Behaviour
Surprisingly weak, fluttery flight.

Prefers to settle amongst tall vegetation rather than on the ground.

Similar species
The banded wings make both sexes unmistakable.

Records
This species has a patchy European distribution. Isolated pockets in The Netherlands and northern Germany. Its main range is in hilly areas from northern Italy and Switzerland eastwards. One British record (Gwent, August 1995) during the massive darter influx.

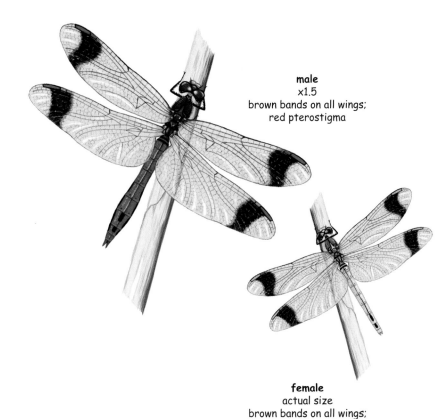

male
x1.5
brown bands on all wings;
red pterostigma

female
actual size
brown bands on all wings;
yellowish pterostigma

Scarlet Darter

Crocothemis erythraea

A distinctive but very rare vagrant from southern Europe and North Africa.

Flight period

In Europe, two generations a year, between April and November.

Description L 41–47mm, WS 66–72mm

Male In general shape resembles a chaser. Brilliant scarlet-red abdomen with fine black line down centre. Deep red-brown thorax, eyes and face. Bright red veins along leading edge of each wing. Wings also have yellow suffusion at bases, larger on hindwing. Long yellowish-brown pterostigma framed with black. Legs dull red.

Female Resembles a chaser or skimmer. Generally grey-brown in colour with pale shoulder stripes and a distinctive pale stripe between the bases of the wings. Abdomen has three black stripes along its length and orange sides.

Similar species

Males should not be confused with any other British dragonfly, but females could be mistaken for either a chaser or a skimmer. Note the shape and colour of the abdomen (with dark line down centre), yellow wing-bases and long yellowish-brown pterostigma.

Behaviour

Adults perch on tall pool-side vegetation or on the ground. Flight is fast, with frequent hovers.

Records

There have been only five records of this southern European/North African species since the first in 1995 – Cornwall (August 1995 and August 1998), Isle of Wight (September 1997), Devon (June 2000) and Hampshire (June 2002).

Species

all insects
yellow at base of hindwings (more extensive on male);
golden pterostigma bordered with black veins

female
actual size

male
x1.5
vivid red eyes,
thorax and
abdomen; red veins
along front edge of
all four wings

SITE GUIDE

Your site-by-site guide to the best dragonfly sites in Britain

Locations of the main sites featured in the *Site Guide*. Each numbered spot on the map below refers to map number on the page right.

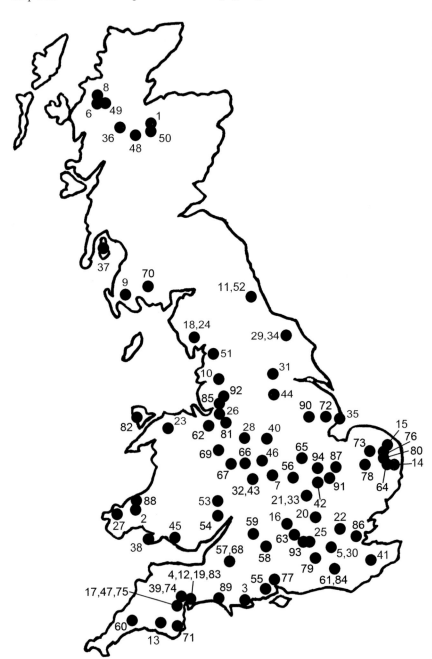

Site Guide

Site Guide

ABERNETHY FOREST
Speyside, Highland
RSPB | www.rspb.org.uk, Scottish Natural Heritage | www.snh.org.uk

NH 960 180
OS Map 36

Species
Good numbers of many northern species including several Scottish specialities:
Large Red Damselfly
Northern Damselfly
Common Blue Damselfly
Common Hawker
Golden-ringed Dragonfly
Northern Emerald
Four-spotted Chaser
Black Darter
White-faced Darter

Habitat
Abernethy Forest is part of the remaining Caledonian pine forest. The forest floor is greatly undulating with many boggy areas; there are also several areas of standing water including lochs and lochans. *Sphagnum* bogs, rich in insect life, are common throughout the area.

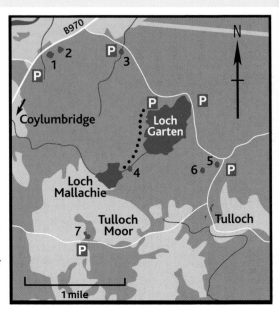

Location
Abernethy Forest lies *c*.6 miles north-east of Aviemore.

Access & Areas to Search
The area is accessed from the B970 Coylumbridge to Nethy Bridge road.

Pool 1   **Abernethy Forest Wood**   **NH 954 192**
A small, circular, well-vegetated pool with *Sphagnum* surrounded by trees which is good for **Northern Damselfly**. **Northern Emerald** has been seen here.

Park in Abernethy Forest Wood car park (NH 953 191) on the B970 opposite the turn to Boat of Garten. Take the footpath behind the notice board (running parallel with the road). The pool is on your right after about 120m.

Pool 2   **Abernethy Forest Wood**   **NH 956 194**
Larger than Pool 1, this is a U-shaped pool with a small wooded island. **Northern Emerald** has been seen here.

Proceed past Pool 1, continue over a small wooden footbridge (after *c*.150m) and then head right, through the trees, to the pool.

Pool 3   **Abernethy Forest Wood**   **NH 967 192**
A large, open, woodland pool with *Sphagnum* areas. Holds good numbers of Common Blue and **Northern Damselflies**. **Northern Emerald** has been seen.

Take the road signed for the RSPB Ospreys (off B970) and park along the road either side of the pool (do not obstruct gateways). Alternatively, you can park in the RSPB Loch Garten car park and walk back along the road.

Pool 4   **Abernethy Forest**   **NH 967 176**
A marsh pool and bog with stunted pines good for **Northern Emerald**.

Park in the Loch Garten car park and follow the marked trail towards Loch Mallachie. The marshy pool is left of the trail just before Loch Mallachie.

Pool 5   **Abernethy Forest**   **NH 982 175**
This is a tiny, circular pool in a heather bog and is particularly good for **White-faced Darter**. **Northern Emerald** has been seen here.

East of the Osprey centre take the next right (signed Tulloch). Park on the left before the cottage at NH 982 174. Walk back to the T-junction, turn left and then left again, through the trees along a narrow path, to a tiny fenced pool. Do not enter the fenced area. Caution – boggy and uneven ground.

Pool 6   **Abernethy Forest**   **NH 979 171**
This is another area to search for **Northern Emerald**. Males patrol the open pools in the *Sphagnum* areas.

Parking as for Pool 5 at NH 982 174. Walk away from the T-junction to Gate House Cottage (towards Tulloch). Turn right immediately after the cottage and walk down the slope through the trees alongside a wire fence. At the bottom, head out from the end of the fence in the direction of 10 o'clock. Continue through the trees until you come to an open boggy area with scattered trees and open *Sphagnum* pools. Caution – boggy and uneven ground.

Pool 7   **Tulloch Moor**   **NH 961 164**
Continue past Gate House Cottage and take the next right signed Tulloch Moor. After *c*.2.5 miles, park in the grass pull-in on the right opposite a farm track at NH 960 162. The pool is at 2 o'clock from the pull-in through the heather. The small pool opposite the parking area is also worth checking.

Timing
Northern Damselfly, **Northern Emerald** and **White-faced Darter** are the main interest species within these sites, and all three species should be seen during a visit in July, although numbers of White-faced Darter do begin to drop from mid-month. All other species, and other Scottish specialities at other sites (Azure Hawker and Highland Darter) should be seen during this period.

Additional Information
You can spend a whole day moving between these sites or combine with a visit to Loch Gamhna. Waterpoof boots or wellingtons and insect repellent are essential. Abernethy Information Centre in Nethybridge village is open between April and October. RSPB visitor facilities, including Osprey viewing, at Loch Garten, where an entrance fee for non-RSPB members applies.

Other Wildlife
An outstanding area. Other wildlife to look out for includes Scotch Argus and Large Heath butterflies, Goldeneye, Osprey, Crested Tit and Red Squirrel.

AFON BRYNBERIAN
near Cardigan, Pembrokeshire

SN 099 347
OS Map 145

Species
Beautiful Demoiselle
Small Red Damselfly
Southern Damselfly
Scarce Blue-tailed Damselfly
Golden-ringed Dragonfly
Keeled Skimmer

Habitat
Moorland with streams.

Location
The moorland area around Afon Brynberian lies *c*.4 miles south-east of Newport.

Leave the A487 (Newport to Eglwyswrw road) just west of Eglwyswrw along the B4329. Follow this road south for *c*.3 miles and park carefully in wide entrance to gated farm track on your left at SN 092 345. Alternatively, park in Brynberian.

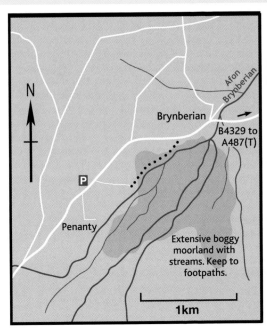

Access & Areas to Search
From the gate, walk down the track (public footpath) and through the farm buildings to the moorland area (close all gates). Follow public footpaths as indicated on OS Map 145. Search streams around footpaths.

Caution should be taken in this extremely boggy area.

Timing
End June to end July for all species.

Additional Information
A superb moorland site. Good waterproof walking boots or wellingtons recommended.

This site can be combined with Dowrog Common and the Welsh Wildlife Centre.

ARNE
near Wareham, Dorset
RSPB | www.rspb.org.uk

SY 972 878
OS Map 195

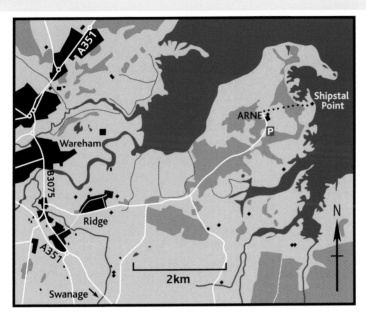

Species
Small Red Damselfly
Migrant Hawker
Downy Emerald
Black Darter

Habitat
Lowland heath with scattered mixed woodland.

Location
Arne reserve lies on the southern edge of Poole Harbour, *c.*3 miles east of Wareham.

Leave the A35 (the Dorchester to Poole road) north of Wareham and take the A351 towards Swanage. On the south side of Wareham, take left turn along the minor road to Ridge and follow the signs for Arne.

Access & Areas to Search
Watch the man-made ponds en-route to the hide at Shipstal Point.

Timing
Mid-July to the end of August for most species except **Downy Emerald**, which is an early flyer from the end of May to early July.

Additional Information
This site can be combined with one or more sites in the New Forest.

Other Wildlife
Heathland bird species include Dartford Warbler, Hobby and Nightjar.

AYLESBEARE COMMON

SY 057 898

near Exeter, Devon

OS Map 192

RSPB | www.rspb.org.uk

Site Guide

Species

Over 20 species including:
Southern Damselfly
Hairy Dragonfly
Emperor Dragonfly
Golden-ringed
  Dragonfly
Keeled Skimmer

Habitat

Wet and dry
heathland.

Location

Aylesbeare Common
lies *c*.8 miles to the
east of Exeter.

The reserve lies 6
miles (9.5 km) east
of Junction 30 of the
M5 off the A3052.
Travel 0.5 mile
past the Halfway Inn, then turn right towards Hawkerland and the car park is
immediately on the left.

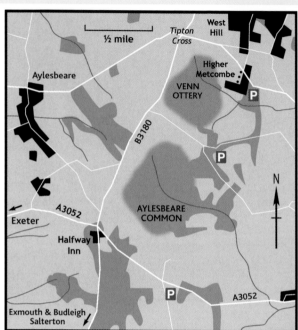

Access & Areas to Search

Park at SY 059 903. Keep to public footpaths and other marked trails.

Timing

Mid-May to mid-June for **Hairy Dragonfly**, July for **Southern Damselfly** and
early June to mid-July for **Keeled Skimmer**.

Additional Information

Parking is free. There is a wheelchair-friendly access track.

This site can be combined with any of the many other sites in the area including
Chudleigh Knighton Heath, Colaton Raleigh Common, Haldon Forest, Little
Bradley Ponds, Slapton Ley, Stafford Bridge, Stover Country Park and Venn
Ottery (also butterflies).

Other Wildlife

Heathland bird species include Dartford Warbler, Hobby and Stonechat. Thirty-
five species of butterfly have been recorded.

BEDFONT LAKES COUNTRY PARK   TQ 084 729

near Hounslow, Greater London   **OS Map 176**

managed by Hounslow Community Initiatives Partnership | www.hounslow.info

Species

Good numbers of
commoner species
including:
Common Blue
 Damselfly
Emperor Dragonfly
Four-spotted Chaser
Black-tailed Skimmer
Common Darter

Habitat

Open lakes (old
gravel workings) with
shallows, surrounded
by rolling meadows
and woodlands.

Location

Bedfont Lakes Country
Park lies just east of
Staines within the M25
ring.

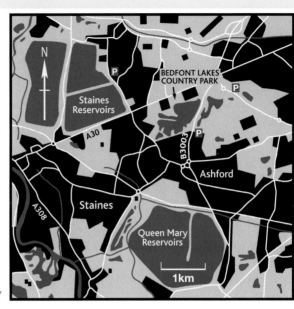

Leave the M25 at Junction 13 and take the A30 towards London. Go through
the Crooked Billet traffic-light complex and over another set of traffic lights by
Ashford Hospital to the Clockhouse Roundabout, where you take the fourth
exit into Clockhouse Lane (B3003). The visitor centre is on the left-hand side
(signed).

Access & Areas to Search

From the free car park follow the footpaths around each of the lakes. There is an
information centre and toilet facilities with disabled access.

Timing

A visit in July will see the greatest variety of species on the wing.

Additional Information

A small number of **Red-veined Darters** appeared at this site in 1996.

This site can be combined with Esher and Fairmile Commons.

Site Guide

BEINN EIGHE NNR
near Kinlochewe, Highland

NH 001 650
OS Map 19

National Nature Reserve managed by Scottish Natural Heritage | www.snh.org.uk

Species
Azure Hawker
Common Hawker
Golden-ringed
  Dragonfly
Northern Emerald
Highland Darter
Black Darter
White-faced Darter

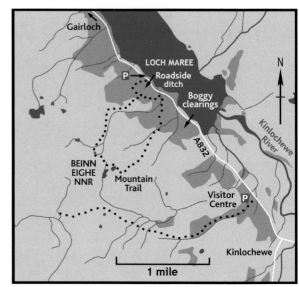

Habitat
Boggy clearings along the wooded foot slopes of the mountains.

Location
Beinn Eighe is a huge mountainous area flanking Loch Maree, to the north-west of Kinlochewe along the A832.

From Kinlochewe take the A832 north-west along the western side of Loch Maree. After *c*.2.5 miles park in the car park on the loch side of the road (NH 001 650).

Access & Areas to Search
Walk north along the road and search the *Sphagnum* roadside ditch on the west side at NG 998 653. Walk south along the road for *c*.0.3 miles, and search the open boggy area on the west side of the road at NH 004 647.

Northern Emerald occurs throughout the area and is relatively easy to see around the boggy areas or along the roadside ditch, where it breeds.

Timing
Mid- to end of July should see all the species mentioned above on the wing.

Additional Information
Waterproof boots and insect repellent essential. Public toilets at Beinn Eighe Centre at NH 019 629, 1 mile north-west of Kinlochewe. Reserve leaflet and booklet available.

This site can be easily combined with Bridge of Grudie and Loch Coulin & Loch Clair.

Other Wildlife
Golden Eagle, Pine Marten and Red Deer all occur in the area.

BRANDON MARSH
near Coventry, Warwickshire
Warwickshire Wildlife Trust | www.warwickshire-wildlife-trust.org.uk

SP 386 754
OS Map 140

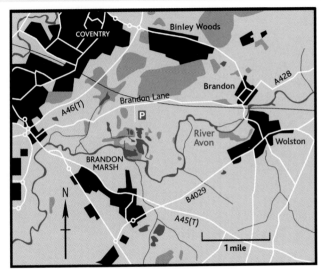

Species
18 species recorded including:
Emerald Damselfly
White-legged Damselfly
Large Red-eyed Damselfly
Small Red-eyed Damselfly
Migrant Hawker
Brown Hawker
Emperor Dragonfly
Broad-bodied Chaser
Ruddy Darter

Habitat
Pools, marsh, grassland, woodland.
West Marsh and Pool is managed for
dragonflies.

Location
The site lies on the banks of the River Avon, *c.*1 mile south-east of Coventry.

From the Toll Bar Island roundabout where the A45 and A46 meet, follow the
A45 south-east away from Coventry (towards Ryton-on-Dunsmore and M45)
for *c.*200m, then turn left after a petrol station into Brandon Lane. The Nature
Centre and car park are *c.*1.5 mile along this road on the right-hand side.

Timing
A visit in July will see the greatest variety of species on the wing.

Additional Information
Reserve open 9am–5pm weekdays, 10am–5pm weekends. Nature trail, visitor
centre and tearoom. Disabled access from centre. Charge for non-members.

This site can be combined with other Midlands sites including Feckenham
Wylde Moor, Ipsley Alders Marsh, Kingsbury Water Park and Saltwells.

Other Wildlife
Marbled White butterfly, 224 bird species recorded up to 2005.

BRIDGE OF GRUDIE
Loch Maree, near Kinlochewe, Highland

NH 965 678
OS Map 19

Site Guide

Species
Northern Damselfly
Azure Hawker
Common Hawker
Golden-ringed Dragonfly
Northern Emerald
Highland Darter
Black Darter
White-faced Darter

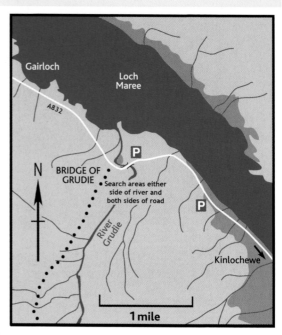

Habitat
Open boggy areas with stony outcrops either side of River Grudie and around shores of Loch Maree.

Location
Bridge of Grudie lies on the western edge of Loch Maree, along the A832.

From Kinlochewe take the A832 north-west along the western side of Loch Maree. After *c*.9 miles you will come to Bridge of Grudie. Park on the north side of the bridge (room for 3–4 vehicles) or at NG 982 671 and walk back along the road. Park with care along soft roadside verges.

Access & Areas to Search
All species occur throughout the boggy areas either side of the road and either side of the river. Also check the wet areas/pools between the road and the loch further west along the road, before Slattadale Forest. **Azure Hawker** and **Highland Darter** also occur along the rides of the forest (see parking areas and picnic sites on OS map). The sheltered clearing north of the bridge (small shaded area on map) can also be very good for **Northern Emerald** and teneral and feeding insects of other species.

Timing
The key species at this site is **Azure Hawker**, which is on the wing during June and July. A visit mid- to late July should see all species mentioned, although the later in July the better for **Highland Darter**.

Additional Information
Waterproof boots and insect repellent essential. Public toilets at Beinn Eighe Centre at NH 019 629, 1 mile north-west of Kinlochewe.

This site can be combined with Beinn Eighe and Loch Coulin & Loch Clair.

BRIGTON POND
near Newton Stewart, Dumfries & Galloway
Forestry Commission Scotland | www.forestry.gov.uk/scotland

NX 359 754
OS Map 77

Species
Common Hawker (inc. blue female form)
Golden-ringed Dragonfly
Black Darter

Habitat
Disused quarry, conifer wood, scrub, rides.

Location
Brigton Pond is situated in the Galloway Forest Park *c.*8 miles north-west of Newton Stewart.

From Newton Stewart, take the A714 north-west towards Girvan. Parking is available along the minor Minnigaff to Bargrennan road, either adjacent to the pond at NX 359 754 or next to the bridge at NX 361 750.

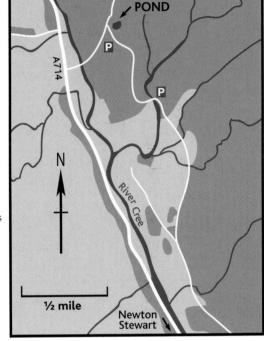

Access & Areas to Search
Search the pond and the surrounding areas, as well as rivers and streams in the locality.

Timing
A visit in July would see the three main-interest species plus several other species of dragonfly.

Additional Information
Part of Galloway Forest Park, managed by Cree Valley Community Woodland Trust (www.creevalley.com/minnoch_trool.htm). There are many other similar sites within the Galloway Forest Park and many of the woodland streams are also worth exploring – see OS Map 77.

The nearby Glen Trool Visitor Centre (at NX 372 786) is open 10am–5pm and has toilets and a tearoom.

Other Wildlife
Goosanders and Dippers breed on the rivers in the area. Many species of butterfly occur throughout the forest, and this site is only several miles north of Wood of Cree RSPB reserve, where 21 species have been recorded.

Site Guide

BROCK VALLEY
near Garstang, Lancashire
Lancashire County Council | www.lancashire.gov.uk

SD 560 440
OS Map 102

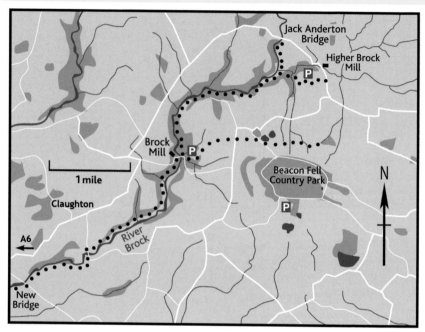

Species
Common Hawker
Golden-ringed Dragonfly

Habitat
Upland, river, marsh, woodland.

Location
The Brock Valley lies *c*.7 miles north-east of Preston.

From Junction 1 of the M55 follow the A6 north to Bilsborrow. Continue through village, and after *c*.1.5 miles, take minor road east over M6 motorway signed for Claughton. Follow the signs for Claughton and then for Brock Mill.

Parking at Brock Mill at SD 549 430 or at Higher Brock Mill at SD 572 447.

Access & Areas to Search
Follow the footpaths from either parking site along the River Brock.

Timing
A visit in July would see the main species of interest plus other dragonflies.

Additional Information
The Bowland Visitor Centre (toilets, café, information on trail along River Brock; open 9.30am–6pm daily) is at Beacon Fell Country Park (see map).

Other Wildlife
Dipper and Grey Wagtail on the river.

BURNHOPE POND
near Durham, County Durham
Durham Wildlife Trust | www.durhamwt.co.uk

NZ 182 483
OS Map 88

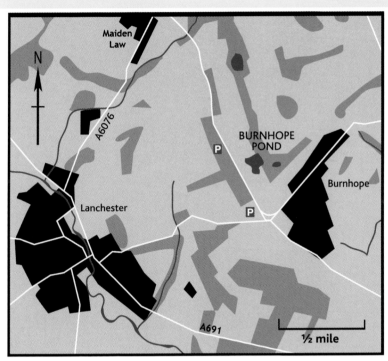

Species
Common Hawker
Southern Hawker
Black Darter

Habitat
Pond and marsh in the centre of a species-rich meadow; plantation with smaller ponds to the east.

Location
The reserve lies *c*.6 miles north-west of Durham.

Leave Durham city north-west along A691. In Lanchester, take minor road by church eastwards and, at crossroads, turn left towards Maiden Law. Limited parking on west side of road. Access reserve through gate in north-west or south-west corners of field and follow public footpath.

Access & Areas to Search
Search the pond for **Black Darter** and other species. The plantation edge is worth searching for feeding insects.

Timing
Black Darter is on the wing from mid-July to mid-September.

Additional Information
There are no facilities on the reserve. This site can be combined with Low Barns Nature Reserve (centre and tea shop).

BYSTOCK POOLS NATURE RESERVE

near Exmouth, Devon

Devon Wildlife Trust | www.devonwildlifetrust.org

SY 034 844

OS Map 192

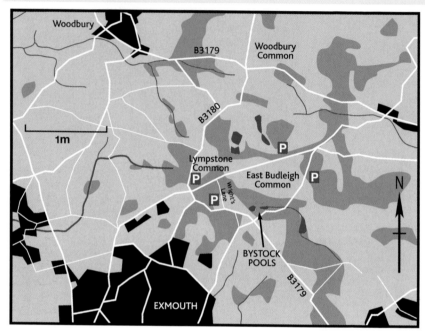

Species
Golden-ringed Dragonfly
Downy Emerald

Habitat
Heath, woodland, scrub, pools.

Location
Bystock Pools is *c*.6 miles south-east of Exeter and *c*.1 mile north of Exmouth.

Leave Exeter along the A376. Turn left along the B3179 at Clyst St George, through Woodbury then, on leaving the village, take the first right turn signposted Exmouth and Budleigh Salterton. Continue for 0.7 miles to the T-junction and turn right onto the B3180. After *c*.1 mile take the unsigned road on the left opposite the right turn for Exmouth, then turn right into Wright's Lane. Reserve entrance is on the left-hand side. Park carefully by gate.

Timing
Downy Emerald is on the wing from late May to mid-July. A visit during late June or early July would be the best time to see this species, **Emperor** and **Golden-ringed Dragonflies** plus many other, commoner species.

Additional Information
This site can be combined with any of the many other sites in the area, including Aylesbeare Common (also good for butterflies), Colaton Raleigh Common and Venn Ottery (also butterflies).

The nearest facilities are in Exmouth town centre.

CADOVER BRIDGE
near Plymouth, Devon

part of Dartmoor National Park | www.dartmoor-npa.gov.uk

SX 556 647
OS Map 202

Species
Scarce Blue-tailed
  Damselfly
Emperor Dragonfly
Golden-ringed
  Dragonfly

Habitat
Moorland pools and
river.

Location
Cadover Bridge is *c*.4
miles north-east of
Plymouth on the edge
of Dartmoor.

From Plymouth
take the A386 north
towards Yelverton.
At Roborough take
the minor road east
to Bickleigh. Just after
Bickleigh take the
minor road north to
Shaugh Prior. Follow
the signs for Wotter

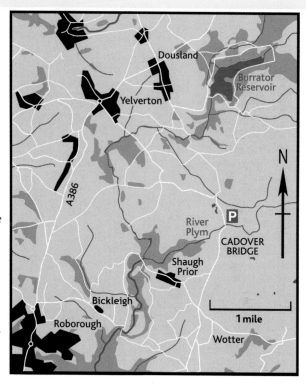

and, at the crossroads, turn north up the minor road towards Yelverton. You
will reach the bridge after *c*.1.5 miles.

Access & Areas to Search
Park in the car park on the east side of the road, north of the bridge (opposite a
house with trees). Search the nearby moorland pools, surrounding marshy areas
and river.

Timing
Scarce Blue-tailed Damselfly has a long flight period, from early June to mid-
August. A visit during late June or early July should allow you to see Scarce
Blue-tailed Damselfly, Emperor and **Golden-ringed Dragonflies** and can easily
be combined with other south Devon sites.

Additional Information
This site can be combined with any of the many other sites in the area including
Chudleigh Knighton Heath, Haldon Forest, Little Bradley Ponds, Slapton Ley,
Stafford Bridge and Stover Country Park.

CARLTON MARSHES
near Lowestoft, Suffolk
Suffolk Wildlife Trust | www.suffolkwildlife.co.uk

TM 508 920
OS Map 134

Site Guide

Species
15 species recorded including:
Variable Damselfly
Hairy Dragonfly
Norfolk Hawker
Scarce Chaser

Habitat
Extensive grazing marshes and mixed fen with well-vegetated dykes.

Location
Carlton Marshes is *c.*2 miles from the western edge of Lowestoft and is at the southern tip of the Norfolk and Suffolk Broads.

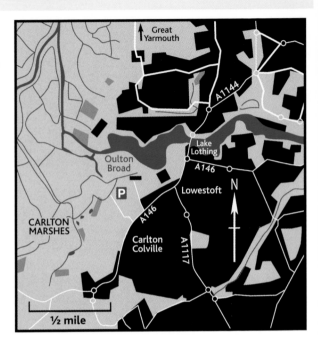

From Lowestoft, take the A146 towards Beccles. At Carlton Colville turn right into Burnt Hill Lane at TM 512 917. Continue down the lane, over the railway and park at the car park and reserve centre.

Access & Areas to Search
Enter the reserve through the gate at the bottom of the car park and turn left towards the pools. Search the dykes to the north of the pools for **Norfolk Hawker, Hairy Dragonfly** and **Scarce Chaser**. **Variable Damselfly** is best looked for along the dyke on the left between the entrance and the pools.

Timing
Variable Damselfly flies from mid-May to early August. **Hairy Dragonfly** is on the wing from mid-May to the end of June. **Norfolk Hawker's** short flight period is from early/mid-June to early July. **Scarce Chaser** flies between mid-June and mid-July.

Additional Information
Carlton Marshes is home to the Suffolk Broads Wildlife Centre. Toilets at the information centre. It can be combined with other Broadland sites, including Catfield Fen, River Waveney, Strumpshaw Fen and Upton Broad & Marshes.

Other Wildlife
Marsh Harrier, Cetti's Warbler and Bearded Tit. The dykes hold Water Voles and the rare and protected plant the Water Soldier. Swallowtail butterfly.

CATFIELD FEN
near Stalham, Norfolk
Butterfly Conservation | www.butterfly-conservation.org

TG 367 215
OS Maps 133/134

Species
Hairy Dragonfly
Migrant Hawker
Common Hawker
Brown Hawker
Norfolk Hawker

Habitat
Open water, reed
and sedge beds,
dykes, fen, and
carr woodland.

Location
Catfield Fen lies
*c.*10 miles north-
east of Norwich
and *c.*15 miles
north-west of
Great Yarmouth.

From Norwich
take the A1151
north-eastwards
to Hoveton. From

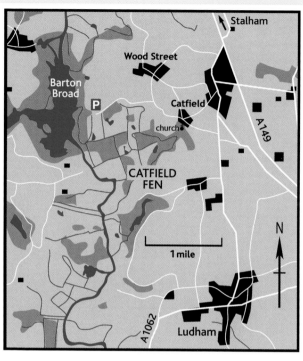

Hoveton take the A1062 to Ludham, then turn left along the minor road to the
village of Catfield. The reserve is 1 mile west of the village. Go past the church
and follow the road round before taking a track on the left to the fen. The car park
is at TG 367 215 and is in Fenside Lane.

Timing
Norfolk Hawker and **Hairy Dragonfly** are best looked for from late May and
throughout June. **Common** and **Brown Hawkers**, and many other common
species, can be seen throughout July and August. **Migrant Hawker** flies from late
July through to mid-September.

Access & Areas to Search
Visitors are asked to exercise extreme caution when visiting this reserve as the
reed fen has hidden ditches and water holes. For reasons of safety, the main part of
the reserve must be visited only on open days. However, the path along the rond
(raised bank) around the west and south sides of the site offers good views and is
always open, but even here care must be taken to stay in the centre of the path as
the bordering dyke has soft banks and deep water.

Additional Information
Swallowtail butterfly.

CHOLSEY MARSH & RIVER THAMES   SU 601 855
near Wallingford, Oxfordshire   OS Maps 174/175

Species
Banded Demoiselle
White-legged
  Damselfly
Club-tailed Dragonfly

Habitat
Marsh, reedbed, scrub,
river.

Location
Cholsey Marsh lies next
to the River Thames
*c.*2 miles south of
Wallingford.

Just south of
Wallingford take the
A329 south. Park near
the Papist Way / A329
crossroads (sign Cholsey
town centre). On foot,
follow Papist Way down to the River Thames.

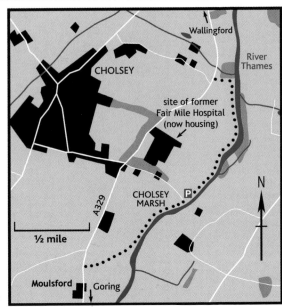

Alternatively, park in Moulsford (just south of Cholsey) and take footpath just
north of the village across fields to the river.

Access & Areas to Search
Follow riverside footpaths in either direction from the car park. Keep to signed
rights of way.

From Moulsford end, follow footpath north of village, down lane, across fields
and northwards along the river footpath.

Timing
All three of the above species, plus other, commoner dragonflies, can be seen
during a visit in mid-June.

Additional Information
This site can be combined with the River Thames at Goring.

CHUDLEIGH KNIGHTON HEATH
near Bovey Tracey, Devon
Devon Wildlife Trust | www.devonwildlifetrust.org

SX 837 776
OS Map 191

Species
Over 12 species including:
Emerald Damselfly
Large Red Damselfly
Scarce Blue-tailed Damselfly
Common Hawker
Southern Hawker
Emperor Dragonfly
Keeled Skimmer

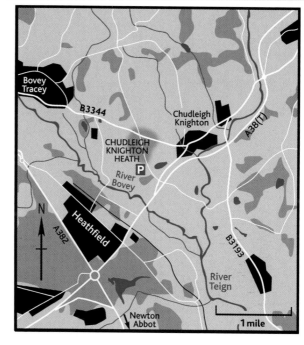

Habitat
Wet and dry heathland, scrub, pools.

Location
Chudleigh Knighton Heath is *c.*12 miles south of Exeter.

From Exeter, head south towards Plymouth on the A38. Leave the A38 at the Chudleigh Knighton turn and follow the B3344 through Chudleigh Knighton towards Bovey Tracey. The B3344 bisects the heath just west of Chudleigh Knighton. Roadside parking at SX 838 770 by the public bridleway sign.

Access & Areas to Search
Check the small pools on the west side of the minor road by the parking area. Note that several public rights of way border or cross the heath. Keep strictly to footpaths – access to parts of the heath not served by these rights of way is by permit only and anyone requiring a permit should apply in writing to the Devon Wildlife Trust.

Timing
A visit to this site during July should see all of the above species plus other commoner dragonflies.

Additional Information
Open all year from dawn until dusk. Can be combined with any of the many other good dragonfly and butterfly sites in south Devon (see gazetteer).

Other Wildlife
Nightjar, Stonechat and Great Crested Newts. One of only two sites in the country for, Narrow-headed Wood Ants.

Site Guide

CLAIFE HEIGHTS

SD 382 976
OS Maps 96/97

near Ambleside, Cumbria
National Trust | www.nationaltrust.org.uk

Site Guide

Species
Golden-ringed
  Dragonfly
Downy Emerald
Black Darter
White-faced Darter

Habitat
Mires, tarns,
moorland, oak
woodland.

Location
Claife Heights
is a large area of
hillside forest on
the west shore
of Windermere,
*c.*8 miles south of
Ambleside.

From Ambleside,
take the A593 south
towards Coniston.
After *c.*1 mile, take
the B5286 south, then the B5285 through Hawkshead to Near Sawrey and park
in village.

Access & Areas to Search
From Near Sawrey, follow footpath north through the area. The walk takes you
past several tarns on the way to the two small tarns marked on the map.

Golden-ringed Dragonfly can be encountered around most tarns, along streams
in the area and along the forest tracks. **Downy Emerald, Black Darter** and
White-faced Darter are best looked for around the standing water of the tarns,
in particular the two small tarns marked on the map.

Additional Information
You can do a circular walk (*c.*4 miles) from Near Sawrey, through the area and
return along the main forest track to Far Sawrey and walk back to Near Sawrey
along the road (*c.*0.5 mile). Tea shops in Near Sawrey and public houses in Near
Sawrey and Far Sawrey.

A walk to the tarn at SD 375 980 will take at least an hour.

Stout footwear and an OS map of the area are strongly recommended.

This site can be combined with Cunsey Beck.

COLATON RALEIGH COMMON

near Exmouth, Devon

Clinton Devon Estates | www.clintondevon.co.uk

SY 050 868

OS Map 192

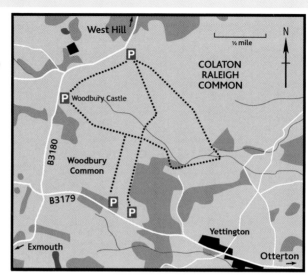

Species

Lowland heath species including:
Southern Damselfly
Emperor Dragonfly
Golden-ringed Dragonfly

Habitat

Fast-flowing stony-bottomed stream and bogs in heather heathland.

Location

The area lies *c.*5 miles east of Exeter and is accessed via Woodbury Castle and Common.

From Exeter take the A376 towards Exmouth. Towards the end of the dual carriageway section, take the B3179 to Woodbury. Continue through the village to the T-junction and turn left along the B3180 towards West Hill. After *c.*0.25 miles, park on the right in the Woodbury Castle car park at SX 032 875. Alternative parking further along B3180 or along the B3179 towards Otterton.

Access & Areas to Search

From the Woodbury Castle car park, take the track east across the heath. As you approach a piece of woodland on the right, a small track leads down to the left to a stream with a small footbridge. Search this area. Go back up to the small plantation and turn left, along the plantation edge and then turn left immediately after the plantation along the footpath which follows the course of the stream. **Southern Damselfly** occurs along the stream. **Emperor** and **Golden-ringed Dragonflies** can be seen throughout the area.

Timing

Southern Damselfly is on the wing from mid-June to mid-August. **Emperor** and **Golden-ringed Dragonflies** can be seen throughout July and August.

Additional Information

This site can be combined with any of the many other sites in the area including Aylesbeare Common (also good for butterflies), Bystock Pools, Chudleigh Knighton Heath, Haldon Forest, Little Bradley Ponds, Slapton Ley, Stafford Bridge, Stover Country Park and Venn Ottery (also butterflies).

COLLEGE LAKE
near Tring, Buckinghamshire

SP 933 139
OS Map 165

Berkshire, Buckinghamshire and Oxfordshire Wildlife Trust | www.bbowt.org.uk

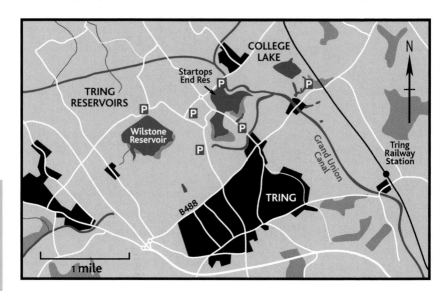

Species
Azure Damselfly
Migrant Hawker
Southern Hawker
Brown Hawker
Emperor Dragonfly

Four-spotted Chaser
Common Darter
Ruddy Darter

Habitat
Chalk pit, grassland, marsh.

Location
College Lake lies *c.*6 miles east of Aylesbury and *c.*2 miles north-east of Tring.

From Tring take the B488 north to Bulbourne. Cross the canal bridge and the reserve entrance is after *c.*250m on the left. Car park and visitor centre.

Access & Areas to Search
Follow footpaths. The well-vegetated channel on the west side of the site is very good for **Ruddy Darter.**

Timing
July and August.

Additional Information
Reserve open 10am–5pm. Obtain permit from warden's office by the car park.

A walk westwards along the Grand Union Canal takes you to Tring Reservoirs, which are good for birds and dragonflies.

COPLE PITS
Bedford, Bedfordshire
TL 103 492
OS Map 153
The Wildlife Trust for Bedfordshire, Cambridgeshire, Northamptonshire & Peterborough
| www.wildlifebcnp.org

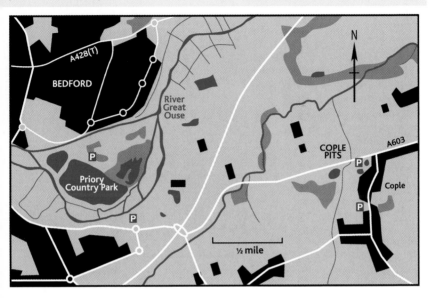

Species
Azure Damselfly
Migrant Hawker
Southern Hawker
Brown Hawker
Emperor Dragonfly
Ruddy Darter

Habitat
Disused gravel workings, now a series of 11 small water-filled pits in woodland and scrub

Location
Cople Pits reserve lies on the eastern outskirts of Bedford, just off the A603.

Approaching from Bedford along the A603, park in the lay-by just before the turn to Cople village, follow the public footpath sign and turn left at the Wildlife Trust notice board.

Access & Areas to Search
Follow footpaths around pits and through clearing in scrub.

Timing
July and August.

Additional Information
Nearby Priory Country Park is also worth exploring for dragonflies and butterflies.

This site can be combined with Felmersham Gravel Pits.

Site Guide

CORNMILL MEADOWS DRAGONFLY SANCTUARY

TL 380 013
OS Map 166

near Waltham Abbey, Essex
part of Lee Valley Park | www.leevalleypark.org.uk

Species

Over 20 species including:
Banded Demoiselle
White-legged Damselfly
Large Red-eyed Damselfly
Hairy Dragonfly
Migrant Hawker
Brown Hawker
Emperor Dragonfly

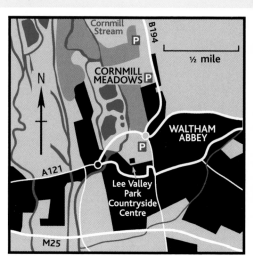

Habitat

Open grass meadows and thin woodland with slow-flowing watercourses.

Location

Cornmill Meadows is on the northern outskirts of Waltham Abbey.

Leave the M25 at Junction 26 and follow the A121 to Waltham Abbey. From Waltham Abbey take the B194 north towards Lower Nazeing. Park in the car park on your left after *c.*0.5 miles.

Access & Areas to Search

From the car park follow the footpaths (several) to the meadows. There is a 1.5-mile perimeter path around the sanctuary. **White-legged Damselfly** is abundant along the main watercourse running parallel with the car park/main road, and is best looked for away from the water's edge, particularly around nettle areas. **Hairy Dragonfly** occurs throughout the site.

Timing

Hairy Dragonfly flies from May to early July; the other species July–August.

Additional Information

Additional parking at the Abbey Gardens pay and display coach park off the large roundabout in Waltham Abbey (junction of A121 and B194). A footpath leads to the meadows from here via a wooden bridge over a stream and a subway. Toilets are next to the car park.

The nearby Lee Valley Park Information Centre is reached by continuing another 1.5 miles north along the B194 from the Cornmill Meadows car park and taking Stubbins Hall Lane on the left at the sharp right-hand bend. The centre is open from 10am until 4pm daily and has refreshments and toilets.

With over 20 species of damselfly and dragonfly, this is regarded as the best dragonfly site in the Hertfordshire, Essex and Greater London area.

CORS BODGYNYDD
near Betws-y-Coed, Conwy
North Wales Wildlife Trust | www.wildlifetrust.org.uk/northwales

SH 767 597
OS Map 115

Species
Four-spotted Chaser
Keeled Skimmer

Habitat
Open moorland bog.

Location
The site lies between the two large lakes, Llyn Geirionydd and Llyn Bodgynydd, *c.*3 miles north-west of Betws-y-Coed.

From Betws-y-Coed, take the A5 west to Ty-hyll. Turn off here north towards Swallow Falls. Go past the falls and then take the next minor road on the left (towards Llyn Geirionydd) and the site is to the west of this road at SH 767 597.

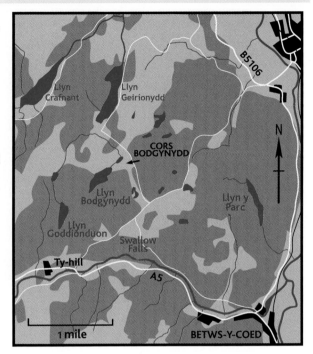

Access & Areas to Search
Park carefully along roadside. Search the moorland bog along the road.

Timing
Keeled Skimmer is on the wing throughout July, when **Four-spotted Chaser** will also be present.

Additional Information
Part of the Snowdonia National Park, leased from the Forestry Commission (www.forestry.gov.uk) and managed by North Wales Wildlife Trust.

This site can be combined with Valley Lakes, Ynys Môn (Anglesey).

Other Wildlife
Nightjar.

CUNSEY BECK
near Lake Windermere, Cumbria
part of the Lake District National Park | www.lake-district.gov.uk

SD 374 938
OS Map 97

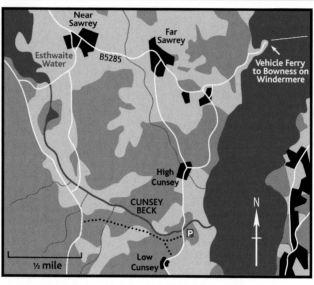

Species
Acid-soil species including:
Beautiful Demoiselle
Golden-ringed Dragonfly

Habitat
Well-vegetated moorland stream.

Location
Cunsey Beck runs between Esthwaite Water and Lake Windermere *c*.10 miles (by road) south of Ambleside.

Leave Ambleside on the A593 towards Coniston. After *c*.0.5 miles take the B5286 south, then the B5285 towards Hawkshead, through Near Sawrey towards the vehicle ferry to Bowness-on-Windermere. At Far Sawrey take the minor road south, through High Cunsey towards Low Cunsey. Where this minor road bridges the beck, park on the roadside verge at SD 382 935.

Access & Areas to Search
A public footpath runs along the beck.

Timing
Both species mentioned above can be seen during mid-June to late July.

Additional Information
This site can be combined with Claife Heights. Tea shops in Near Sawrey and public houses in Near Sawrey and Far Sawrey.

DECOY HEATH
near Reading, Berkshire
Berkshire, Buckinghamshire and Oxfordshire Wildlife Trust | www.bbowt.org.uk

SU 613 635
OS Map 175

Species
Over 20 species breed
annually including:
Scarce Blue-tailed
Damselfly
Migrant Hawker
Golden-ringed Dragonfly
Downy Emerald
Brilliant Emerald
Keeled Skimmer

Habitat
A mosaic of wet and dry
heath, woodland, scrub
and open water areas.

Location
Decoy Heath lies *c*.8 miles
south-west of Reading.

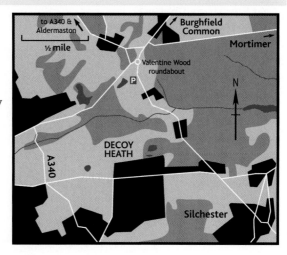

Leave the M4 at Junction 12 and follow the A4 towards Newbury. After *c*.3
miles take the left fork, A340 towards Heath End. Drive through Aldermaston
and turn left at the fork signed for Silchester. Continue for *c*.2 miles and turn
right at the T-junction. At the Valentine Wood roundabout take the Silchester
exit. The reserve car park is *c*.200m on the right opposite a factory entrance.

Access & Areas to Search
From the car park follow the path down to the reserve. Search the wet heath and
scrub fringe areas in particular.

Timing
All the main-interest species should be seen on a visit during the first half of
July. Migrant Hawker flies from mid-July.

Additional Information
Decoy Heath is Berkshire's premier dragonfly site with over 20 species regularly
breeding and is also one of the county's top butterfly sites.

This site can be combined with Wildmoor Heath.

DELAMERE FOREST
BLACK LAKE CWT
HATCH MERE CWT
near Frodsham, Cheshire
Cheshire Wildlife Trust | www.wildlifetrust.org.uk/cheshire

SJ 537 709
SJ 555 721
OS Map 117

Site Guide

Species
Variable Damselfly
Hairy Dragonfly
Common Hawker
Black Darter

Habitat
Black Lake An acidic
woodland lake.
Hatch Mere Lake.

Location
Delamere Forest
lies *c*.7 miles south
of Runcorn and
c.7 miles west of
Northwich.

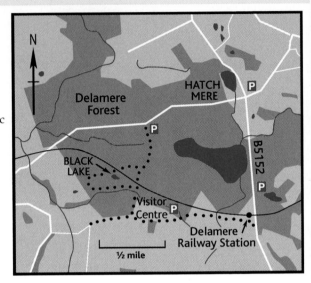

Black Lake is
reached off the A54
Chester to Middlewich road. Leave the A54 at the B5152 and head north to
Delamere. Go through Delamere, past the train station, to Hatchmere, then take
the minor road west towards Mouldsworth. Park on the south side of the road
at the Barnsbridge Gate visitor car park at SJ 542 715.

Hatch Mere lies off the B5152 as indicated on the map above.

Access & Areas to Search
Black Lake From the car park, take the footpath trail south, over the railway
and round to the right. View the pool from the footpath – do not attempt to
approach the pool, much of the vegetation is floating and will give way if
walked on. Note that **White-faced Darter** no longer occurs at this site.

Hatch Mere From car park, cross road and walk paths around the mere.

Timing
Variable Damselfly and **Hairy Dragonfly** can both be seen during June. August
is best for both **Common Hawker** and **Black Darter**.

Additional Information
Black Lake can also be accessed via the Delamere Forest Park Visitor Centre at
Linmere (SJ 548 704). Café and toilets at the visitor centre. There are also toilets
at Hatch Mere. Delamere Forest can be combined with Warrington sites and
Vale Royal Locks.

Owned by the Forestry Commission (www.forestry.gov.uk).

DOWROG COMMON
near St David's, Pembrokeshire
owned by the National Trust | www.nationaltrust.org.uk
managed by The Wildlife Trust of South and West Wales | www.welshwildlife.org

SM 770 270
OS Map 157

Species
Beautiful Demoiselle
Small Red Damselfly
Southern Damselfly
Scarce Blue-tailed
  Damselfly
Hairy Dragonfly
Emperor Dragonfly
Golden-ringed
Dragonfly
Four-spotted Chaser

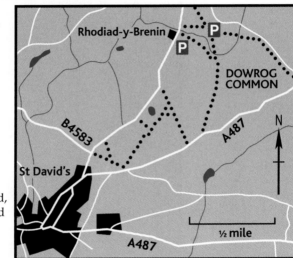

Habitat
Wet and dry heathland,
grassland, bog, fen and
pools.

Location
Dowrog Common is *c*.2
miles north-east of St David's.

From St David's take the minor road to Rhodiad-y-Brenin. The common lies immediately west of here on the right-hand side of the minor road. Park in the pull-in on the right by the entrance to the public footpath immediately before the village at SM 766 270, or continue through Rhodiad-y-Brenin and take the next right down very narrow gated road and park on the right just before the bridge at SM 771 275.

Access & Areas to Search
Keep to the paths throughout the site to avoid damaging the sensitive bogland plant community.

Timing
Most species should be easy to see during a visit from mid-June to end of July.

Additional Information
An extremely wet site for which waterproofs and wellingtons are strongly recommended. **Yellow-winged Darters** bred on the reserve in 1996 following the autumn 1995 influx.

This site can be combined with Afon Brynberian and the Welsh Wildlife Centre.

Other Wildlife
Grasshopper Warbler, Sedge Warbler and Reed Bunting. Otter.

DOXEY MARSHES
Stafford, Staffordshire
Staffordshire Wildlife Trust | www.staffordshirewildlife.org.uk

SJ 915 239
OS Map 127

Species
Banded Demoiselle
Emerald Damselfly
Azure Damselfly
Brown Hawker
Broad-bodied
    Chaser

Habitat
Riverside marsh and pools.

Location
Doxey Marshes lies alongside the River Sow on the northern outskirts of Stafford.

Car park just south of Junction 14 of M6, at end of Creswell Farm Drive off the A5013 (Eccleshall Road).

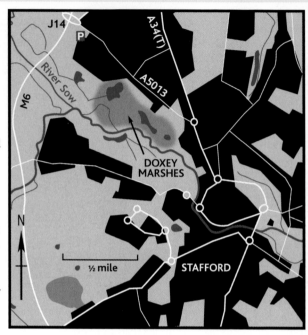

Access & Areas to Search
Follow paths around the reserve.

Timing
All the species mentioned above can be seen during a visit in the latter half of July.

Additional Information
Information boards and nature trails. The majority of paths have a firm surface and are suitable for wheelchairs and pushchairs.

Stafford town centre, with its cafés and pubs, is within easy walking distance of the reserve.

Other Wildlife
Otters may be seen from the old bird hide at Tillington Flash in the mornings and early evenings.

DUNDALE POND, LEVISHAM MOOR
near Pickering, North Yorkshire
part of the North Yorkshire Moors National Park | www.moors.uk.net

SE 828 918
OS Map 94

Species
Emerald Damselfly
Large Red Damselfly
Common Blue Damselfly
Blue-tailed Damselfly
Golden-ringed Dragonfly
Black Darter

Habitat
Moorland with ponds and streams.

Location
Dundale Pond lies within Levisham Moor, *c.*8 miles north of Pickering.

Leave the A169 Pickering to Whitby road at Lockton (*c.*5.5 miles north of Pickering) and follow the signs to Levisham. In Levisham village, take the right-hand fork at The Horseshoe Inn. This minor road (Limpsey Gate Lane) turns into a rough grass track. Park at the bottom at SE 830 915.

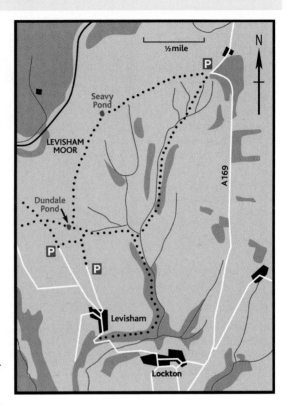

Access & Areas to Search
From the car, follow the path down the moorland slope to Dundale Pond at SE 828 918. Search the pond, feeder stream and surrounding vegetation.

By following the track due north from Dundale Pond, you come to Seavy Pond (SE 833 934). The water level of this pond is very variable as it is higher up than Dundale Pond, and is only worth visiting in a wet year.

Timing
Mid-July through August.

Additional Information
Waterproof walking boots recommended.

This site can be combined with nearby Fen Bog and Ellerburn Bank (for butterflies).

ESHER COMMON & FAIRMILE COMMON

TQ 130 623
TQ 125 615
OS Map 187

near Esher, Surrey
Elmbridge Borough Council | www.elmbridge.gov.uk

Species
Banded Demoiselle
White-legged Damselfly
Small Red Damselfly
Large Red-eyed Damselfly
Downy Emerald
Brilliant Emerald
Black-tailed Skimmer

Habitat
Grassland with ponds, scrub.

Location
These two commons lie on the southern outskirts of Esher, to the north and south of the A3.

Parking along the A307 south of Esher in small car park at TQ 125 625, next to Blackhills private road.

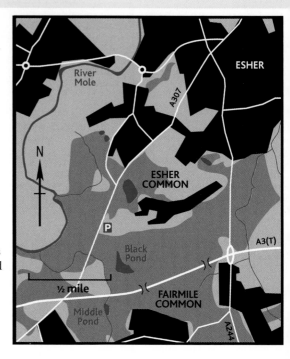

Access & Areas to Search
The commons are connected by two footbridges which cross the A3.

Brilliant Emerald occurs on Middle Pond (TQ 127 618) on Fairmile Common and should also be looked for on Black Pond (TQ 128 623) on Esher Common. All the other species should be easy to see around the various water bodies on both commons.

Timing
A visit to the area in the first half of July should see all the above species on the wing.

Additional Information
This site can be combined with Bedfont Lakes Country Park.

Other Wildlife
Silver-studded Blue butterfly on Fairmile Common.

FAIRBURN INGS
near Castleford, West Yorkshire
RSPB | www.rspb.org.uk

SE 451 277
OS Map 105

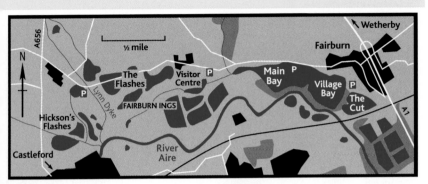

Species
Emerald Damselfly
Azure Damselfly
Common Blue Damselfly
Migrant Hawker
Brown Hawker
Four-spotted Chaser
Common Darter

Habitat
Variety of open pools, streams and marsh surrounded by grassland and woodland.

Location
Fairburn Ings lies on the northern outskirts of Castleford and *c*.4 miles from Junction 33 (Ferrybridge/A1) of the M62.

The reserve is accessed from the east off the A1 (Fairburn turn) and from the west off the A656 (Fairburn/Allerton Bywater crossroads). Car parking at the visitor centre, Lynn Dyke (SE 432 274) or in village (SE 470 278).

Access & Areas to Search
The area around the visitor centre is excellent, with a raised wooden boardwalk which takes you around a small wetland area with small pond. Suitable for wheelchair access. Species include **Azure Damselfly**.

The footpath along Lynn Dyke to Hickson's Flashes is also a good area. Species include **Emerald Damselfly**.

Timing
A visit during the second half of July should see most of the above species mentioned, plus other common species.

Additional Information
Toilets, drinks and snacks available at the visitor centre. This site can be combined with Johnny Brown's Common.

FECKENHAM WYLDE MOOR

near Redditch, Worcestershire
Worcestershire Wildlife Trust | www.worcswildlifetrust.co.uk

SP 012 606
OS Map 150

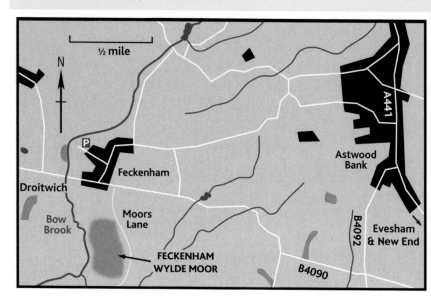

Species

Large Red Damselfly
Azure Damselfly
Common Blue Damselfly
Blue-tailed Damselfly
Southern Hawker
Brown Hawker
Emperor Dragonfly

Four-spotted Chaser
Broad-bodied Chaser
Black-tailed Skimmer

Habitat

Fen, reedbed and pools.

Location

The reserve lies *c*.3 miles south of Redditch.

From Redditch take the A441 south to Astwood Bank, then the B4092 to Edgiock and the B4090 west to Feckenham. Park in the public car park in the village (signed). From the car park turn right down the High Street and then left at the T-junction along Alcester Road. Take the first right along Moors Lane (footpath signed to Morton Underhill) and follow track south to reserve entrance on your right.

Access & Areas to Search

Follow circular walk around the reserve. Small pools and hide overlooking small lake provide excellent viewing of all species.

Timing

A visit during July will provide the widest selection of species.

Additional Information

This is a wet site so waterproof boots or wellingtons are strongly recommended.

FELMERSHAM GRAVEL PITS
SP 991 584
OS Map 153

near Rushden, Bedfordshire

The Wildlife Trust for Bedfordshire, Cambridgeshire, Northamptonshire & Peterborough
| www.wildlifebcnp.org.uk

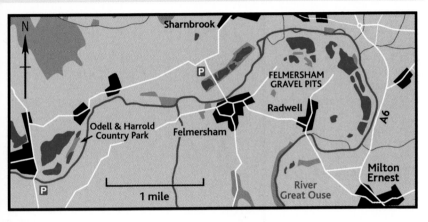

Species

White-legged Damselfly
Large Red-eyed Damselfly
Hairy Dragonfly
Migrant Hawker
Southern Hawker
Brown Hawker
Emperor Dragonfly
Black-tailed Skimmer
Ruddy Darter

Habitat

Lakes, river, woodland and grassland on former gravel workings.

Location

Felmersham Gravel Pits reserve lies *c*.5 miles north-west of Bedford.

Leave the A6 north of Bedford at Milton Ernest and follow the road to Felmersham village, then follow the signs towards Sharnbrook, over the River Great Ouse. Car park *c*.500 m beyond bridge on left at SP 987 583.

Access & Areas to Search

There is an extensive network of paths around the pits either side of the minor Felmersham to Sharnbrook road.

Timing

Mid-June to end of July for the widest selection of species, but **Hairy Dragonfly** is on the wing earlier, during May and June.

Additional Information

This site can be combined with Cople Pits or Priory Country Park.

Other Wildlife

White-letter Hairstreak butterfly.

FEN BOG

near Pickering, North Yorkshire

Yorkshire Wildlife Trust | www.yorkshire-wildlife-trust.org.uk
part of North Yorkshire Moors National Park | www.moors.uk.net

SE 853 981
OS Map 94

Species

Golden-ringed Dragonfly
Keeled Skimmer
Black Darter

Habitat

Boggy grass moorland.

Location

Fen Bog lies west of the A169, midway between Pickering and Whitby.

Park on the west side of the A169 in the large rough parking area just north of Eller Beck Bridge at SE 856 984.

Access & Areas to Search

From the car park follow the track west down the slope to the valley bottom. Search the wet grassland to the left of the path before the railway line at SE 853 981, and the stream running parallel with the railway line.

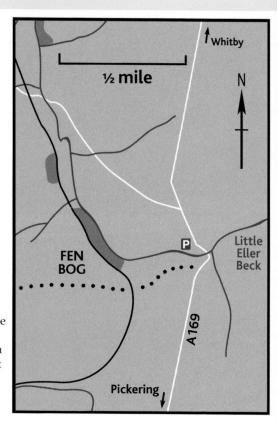

Timing

A visit in July should allow you to see all the main species at this site.

Additional Information

This is a Special Area of Conservation (SAC) and the bog has a fragile plant community so view only from the footpath/track to avoid damaging the bog flora.

Other Wildlife

Small Pearl-bordered and Dark Green Fritillaries and Large Heath butterflies also present.

This site can be combined with nearby Dundale Pond and Ellerburn Bank (for butterflies).

GIBRALTAR POINT
near Skegness, Lincolnshire
Lincolnshire Wildlife Trust | www.lincstrust.org.uk

TF 556 580
OS Map 122

Species
12 species including:
Common Blue Damselfly
Migrant Hawker
Common Hawker
Southern Hawker
Emperor Dragonfly
Black-tailed Skimmer
Common Darter

Habitat
Coastal sand dunes,
scrub, ponds.

Location
Gibraltar Point is *c*.3 miles
south of Skegness.

In Skegness, follow signs
for seafront and then the
signs for Gibraltar Point
Nature Reserve.

Access & Areas to Search
The best area on the
reserve is the ponds at TF
560 588. Migrant Hawker
and Common Darter
can be found along the
coastal scrub areas in late
summer and autumn.

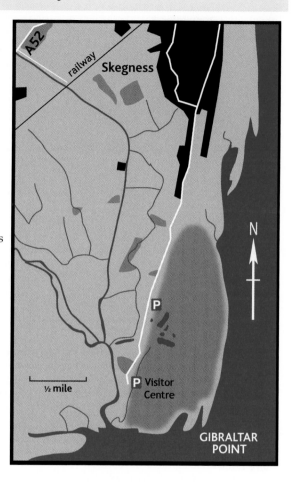

A good site to look for migrant species. **Yellow-winged Darter** has been seen
here during invasion years.

Timing
July–August.

Additional Information
Several car parks (charge). Visitor centre (10am–5pm daily), toilets and café.

This site can be combined with nearby Snipe Dales and Whisby Nature Park.

Other Wildlife
Breeding terns. Reintroduced colony of Natterjack Toads. Water Shrew.

GLEN AFFRIC

NH 197 234

near Inverness, Highland

OS Map 25

managed by Forest Enterprise | www.forestry.gov.uk

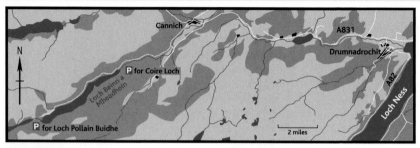

Species

Northern species including:
Azure Hawker
Common Hawker
Golden-ringed Dragonfly
Downy Emerald
Brilliant Emerald
Northern Emerald
Four-spotted Chaser

Highland Darter
Black Darter
White-faced Darter

Habitat

A vast glen containing open lochans, bogs and pools, including many *Sphagnum*-rich areas within remnant Caledonian pine forest.

Location

Glen Affric lies *c.*30 miles south-west of Inverness.

From Inverness take the A82 south to Drumnadrochit then take the A831 west to Cannich. At Cannich take the minor road south-west signed Glen Affric. After 2 miles, turn right at the Fasnakyle power station. The Dog Falls car park is a further 2.5 miles and the River Affric car park a further 10 miles along this road.

Access & Areas to Search

Coire Loch

NH 294 282

Park at the Dog Falls car park (NH 286 283). From the car park, follow the yellow circular trail (*c.*3.25 miles) to Coire Loch. The loch itself is one of Scotland's best dragonfly sites, where you should search for both **Brilliant** and **Northern Emeralds** (care should be taken when separating the three emerald species that occur in the general area) and **White-faced Darter**. The forest track just above the loch on your return is the best area to search for both **Highland Darter** and **Azure Hawker**.

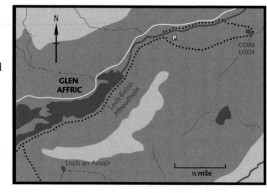

Brilliant Emerald has been recorded from many of the small lochans within Glen Affric, including Loch an Amair. From the Dog Falls car park, follow the forest tracks south-west along the south shore of Loch Beinn a Mheadhoin as indicated on the Coire Loch map.

Loch Pollain Buidhe   **NH 190 225**

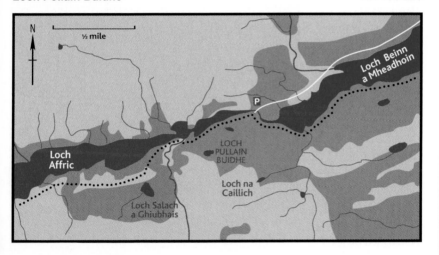

Park at the River Affric car park at the bottom of Glen Affric. From the car park take the path over the bridge, south-west along Loch Affric to a deer fence and gate at NH 187 227. Turn left up the hill and follow the fence to the loch. **Brilliant Emerald** is best looked for here, but care should be taken as **Downy Emerald** also occurs throughout the area. **White-faced Darter** also occurs here. **Azure Hawker** and **Highland Darter** can be seen along the track.

Timing
A July visit would offer the best chance of seeing all of the main species.

Additional Information
Scotland's premier dragonfly site. **Azure Hawker** and **Highland Darter** can be seen along the stony forest tracks and rides throughout the area. **Brilliant** and **Downy Emeralds** occur on many of the small lochans in the locality. **Northern Emerald** is scarce throughout the Glen but can be encountered at any *Sphagnum*-rich pools and is best looked for around Coire Loch.

The Glen contains extensive moorland and forest areas with many lochans, pools and streams which host all of the species found here. Explore any water body identifiable on the OS map, especially *Sphagnum*-rich areas with pools.

Toilets and information available at each car park. Waterproof walking boots and insect repellent essential.

Other Wildlife
Golden Eagle, Wood Warbler, Crested Tit, crossbills, Pearl-bordered Fritillary butterfly and Pine Marten occur throughout the area.

GOATFELL
NR 991 416
near Brodick, Isle of Arran, North Ayrshire
OS Map 69
National Trust for Scotland | www.nts.org.uk

Species
Large Red Damselfly
Common Hawker
Golden-ringed Dragonfly
Highland Darter

Habitat
Mountain heathland, dry and wet grass and heather moor.

Location
Goatfell lies *c*.4 miles north of Brodick on the Isle of Arran.

The Isle of Arran can be reached by ferry (crossing 55 minutes – *c*.£48 for cars, *c*.£8 foot passenger) from Ardrossan, near Kilmarnock (*c*.20 miles south-west of Glasgow), to Brodick (Arran), or from Claonaig, on Kintyre (*c*.25 miles north of Campbeltown), to Lochranza (Arran). A bus service meets the ferry for foot passengers. Cars – on Arran, make your way to Brodick Castle and Country Park, which is situated off the A481 north of Brodick. Park in the visitor centre car park.

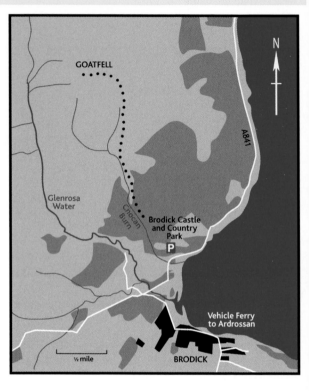

Follow the footpath from Brodick Country Park at NS 005 382 along Cnocan Burn up to Goatfell. A walk to the summit will take 5 hours there and back.

Access & Areas to Search
Most species can be found along Cnocan Burn. **Common Hawker, Golden-ringed Dragonfly** and **Highland Darter** also found in the country park.

Timing
A visit during mid-July to mid-August should see all the above species.

Additional Information
Toilets, café and ranger service at the country park.

Other Wildlife
Ptarmigan (most southerly point in Britain), Golden Eagle and Raven. Heath Spotted Orchid.

THE GOWER PENINSULA
BROAD POOL & BOG WTS&WW
OXWICH NNR CCW
near Swansea
Wildlife Trust of South and West Wales | www.welshwildlife.org
Countryside Council for Wales | www.ccw.gov.uk

SS 510 910
SS 502 865
OS Map 159

Species
Beautiful Demoiselle
Hairy Dragonfly
Emperor Dragonfly
Golden-ringed Dragonfly

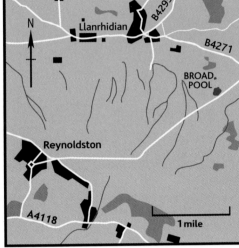

Broad Pool & Bog
Heathland pond and bog.

Leave the A4118 west of
Swansea and head west along
the B4271 to Cillibion, then take
the minor road south-west to
the roadside pool.

Search the pool and
surrounding bog. Over 14
species recorded including
Large Red Damselfly, Emperor
Dragonfly and **Golden-ringed Dragonfly**.

Oxwich NNR
Sand dunes, marsh, woodland.

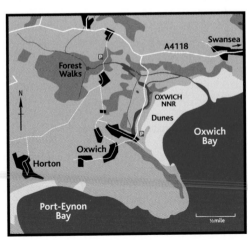

Oxwich NNR lies north-east of
Oxwich, *c.*10 miles south-west
of Swansea off the A4118. Car
park on site (charge).

Follow reserve footpaths and
around the dune areas. Species
include **Beautiful Demoiselle,**
Large Red Damselfly, **Hairy
Dragonfly** and Emperor
Dragonfly.

Timing
Hairy Dragonfly is on the wing
from mid-May to the end of June, but the other species are best looked for during July.

Additional Information
Oxwich is also very good for butterflies, as are the nearby sites at Welsh Moor
and Gelli-hir Wood (for butterflies). Can be combined with Kenfig NNR.

HALDON FOREST

near Exeter, Devon
Forest Enterprise | www.forestry.gov.uk

SX 880 840
OS Map 192

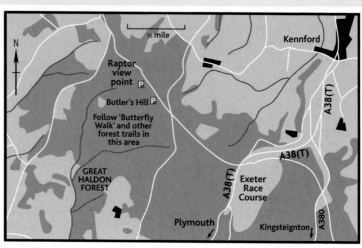

Species
Beautiful Demoiselle
Emperor Dragonfly
Golden-ringed Dragonfly
Broad-bodied Chaser

Habitat
Coniferous forest with some deciduous stands, with open rides, glades
and managed butterfly meadows.

Location
Haldon Forest is *c*.4 miles south-west of Exeter.

On the A38, take the Dunchideock turn (at Exeter Race Course) off the dual
carriageway and follow signs for 'Forest Walks'. Buller's Hill car park is signed
at its entrance and is *c*.1 mile from the A38, on the left-hand side. Alternative
parking at the Forest Enterprise Raptor View Point further west along the road
at SX 877 854.

Access & Areas to Search
From the **Buller's Hill** car park take the Green 'Butterfly Walk' trail (3-mile
loop). This leads you down to the managed butterfly meadows at SX 871 844,
where there is a large pond. The pond is the best place to look for **Beautiful
Demoiselle** and **Golden-ringed Dragonfly**. Numerous streams and drainage
channels along the paths and rides. From the **Raptor View Point** take the path
down the slope at the entrance to the 'viewing area'. From here you can join the
Green 'Butterfly Walk' trail to the butterfly meadows.

Timing
June through July is a good time to look for most species.

Other Wildlife
Over 30 species of butterfly including Pearl-bordered and Silver-washed
Fritillaries. Birds include Honey-buzzard, Peregrine, Hobby and Nightjar.

Site Guide

HILTON GRAVEL PITS
near Burton-on-Trent, Derbyshire
Derbyshire Wildlife Trust | www.derbyshirewildlifetrust.org.uk

PARKING **SK 245 314**
OS Map 128

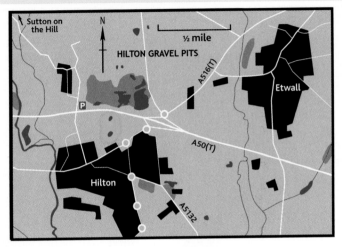

Species
Banded Demoiselle
Large Red-eyed Damselfly
Azure Damselfly
Migrant Hawker
Brown Hawker
Emperor Dragonfly
Common Darter
Ruddy Darter

Habitat
Disused gravel pits surrounded by marsh, scrub and woodland.

Location
The reserve lies between Burton-on-Trent and Derby.

Leave the A50 at the Hilton and Etwall turn and follow signs to Hilton. In the village, head north along the road signed for Sutton (Sutton Lane), go over the road bridge and take the next right (signed dead end) and right again. Park at the end, opposite the reserve entrance.

Access & Areas to Search
Follow the footpaths around the open-water areas. Do not climb down the banks as these are unstable and the water is deep. The reserve has a viewing platform.

Timing
There will always be something on the wing at this site from mid-May through to the end of September, but the most profitable time to visit is during July.

Additional Information
This is Derbyshire's (and the north Midlands') premier dragonfly site with over 16 species recorded. The path along the southern edge of the reserve is suitable for wheelchairs.

HOTHFIELD COMMON LNR
near Ashford, Kent
Kent Wildlife Trust | www.kentwildlifetrust.org.uk

TQ 970 457
OS Map 189

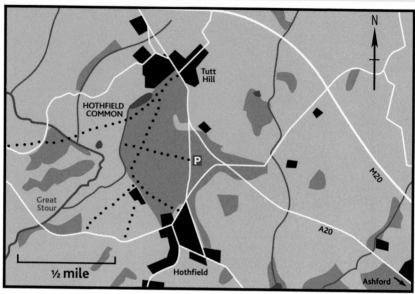

Species
Azure Damselfly
Migrant Hawker
Keeled Skimmer
Ruddy Darter

Habitat
Boggy heathland with woodland.

Location
Hothfield Common lies between Ashford (*c*.3 miles) and Charing (*c*.2 miles).

Follow the A20 from Ashford and after 3 miles turn south along the minor road towards Hothfield village. Take the next right turn and the car park is on the right at TQ 972 458, opposite the reserve entrance (do not use the car park nearest the football field).

Access & Areas to Search
From the car park cross the road to enter the reserve and follow the extensive network of paths around the series of bogs.

Timing
A visit in July should see all of the above species.

Additional Information
Wheelchair access is via equestrian gates opposite the main car park; however, the paths and boardwalks are narrow in places. Public toilets are situated just off the A20 lay-by on the edge of the wooded area of the reserve called 'The Triangle'.

HOUGHTON MILL

TL 284 717
OS Map 153

near Huntingdon, Cambridgeshire
National Trust | www.nationaltrust.org.uk

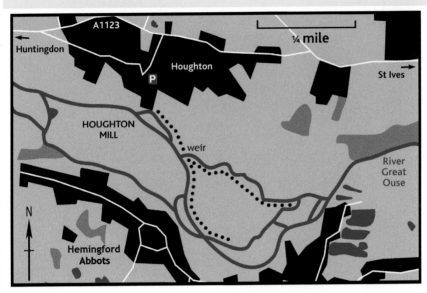

Site Guide

Species

The watercourses around this section of the River Ouse are particularly rich in dragonflies:
White-legged Damselfly
Large Red-eyed Damselfly
Scarce Chaser

Habitat

Open river and linked, vegetated watercourses surrounded by pasture with scattered scrub.

Location

This site lies *c*.3 miles east of Huntingdon.

Leave the A1123 east of Huntingdon at the National Trust (brown) signs for Houghton Mill. Continue through the village following the signs and park at the caravan-site car park (charge) in Mill Street. Limited roadside parking by the church is often taken up at weekends at this popular spot.

Access & Areas to Search

From the car park, public footpaths run east and west along the River Ouse and linked watercourses.

The main area to concentrate on is the well-vegetated waterway to the left (east) after the second of the bridges at the weir. **Large Red-eyed Damselfly** can be found along the main river stretch at the weir, whilst **Scarce Chaser** and **White-legged Damselfly** are common along both banks of the waterway on the left. Pay particular attention to nettle clumps and bramble patches.

Timing

All species above, plus several others, are on the wing throughout June.

IPSLEY ALDERS MARSH
Winyates Green, Redditch, Worcestershire
Worcestershire Wildlife Trust | www.worcswildlifetrust.co.uk

SP 076 677
OS Map 150

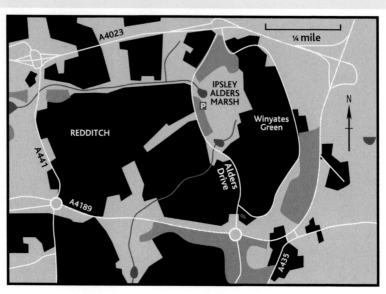

Species
Large Red-eyed Damselfly
Black Darter

Habitat
Woodland, wet meadow, ponds.

Location
This small nature reserve lies within the eastern outskirts of Redditch.

The reserve entrance is situated halfway along Alders Drive, Winyates, which links the A4023 (to the north of the site) with the A4189 (to the south). Park on the roadside verge or on roads nearby.

Timing
Large Red-eyed Damselfly has a long flight period, from the end of May to early August. **Black Darter** is best looked for from mid-July to mid-September. Many other, common species will be found during these two periods, with July being the best month.

Access & Areas to Search
Follow paths around site, but the stream area is particularly worth exploring.

Additional Information
Waterproof footwear recommended. The marsh can be very boggy in places so keep to the paths.

This site can be combined with nearby Feckenham Wylde Moor.

JOHNNY BROWN'S COMMON
near Barnsley, South Yorkshire
Wakefield Metropolitan District Council | www.wakefield.gov.uk

SE 460 125
OS Map 111

Species
*Over 15 species
including:*
Large Red Damselfly
Azure Damselfly
Migrant Hawker
Common Hawker
Brown Hawker
Emperor Dragonfly
Broad-bodied Chaser
Black-tailed Skimmer
Common Darter
Ruddy Darter

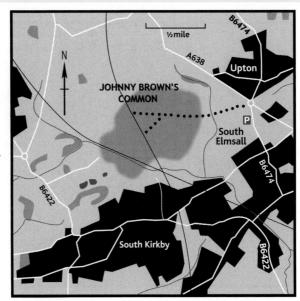

Habitat
Reclaimed colliery
site now containing
meadows, ponds,
marsh and scrub.

Location
The area is situated *c*.6 miles north-east of Barnsley.

Leave Barnsley northwards along the A628. At the roundabout in Ackworth
Moor Top, take the A638 south-eastwards to the roundabout (junction of A638
and B6474) at Upton. Park in car park *c*.100m south of the roundabout, along the
B6474.

Access & Areas to Search
From the car park, walk back to the roundabout and follow the disused railway
west from the roundabout. A very good pond is situated down this track on the
right-hand side. Further ponds to explore can be found by continuing down the
track and taking the left fork.

Timing
A visit at any time from the end of May to early September will be rewarding,
but the maximum number of species will be on the wing from late June to early
August.

Additional Information
Managed as a local community green space by the South Kirkby, South Elmsall
and Upton Area (SESKU) Environment Group, Broad Lane Business Centre,
Westfield Lane, South Elmsall, West Yorkshire WF9 2JX; tel. 01977 609 939.
SESKU produces a leaflet 'The Dragonflies of the SESKU Ringway'.

Site Guide

Site Guide

KENFIG NNR
near Porthcawl, Bridgend
Countryside Council for Wales | www.ccw.gov.uk
managed by Bridgend County Borough Council | www.bridgend.gov.uk

SD 800 815
OS Map 170

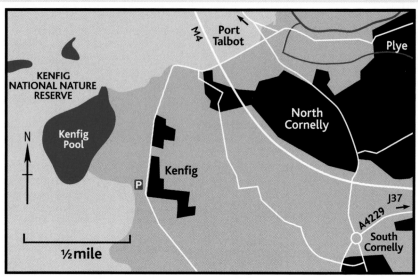

Species
Up to 20 species including:
Hairy Dragonfly
Emperor Dragonfly
Keeled Skimmer
Ruddy Darter

Habitat
Extensive dune system and ponds including the large open Kenfig Pool.

Location
Kenfig NNR is situated *c.*2 miles north of Porthcawl.

Leave the M4 at Junction 37 and follow the A4229 towards Porthcawl. Take the right turn south of South Cornelly (off map) to Kenfig village. Car park (free), visitor centre, with toilets and gift shop, along this minor road.

Access & Areas to Search
Follow the numerous footpaths running around the pool and across the adjacent dunes.

Timing
Most of the reserve's species are best looked for during July. **Hairy Dragonfly**, however, is best looked for from mid-May to late June.

Additional Information
Leaflet available from visitor centre. Wheelchair access to the visitor centre, but difficult to the dunes.

This site can be combined with sites on the Gower.

KINGSBURY WATER PARK
near Tamworth, Warwickshire
Warwickshire County Council | www.warwickshire.gov.uk

SP 210 960
OS Map 139

Species
Over 10 species including:
**Large Red-eyed
   Damselfly**
Migrant Hawker
Southern Hawker
Brown Hawker
Emperor Dragonfly

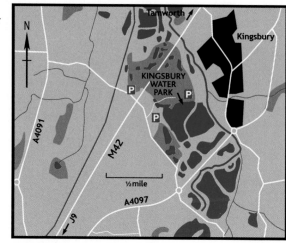

Habitat
Lakes and pools,
grassland, scrub,
woodland on former
gravel workings.

Location
The park lies *c*.5 miles
south of Tamworth and
c.2 miles from Junction 9 of the M42.

From the M42 Junction 9, take the A4097 towards Tamworth. After *c*.1.5 miles, take the minor road (Bodymoor Heath Lane) on the left signed for the water park. The car park (small charge) for the nature reserve is at the Broomey Croft entrance, which is on the right just after this road passes over the M42.

Timing
A visit any time from June to August would be productive. **Large Red-eyed Damselfly** flies from late May to the end of August; **Emperor Dragonfly** from early June to mid-August; **Brown Hawker** from mid-June to end of August; **Southern Hawker** during July to September; and **Migrant Hawker** from mid-July to mid-September.

Additional Information
Tea shop, toilets and children's farm at the nature reserve entrance. West Midland Bird Club mans a visitor centre next to the car park at weekends.

Watersports take place south of the M42 and quieter activities, including nature reserve area, are to the north of the motorway.

LITTLE BRADLEY PONDS
near Bovey Tracey, Devon
Devon Wildlife Trust | www.devonwildlifetrust.org

SX 829 778
OS Map 191

Species
Over 20 species including:
Beautiful Demoiselle
Scarce Blue-tailed Damselfly
Hairy Dragonfly
Downy Emerald
Four-spotted Chaser
Keeled Skimmer
Ruddy Darter

Habitat
Two large ponds, scrub.

Location
This reserve lies off the B3344 between Chudleigh Knighton and Bovey Tracey.

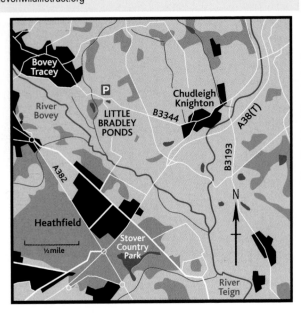

Leave the A38 at the Chudleigh Knighton turn. In Chudleigh Knighton, take the B3344 towards Bovey Tracey. After *c*.1 mile, turn south along the minor road towards Bradley. The car park is immediately on the left and the two ponds lie on either side of the road.

Access & Areas to Search
Both ponds are accessed from the minor road just off the B3344. Access to the newer pond is via a stile. Footpaths take you around both ponds.

Timing
Both **Hairy Dragonfly** and **Downy Emerald** are on the wing from May to early July. Both **Scarce Blue-tailed Damselfly** and **Keeled Skimmer** are on the wing from late May to the end of August, and **Ruddy Darter** is on the wing from the end of June through to September. Early July would be the best time to visit.

Additional Information
This is one of the top two sites in Devon for dragonflies, with over 20 species recorded. It can be combined with any of the many other sites in the area including Aylesbeare Common (also butterflies), Bystock Pools, Chudleigh Knighton Heath, Colaton Raleigh Common, Haldon Forest, Slapton Ley, Stafford Bridge, Stover Country Park and Venn Ottery (also butterflies).

LOCH BRAN
near Inverness, Highland
Scottish Natural Heritage | www.snh.org.uk

NH 507 192
OS Map 34/35

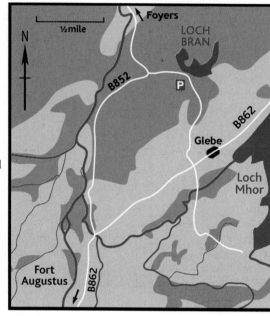

Species
Up to 10 species including:
Emerald Damselfly
Common Blue Damselfly
Golden-ringed Dragonfly
Brilliant Emerald
Four-spotted Chaser
Highland Darter
Black Darter

Habitat
Lochan with bog situated within coniferous forest.

Location
Loch Bran is a small loch on the east shore of Loch Ness, *c.*17 miles south of Inverness.

Take the B852 from Inverness south along the east shore of Loch Ness to Foyers. From Foyers, take the third minor road on the left, towards Glebe. This minor road joins the B862. Park midway along this minor road at NH 507 192.

Access & Areas to Search
Follow the various forest tracks to the different lochans.

Timing
Brilliant Emerald is on the wing throughout July and **Highland Darter** is on the wing from mid-July (but towards the end of July is best for this species). A visit from mid- to late July should see all the species mentioned above on the wing.

Additional Information
Take care by the water's edge as this site is very boggy.

Brilliant Emerald is the *only* species of emerald found here. Loch Bran is possibly the best loch to look for the species in Scotland, but it has been recorded from many of the lochans in the area.

This site can be combined with Abernethy Forest, Glen Affric or Loch Gamhna.

LOCH COULIN & LOCH CLAIR
near Kinlochewe, Highland
Scottish Natural Heritage | www.snh.org.uk

NH 003 582
OS Map 25

Species
An excellent area holding several key Scottish species:
Large Red Damselfly
Common Blue
  Damselfly
Azure Hawker
Common Hawker
Golden-ringed
  Dragonfly
Northern Emerald
Highland Darter

Habitat
Lochs surrounded by open, mountainous country including blanket bog and birch woodland.

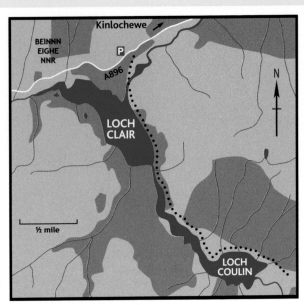

Location
Loch Coulin and **Loch Clair** lie south of the A896, *c*.3 miles south-west of Kinlochewe, at the foot of the Beinn Eighe NNR.

From Kinlochewe, take the A896 south-west for *c*.3 miles. Park on right-hand side of the road in pull-in opposite the Coulin Estate road at NH 003 582.

Access & Areas to Search
Walk down the Coulin Estate road, across the bridge and down the east side of Loch Clair to the swing gate at NH 004 560. Continue through the gate (do not cross over the bridge – private).

Azure Hawker occurs throughout the area but is best looked for beyond the swing gate. **Highland Darter** is best looked for around rocky areas close to the loch shores whilst **Northern Emerald** has been seen around the *Sphagnum* bog and forest areas of Loch Coulin.

Timing
A visit in mid-July is the best time. **Azure Hawker** is best looked for before the end of July and **Highland Darter** is at its peak from the end of July.

Additional Information
Waterproof walking boots advisable and insect repellent essential.

This site can be easily combined with Bridge of Grudie and Beinn Eighe.

LOCH GAMHNA
Loch an Eilein, near Aviemore, Highland
Forestry Commission Scotland | www.forestry.gov.uk/scotland and
Scottish Natural Heritage | www.snh.org.uk

NH 891 070
OS Map 36

Species
Golden-ringed Dragonfly
Highland Darter
Black Darter

Habitat
Small loch lying in
Caledonian pine forest.
Stony ground with
heather.

Location
Loch Gamhna is a small,
shallow loch directly south
of Loch an Eilein, *c*.4 miles
south of Aviemore.

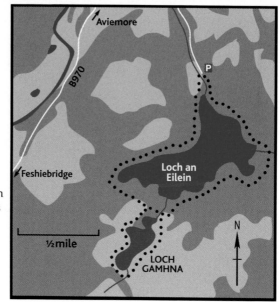

From Aviemore take the
B970 to Inverdruie, where
you turn left, continuing
along the B970 south
towards Feshiebridge.
After *c*.1 mile, take the left turn signed Loch an Eilein. Park in the car park at
NH 897 085 (charge).

Access & Areas to Search
From the Loch an Eilein car park follow the path along the western side of Loch
an Eilein. At the junction with a seat, turn right and follow the path around and
down towards Loch Gamhna.

Highland Darter can be found almost anywhere in the area but is best looked
for along the footpath on the western side of Loch Gamhna.

Timing
Highland Darter is on the wing from early July into October, but towards the
end of July is best and most other Scottish specialities are still on the wing.

Additional Information
Light refreshments and toilets available at the visitor centre at Loch an Eilein.

This site can be easily combined with Abernethy Forest sites or Loch Bran.

Other Wildlife
Ospreys fish at Loch an Eilein.

Site Guide

LORD'S LOT WOOD & BOG
near Carnforth, Lancashire
The Wildlife Trust for Lancashire, Manchester & North Merseyside |
www.lancswt.org.uk

SD 546 705
OS Map 97

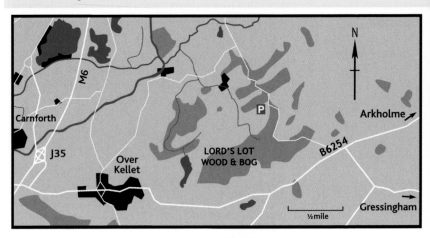

Species
Common Hawker
Black Darter

Habitat
Sphagnum bog, mixed woodland.

Location
This site lies *c.*3 miles east of Carnforth.

Leave the M6 at Junction 35 for Carnforth. From Carnforth, take the B6254
through Over Kellet. At the next (staggered) crossroads (right turn signed to
Gressingham), turn left along Borwick Road. Car park and picnic site at SD 547
710 at north end of wood. The best access point to the reserve is south of this car
park, via a track leading south-west into the wood (at SD 549 707, just north of a
lay-by).

Access & Areas to Search
Follow footpaths through the wood. The bog itself is hazardous as it is a raft
of *Sphagnum* and cottongrass floating on deep water. For this reason, and also
because the habitat is easily damaged by trampling, do not venture out into the
bog. It is best viewed from the birch scrub along the eastern side. Do not use the
dam as a footpath for reasons of safety.

Timing
Both **Black Darter** and **Common Hawker** are on the wing from July to
September.

LOW BARNS
near Bishop Auckland, County Durham
Durham Wildlife Trust | www.durhamwt.co.uk

NZ 160 315
OS Map 92

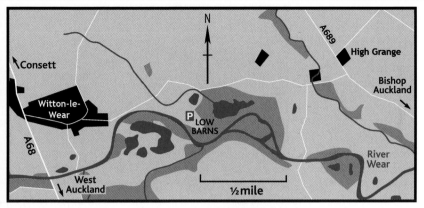

Species
Banded Demoiselle
Blue-tailed Damselfly
Common Hawker
Southern Hawker
Common Darter

Habitat
Lakes and ponds within woodland and
grassland beside the River Wear.

Location
The reserve lies *c*.3 miles west of Bishop Auckland.

From the A68 west of Bishop Auckland take the road to Witton-le-Wear. On the
east of the village follow the signs for the reserve at the right turn at the Victoria
public house and continue over the level crossing. The reserve entrance and car
park are *c*.0.5 mile further on.

Alternatively, take the minor road heading west off the A689 near High Grange
for *c*.0.75 mile.

Access & Areas to Search
Follow footpaths around reserve.

Timing
July–August.

Additional Information
Visitor centre, coffee shop and toilets. The reserve is accessible to wheelchair users.
Headquarters of the Durham Wildlife Trust.

This site can be combined with Burnhope Pond.

Other Wildlife
Dingy Skipper and Ringlet butterflies, Redstart, Pied Flycatcher and Otter.

Site Guide

LUGG MEADOW & LUGG MILLS

SO 527 411

Hereford, Herefordshire

OS Map 149

Herefordshire Nature Trust | www.wildlifetrust.org.uk/hereford

Species
Banded Demoiselle
Club-tailed Dragonfly

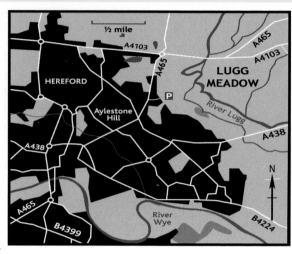

Habitat
Ancient hay meadows alongside the River Lugg.

Location
The reserve is situated on the north-eastern outskirts of Hereford.

From the A465, at Aylestone Hill, in north-eastern Hereford, turn east into Walney Lane, *c.*0.5 mile from the A4103/A465 roundabout. Park in lay-by at bottom of the lane

Access & Areas to Search
From the car, continue down to the reserve and the riverside path. Note that, although access to Upper Lugg Meadow is unrestricted, the hay crop must not be entered between April and the end of July. Take care when walking alongside the river as some of its banks are vertical cliffs. Lugg Mills is an 8-acre island at the northern end of the reserve formed by the confluence of the Lugg and Little Lugg rivers. Banded Demoiselle may be seen here.

Alternative access on foot from the Lugg Bridge on A4103 and follow path along the River Lugg.

Timing
Club-tailed Dragonfly flies from late May to late June and **Banded Demoiselle** is on the wing from early June to early August.

Additional Information
Leaflet available from Herefordshire Nature Trust.

This site can be combined with Nagshead.

Other Wildife
Curlew and Skylark breed in the meadows and Kingfisher and Sand Martin in the river banks. Otters visit the reserve.

NAGSHEAD
near Chepstow, Gloucestershire
RSPB | www.rspb.org.uk, Forest Enterprise | www.forestry.gov.uk

SO 606 080
OS Map 162

Species
Up to 20 species have been recorded here, including:
Beautiful Demoiselle
White-legged Damselfly
Large Red-eyed
   Damselfly
Southern Hawker
Emperor Dragonfly
Club-tailed Dragonfly
Golden-ringed
   Dragonfly

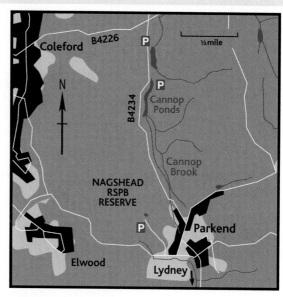

Habitat
Small pools and fast-flowing river tributary of the River Severn within mature deciduous woodland.

Location
Nagshead lies *c*.10 miles north-east of Chepstow.

From Chepstow take the A48 to Lydney and then the B4234 north towards Upper Lydbrook. At Parkend, head west from the village along the minor road to Coleford. The reserve entrance is signposted on the right just outside Parkend. Information centre and car park are 500m up the entrance track.

Access & Areas to Search
There are a number of ponds at the information centre and around the hide. **Club-tailed Dragonfly** can be found feeding along forest tracks and rides, particularly close to the river. Search along the fast-flowing stream/river areas for **Beautiful Demoiselle**. Cannop Ponds and Brook are also worth visiting, especially for **White-legged** and **Large Red-eyed Damselflies**.

Timing
Club-tailed Dragonfly is on the wing from late May to late June, whilst a visit any time during June to August should see many species on the wing.

Additional Information
Information centre (with toilets) open at weekends and Bank Holidays.

This site can be combined with Lugg Meadows & Luggs Mills.

Other Wildlife
Thirty-five species of butterfly also occur throughout the area. Nesting Redstarts, Wood Warblers and Pied Flycatchers.

Site Guide

NEW FOREST 1
CROCKFORD BRIDGE
HATCHET MOOR & POND
BEAULIEU ROAD STATION
near Lyndhurst, Hampshire
part of the New Forest National Park | www.newforestnpa.gov.uk

SZ 351 990
SU 365 012
PARKING **SU 346 064**
OS Map 196

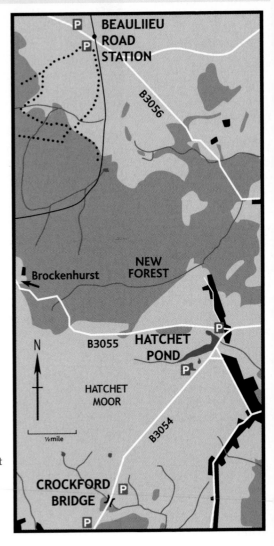

Species

The New Forest supports good populations of acid-soil-loving insects:

Beautiful Demoiselle
Large Red Damselfly
Small Red Damselfly
Large Red-eyed Damselfly
Southern Damselfly
Common Blue Damselfly
Scarce Blue-tailed Damselfly
Blue-tailed Damselfly
Emperor Dragonfly
Broad-bodied Chaser
Black-tailed Skimmer
Keeled Skimmer

Habitat

Crockford Bridge Stony-bottomed, medium-flowing stream fringed by boggy heathland.

Hatchet Moor & Pond
Large and small open lake and ponds fed by medium-flowing, stony-bottomed stream adjacent to boggy heathland.

Beaulieu Road Station Wet and dry heath, woodland, scrub, ponds and streams.

Location

These three sites lie within the New Forest, *c.*3–5 miles south-east of Lyndhurst.

Crockford Bridge lies *c.*1.5 miles south of Hatchet Moor on the B3054.

Hatchet Moor & Pond lies at the junction of the B3055 and B3054, *c.*4.5 miles east of the A337 Lyndhurst to Lymington road.

Beaulieu Road Station lies along the B3056 Lyndhurst to Beaulieu road. The main (Shatterford) car park is on the left on the Lyndhurst side of the railway bridge (SU 346 064). Other car parks before the bridge on the right (SU 352 064) and further along towards Lyndhurst on the right (SU 345 067).

Access & Areas to Search
Crockford Bridge
Park at Crockford Clump car park at SZ 352 993. Cross over the road and walk down to the bridge and follow the north bank of the stream.

Southern Damselfly is the commonest insect along the stream and can easily be found west of the bridge in the low emergent vegetation of the more open stretches of the stream. Southern Damselfly also disperses into the adjacent heathland. **Beautiful Demoiselle** can easily be found around bushes providing shade over the water. **Keeled Skimmer** occurs along open stretches and throughout the adjacent heathland bogs.

Hatchet Moor & Pond
Park at Hatchet Moor car park at SU 365 000. Follow the southern shore of Hatchet Pond (the large open water body) to the extreme south-western corner, where the feeder stream enters the pond. Search the immediate boggy areas and along the stream up to the obvious track that fords it (very pale stony ground area).

Scarce Blue-tailed Damselfly occurs in small numbers throughout the boggy areas at the mouth of the feeder stream to Hatchet Pond. **Southern Damselfly** is found along the feeder stream from around 60m from the mouth. This species slowly replaces **Common Blue Damselfly** the further away from the mouth you walk. **Blue-tailed Damselfly** also occurs here. **Keeled Skimmer** is abundant along the stream.

Beaulieu Road Station
From the main car park, search the pools and streams along the footpath that runs parallel with the railway.

Timing
All the main-interest species are on the wing from end June to end July.

Additional Information
Small Red-eyed Damselfly has been recorded in the area. A similar range of species can be found at the New Forest 2 sites (Latchmore Bottom, Black Water, Ober Water and Mill Lawn Brook), some of which can be combined with this site in the same day. The Lyndhurst Visitor Information Centre provides information for visitors to the New Forest and is open daily, 10am–5pm, at The Main Car Park, High Street, Lyndhurst.

Other Wildlife
An excellent area for heathland species. Butterflies include Purple Hairstreak, Silver-studded Blue, Small Pearl-bordered and Dark Green Fritillaries and Grayling and birds include Honey-buzzard, Hobby, Woodlark, Redstart, Stonechat, Wood Warbler and Common Crossbill.

Site Guide

NEW FOREST 2

LATCHMORE BOTTOM	**SU 185 125**
BLACK WATER	**SU 260 050**
OBER WATER	**SU 270 029**
MILL LAWN BROOK	**SU 223 033**
near Ringwood, Hampshire	OS Map 195

part of the New Forest National Park | www.newforestnpa.gov.uk

Species

The New Forest supports good populations of acid-soil-loving insects:

Beautiful Demoiselle
White-legged Damselfly
Large Red Damselfly
Small Red Damselfly
Southern Damselfly
Azure Damselfly
Common Blue Damselfly
Scarce Blue-tailed
   Damselfly
Blue-tailed Damselfly
Emperor Dragonfly
Golden-ringed Dragonfly
Broad-bodied Chaser
Keeled Skimmer

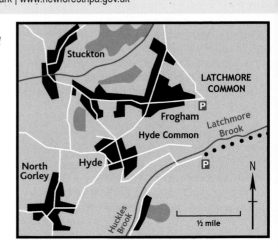

Habitat

Stony-bottomed, medium-flowing streams, seepages and boggy heathland.

Location

These sites lie within the New Forest near Ringwood.

Latchmore Bottom lies east of the A338 north of Ringwood.

Black Water lies north-west of Brockenhurst and is accessed from the minor road runing from Brockenhurst to the A35.

Ober Water lies to the west of Brockenhurst and is crossed by the minor road from Brockenhurst to the A35 and by the A35 itself.

Mill Lawn Brook is part of Ober Water (above) and lies to the north-east of Bisterne Close (east of Burley).

Access & Areas to Search
Latchmore Bottom

Park in car parks east of Hyde Common at SU 181 123 (past Ogdens Farm, via bumpy track) and SU 178 128. Search the heath to the east of car parks, paying particular attention to Latchmore Brook, and Huckles Brook to the west. All the species occur along these brooks and in the surrounding wet heathland.

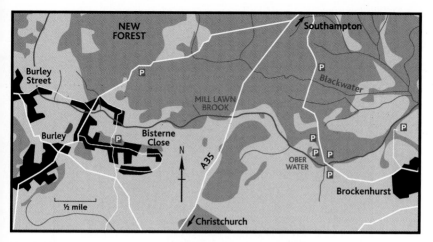

Black Water
Car park at Rhinefield at SU 268 048. Search damp areas along Black Water.

Ober Water
Several car parks around the minor road at SU 270 030. Walk the stream in both directions concentrating on the more open areas. Search areas of damp heath. **White-legged Damselfly** occurs only along the Ober Water within the New Forest.

Mill Lawn Brook
Park in the car park east of Burley village at SU 223 033. Walk east along the stream. Species include **Southern, Scarce Blue-tailed** and **Small Red Damselflies**.

Timing
All the main species are on the wing from end June to end July.

Additional Information
A similar range of species can be found at the New Forest 1 sites (Hatchet Pond, Crockford Bridge and Beaulieu Road Station – see pp. 194–195), which can be combined with this site in the same day. The Lyndhurst Visitor Information Centre provides information for visitors to the New Forest and is open daily, 10am–5pm, at The Main Car Park, High Street, Lyndhurst.

Other Wildlife
An excellent area for heathland species. Butterflies include Purple Hairstreak, Silver-studded Blue, Small Pearl-bordered and Dark Green Fritillaries and Grayling; birds include Hobby, Honey-buzzard, Woodlark, Redstart, Stonechat, Wood Warbler and Crossbill.

Site Guide

PITSFORD RESERVOIR
near Northampton, Northamptonshire

SP 780 708
OS Maps 141/152

Anglian Water | www.anglianwater.co.uk, The Wildlife Trust for Bedfordshire,
Cambridgeshire, Northamptonshire & Peterborough | www.wildlifebcnp.org.uk

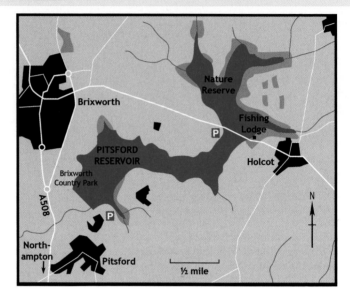

Species
Over 15 species including:
Emerald Damselfly
Azure Damselfly
Common Blue Damselfly
Blue-tailed Damselfly
Migrant Hawker
Southern Hawker
Brown Hawker

Emperor Dragonfly
Common Darter
Ruddy Darter

Habitat
Reservoir with wet margins, mixed
plantation, grassland.

Location
The reservoir is 5 miles north of Northampton between the A508 and the A43.
The reserve lies north of the minor road between Brixworth and Holcot villages.
There is a public car park at the western end of the causeway.

Access & Areas to Search
Follow footpaths around the nature reserve, which is the best area to search for all
the above species. There is further parking at the picnic site just north of Pitsford
village. Follow footpaths from here to reservoir edge.

Additional Information
Permits (free to Trust members) available from the Fishing Lodge at the eastern
end of the causeway. Alternatively, contact the Northamptonshire office of the
Wildlife Trust before a visit for a permit and information about the reserve (tel.
01604 405 285; northamptonshire@wildlifebcnp.org). Brixworth Country Park
(www.northamptonshire.gov.uk), at the western arm of the reservoir, has some
good dragonfly ponds as well as a visitor centre, toilets, café and easy-access
trails.

PRIDDY MINERIES
near Wells, Somerset
formerly Somerset Wildlife Trust | www.somersetwildlife.org

ST 547 515
OS Map 182

Species
Large Red-eyed
  Damselfly
Common Hawker
Emperor Dragonfly
Downy Emerald
Four-spotted Chaser
Black Darter

Habitat
Grassland/
heathland mosaic
with pools on site
of disused lead
workings.

Location
The reserve lies *c.*3
miles north of Wells.

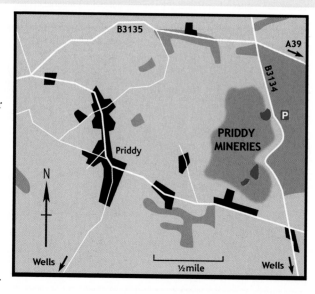

Leave Wells north-east along the A39 towards Chewton Mendip. At Green Ore, turn left along the B3135. At the crossroads with the B3134 (on your right), turn left. Parking after *c.*0.5 mile by the northernmost pond at ST 547 515.

Alternatively, from the A39 at Hill Grove, take the minor road west towards Priddy (signed 3 miles) and then turn right at the crossroads towards Harptree and Burrington. Car park and roadside parking at ST 547 515.

Access & Areas to Search
Large pool immediately by roadside parking area; smaller pools along footpaths to south at ST 546 508.

Additional Information
Information boards. Note that the lease for the reserve had not been extended at the time of writing, so Somerset Wildlife Trust is currently not the site manager.

This site can be combined with Shapwick Heath.

200 *Watching British Dragonflies*

RAMSBURY MEADOW
near Marlborough, Wiltshire

SU 273 714
OS Map 174

owned by Wiltshire Wildlife Trust | www.wiltshirewildlife.org;
leased and managed by Ramsbury Parish Council | www.ramsbury.org

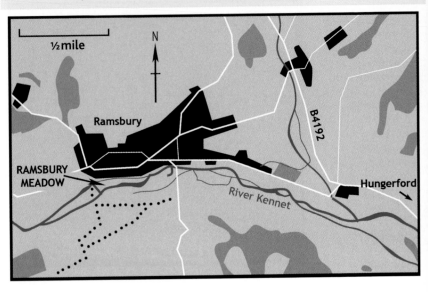

Species
Common species including:
Emerald Damselfly
Common Blue Damselfly
Southern Hawker
Common Darter

Habitat
Former water meadow with pond alongside the River Kennet.

Location
Ramsbury Meadow lies *c.*7 miles east of Marlborough.

Leave Marlborough along the minor road through Mildenhall to Ramsbury. Park carefully in the High Street. On foot, take the path running down the side of the fire station and cross the bridge over the stream to the reserve.

Access & Areas to Search
A boardwalk across the meadow leads to viewing platforms overlooking the river and the pond.

Timing
July and August are the best months to visit the reserve for dragonflies.

Additional Information
Pubs and shops in Ramsbury village; toilets in the High Street.

Site Guide

RAVENSROOST WOOD & MEADOWS   SU 024 876
near Swindon, Wiltshire   **OS Map 173**
Wiltshire Wildlife Trust | www.wiltshirewildlife.org

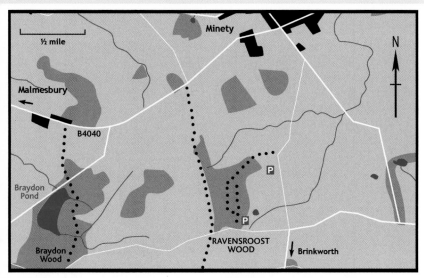

Species
Emerald Damselfly
Common Blue Damselfly
Migrant Hawker
Emperor Dragonfly
Common Darter
Ruddy Darter

Habitat
Mature deciduous woodland of
mainly oak and hazel, flower-rich
meadows and ponds.

Location
Ravensroost Wood lies *c*.6 miles to the west of Swindon.

Leave the A149 at Cricklade and continue along the B4040 to Minety. At Minety,
take the turn for Wootton Bassett and Brinkworth at the Turnpike Inn. Take the
next right signed for Brinkworth. After 1.5 miles, turn right at the crossroads.
The small car park is on the right after 0.5 mile at the start of the wood (SU 024
876).

Access & Areas to Search
Follow the path from the car park through the woodland. Small ponds are
situated near Robinswood Farm and along Jack Smith Ride (see information
boards or WWT leaflet). Dragonflies hunt along the woodland rides.

Timing
Mid-July to mid-August.

Other Wildlife
Butterflies include Brown Hairstreak, White Admiral and Silver-washed
Fritillary; birds include Marsh Tit.

RED MOOR
near Lostwithiel, Cornwall
Cornwall Wildlife Trust | www.cornwallwildlifetrust.org.uk

SX 065 611
OS Map 200

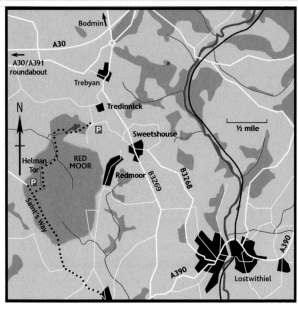

Species
13 species recorded including:
Small Red Damselfly
Scarce Blue-tailed Damselfly

Habitat
Lowland heath, pools, bog, carr.

Location
The reserve lies between Bodmin and Lostwithiel.

From the A30/A391 roundabout, south-west of Bodmin, take the A389 towards Bodmin. Turn right under the A30 and follow this minor road to Fenton Pits, then take the left fork to Tredinnick. Limited parking south-west of Treddinnick near the track leading off a triangle formed in the roads at SX 077 622. Alternatively, reach the same spot via the B3268 and B3269 north-west of Lostwithiel or park in the small car park at Helman Tor and follow the path from here.

Access & Areas to Search
Follow footpath heading south-west of the triangle (see map) to Helman Tor.

Timing
Small Red Damselfly and **Scarce Blue-tailed Damselfly** can be seen from early June to late August.

Other Wildlife
Nightjar, Tree Pipit and Willow Tit breed on the reserve.

RIVER ARUN, NEW BRIDGE
near Billingshurst, West Sussex

TQ 069 260
OS Map 197

Species
Over 15 species have been recorded including:
White-legged Damselfly
Large Red-eyed Damselfly
Hairy Dragonfly
Brown Hawker
Club-tailed Dragonfly
Downy Emerald
Scarce Chaser

Habitat
Richly vegetated disused stretch of the Wey & Arun Canal and the River Arun.

Location
New Bridge is situated along the A272 between Billingshurst and Petworth.

Park sensibly at the bridge at TQ 069 260 (room for 6–8 cars).

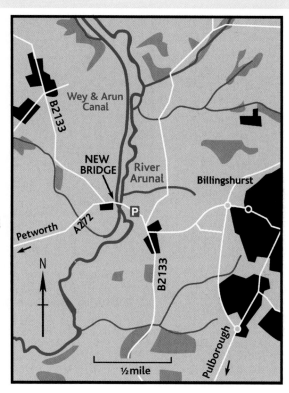

Site Guide

Access & Areas to Search
Search north and south of the bridge by walking along the banks of both the canal and the river. **Scarce Chaser** occurs on both the canal and the river, whilst **Hairy Dragonfly** and **Downy Emerald** both prefer the canal, and **White-legged Damselfly** prefers the river. It is worth searching the dense areas of dock in the grazed fields that separate the canal from the river for roosting insects. **Club-tailed Dragonfly** is an infrequent visitor to the site from populations that occur further south along the River Arun. **Brilliant Emerald** occasionally recorded.

Timing
A visit in early to mid June should give you a chance of seeing all the main species, of which **White-legged Damselfly** is usually the latest to emerge.

Additional Information
This is undoubtedly one of southern England's top dragonfly sites in terms of number of species and sheer numbers of insects. Huge concentrations of **Banded Demoiselle** and **White-legged Damselfly** are particularly noteworthy as is the density at which **Scarce Chaser** occurs at this site.

RIVER DEE, FARNDON
Cheshire
Cheshire County Council | www.cheshire.gov.uk

SJ 413 545
OS Map 117

Species
Banded Demoiselle
White-legged
   Damselfly
Club-tailed Dragonfly

Habitat
Stretch of River Dee
with adjacent farmland.

Location
Farndon is situated
*c.*8 miles north-east of
Wrexham.

From Wrexham take
the A534 to Holt, then
the B5130 to Farndon.
Just before the town,
park around the River
Dee bridge at SJ 414
541.

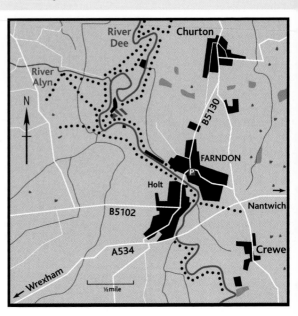

Access & Areas to Search
Walk the north-east bank of the River Dee up to a mile north and south of
Farndon, searching riverside vegetation and bushes for perched insects,
sheltered tree and bush lines for feeding individuals and the water's edge for
patrolling males.

Timing
Club-tailed Dragonfly is best looked for from the end of May to mid-June.
White-legged Damselfly is best looked for from mid-June to mid-July. **Banded
Demoiselle** will be on the wing during these periods.

Additional Information
This can be a difficult site as there is only a small to medium population of **Club-
tailed Dragonfly**, so be prepared to wait some time before you find one. White-
legged Damselfly found along the river in 2007 (new species for the county).

RIVER EXE, STAFFORD BRIDGE
Exeter, Devon

SX 921 962
OS Map 192

Species
Lowland river species including:
Beautiful Demoiselle
Banded Demoiselle
White-legged Damselfly

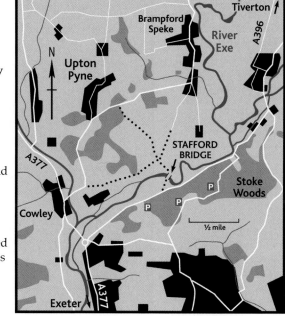

Habitat
Slow-flowing stretch of the River Exe with lush marginal vegetation surrounded by pasture with scattered bushes and rank vegetation clumps (nettles and brambles).

Location
Stafford Bridge is situated on the River Exe *c.*2 miles north of Exeter.

From Exeter take the A377 towards Crediton. At the Cowley Bridge roundabout take the A396 towards Tiverton. After *c.*1 mile leave the road to the left down a gated track leading to the river. Park at the railway bridge at the river.

Access & Areas to Search
Search around the bridge, including bushes and nettlebeds, for **White-legged Damselfly**. Keep to footpaths.

Timing
Mid-June to the end of July.

Additional Information
This site can be combined with any of the many other sites in the area including Aylesbeare Common (also butterflies), Bystock Pools, Chudleigh Knighton Heath, Colaton Raleigh Common, Haldon Forest, Little Bradley Ponds, Slapton Ley, Stover Country Park and Venn Ottery.

RIVER THAMES, GORING
near Goring, Berkshire

SU 616 794
OS Map 175

Species
Banded Demoiselle
**White-legged
    Damselfly**
Large Red-eyed
    Damselfly
Club-tailed Dragonfly

Habitat
Riverside meadows and
hedgerows.

Location
This site lies *c*.1 mile
south of Goring.

In Goring, take
the minor road
(Gatehampton Road)
alongside the railway
station then turn right
at the fork and follow
this to the railway and
down to the river to
park.

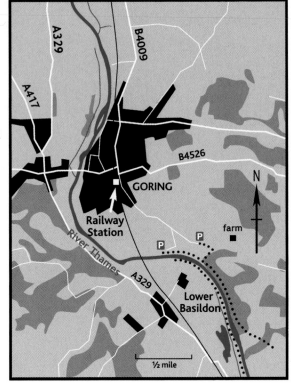

Access & Areas to Search
From the parking area, follow the riverside footpath south. Search the riverside
and also the footpath which runs away from the river along the northern edge
of the wood to the BBOWT Hartslock reserve.

Parking also at SU 615 797 by track to Upper Gatehampton Farm (keep track
clear at all times). Walk along the track, through gate on right and then through
the BBOWT Hartslock reserve (www.bbowt.org.uk) to River Thames.

Additional Information
One of the best sites for **Club-tailed Dragonfly**.

Other Wildlife
The Hartslock Nature Reserve is a chalkland site and has several species of
orchid, including Bee, Pyramidal and Common Spotted Orchids, Common
Twayblade and White Heleborine.

Site Guide

RIVER WAVENEY, GELDESTON
near Beccles, Norfolk/Suffolk border

TM 390 907
OS Map 134

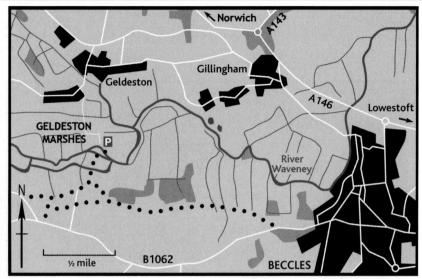

Species
Banded Demoiselle
Azure Damselfly
Hairy Dragonfly
Norfolk Hawker
Scarce Chaser

Habitat
Riverside grazing marshes with well-vegetated dykes.

Location
The village of Geldeston lies *c*.2 miles north-west of Beccles.

From Beccles take the A146 north to Gillingham then the minor road west signed for Geldeston. At the north-west end of Geldeston village, turn left down Geldeston Hill (signed for Ellingham), straight on at the crossroads onto Station Road and at the right-hand bend take the track on the left. Continue down track and park at or near to the Locks Inn.

Access & Areas to Search
From the pub, cross over footbridge and turn left. Search along the riverside and along the dykes running at right angles to the river and along New Dyke, which runs parallel to the river.

Timing
Hairy Dragonfly is an early flying species, on the wing from mid-May to the end of June. **Norfolk Hawker** has a very short flight period from early/mid-June to early July. **Scarce Chaser** is on the wing throughout June.

Additional Information
The Locks Inn is open throughout the summer, from Easter weekend, for refreshments.

RUTLAND WATER
EGLETON RESERVE
LYNDON RESERVE

SK 878 075
SK 894 058

near Oakham, Rutland
OS Map 141

Leicestershire & Rutland Wildlife Trust | www.rutlandwater.org.uk
Anglian Water | www.anglianwater.co.uk

Site Guide

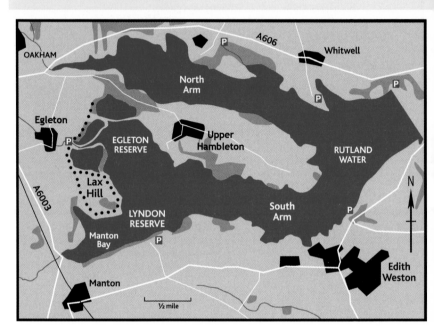

Species

Most common species including:

Large Red Damselfly
Azure Damselfly
Common Blue Damselfly
Migrant Hawker
Southern Hawker

Brown Hawker
Emperor Dragonfly
Four-spotted Chaser
Broad-bodied Chaser
Black-tailed Skimmer
Common Darter

Habitat

Huge reservoir with grassland, scrub, woodland.

Location

Rutland Water is situated between Oakham and Stamford west of the A1.

Leave the A1 at the Oakham and Stamford turn and take the A606 west towards Oakham. Access to the two nature reserve sites as below.

Access & Areas to Search
Egleton Reserve and the Anglian Birdwatching Centre

Signed from both the A6003 south of Oakham and the A606 east of Oakham. Follow signs through Egleton village to the reserve car park.

Anglian Birdwatching Centre includes toilets and shop (selling cold drinks and confectionery). Nature trails and hides. Entrance fee for non-Trust members. Day permits must be obtained from the visitor centre.

Marked nature trails run in either direction from the centre. Although the trails do not take you to the water's edge, the sheltered paths and field edges provide good feeding areas for many medium- and large-sized dragonflies such as darters and hawkers. Many species can be seen from the many hides along these trails.

The trail towards Lax Hill is possibly the better of the two walks, and contains several narrow wet ditches frequented by damselflies and dragonflies.

Lyndon Reserve
Leave the A606 at Empingham and head south-west along the minor road signed for Rutland South Shore, Edith Weston and Manton. Drive to Edith Weston and, at the T-junction, turn right towards Manton. Continue along this road for *c.*2 miles to the Lyndon Nature Reserve car park on the right-hand side (opposite turn to Lyndon village). Visitor centre, toilets, refreshments. Charge for non-Trust members. Note that the reserve is closed on Mondays, unless a Bank Holiday. Day permits must be obtained from the visitor centre.

The car park area is excellent with a small pond at the information centre entrance, which is very good for many species.

Follow the nature trail from the centre towards Manton Bay. Many species can be found feeding along the path and from the hides.

Timing
A visit during July and August will see most species.

Additional Information
England's largest inland water body is internationally recognised as a Ramsar site for wintering wildfowl. The reservoir is owned by Anglian Water and the nature reserves are managed by LRWT. The reserve areas are excellent at any time of year for birdwatching, and very good during the summer months for many common species of dragonflies and butterflies. Information about recent sightings is available from both reserve information centres.

From 1996 to 2001, Ospreys were released annually within the reserve areas in an attempt to establish them as an English breeding species. As a result, Ospreys can be enjoyed when you visit the area insect watching. Returning birds are present from April to September. Birds first bred here in 2001, and in 2007 a pair bred in Manton Bay, the nest easy viewable from the Lyndon reserve. For more information on Ospreys, visit the Anglian Birdwatching Centre at the Egleton Reserve.

Rutland Water is surrounded by a signed cycle route and bicycles are available for hire from the Cycle Centre at Whitwell, along the North Arm of the reservoir.

SALTWELLS LNR
Dudley, West Midlands
Dudley Metropolitan Borough Council | www.dudley.gov.uk

SO 935 868
OS Map 139

Species
Over 20 species including:
Emerald Damselfly
Large Red Damselfly
Variable Damselfly
Migrant Hawker
Common Hawker
Brown Hawker
Emperor Dragonfly
Broad-bodied Chaser
Ruddy Darter
Black Darter

Habitat
A mosaic of grassland, woodland and scrub with pools and streams.

Location
Saltwells Local Nature Reserve lies within the urban conurbation of the Borough of Dudley.

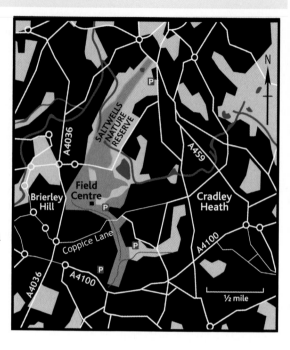

Leave the M5 at Junction 3 and take the A456 west to Hagley, then the A491, and the A4036 at the Pedmore roundabout. After *c*.2.5 miles, go past the A4100 exits (staggered first on the right then on the left) to the next roundabout and take the third exit into Coppice Lane. Continue over the bridge then turn left into Saltwells Lane (signed for Saltwells Inn) and park in the reserve car park at SO 935 869. Other car parks as indicated on map.

Access & Areas to Search
Search the streams and pools reached by the extensive network of paths.

Timing
With so many species to see, this site has something to offer from mid-May to the end of September. For the more interesting species, **Variable Damselfly** flies throughout June and July, **Migrant Hawker** August–September, **Common Hawker** July–September and **Black** and **Ruddy Darters** July–August.

Additional Information
This nationally important site boasts 18 species recorded annually. It is one of the largest urban nature reserves in the country. Additional information can be obtained from the reserve wardens (tel. 01384 812 795). Excellent information leaflets available, including one dedicated to dragonflies and where to find each species around the reserve.

SEVERN VALLEY COUNTRY PARK
near Bridgnorth, Shropshire

SO 755 838
OS Map 138

Bridgnorth District Council | www.bridgnorth-dc.gov.uk
Shropshire County Council | www.shropshire.gov.uk

Species
Banded Demoiselle
White-legged
   Damselfly
Large Red Damselfly
Emperor Dragonfly
Club-tailed Dragonfly

Habitat
Wood, scrub, meadow,
river and ponds.

Location
The country park
lies *c*.5 miles south of
Bridgnorth.

Take the A442 south of
Bridgnorth to Alveley
and follow the brown
signs to the visitor
centre and car park. Also
reached on foot from
Highley on west side of
River Severn. The Severn
Valley Railway has a
request stop in the park
(ask for Country Park
Halt).

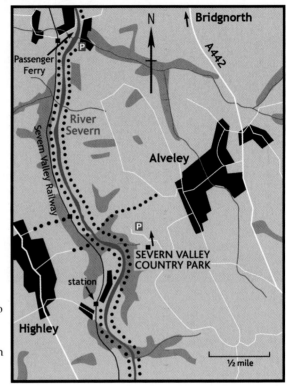

Access & Areas to Search
Access to River Severn along footpaths. Both **Club-tailed Dragonfly** and
Banded Demoiselle found along riverbanks and Club-tailed Dragonfly
throughout the country park. Search for **White-legged Damselfly** along the
river section. There are six ponds situated on the slopes down to the River
Severn, which are excellent for many species.

Timing
White-legged Damselfly and **Club-tailed Dragonfly** can be seen during June.

Additional Information
A wildlife pond adjacent to the car park has wheelchair access. Visitor centre
(open Wednesday to Sunday and Bank Holidays from noon until 5pm), toilets
and teashop (open weekends and Bank Holidays 2pm–5pm).

Other Wildlife
Otters and dormice.

SHAPWICK HEATH
near Glastonbury, Somerset
Natural England | www.naturalengland.org.uk

ST 423 411
OS Map 182

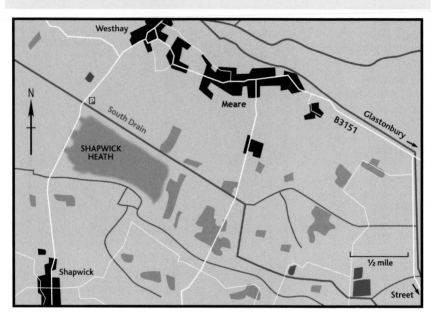

Species
Over 15 species including:
Banded Demoiselle
Large Red-eyed Damselfly
Hairy Dragonfly
Four-spotted Chaser
Broad-bodied Chaser
Ruddy Darter

Habitat
Marsh, fen, peat cuttings.

Timing
Late June and early July will offer the most species. **Hairy Dragonfly** is best looked for in the first half of June.

Location
Shapwick Heath lies *c.*4 miles west of Glastonbury.

Leave the A39 west of Glastonbury at Shapwick. Proceed north through the village. The nearest car park is at the Peat Moors Centre, *c.*0.25 mile north of the main entrance to Shapwick Heath.

Access & Areas to Search
From the car park walk south along the minor road and then east along the bridleway (cycle route to Glastonbury) along the South Drain. Several paths on right lead onto the reserve. Keep to footpaths.

Additional Information
Interpretation panels and waymarked paths to hides, one of which has disabled access. Nearby Westhay Heath (see OS Map 182) holds similar species. This site can be combined with Priddy Mineries.

SHREWSBURY AREA
RIVER SEVERN, ATCHAM
BERRINGTON POOL

SJ 538 084
SJ 526 073

Shropshire
OS Map 126
Berrington Pool is National Trust I www.nationaltrust.org.uk

Species
River Severn, Atcham
Banded Demoiselle
White-legged
Damselfly
Club-tailed Dragonfly

Berrington Pool
Variable Damselfly
Large Red-eyed
Damselfly
Downy Emerald

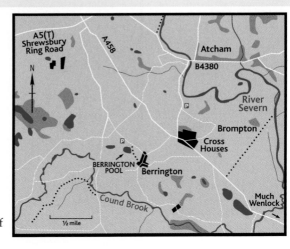

Habitat
Well-vegetated stretch of
River Severn at Atcham
and a large vegetated
pool at Berrington.

Location
Atcham lies *c*.2 miles to the south-east of Shrewsbury.

From the Shrewsbury A5 southern ring road, take the B4380 to Atcham. At
Atcham, take the minor road south towards Cross Houses. Park in the car park
at SJ 538 084 where the river is closest to the road.

Berrington Pool is *c*.2 miles from Atcham (and *c*.3 miles south of Shrewsbury).

Leave the A458 at Cross Houses and head west to Berrington. At Berrington
head north-west towards Betton Abbots. Berrington Pool is on the left after 0.25
mile. Limited parking at the pool, or park in Berrington village and follow the
public footpath to the pool.

Access & Areas to Search
Search the well-vegetated banks of the River Severn in both directions. At
Berrington view the pool from the bank.

Nearby Cound Brook is also worth investigating. Follow footpaths.

Timing
A visit before the fishing season (which starts in mid-June) is recommended.

SILVER FLOWE NNR
near Newton Stewart, Dumfries & Galloway
Scottish Natural Heritage | www.snh.org.uk
Forestry Commission | www.forestry.gov.uk

NX 480 820
OS Map 77

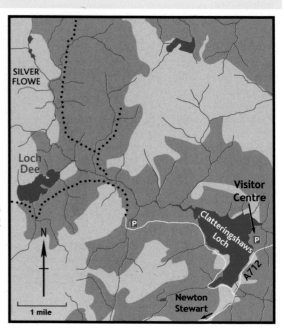

Species
Azure Hawker
Common Hawker
Golden-ringed Dragonfly
Common Darter

Habitat
Coniferous forest with
rides and clearings
leading to blanket bog in
mountain valley.

Location
The Silver Flowe NNR lies
c.7 miles north of the A712
between New Galloway
and Newton Stewart.

Leave the A712 at
the southern tip of
Clatteringshaws Loch and
follow single-track road
towards Loch Dee. Park at
end of road at NX 503 781.

Access & Areas to Search
From the parking area, follow the track north as indicated on map above. Walk
up and down the track, and investigate the forest breaks, especially on the left-
hand side. Look for **Azure Hawker** on lichen-covered rocks and on pale areas of
ground.

To reach the open-bog breeding area, you need to cross a fast-flowing burn with
care. This burn can be difficult to cross and even more so when in spate after
periods of heavy rain.

Timing
Azure Hawker is on the wing during June and July, but mid-July would be
better for the other species.

Additional Information
The blue female form of Common Hawker is recorded regularly here.

Information, tearoom and toilets at Clatteringshaws Visitor Centre along A712
at NX 551 763 (open 10.30am–5.30pm).

Other Wildlife
Scotch Argus and Large Heath butterflies; three different kinds of sundew.

SLAPTON LEY NNR
near Kingsbridge, Devon
Field Studies Council | www.field-studies-council.org

SX 825 440
OS Map 202

Species
Southern Damselfly
Hairy Dragonfly
Southern Hawker
Downy Emerald

Habitat
Lagoon, reebed, scrub.

Location
Slapton Ley lies c.22 miles east of Plymouth and c.30 miles south of Exeter.

At Kingsbridge, take the A379 eastwards to Torcross and then north towards Dartmouth. Car parks along the A379 at SX 828 442 and SX 824 424.

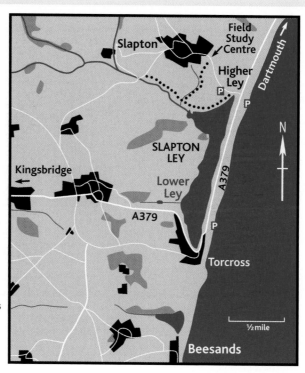

Access & Areas to Search
Follow marked footpaths. Some areas are of restricted access to protect the wildlife. Reedbed Walk requires a permit from Slapton Field Study Centre (SX 823 449) in Slapton village, where there is another car park and further access points.

Timing
Hairy Dragonfly and **Downy Emerald** are both on the wing from mid-May until early July; **Southern Damselfly** is on the wing from late May to early August.

Additional Information
Toilets and picnic areas at both car parks. The Field Studies Council information centre in Slapton village is open seven days a week.

Other Wildlife
The reserve has a good population of breeding Cetti's Warblers.

Site Guide

SNIPE DALES

TF 330 685

near Horncastle, Lincolnshire

OS Map 122

Lincolnshire County Council | www.lincolnshire.gov.uk
Lincolnshire Wildlife Trust | www.lincstrust.org.uk

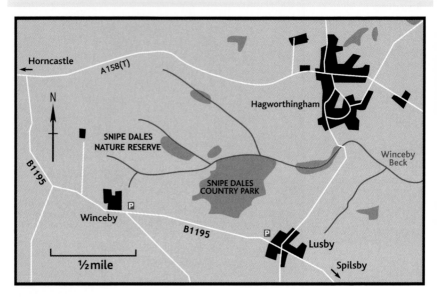

Site Guide

Species

Emerald Damselfly
Common Blue Damselfly
Migrant Hawker
Southern Hawker
Common Darter

Habitat

Woodland and grassland with streams and ponds.

Timing

July through August.

Location

Country Park and Nature Reserve lie *c.*5 miles east of Horncastle off the A158.

Leave the A158 west of Hagworthingham and take the B1195 south (signed Spilsby). Just beyond Winceby, park in either the nature reserve car park (free) at TF 319 683 or the country park car park (pay & display) at TF 330 681.

Access & Areas to Search

Search Winceby Beck, which runs through the nature reserve, and the ponds within the country park. The country park has an easy-access path suitable for wheelchair users leading to central ponds.

Additional Information

Country park car park has toilets, picnic tables and an information office (which is open school summer holidays and at busy weekends).

A variety of signed paths and nature trails lead you around both the nature reserve and the country park. Nature trail leaflet available on site.

This site can be combined with Gibraltar Point or Whisby Nature Park.

SPARHAM POOLS
near East Dereham, Norfolk
Norfolk Wildlife Trust | www.norfolkwildlifetrust.org

TG 075 178
OS Map 133

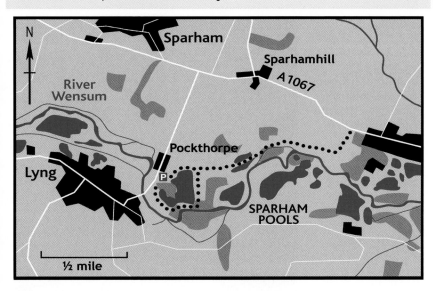

Species
Banded Demoiselle
Large Red-eyed Damselfly
Small Red-eyed Damselfly
Migrant Hawker
Common Hawker
Southern Hawker
Four-spotted Chaser

Habitat
Former gravel workings now flooded to form deep and shallow pools.

Timing
Most species recorded here are on the wing during July, although **Migrant Hawker** occurs from August onwards.

Location
This reserve lies between Norwich (*c.*10 miles) and Fakenham (*c.*10 miles) south of the A1067.

Leave the A1067 between Sparham and Sparhamhill on the minor road towards Lyng. The reserve is immediately south of Pockthorpe on the left-hand side before the road crosses the River Wensum.

Access & Areas to Search
Park in the car park at TG 073 178. Circular walk around the pools and public footpath along the edge of the reserve.

Additional Information
This site can be combined with any of the Broadland sites, such as Catfield Fen, Strumpshaw Fen or Upton Broad & Marshes. The pools are fished from 16 June.

Other Wildlife
Kingfisher and Sand Martin breed in the banks.

STOVER COUNTRY PARK
near Newton Abbot, Devon
Devon County Council | www.devon.gov.uk

SX 834 750
OS Map 191

Species
Over 20 species recorded including over 15 breeding species:
Beautiful Demoiselle
Banded Demoiselle
Small Red Damselfly
Scarce Blue-tailed Damselfly
Hairy Dragonfly
Emperor Dragonfly
Downy Emerald
Keeled Skimmer
Black Darter

Habitat
Lake and ponds, reed bed, lowland heath, woodland.

Location
Stover Country Park lies *c.*15 miles south-west of Exeter.

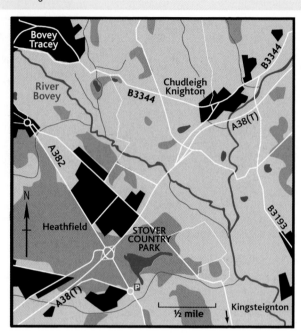

The entrance to the country park is on the A382 Newton Abbot to Bovey Tracey road just south of Drumbridges roundabout (A38/A382 junction).

Access & Areas to Search
Follow network of paths around the site. Best area is around the dragonfly pond on the west side of the park. From the car park, follow the path to the main lake, turn left and follow path around the western side of the lake. The dragonfly pond and immediate area of the lake are excellent for the four species above plus more common species.

Timing
A visit to the site during the second half of June and early July should see the four main species on the wing.

Additional Information
Interpretative Centre and toilets near pay & display car park. Many paths are suitable for wheelchairs. Leaflet available. This site can be combined with many other sites – see gazetteer.

Other Wildlife
Over 35 species of butterfly recorded (inc. Dingy and Grizzled Skippers, Wood White, Brown Hairstreak and five species of fritillary).

Site Guide

STRUMPSHAW FEN
near Norwich, Norfolk
RSPB | www.rspb.org.uk

TG 336 065
OS Map 134

Species
Large Red-eyed Damselfly
Small Red-eyed Damselfly
Hairy Dragonfly
Migrant Hawker
Norfolk Hawker
Scarce Chaser

Habitat
Mixed open fen, grazing marshes.

Location
Strumpshaw lies along the River Yare *c.*5 miles east of Norwich.

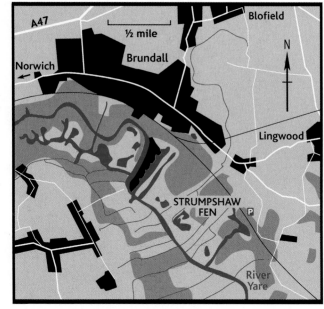

From Norwich take the A47 towards Great Yarmouth. Leave the A47 at Brundall and follow the minor road signed Strumpshaw. Proceed through Brundall, under the railway bridge, and take the next right (Stone Road) and then right again (Low Road). Park in the RSPB car park on your right halfway down lane and follow signs to entrance.

Access & Areas to Search
The best place to search is along the reserve's Summer Walk, which takes you around one of the reserve's many fen meadows with sheltered tree lines for feeding insects and open dykes for breeding. Information from reserve centre.

Timing
Hairy Dragonfly is on the wing from mid-May to early July. **Norfolk Hawker** has a very short flight period, from early/mid-June to early July. A visit in late June or early July should enable you to see both species well.

Additional Information
Free entry to RSPB members. Small charge for non-members. Toilets, sightings information and wheelchair-accessible viewing platform at reception hide. Suitability of paths for wheelchairs and pushchairs depends on weather (for information tel. 01603 715191; email strumpshaw@rspb.org.uk).

Other Wildlife
Swallowtail butterfly can also be seen at this reserve and is on the wing from late May to early July and again in mid-August.

SWANWICK NATURE RESERVE

Southampton, Hampshire

Hampshire & Isle of Wight Wildlife Trust | www.hwt.org.uk

SU 507 097
OS Map 196

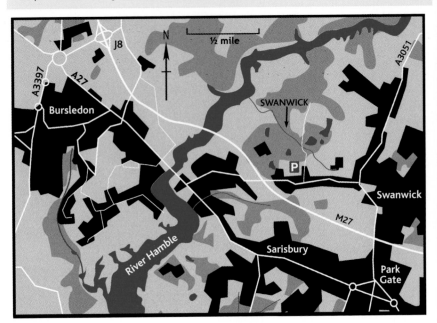

Species

Over 12 species recorded including:
Large Red-eyed Damselfly
Downy Emerald
Broad-bodied Chaser
Black-tailed Skimmer

Habitat

Lakes surrounded by woodland, scrub and meadows on former clay-pit site.

Location

The reserve lies north of the M27 between Southampton and Fareham.

From the west exit at Junction 8 of the M27, take the A27 south towards Fareham. Just after crossing the River Hamble, turn left into Swanwick Lane. Go over the motorway bridge and then turn left into Sopwith Way. Turn right at the mini-roundabout and park in car park at the Study Centre.

Access & Areas to Search

Follow footpaths around the reserve. There is an easy-access path. The Study Centre and toilets are open Saturday and Sunday, 2–5pm.

Additional Information

Leaflet available from Hampshire Wildlife Trust.

This site can be combined with any of the sites in the New Forest.

Other Wildlife

Nightingale and Cetti's Warbler.

Site Guide

THOMPSON COMMON
near Watton, Norfolk
Norfolk Wildlife Trust | www.norfolkwildlifetrust.org

TL 936 956
OS Map 144

Species
Emerald Damselfly
Scarce Emerald Damselfly
Large Red-eyed Damselfly
Small Red-eyed Damselfly
Hairy Dragonfly
Emperor Dragonfly
(Yellow-winged Darter)

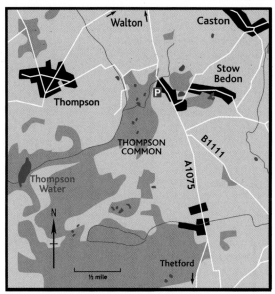

Habitat
Oak woodland, scrub,
grassland and pingos
(small pools formed at the
end of the Ice Age).

Location
Thompson Common
lies *c.*10 miles north of
Thetford and *c.*3 miles
south of Watton.

Park in the Great Eastern Pingo Trail car park behind the lay-by just north of Stow
Bedon village, on the west side of the A1075.

Access & Areas to Search
Turn right at the entrance through the gate that leads to a wooded area and
follow the Great Eastern Pingo Trail through the reserve. The pingos beyond the
wood hold **Scarce Emerald Damselfy**, Broad-bodied Chaser, darters, including
Ruddy Darter. The large meadow pond is excellent and also holds all the larger
dragonfly species. Beyond the meadow, leave the reserve along the lane before
rejoining the reserve in another field dotted with ponds which are again good
for most species. At the end of this field, go through the gate and down a track
to Thompson Water, which is the best place to search for **Large Red-eyed
Damselfly**, as well as many other species. Avoid trampling vegetation and, as
always, be very careful in such wet areas.

Timing
Scarce Emerald Damselfly flies from the last week of June, and it is usually
another 2–3 weeks, in mid-July, when **Emerald Damselfly** appears. Although
you could visit early in the season to avoid confusion of Scarce Emerald with
Emerald, it is worth visiting when Emerald Damselfly is on the wing so that
the differences between the two species can be appreciated (females are easy to
separate but males are difficult). Numbers of Scarce Emerald are at a peak during
the first two weeks of Emerald Damselfly's flight period.

Additional Information
Yellow-winged Darters bred here in 1997, after the 1995 invasion.

THURSLEY COMMON NNR
near Farnham, Surrey
Natural England | www.naturalengland.org.uk

SU 904 415
OS Map 186

Species
This is arguably the top British dragonfly site with up to 26 species regularly breeding, including:
Beautiful Demoiselle
Large Red Damselfly
Small Red Damselfly
Small Red-eyed Damselfly
Emperor Dragonfly
Golden-ringed Dragonfly
Downy Emerald
Brilliant Emerald
Four-spotted Chaser
Keeled Skimmer
Black Darter

Habitat
Open lowland heath, bog, open shallow pools, slow- and fast-flowing runnels and streams, large tree-edged lake (The Moat) and woodland.

Location
Thursley Common lies *c.*7 miles south-west of Guildford.

Take the B3001 Farnham–Milford road to Elstead. At Elstead take the minor road south towards Thursley. The car park is on this minor road *c.*2 miles south of Elstead on the left-hand side, at SU 899 417.

Access & Areas to Search
Network of footpaths and boardwalks take you around the lake (The Moat), heath and woodland areas.

The Moat
The Moat is the large tree-edged lake by the car park. Both **Downy Emerald** and **Brilliant Emerald** are easy to find patrolling the margins in sunny weather. As soon as it gets dull they will disappear into nearby trees.

Search the edges of The Moat along the car park edge, particularly the small bushes for damselflies, including **Small Red Damselfly**.

Stream
From the car park, head out to the heath, turn left following the path/track towards Pudmore Pond. This path/track crosses a stream which is particularly good for **Keeled Skimmer** (occurring around the path and bridge), whilst both **Golden-ringed Dragonfly** and **Beautiful Demoiselle** prefer the faster-flowing stream itself. View from the bridge or search upstream of the bridge for these last two species.

Boardwalk
A raised, wooden boardwalk criss-crosses the wet heath and provides excellent views of the many shallow pools and runnels, providing exceptionally close views of most species. **Four-spotted Chaser**, **Keeled Skimmer** and **Black Darter** are all common throughout the area, as are the commoner southern damselfly species. The larger open pools can be viewed with binoculars and telescope.

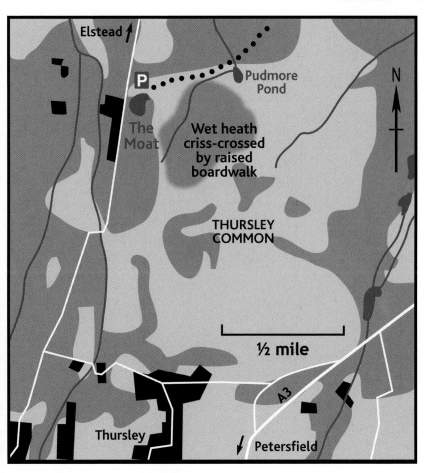

White-faced Darter used to breed around Pylon Island/Pudmore Pond and nearby pools, but single individuals have been reliably recorded on only a couple of occasions since 1992.

Timing
From late May onwards, insects will be on the wing, but the first two weeks of July will offer the most species, including all the scarcer species.

Additional Information
Small Red-eyed Damselfly recorded here, but as at other sites, status is unclear. Leaflet available from Natural England's Sussex and Surrey Team (Phoenix House, 32–33 North Street, Lewes BN7 2PH; tel. 01273 476595) or on site.

Other Wildlife
The area is particularly good for birds, with Hobby, Nightjar and Dartford Warbler all present. Butterflies include Silver-studded Blue, Purple Emperor and Grayling and the whole area has interesting flora.

UPTON BROAD & MARSHES

TG 385 135

near Acle, Norfolk

OS Maps 133/134

Norfolk Wildlife Trust | www.norfolkwildlifetrust.org.uk

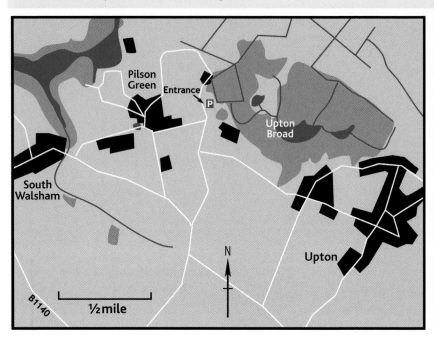

Site Guide

Species

One of Norfolk's, and the country's top sites. Species include:

Large Red Damselfly	Brown Hawker
Large Red-eyed Damselfly	**Norfolk Hawker**
Azure Damselfly	Emperor Dragonfly
Variable Damselfly	Four-spotted Chaser
Hairy Dragonfly	Black-tailed Skimmer
Migrant Hawker	Common Darter
Southern Hawker	Ruddy Darter

Habitat

Open broadland fen with dykes, alder carr and oak woodland.

Location

Upton Broad and Marshes is *c.*9 miles east of Norwich.

From Norwich take the A47 Great Yarmouth road. At Acle take the B1140 north towards South Walsham and then the third turning on the right towards Pilson Green. East of the village, turn left into Low Road (look for 'no through road' sign). The (free) reserve car park is 200m along on the right.

Access & Areas to Search

There are a number of waymarked paths from which insects can be readily seen.

From the car park, go through the gate and over a bridge to the information sign. The tiny ponds (some only a couple of feet across) in this area are excellent for most damselflies, including **Variable Damselfly,** plus larger species such as **Emperor** and **Common Darter**. The boardwalk on your right is excellent for **Black-tailed Skimmers** and both **Common** and **Ruddy Darters**, and you can look for **Large Red-eyed Damselflies** from the viewing platform. Continue along the grass path looking out for larger species such as hawkers, including **Norfolk Hawker**, and **Hairy Dragonfly**. For the last two species search along the dykes for patrolling males or along sheltered grass paths, tree and scrub edges for feeding individuals.

Timing

Hairy Dragonfly is an early flying species, on the wing from mid-May to the end of June. **Norfolk Hawker** has a very short flight period, from early/mid-June to early July, whilst **Variable Damselfly** can be seen throughout June and July. All the other species can be seen during July–August.

Additional Information

This is one of the top ten British sites for dragonflies.

Upton Broad and Marshes can be combined with any of the other Broadland sites including Carlton Marshes, Catfield Fen and the River Waveney at Geldeston. Sparham Pools is also nearby.

Other Wildlife

Butterflies include Swallowtail and White Admiral. Birds include Marsh Harrier, Hobby, Yellow Wagtail and Cetti's Warbler. Marsh Helleborine, Milk Parsley, Bog Pimpernel and Water Soldier are just some of the interesting plant species which grow on the reserve.

Site Guide

VALE ROYAL LOCKS
near Hartford, Cheshire
Vale Royal Borough Council | www.valeroyal.gov.uk
British Waterways | www.waterscape.com

SJ 641 706
OS Map 118

Species
Banded Demoiselle
Large Red Damselfly
Large Red-eyed
 Damselfly
Hairy Dragonfly
Brown Hawker
Four-spotted Chaser

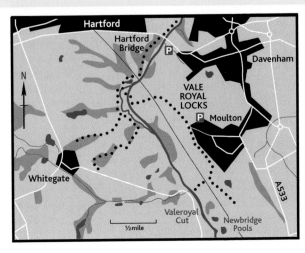

Habitat
Well-vegetated
riverbank.

Location
The site lies along the
Weaver Navigation
channel *c.*8 miles
north-west of Crewe.

From Middlewich, take the A533 towards Davenham and then the turn to
Moulton. Park at the north of the village and follow the footpath to the locks.

Access & Areas to Search
Walk the west side of the riverbank above and below the locks.

A walk north of Hartford Bridge, on the west side of the channel, will bring
you to the Marshall's Arm LNR (also accessed on foot from the end of Stones
Manor Lane in Hartford or at the end of Saxons Lane (where there is wheelchair
access), in Northwich), where Hairy Dragonfly may also be found, along with
other dragonfly species.

Timing
Hairy Dragonfly is an early flying species, on the wing from mid-May to the
end of June. A visit during the first half of June is recommended, before the start
of the fishing season.

Additional Information
This site can be combined with sites in the Warrington area and Delamere
Forest.

Site Guide

VALLEY WETLANDS
near Caergeiliog, Ynys Môn (Anglesey)
RSPB | www.rspb.org.uk

SH 313 765
OS Map 114

Species
Variable Damselfly
Four-spotted Chaser

Habitat
Large and small
reed-fringed lakes,
marsh.

Location
Valley Wetlands
lies *c*.5 miles east of
Holyhead and *c*.15
miles west of Bangor.

From Bangor, take
the A55 towards
Holyhead. Leave
the A55 where it
joins the A5 between

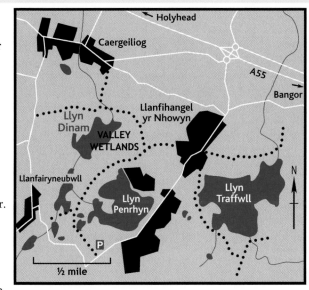

the villages of Bryngwran and Caergeiliog and head south on the minor road
signed RAF Valley. The reserve car park is 2 miles down this minor road on the
right-hand side and opposite the Valley Airfield Barracks.

Access & Areas to Search
Follow paths around the lakes. Note that the paths are unimproved and may
not be suitable for all visitors.

Timing
Variable Damselfly is on the wing during June and July, when many other
species, including **Four-spotted Chaser**, can also be seen.

Other Wildlife
Gadwall, Marsh Harrier, Cetti's, Sedge and Reed Warblers.

VENN OTTERY
near Exeter, Devon
Devon Wildlife Trust | www.devonwildlifetrust.org

SY 065 920
OS Map 192

Species
Emperor Dragonfly
Golden-ringed Dragonfly
Keeled Skimmer

Habitat
Wet and dry heathland, raised bog, scrub, carr, woodland.

Location
Venn Ottery lies *c.*9 miles east of Exeter.

Leave Exeter along the A3052 towards Newton Poppleford. After *c.*7.5 miles, leave the A3052 at Halfway Inn and head north along the B3180 towards West

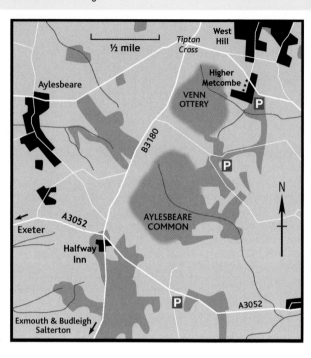

Hill. After *c.*1.5 miles, turn right at the crossroads towards Tipton Cross. After another 0.5 mile, after passing a left-hand fork, you will come to a crossroads, signed Broad Oak and West Hill on the left, where there is a public footpath on the right at SY 067 924. Park carefully on the roadside verge.

Access & Areas to Search
From the parking area, follow the public footpath for 200m to a T-junction. Turn right here for the nature reserve (away from public footpath). After another 200m (ignore 'No public access' signs as there is a right of way to the reserve), walk through the gateway to 'Furzelands'. Just before the next gateway, turn left into a track to the reserve entrance at SY 064 923.

Timing
Both main species, plus many commoner species, can be seen during July, but a visit any time between mid-June and late August will be rewarding.

Additional Information
Parts of the reserve are very wet. Do not disturb grazing livestock.

This site can be combined with any of the many other sites in the area, including Aylesbeare Common (also butterflies), Bystock Nature Reserve, Chudleigh Knighton Heath, Colaton Raleigh Common, Haldon Forest, Little Bradley Ponds, Slapton Ley, Stafford Bridge and Stover Country Park.

WARNHAM LNR
near Horsham, Sussex
Horsham District Council | www.horsham.gov.uk

TQ 168 323
OS Map 187

Species
23 species recorded including:
Banded Demoiselle
Large Red-eyed Damselfly
Downy Emerald
Brilliant Emerald

Habitat
Mill pond, brooks, reed fringe, meadows, scrub, woodland.

Location
This site lies on the northern outskirts of Horsham.

Car park off the B2237 on north-western edge of Horsham (just off A24 roundabout).

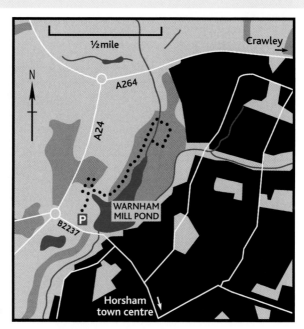

Access & Areas to Search
Reserve open daily 10am–6pm. Follow waymarked trails around the reserve. The western side of the main lake and the feeder stream to the north are the best areas to search.

Timing
A visit during July should allow you to see all the above species.

Additional Information
An entry permit must be purchased (nominal charge) from the visitor centre for each adult; entry is free for children. Visitor centre and café (offering light refreshments) open 10am–4pm at weekends, Bank Holidays, school holidays and daily from 1 July until 30 September. Toilets (including disabled access) and baby-changing facilities. Paths suitable for wheelchairs and pushchairs. This site can be combined with the River Arun at New Bridge.

Other Wildlife
Butterflies include Brown and Purple Hairstreaks, White Admiral and Silver-washed Fritillary; breeding birds include Common Tern and Cetti's Warbler.

WARRINGTON AREA
RISLEY MOSS LNR (CCC)
RIXTON CLAYPITS LNR (WRS)
Cheshire

SJ 664 921
SJ 684 900
OS Map 109

Cheshire County Council | www.cheshire.gov.uk
Warrington Ranger Service | www.warrington.gov.uk

Species
Both sites have over 15 species including:
Common Hawker
Emperor Dragonfly
Ruddy Darter
Black Darter

Habitat
Risley Moss is a remnant raised bog in a wooded area.

Rixton Claypits is a reclaimed clay workings with ponds, meadows and woodland.

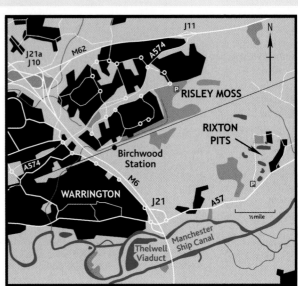

Location
Risley Moss lies on the north-eastern outskirts of Warrington between the M6 and M62 motorways.

From M62 Junction 11, take the A574 towards Warrington. Take the first exit at the first roundabout and go straight across the second and third roundabouts. The car park and centre (toilets) are immediately after the third roundabout.

Rixton Claypits lies *c.*2 miles to the east of Warrington.

From M6 Junction 21, take the A57 towards Irlam. The visitor centre and car park are *c.*2 miles along this road on the left (beyond Moat Lane).

Access & Areas to Search
Risley Moss – keep to marked footpaths. The bog is accessible only on ranger-led guided walks (contact the rangers on 01925 824 339) but the trails in the woodland alongside the bog are accessible at all times. The reserve is open Mon–Thurs 9am–5pm and 10am–6pm at weekends and Bank Holidays.

Rixton Claypits – walk around the ponds following the footpaths. The ground is uneven in many places and there are steep slopes.

Timing
A visit in August should provide both **Black Darter** and **Common Hawker**.

WAT TYLER COUNTRY PARK
near Basildon, Essex
Basildon District Council Countryside Services | www.basildon.gov.uk

TQ 745 873
OS Map 178

Species
Emerald Damselfly
**Scarce Emerald
    Damselfly**
Large Red-eyed
    Damselfly
Hairy Dragonfly
Southern Hawker
Emperor Dragonfly
Broad-bodied Chaser
Black-tailed Skimmer

Habitat
Scrub, grassland,
streams, ponds and
freshwater marsh
alongside saltmarsh
and tidal creeks.

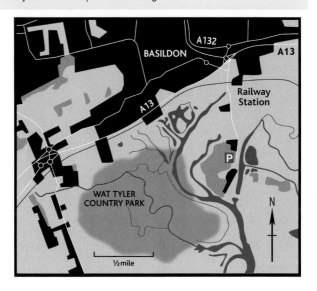

Location
The country park is situated on the southern outskirts of Basildon.

Follow signs off A13 past Pitsea railway station to car park.

Access & Areas to Search
A marked (numbered) trail from the car park takes you around the park. Collect
leaflet from dispenser by toilet block/warden's office.

Search the pond opposite the café/shops and the ponds around posts 1–3, 9–10,
17–20 and 28. **Scarce Emerald Damselfly** occurs around posts 1–3 (opposite
café), along the ditch between posts 24–28 and around the ponds by posts 9, 10
and 28.

Timing
Scarce Emerald Damselfly is on the wing from mid-June until early August but
occurs in its best numbers during July.

Additional Information
Park open daily 9am–6pm. Enquiries tel. 01268 550 088 (Monday–Friday).

Toilets by park office at car park entrance. Café. A trail suitable for wheelchair
users runs between points 23 and 28. Other attractions include National
Motorboat Museum, craft shops, adventure play area and miniature railway.

This site can be combined with Cornmill Meadows.

Site Guide

WELNEY WILDFOWL REFUGE
near Ely, Norfolk
Wildfowl & Wetlands Trust | www.wwt.org.uk

TL 546 946
OS Map 143

Species
Banded Demoiselle
Large Red-eyed Damselfly
Small Red-eyed Damselfly
Variable Damselfly
Hairy Dragonfly
Brown Hawker
Emperor Dragonfly
Broad-bodied Chaser

Habitat
Grazing marsh, open water, reedbed.

Location
Welney lies *c*.10 miles north of Ely and *c*.9 miles south-west of Downham Market.

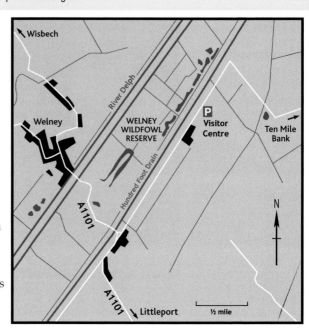

From Ely take the A10 north to Littleport, then follow the signs west along the A1101 for the reserve. Park at visitor centre.

Access & Areas to Search
The walk to Friends Hide takes you along a wide dyke rich in dragonflies. The Summer Walk (when open) is excellent. Pond at the visitor centre.

Timing
Hairy Dragonfly is an early flyer, on the wing from mid-May to the end of June. **Variable Damselfly** flies from late May to the end of September. **Large Red-eyed Damselfly** flies from June to mid-August, whilst the similar **Small Red-eyed Damselfly** emerges later, from mid-July, and flies until mid-September. A visit during the first half of June is recommended.

Additional Information
Charge for non-WWT members. Tearoom and toilets. Reserve open until dusk. Weekend walks (2 hrs), from 11am and 2pm, run April–July (breeding waders and ditch-side fauna and flora) and 1 July–September (to areas of the reserve not normally accessible to see dragonflies and other wildlife); pre-book (tel. 01353 860 711). Wheelchair (available for hire – phone beforehand) access to the visitor centre, reedbed boardwalk and main hides.

This site can be combined with Houghton Mill or Wicken Fen.

WELSH WILDLIFE CENTRE & TEIFI MARSHES

SN 185 455
OS Map 145

near Cardigan, Ceredigion
The Wildlife Trust of South and West Wales | www.welshwildlife.org

Species
Beautiful Demoiselle
Azure Damselfly
Common Blue Damselfly
Scarce Blue-tailed Damselfly
Blue-tailed Damselfly
Southern Hawker
Emperor Dragonfly
Golden-ringed Dragonfly
Broad-bodied Chaser

Habitat
Wood, meadow, wetland
(tidal and fresh water).

Location
The Welsh Wildlife Centre
and Teifi Marshes Nature
Reserve are situated on the
outskirts of Cardigan.

Leave Cardigan south
along the A478 to Pen-y-
bryn then take the minor

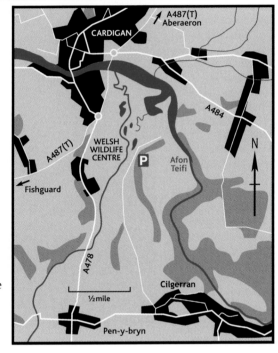

road east towards Cilgerran. Just short of the village, take the signed minor road
north to the centre.

Access & Areas to Search
Follow footpaths around the reserve. Information about recent sightings
available from the visitor centre.

Additional Information
June–July is the best time to visit for the main (and other) species.

Additional Information
The reserve and visitor centre are open 10.30am–5pm daily. Tearoom and toilets
at the visitor centre. Wildlife adventure playground. Car parking charge for
non-Trust members. Wheelchair loan available. Tel. 01239 621 600 for further
information on the Welsh Wildlife Centre.

This site can be combined with Afon Brynberian and Dowrog Common.

Other Wildlife
Mammals include Water Buffalo used to graze the wetland and Water Shrew.
Live camera link to the inside of an Otter's holt. Cetti's Warbler breeds.

WEST BEXINGTON
near Bridport, Dorset
Dorset Wildlife Trust | www.dorsetwildlife.co.uk

SY 525 870
OS Map 194

Species
Migrant Hawker
Southern Hawker
Brown Hawker
Emperor Dragonfly
Golden-ringed Dragonfly
Common Darter
(Red-veined Darter)

Habitat
Pool, reedbed, wet meadow, scrub and shingle beach.

Location
West Bexington Nature Reserve is situated along the coastal strip between Bridport (*c*.6 miles) and Abbotsbury (*c*.3 miles).

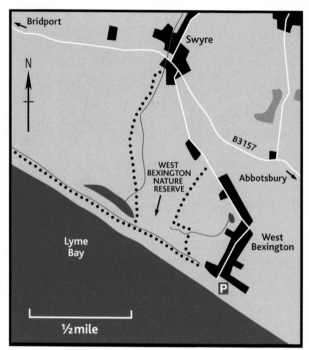

Turn off the Bridport–Abbotsbury road (B3157) at Swyre for West Bexington and follow road down to beach car park (pay & display) at SY 527 866.

Access & Areas to Search
From the car park, walk west along the coastal path (shingle beach) for *c*.200m to reserve entrance on right. Walk through the reedbed, over the field to the raised pond in the second field.

Timing
The pond is at its best during July and August. Migrant **Red-veined Darters** have bred here.

Additional Information
Café and toilets at the car park. Public house in West Bexington.

Other Wildlife
Cetti's Warblers and Bearded Tits breed in the reedbed.

WHISBY NATURE PARK
near Lincoln, Lincolnshire
Lincolnshire Wildlife Trust | www.lincstrust.org.uk
Lincolnshire County Council | www.lincolnshire.gov.uk

SK 914 661
OS Map 121

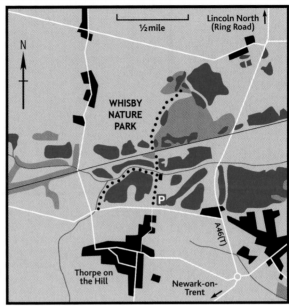

Species
Over 20 species including:
Four-spotted Chaser
Black-tailed Skimmer
Common Darter
Ruddy Darter

Habitat
Flooded gravel pits, grassland, scrub.

Location
Whisby Nature Park lies on the western outskirts of Lincoln.

Signed from the western Lincoln bypass (A46). Car park (no charge) situated off A46 along minor road (Moor Lane) just north of Thorpe on the Hill.

Access & Areas to Search
From the car park walk past the Natural World complex to the reserve entrance. Follow waymarked paths around the site. Paths are hard-surfaced and suitable for wheelchairs.

Timing
A visit during July–August will see all the above species plus many other common species.

Additional Information
Both **Black-tailed Skimmer** and **Ruddy Darter** are getting towards their northern limit here. **Lesser Emperor** recorded here in 2006.

The Natural World Centre (operated by North Kesteven District Council – www.n-kesteven.gov.uk) has a café, toilets and visitor centre. Dogs are allowed at the park, but must be kept on leads.

This site can be combined with Snipe Dales and Gibraltar Point.

Other Wildlife
Water Ladybird; Purple Hairstreak, Brown Argus and Wall Brown butterflies; breeding Nightingale, Lesser Whitethroat and Willow Tit.

WICKEN FEN NNR
near Ely, Cambridgeshire
National Trust owned National Nature Reserve | www.nationaltrust.org

TL 563 705
OS Map 154

Species
18 species have been recorded including:
Large Red-eyed Damselfly
Variable Damselfly
Hairy Dragonfly
Brown Hawker
Emperor Dragonfly
Ruddy Darter

Habitat
A rich mix of fen habitat including grazing marsh, reedbeds, dykes, deciduous woodland and a large lake.

Location
The village of Wicken lies *c*.8 miles north of Cambridge along the A1123, between Soham and Stretham.

Leave the A1123 in Wicken village at the National Trust sign for Wicken Fen. Follow signs down the minor road (Lode Lane) to reserve car park (charge).

Access & Areas to Search
All species can be seen both on and off the reserve. On the reserve, search the lodes and paths. Off the reserve **Hairy Dragonfly** and **Large Red-eyed Damselfly** can be easily seen along Wicken Lode and the New River footpaths. **Variable Damselfly** is best looked for along the footpath which runs along the northern edge of the reserve, opposite the car park.

Timing
The first two weeks of June see **Hairy Dragonfly** and **Variable Damselfly** on the wing, whilst the end of June to the end of July is the best period for **Emperor Dragonfly** and other commoner species.

Additional Information
Entrance to the reserve is free to National Trust members. Charge for non-members. Dragonfly walks and identification courses are held on some weekends in the summer (tel. 01733 204 286 for more information). The boardwalk nature trail is suitable for pushchairs and wheelchairs.

The reserve visitor centre and café are open 10am–5pm daily. Toilets, baby-changing and feeding facilities available.

WIGAN FLASHES LNR

SD 580 040

OS Map 108

The Wildlife Trust for Lancashire, Manchester and North Merseyside | www.lancswt.org.uk,
Wigan Borough Council | www.wigan.gov.uk

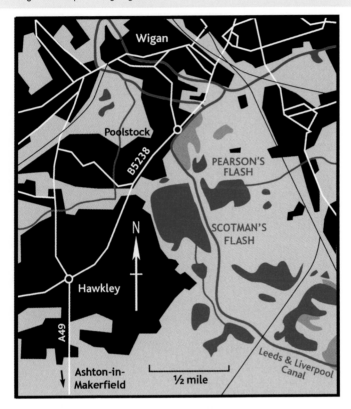

Species
Emerald Damselfly
Large Red Damselfly
Brown Hawker
Four-spotted Chaser
Broad-bodied Chaser

Habitat
Pools, canal, fen, wet woodland and
scrub.

Timing
July–August.

Location
The flashes are on the southern outskirts of Wigan.

Leave the M6 at Junction 25 and head north on the A49. Turn right onto the
B5238 (Poolstock Lane). Park in Poolstock.

Access & Areas to Search
Entrances off Poolstock Lane (along canal), Carr Lane (Hawkley Hall School, at
west end of Poolstock Lane), and off A573. Disabled access along canal. There
are no facilities on site but Wigan town centre is within walking distance.

WILDMOOR HEATH
near Bracknell, Berkshire

SU 845 630
OS Map 175

Berkshire, Buckinghamshire and Oxfordshire Wildlife Trust | www.bbowt.org.uk

Species
Scarce Blue-tailed
  Damselfly
Southern Hawker
Brown Hawker
Emperor Dragonfly
Golden-ringed Dragonfly
Downy Emerald
Brilliant Emerald
Keeled Skimmer

Habitat
Wet and dry heath,
woodland, scrub with open
water.

Location
Wildmoor Heath lies on
the northern outskirts
of Sandhurst, between
Owlsmoor and Crowthorne.

The car park at SU 838
631 is situated along Crowthorne Road south of the school on the outskirts of
Crowthorne.

Access & Areas to Search
From the car park, follow the main path eastwards for *c.*250m to an open, wet
area on your right. Search this area, but care must be taken as the ground is very
boggy. Further along the main path, turn left at the cross-paths and search the
small pools and wet heath.

Additional Information
This site is very wet and wellingtons are strongly recommended.

This site can be combined with Decoy Heath.

Other Wildlife
Raft Spider; Sand Lizard was reintroduced here in 2006 after an absence of 30
years in the county of Berkshire.

WOODWALTON FEN NNR
Near Ramsey, Cambridgeshire
Natural England | www.naturalengland.org.uk

TL 235 849
OS Map 142

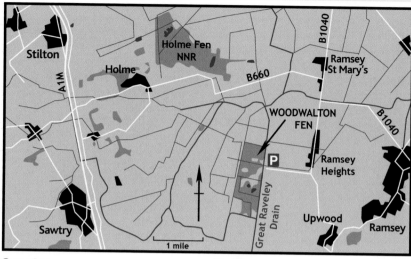

Species
18 species have been recorded including:
Hairy Dragonfly
Scarce Chaser
Common Darter
Ruddy Darter

Habitat
Fen with interconnecting dykes, lakes, reedbed, woodland and grassland. This is one of two main sites (with Holme Fen NNR) on which the Great Fen Project is being centred.

Location
Woodwalton Fen lies midway between Peterborough and Huntingdon.

From the B1040 take the minor road running between Ramsey St Mary's and Upwood. At the southern end of Ramsey Heights village, take the track signposted 'Countryside Classroom'. Drive to the end of the track and park on the bank on the right. Do not block the track or gateways.

Access & Areas to Search
Most species, including **Scarce Chaser**, may be seen along the Great Raveley Drain, which runs along the entire eastern edge of the reserve.

Timing
A visit in June should allow you to see both **Hairy Dragonfly** and **Scarce Chaser**. **Ruddy Darter** flies from late June.

Additional Information
Keep to paths. Beware of deep dykes and biting insects.

Other Wildlife
Chinese Water Deer. Breeding birds include Woodcock, Long-eared Owl, Lesser Spotted Woodpecker, Nightingale and Grasshopper Warbler. Wide variety of fenland plants and flowers.

SITE GAZETTEER
Your county-by-county guide to where to watch dragonflies
in Britain and Northern Ireland

Sites with no species information have been selected from reserve leaflets, handbooks, websites and other literature on the basis that the reserve manager/ owner has indicated that dragonflies (unspecified) are a feature of the site.

ENGLAND

County/Regional Recorders
Details of recorders at
WWW.DRAGONFLYSOC.ORG.UK
WWW.ATROPOS.INFO/DRAGONFLY.HTML

Forest Enterprise England
(agency of the Forestry Commission)
340 Bristol Business Park, Coldharbour
Lane, Bristol BS16 1EJ
TEL 0117 906 6000
WWW.FORESTRY.GOV.UK

National Biodiversity Network
WWW.SEARCHNBN.NET

The National Trust
General Office: PO Box 39, Warrington
WA5 7WD
TEL 0870 458 4000
EMAIL enquiries@thenationaltrust.
org.uk
WWW.NATIONALTRUST.ORG.UK

Natural England
Northminster House, Peterborough
PE1 1UA
TEL 0845 600 3078
EMAIL enquiries@naturalengland.
org.uk
WWW.NATURALENGLAND.ORG.UK

Royal Society for the Protection of Birds (RSPB)
The Lodge, Potton Road, Sandy,
Bedfordshire SG19 2DL
TEL 01767 680551
WWW.RSPB.ORG.UK

The Wildlife Trusts
The Kiln, Waterside, Mather Road,
Newark NG24 1WT
TEL 0870 036 7711
EMAIL enquiry@wildlifetrusts.org
WWW.WILDLIFETRUST.ORG.UK

BEDFORDSHIRE

The Wildlife Trust for Bedfordshire, Cambridgeshire, Northamptonshire & Peterborough (WTBCNP)
Bedfordshire Office: Priory Country
Park, Barkers Lane, Bedford MK41 9SH
TEL 01234 364213
EMAIL bedfordshire@wildlifebcnp.org
WWW.WILDLIFEBCNP.ORG

The National Trust Regional Office: East of England
Westley Bottom, Bury St Edmunds,
Suffolk IP33 3WD
TEL 01284 747500

Bedford Borough Council
Riverside House, Horne Lane, Bedford
MK40 1PY
TEL 01234 227407
WWW.BEDFORD.GOV.UK

County atlas/book
Dragonflies of Bedfordshire. Steve Cham,
2004, Bedfordshire Natural History
Society

Websites
Bedfordshire Odonata
WWW.MAKEHAM.ORG

ARLESEY OLD MOAT AND GLEBE MEADOWS
near Arlesey
OS Map 153. TL 189 373.
Moat and river.
From the A507, turn south into minor road
c.250m west of railway crossing in Church
End. Park carefully on verge near gate to
reserve after sharp left-hand bend (do not
obstruct gates). Follow the riverside path
and walk down to the southern end of
Glebe Meadow to the L-shaped moat.
Species inc. Banded Demoiselle.
WTBCNP

Gazetteer

Gazetteer

COPLE PITS
near Bedford
OS Map 153. TL 103 492.
See main site section page 159.
Disused gravel pits, scrub.
Cople Pits lies on the eastern outskirts of Bedford just off the A603.
Species inc. Migrant and Brown Hawkers, Ruddy Darter.
WTBCNP

DROPSHORT MARSH
near Dunstable
OS Map 166. TL 007 276.
Marshy grassland and bog.
The reserve lies 0.25 mile south of Toddington and is adjacent to the A5120 road to Dunstable. Limited parking along the verge on the eastern side of the road, opposite the reserve entrance. Do not obstruct field entrances. Follow path through metal gate and along higher ground by fence.
Species recorded inc. Small Red-eyed Damselfly, Migrant and Brown Hawkers.
WTBCNP

FELMERSHAM GRAVEL PITS
near Rushden
OS Map 153. SP 991 584.
See main site section page 171.
Disused gravel workings.
Felmersham Gravel Pits lies c.5 miles north-west of Bedford off the A6.
Species inc. White-legged and Large Red-eyed Damselflies, Migrant and Brown Hawkers, Emperor Dragonfly, Ruddy Darter.
WTBCNP

PRIORY COUNTRY PARK
Bedford
OS Map 153. TL 076 492.
Lakes, water meadows, river, scrub, woodland.
Country park on the south-eastern outskirts of Bedford signed off the A603. Parking, visitor centre and toilets. Disabled access and guided walks.

Species inc. Banded Demoiselle, Large Red, Azure, White-legged and Large Red-eyed Damselflies, Hairy Dragonfly, Migrant and Brown Hawkers, Ruddy Darter.
BEDFORD BOROUGH COUNCIL

BERKSHIRE

The Berkshire, Buckinghamshire & Oxfordshire Wildlife Trust (BBOWT)
Head Office: The Lodge, 1 Armstrong Road, Littlemore, Oxford OX4 4XT
Berkshire Office: TEL 01628 829574
EMAIL info@bbowt.org.uk
WWW.BBOWT.ORG.UK

The National Trust Regional Office: Thames & Solent
Hughenden Manor, High Wycombe, Bucks HP14 4LA
TEL 01494 528051

ANKERWYCKE
near Wraysbury
OS Map 176. TQ 006 731.
Parkland and ponds by River Thames.
This site lies on the north bank of the River Thames. Small car park with information board off Magna Carta Lane.
Species inc. White-legged Damselfly, Club-tailed Dragonfly.
NATIONAL TRUST

BAYNES RESERVE
near Newbury
OS Map 174. SU 504 657.
Woodland, open areas, streams.
From Thatcham (east of Newbury) take the minor road south past Thatcham Station and then the right fork into Bury's Bank Road at Crookham Common. After c.0.5 mile take the track on your right, at SU 511 649, past Thatched Lodge to car park. Reserve is straight ahead.
15 species have been recorded.
BBOWT

BOWDOWN WOODS
near Newbury
OS Map 174. SU 501 656.
Woodland, heath, scrub, streams.
Head south from Newbury on A34, turn
left at roundabout to Greenham and
continue for c.1.5 miles down Bury's Bank
Road. Three tracks on north side of road
lead to three car parks.
BBOWT

BRAY PIT
near Maidenhead
OS Map 175. SU 906 787.
Gravel pit.
From Maidenhead, take the A308 south
through Bray Wick, under the M4, then
left after the Brayfield Arms down Monkey
Island Lane. Continue past the marina and
turn left into the water sports area, past the
sailboard clubhouse and park at end. Leaflet
available.
BBOWT

BUCKLEBURY COMMON
near Thatcham
OS Map 174. SU 555 688.
Heathland, ponds and woodland.
Area lies c.2 miles north-east of Thatcham.
Car park along minor road at SU 555 698.
BUCKLEBURY ESTATE

DECOY HEATH
near Reading
OS Map 175. SU 613 635.
See main site section page 163.
Wet and dry heath, woodland, scrub,
open water.
Decoy Heath lies c.8 miles south-west of
Reading.
Species inc. Scarce Blue-tailed
Damselfly, Golden-ringed Dragonfly,
Downy and Brilliant Emeralds, Keeled
Skimmer.
BBOWT

ENGLEMERE POND
near Bracknell
OS Map 175. SU 901 684 (car park).
Wet and dry heath, woodland, scrub,
open water.

The site is immediately south of the A329
between Bracknell and Ascot. Car park off
the B3017 west of the pond.
17 species inc. Large Red-eyed
Damselfly, Downy Emerald.
BRACKNELL FOREST BOROUGH COUNCIL
WWW.BRACKNELL-FOREST.GOV.UK

FINCHAMPSTEAD RIDGES AND SIMON'S WOOD
near Wokingham
OS Maps 175/186. SU 808 634.
Heathland, ponds, and mixed
woodland.
These two sites lie c.0.75 mile west of
Crowthorne station and are adjacent to the
B3348. There is a large car park at Simon's
Wood at SU 812 635. Pay particular
attention to Heath Pool and Spout Pond.
Species inc. Emerald and Azure
Damselflies.
NATIONAL TRUST

HAYMILL VALLEY LNR
Lynch Hill, Slough
OS Map 175. SU 942 816.
Pond, reedbed, woodland.
From Junction 7 of M4, turn right along
A4 towards Slough for c.0.5 mile, then left
at Burnham station, and left again at the
junction with Burnham Lane. At the
Harvest pub, take the right fork down
Haymill Road then into Whittaker Road at
the mini-roundabout. Reserve access at the
junction of Whittaker Road and Littlebrook
Avenue.
BBOWT

LODDON RESERVE
Twyford
OS Map 175. SU 785 758.
Gravel pit, scrub.
Public car park situated on the west side of
Twyford in Polehampton Close off Old Bath
Road. Walk west along Old Bath Road, over
the railway, to the access path just before
the factory on the left. Leaflet available.
BBOWT

MAIDENHEAD COMMONS AND COCK MARSH
near Maidenhead
OS Map 175. SU 884 867.
Ponds and calcareous marsh, river and woodland.
Small car parks at Cookham Moor (SU 893 854) and Winter Hill (SU 870 860). Follow footpaths and bridleways.
Species inc. Variable Damselfly.
NATIONAL TRUST

MOOR COPSE
near Reading
OS Map 175. SU 633 738.
Woodland, river (Pang).
Reserve situated on eastern side of A340 Theale to Pangbourne road. Just before the road crosses the M4, turn left and park in the lay-by (SU 635 742). Leaflet available.
Species inc. Beautiful and Banded Demoiselles, Common and Brown Hawkers, Ruddy Darter.
BBOWT

RIVER THAMES
Goring
OS Map 175. SU 616 794.
See main site section page 206.
Riverside.
This site lies c.1 mile south of Goring.
Species inc. Banded Demoiselle, Club-tailed Dragonfly.

RIVER THAMES
Pangbourne
OS Map 175. SU 636 768.
Riverside.
Park in Pangbourne or in small car park on the A329 between Pangbourne and Streatley at SU 623 771. Follow footpaths along river.
Species inc. Banded Demoiselle, White-legged and Large Red-eyed Damselflies, Club-tailed Dragonfly.

SILCHESTER COMMON & PAMBER HEATH
near Tadley
OS Map 175. SU 620 622.
Heath, bog, birch scrub.
Park at SU 617 623 along Impstone Road in Pamber Heath and follow tracks.
Over 20 species recorded inc. Beautiful Demoiselle, White-legged, Small Red and Scarce Blue-tailed Damselflies, Common Hawker, Hairy and Golden-ringed Dragonflies, Downy Emerald, Black Darter.
SILCHESTER PARISH COUNCIL

SNELSMORE COMMON COUNTRY PARK
near Newbury
OS Map 174. SU 460 710.
Heathland, ponds, woodland.
Parking off B4494 at SU 463 712.
Species inc. Migrant and Common Hawkers.
WEST BERKSHIRE COUNCIL

SOLE COMMON
near Newbury
OS Map 174. SU 413 707.
Heath, pond, *Sphagnum* bog, woodland.
Leave Newbury west along the A4 and take the B4000 north towards Wickham for c.2.5 miles, then turn right down the Boxford road and park on roadside after c.350m by track on left.
BBOWT

THATCHAM REED BEDS
near Newbury
OS Map 174. SU 507 665.
Lakes with reedbeds and stretch of Kennet & Avon Canal.
Park in Thatcham. Keep to footpaths. RSPB Nature Discovery Centre and toilets (disabled access).
Species recorded inc. Beautiful and Banded Demoiselles, Common Hawker, Black Darter.
WEST BERKSHIRE DISTRICT COUNCIL, RSPB

THEALE GRAVEL PITS
near Reading
OS Map 175. SU 649 699.
Gravel pits and stretch of Kennet &
Avon Canal.
Roadside parking. Keep to public footpaths.
Species inc. Banded Demoiselle, Broad-
bodied Chaser, Black-tailed Skimmer.

WILDMOOR HEATH
near Bracknell
OS Map 175. SU 845 630.
See main site section page 236.
Wet and dry heath, woodland, scrub,
open water.
*Wildmoor Heath lies on the northern
outskirts of Sandhurst at Owlsmoor.*
Species inc. Scarce Blue-tailed
Damselfly, Golden-ringed Dragonfly,
Downy and Brilliant Emeralds.
BBOWT

WOKEFIELD COMMON
near Reading
OS Map 175. SU 651 658.
Heathland, ponds and woodland.
Parking at SU 648 658.
READING BOROUGH COUNCIL
WWW.READING.GOV.UK

BUCKINGHAMSHIRE

**The Berkshire, Buckinghamshire &
Oxfordshire Wildlife Trust (BBOWT)**
The Lodge, 1 Armstrong Road,
Littlemore, Oxford OX4 4XT
TEL 01865 775476
EMAIL info@bbowt.org.uk
WWW.BBOWT.ORG.UK

**The National Trust Regional Office:
Thames & Solent**
Hughendon Manor, High Wycombe,
Buckinghamshire HP14 4LA
TEL 01494 528051

Websites
Buckinghamshire & Milton Keynes
Environmental Records Centre
WWW.BUCKSMKERC.ORG.UK/NEWS/INDEX.HTM

BUCKINGHAM CANAL
near Buckingham
OS Map 152. SP 726 350.
Disused canal, open water, marsh.
*Take the A422 north-east from Buckingham
for c.2 miles then the track on left and park
by pumping house.*
Species inc. Southern Hawker.
BUCKINGHAM CANAL SOCIETY
WWW.MKHERITAGE.CO.UK/BCS/

COLLEGE LAKE
near Tring
OS Map 156. SP 933 139.
See main site section page 158.
Chalk pit, grassland, marsh.
Site lies c.2 miles north-east of Tring.
Species inc. Azure Damselfly, Ruddy
Darter.
BBOWT

LITTLE LINFORD WOOD
near Milton Keynes
OS Map 152. SP 834 455.
Ancient woodland, ponds.
*Take the B526 north from Newport Pagnell
and then the left turn signed Haversham
(just before Gayhurst). After c.0.5 mile,
turn right through the farm gate marked
'Dairy Farm' and follow the track under the
motorway, past the farm to the car park at
the wood. Leaflet available.*
BBOWT

PITSTONE FEN
near Tring
OS Map 165. SP 94 14.
Chalk pit, pools, marsh, seepages.
*Permit and access details available from
nearby College Lake (see above).*
Species inc. Brown Hawker, Broad-
bodied Chaser.
BBOWT

RUSHBEDS WOOD
near Bicester
OS Maps 164/165. SP 672 154.
Ancient woodland, ponds.
*Take the A41 Bicester to Aylesbury road,
and at Kingswood turn south-west along
minor road. After c.2 miles turn left at the*

Gazetteer

T-junction. After c.0.25 mile turn right into a track just before the next T-junction. Go through the gateway and over the railway bridge to the car park. Follow rides and public footpath. Leaflet.
Species inc. Migrant Hawker, Broad-bodied Chaser.
BBOWT

WESTON TURVILLE RESERVOIR
near Aylesbury
OS Map 165. SP 864 095.
Reservoir, reed, scrub, woodland.
Park in lay-by along minor road between B4544 (Weston Turville) and A413 (World's End).
Over 13 species recorded inc. Large Red Damselfly, Migrant Hawker, Ruddy Darter.
AYLESBURY VALE DISTRICT COUNCIL, BBOWT

CAMBRIDGESHIRE

The Wildlife Trust for Bedfordshire, Cambridgeshire, Northamptonshire & Peterborough (WTBCNP)
Head Office: The Manor House, Broad Street, Great Camborne, Cambridge CB23 6DH
TEL 01954 713500
EMAIL cambridgeshire@wildlifebcnp.org
Peterborough Office: Second Floor, 4–6 Cowgate, Peterborough PE1 1NA.
TEL 01733 890419
EMAIL peterborough@wildlifebcnp.org
WWW.WILDLIFEBCNP.ORG

Natural England Regional Offices
EMAIL (all offices):
enquiries.east@naturalengland.org.uk
Cambridgeshire: Eastbrook, Shaftesbury Road, Cambridge CB2 2DR
TEL 01223 462727
2nd Floor, City House, 126–128 Hills Road, Cambridge CB2 1PT
TEL 01223 354462
Peterborough: Northminster House, Peterborough PE1 1UA
TEL 01733 890419

Ham Lane House, Ham Lane, Nene Park, Orton Waterville, Peterborough PE2 5UR
TEL 01733 405850

The National Trust Regional Office: East of England
Westly Bottom, Bury St Edmunds, Suffolk IP33 3WD
TEL 01284 747500

Websites
Cambridgeshire Dragonfly Group
CAMDRAGS.BLOGSPOT.COM

THE BOARDWALKS LNR
Peterborough
OS Map 142. TL 180 982.
Ponds, marsh, grassland, scrub along River Nene.
Parking off Thorpe Road/Thorpe Parkway roundabout, along Thorpe Meadows by the Boathouse pub and Butterfly Hotel. Cross the bridge and head straight on to the river and turn left. Access also along river from Peterborough city centre and Orton Staunch.
Species recorded inc. Small Red-eyed Damselfly on dyke by the Boathouse pub in 2006.
PETERBOROUGH CITY COUNCIL
WWW.PETERBOROUGH.GOV.UK

COE FEN
Cambridge
OS Map 154. TL 447 574.
Fen alongside the River Cam.
Park in city centre. Follow Trumpington Street south and turn right at the second roundabout into Fen Causeway. Take footpaths by bridge.
Over 15 species recorded inc. Ruddy Darter.
CAMBRIDGESHIRE COUNTY COUNCIL

FERRY MEADOWS COUNTRY PARK
Peterborough
OS Map 142. TL 146 978.
Park with open water, marsh, streams, grassland, woodland.

Situated off A605 on western outskirts of Peterborough. Large car park (charge at weekends and holiday periods) at TL 148 973. Includes station for Nene Valley Steam Railway.

PETERBOROUGH DEVELOPMENT CORPORATION

FIVE ARCHES PIT
near Sawtry
OS Map 142. TL 204 829.

Pools, reedbed, scrub.

Leave A1 south of Sawtry east along B1090 then take minor road left into Woodwalton. In the village, turn left immediately after railway line into New Road and along to Church End. Park where the road becomes a track and continue on foot to entrance before railway line.

WTBCNP

HOUGHTON MILL
near Huntingdon
OS Map 153. TL 284 717.

See main site section page 181.

Open river and linked, vegetated watercourses surrounded by pasture with scattered scrub.

This site is c.3 miles east of Huntingdon. Species inc. White-legged and Large Red-eyed Damselflies, Scarce Chaser.

NATIONAL TRUST

LATTERSEY LNR
Whittlesey
OS Map 142. TL 282 966.

Disused brick pits.

Leave the A605 in Whittlesey (at the roundabout) and head south along the B1093 (Bellman's Lane). At the T-junction, turn left into New Road and continue to car park on right.

Species inc. Large Red-eyed Damselfly.

WTBCNP

LITTLE PAXTON PITS
near St Neots
OS Map 153. TL 200 635.

Gravel pits, reed fringe, meadows.

The reserve is signed from Little Paxton village (just off A1) and lies to the east of the village, at the end of High Street. Car

park at TL 195 629. *Keep to footpaths as some pits still operative. Information centre, toilets (inc. disabled; 9am–5pm). Some wheelchair access along trails – enquire at visitor centre.*

Over 18 species regularly recorded including White-legged and Variable Damselflies, Hairy Dragonfly, Scarce Chaser, Small Red-eyed Damselfly has been recorded in recent years.

HUNTINGDONSHIRE DISTRICT COUNCIL
WWW.PAXTON-PITS.ORG.UK

MILTON COUNTRY PARK
near Cambridge
OS Map 154. TL 480 620.

Disused gravel pits.

Situated off the junction of the A14/A10 on the northern outskirts of Cambridge. Species inc. Hairy Dragonfly, Migrant Hawker, Emperor Dragonfly, Black-tailed Skimmer.

SOUTH CAMBRIDGESHIRE DISTRICT COUNCIL
WWW.SCAMBS.GOV.UK
WWW.MILTONVILLAGE.ORG.UK

NORWOOD ROAD
March
OS Map 143. TL 417 980.

Disused gravel pit.

Leave March town centre north along B1101 and turn left into Norwood Road after level crossing (second turn). Park carefully along road near reserve entrance.

WTBCNP

OUSE WASHES
near Ely
OS Map 143. TL 470 860.

Grassland (summer grazing) with dykes and marsh.

Leave the A141 between March and Chatteris at Wimblington and take the B1093 to Manea. Follow the signs to the RSPB reserve car park at Welches Dam. Information centre. Stay on lower path to avoid disturbing the birds.

Species inc. Variable Damselfly, Hairy Dragonfly.

RSPB, WTBCNP, WILDFOWL & WETLANDS TRUST

Gazetteer

PARADISE FEN & SKATERS' MEADOWS
Cambridge
OS Map 154. TL 446 573.
Fen alongside the River Cam.
Park in city centre. Follow Trumpington Street south and turn right at the second roundabout into Fen Causeway. Take footpaths by bridge into Paradise Fen. For Skaters' Meadow, go to the southern end of Paradise Fen, turn left onto Granchester Street and view meadow from roadside.
WTBCNP

RAMSEY HEIGHTS COUNTRYSIDE CLASSROOM
near Ramsey
OS Map 142. TL 245 848.
Pools, grassland, scrub.
From Ramsey take the minor road to Upwood then turn right by the school to Ramsey Heights. At the southern edge of the village, take the track on the left signed for Countryside Classroom. The reserve is after c.0.5 mile on the right. Go through the gate to the grassy meadow car park. Park on verge if car park closed. Woodwalton Fen NNR lies at the bottom of the road.
WTBCNP

WICKEN FEN
near Soham
OS Map 154. TL 563 705.
See main site section page 236.
Fen, open water, reedbeds, woodland.
Wicken lies c.8 miles north of Cambridge.
18 species inc. Variable and Large Red-eyed Damselflies, Hairy Dragonfly.
NATIONAL TRUST

WOODWALTON FEN NNR
near Ramsey
OS Map 142. TL 234 848 (parking).
See main site section page 239.
Fen, woodland.
This NNR lies midway between Peterborough and Huntingdon. See main site section, or Ramsey Heights above, for directions.

Over 18 species inc. Large Red-eyed Damselfly, Hairy Dragonfly, Common Hawker, Scarce Chaser, Common and Ruddy Darters.
NATURAL ENGLAND, WTBCNP

WOODWALTON MARSH NNR
near Sawtry
OS Map 142. TL 212 813.
Pools, reedbed, scrub.
Leave A1 south of Sawtry east along B1090 then take minor road left into Woodwalton. In the village, turn left immediately after railway line into New Road. Park in passing place opposite the reserve entrance.
Over 15 species inc. Large Red-eyed Damselfly, Hairy Dragonfly, Common Hawker.
WTBCNP

CHESHIRE

Cheshire Wildlife Trust
Bickley Hall Farm, Bickley, Malpas SY14 8EF
TEL 01948 820728
EMAIL info@cheshirewt.cix.co.uk
www.wildlifetrust.org.uk/cheshire

Cheshire County Council
Countryside Management Service, Phoenix House, Clough Road, Winsford CW7 4BD
TEL 01606 541808
EMAIL countryside@cheshire.gov.uk
WWW.CHESHIRE.GOV.UK

The National Trust Regional Office: Cheshire
Stamford Estates, 18 Market Street, Altrincham WA14 1PH
TEL 0161 928 0075

Natural England Regional Office: Cheshire
Electra Way, Crewe Business Park, Crewe, Cheshire, CW1 6GJ
TEL 01270 754000

Warrington Ranger Service
TEL 01925 443000 and 01925 222494
WWW.WARRINGTON.GOV.UK

Websites
Cheshire Dragonflies and Damselflies
WWW.BROCROSS.COM/DFLY/DFLY.HTM

ANDERTON NATURE PARK
near Northwich
OS Map 118. SJ 649 753 (parking).
Chalk grassland, woodland, ponds.
Head north-west from Northwich on the A533. Just before Barnton take the minor road to Anderton. Follow signs for Anderton Boat Lift, which adjoins the nature park. Car park. Nature walks.
Species inc. Emperor Dragonfly.
CHESHIRE COUNTY COUNCIL

BLACK LAKE, DELAMERE FOREST
near Frodsham, Cheshire
OS Map 117. SJ 537 709.
See main site section page 164.
A small acidic lake with patch of *Sphagnum* moss in woodland.
Delamere Forest lies c.7 miles south of Runcorn and c.7 miles west of Northwich.
Species inc. Common Hawker, Black Darter.
CHESHIRE WILDLIFE TRUST

DANES MOSS
near Macclesfield
OS Map 118. SJ 905 704.
Heathland, peat moss, woodland.
Leave Macclesfield south along the A536. Turn left at the crossroads in Gawsworth and bear left after c.200m down Woodhouse End Road. Park along roadside at SJ 903 701 by the footpath on left. Keep to footpaths.
Over 12 species inc. Common Hawker, Black Darter.
CHESHIRE WILDLIFE TRUST

HATCH MERE, DELAMERE FOREST
near Northwich
OS Map 117. SJ 555 721 (parking).
See main site section page 164.

Lake, woodland.
Delamere Forest lies c.7 miles south of Runcorn and c.7 miles west of Northwich.
Species inc. Variable Damselfly, Hairy Dragonfly.
CHESHIRE WILDLIFE TRUST

LYME PARK
near Stockport
OS Map 109. SJ 965 825.
Parkland, ponds, woodland, moorland.
The park lies c.6.5 miles south-east of Stockport. Entrance off the A6. Open 8am–8.30pm during the summer. Network of paths and trails. Two car parks, NT shops, restaurant and information centre.
Over 10 species inc. Common Hawker, Black Darter.
NATIONAL TRUST

MARBURY COUNTRY PARK
near Northwich
OS Map 118. SJ 651 762 (parking).
Lake, reedbed, woodland.
The country park is between Northwich and Comberbach off the A533 or A559, and is signed from Junction 10 of the M56.
CHESHIRE COUNTY COUNCIL

RISLEY MOSS
near Warrington
OS Map 109. SJ 664 921.
See main site section page 230.
Raised bog, woodland.
Risley Moss lies on the north-eastern outskirts of Warrington between the M6 and M62 motorways.
Species inc. Common Hawker, Black Darter.
WARRINGTON RANGER SERVICE

RIVACRE VALLEY LNR
Ellesmere Port
OS Map 117. SJ 384 778 (parking).
Woodland, scrub, grassland.
The site is south of Junction 7 of the M53 and is accessed off the B5132.
Species inc. Broad-bodied Chaser, Emperor Dragonfly, Ruddy Darter.
ELLESMERE PORT & NESTON BOROUGH COUNCIL

Gazetteer

RIVER DEE
Farndon
OS Map 117. SJ 413 545.
See main site section page 202.
River Dee, farmland.
Situated c.8 miles north-east of Wrexham.
Species inc. Banded Demoiselle, Club-tailed Dragonfly.
CHESHIRE COUNTY COUNCIL

RIXTON CLAY PITS
near Warrington
OS Map 109. SJ 684 900.
See main site section page 230.
Disused clay pits.
The reserve lies c.2 miles from Warrington.
Species inc. Common Hawker, Black Darter.
WARRINGTON RANGER SERVICE

STYAL COUNTRY PARK
near Wilmslow
OS Map 109. SJ 830 832.
River Bollin, deciduous woodland.
Lies c.1.5 miles north-west of Wilmslow off the B5166. Car parks at Quarry Bank Mill (NT) and Twinnies Bridge. Riverside walks. Information boards. Leaflet. NT shop, café, toilets, picnic areas.
NATIONAL TRUST

VALE ROYAL LOCKS
River Weaver, near Hartford
OS Map 118. SJ 641 706.
See main site section page 224.
Well-vegetated riverbank.
The site lies along the Weaver Navigation channel c.8 miles north-west of Crewe.
Species inc. Banded Demoiselle, Large Red and Large Red-eyed Damselflies, Hairy Dragonfly, Brown Hawker, Four-spotted Chaser.
VALE ROYAL BOROUGH COUNCIL
BRITISH WATERWAYS

CORNWALL

Cornwall Wildlife Trust
Five Acres, Allet, Truro TR4 9DJ
TEL 01872 273939
EMAIL info@cornwt.demon.co.uk
WWW.CORNWALLWILDLIFETRUST.ORG.UK

The National Trust Regional Office: Cornwall
Lanhydrock, Bodmin PL30 4DE
TEL 01208 74281

Natural England Regional Office: South West
Ground Floor, Trevint House, Strangeways Villas, Truro TR1 2PA
TEL 01872 265710
EMAIL cornwall@naturalengland.org.uk

BODMIN MOOR
OS Map 201. SX 200 765.
Wet heather moorland, peaty pools.
Many minor roads off A30 give access to the moor. The Bolventor to St Neot road to the south of the A30 (at SX 184 768) gives good access to the moor.
Over 20 species inc. Beautiful Demoiselle, Small Red, White-legged and Scarce Blue-tailed Damselflies, Common Hawker, Golden-ringed Dragonfly, Keeled Skimmer, Ruddy and Black Darters.
NATIONAL TRUST, FOREST ENTERPRISE, NATURAL ENGLAND, PRIVATE OWNERSHIP
WWW.BODMINMOOR.CO.UK

BRENEY COMMON
near St Austell
OS Map 200. SX 056 614.
Wet heath, scrub.
From the A30/A391 roundabout south of Bodmin, turn north towards Lanivet and take the first right under the A30 bridge. Take the next left and at Reperry Cross take the left fork to Trebell Green. Continue to Gurtla. The entrance track is on the left in Gurtla, after the Methodist church and opposite a house called 'The Barn' at SX 054 610. Wheelchair access from the small car park to a pond and heathland; other

paths uneven.
Over 13 species inc. Small Red
Damselfly, Common Hawker,
Golden-ringed Dragonfly, Keeled
Skimmer, Black Darter.
CORNWALL WILDLIFE TRUST

BUDE MARSHES LNR
& BUDE CANAL
Bude
**OS Map 190. SS 207 061 (northern
end of canal path).**
Reedbed, wet woodland, grassland,
pools.
*Park in The Crescent car park in Bude
and take canal footpath. The reserve can
be accessed via footbridge from canal
path. Tourist Information Centre nearby.*
NORTH CORNWALL DISTRICT COUNCIL
WWW.NCDC.GOV.UK

CARNKIEF POND
near Newquay
OS Map 200. SW 784 524.
Damp woodland, bog, pool.
*The pond lies east of the A3075 and south
of the B3285. Access along minor roads
south of Goonhavern at SW 784 524.*
Over 13 species inc. Beautiful
Demoiselle, Small Red and Scarce
Blue-tailed Damselflies, Common
Hawker, Golden-ringed Dragonfly,
Keeled Skimmer, Ruddy and Black
Darters.

CARN MOOR
near Newquay
OS Map 204. SW 794 537.
Wet heath.
*Leave the A3075 east along B3285 at
Goonhavern for c.0.5 mile to the track on
the left (opposite World in Miniature) and
park carefully. Walk down the track, over
the stile and bear left along the private
(permissive) footpath across the field to the
heath. Go through gate in south-west
corner and walk along west bank and
boardwalk.*
CORNWALL WILDLIFE TRUST

CROWDY RESERVOIR
near Camelford
OS Maps 200/201. SX 147 835.
Reservoir, marsh, coniferous
plantation.
Car park at SX 138 834.
SOUTH WEST WATER, FOREST ENTERPRISE

GOSS MOOR NNR
near Newquay
OS Map 200. SW 950 600.
Wet heath.
*Area lies south of A30 and to the east of
Indian Queens. Best accessed just north of
Enniscaven at SW 965 597. Car park near
the A30/B3274 junction.*
Over 15 species inc. Beautiful
Demoiselle, Small Red and Scarce
Blue-tailed Damselflies, Common
Hawker, Golden-ringed Dragonfly,
Keeled Skimmer, Black Darter.
NATURAL ENGLAND

GREENA MOOR
near Bude
OS Map 190. SX 234 963.
Culm grassland, woodland, scrub,
streams.
*Leave the A39 c.5 miles south of Bude and
take the minor road to Week St Mary. In
the village, take the right turn towards
Week Green, then the right-hand fork.
After c.0.75 mile, access reserve along path
on left. Footpaths are uneven and can be
very wet and muddy. Information board.*
CORNWALL WILDLIFE TRUST, PLANTLIFE
WWW.PLANTLIFE.ORG.UK

THE LIZARD & KYNANCE COVE
OS Map 203. SW 701 140.
Damp coastal heath.
*Park in Lizard village or at Kynance and
take footpaths to heath on west side of
A3083. Check streams and pools
throughout the area. Note that some pools
are on private land – use OS map and keep
to footpaths.*
NATIONAL TRUST, NATURAL ENGLAND &
PRIVATE OWNERSHIP

Gazetteer

LOE POOL AND MARSH
near Helston
OS Map 203. SW 647 248.
Lake, rivers and marsh.
Car parks at Helston, Penrose, and Degibna. Footpaths around lake and marsh. Information boards.
NATIONAL TRUST

LOGGAN'S MOOR
near Hayle
OS Map 203. SW 576 389.
Meadow with reedbed and grassland bordered by streams.
Two miles north-east of Hayle on the B3301, park in the lay-by on the south side of the road. Access along track. No footpaths at the site.
Species inc. Beautiful Demoiselle, Golden-ringed Dragonfly.
CORNWALL WILDLIFE TRUST

LOWER LEWDON
near Bude
OS Map 190. SS 256 096.
Culm grassland, woodland, scrub.
Leave Kilkhampton south along B3254 for c.1.5 miles, then turn right to Hessaford. Park after c.0.25 mile and follow waymarked path to reserve.
CORNWALL WILDLIFE TRUST

MARAZION MARSH
near Penzance
OS Map 203. SW 510 313.
Marsh, reedbed.
Situated along the A394 between Long Rock and Marazion. Car park. Boardwalk and marked trail.
Over 20 species recorded inc. Common Hawker, Golden-ringed Dragonfly. Also good for migrant species such as Lesser Emperor and Red-veined Darter.
RSPB

PENDARVES WOOD
near Camborne
OS Map 203. SW 640 376.
Deciduous woodland, lake.

Head south from Camborne along the B3303 for c.1 mile and reserve entrance is on the left. Nature trail.
Over 10 species recorded inc. Small Red Damselfly.
CORNWALL WILDLIFE TRUST

RED MOOR
near Lostwithiel
OS Map 200. SX 065 611 (entrance).
See main site section page 202.
Lowland heath, pools, bog, carr.
Between Bodmin and Lostwithiel.
13 species recorded inc. Small Red and Scarce Blue-tailed Damselflies.
CORNWALL WILDLIFE TRUST

TAMAR LAKES
near Bude
OS Map 190. SS 290 115.
Reservoirs with scrub.
Car park and centre at SS 291 117.
SOUTH WEST WATER

VENTONGIMPS MOOR
near Perranporth
OS Map 200. SW 781 511.
Wet and dry heath, bog, scrub, pools, carr.
Leave the A30 c.1.5 miles south of Zelah along the minor road to Ventongimps. After c.1.5 miles turn left at the T-junction, then take next left. Access is along footpath c.30m along this road. Limited parking near the entrance.
Over 15 species inc. Beautiful Demoiselle, Small Red Damselfly, Common Hawker, Golden-ringed Dragonfly, Keeled Skimmer, Ruddy Darter.
CORNWALL WILDLIFE TRUST

CUMBRIA

Cumbria Wildlife Trust
Plumgarths, Crook Road, Kendal, Cumbria LA8 8LX
TEL 01539 816300
EMAIL mail@cumbriawildlifetrust.org.uk
WWW.WILDLIFETRUST.ORG.UK/CUMBRIA

The National Trust Regional Office: North West
The Hollens, Grasmere, Ambleside
LA22 9QZ
Tel 0870 609 5391

Natural England Regional Offices: North West
Kendal Office: Juniper House, Murley Moss, Oxenholme Rd, Kendal LA9 7RL
Tel 01539 792800
Penrith Office: Agricola House, Cowper Road, Gilwilly Trading Estate, Penrith CA11 9BN
Tel 01768 860700
Email (both offices)
cumbria@naturalengland.org.uk

Websites
Lakeland Wildlife
WWW.LAKELANDWILDLIFE.CO.UK/
DRAGONFLIES.HTM

Wildlife in Cumbria
WWW.WILDLIFEINCUMBRIA.ORG.UK

ASH LANDING
near Ambleside
OS Map 97. SD 386 952.
Woodland, scrub, meadows, ponds.
Park in either the small reserve car park c.0.5 mile along B5285 from the ferry crossing, or in the National Trust car park (c.100m back along the road towards the ferry). Visitor centre.
National Trust

BOWNESS-ON-SOLWAY
near Carlisle
OS Map 85. NY 207 617.
Flooded gravel pits, grassland, carr.
The reserve lies c.10 miles west of Carlisle and c.1 mile west of Bowness-on-Solway village. From Bowness, take the minor road west. The reserve entrance is accessed on foot via a farm track on the left after the turn to Biglands House. Park on the verge on the south side of the road after the bungalow. Do not obstruct farm track. Walk up the track to reserve, which lies on either side of track. A waymarked circular

trail takes you round both sides of the reserve.
Cumbria Wildlife Trust

CLAIFE HEIGHTS
near Ambleside
OS Maps 96/97. SD 382 976.
See main site section page 156.
Mires, tarns, moorland, woodland.
Claife Heights is a large area of hillside forest on the west shore of Windermere, c.8 miles south of Ambleside.
Species inc. Golden-ringed Dragonfly, Downy Emerald, Black and White-faced Darters.
National Trust

CLINTS QUARRY
near Egremont
OS Map 89. NY 008 124.
Limestone grassland, woodland, disused quarry, ponds.
North of Egremont take the A5086 and then the first left towards Moor Row. Space for only two cars in the quarry entrance by the bridge after c.1 mile. Alternative parking in lay-by near junction of A5086/ A595. Leaflet. Strong footwear essential.
Cumbria Wildlife Trust

CUNSEY BECK
near Lake Windermere
OS Map 97. SD 374 938.
See main site section page 162.
Moorland stream.
Site lies c.10 miles south of Ambleside.
Species inc. Beautiful Demoiselle, Golden-ringed Dragonfly.
Part of Lake District National Park

DRUMBURGH MOSS NNR
near Carlisle
OS Map 85. NY 255 586.
Raised bog, heath, pools.
The reserve lies west of Carlisle, just north of the B5307 between Kirkbride and Drumburgh village. Leave the village south on the minor road next to the post office. After c.200m the road becomes a track. Limited parking on verges of track just beyond Moss Cottage at NY 255 591. Do

not block track. Access to reserve through
gate on south side of track and across
disused railway. Leaflet.
Over 10 species inc. Common Hawker,
Emperor and Golden-ringed
Dragonflies, White-faced Darter.
CUMBRIA WILDLIFE TRUST

DUBBS MOSS
near Cockermouth
OS Map 89. NY 103 290.
Fen, woodland.
*Leave Cockermouth along A5086 then turn
right towards Eaglesfield. Take the first
track on the right, Moorland Close (signed
public footpath), and then next right to the
junction. Park on side of track (do not
block). Walk down the hill to the reserve.
Alternative parking in village.*
CUMBRIA WILDLIFE TRUST

GREENDALE MIRES
near Egremont
OS Map 89. NY 143 056.
Streams, mires, tarns, moorland.
*Leave the A595 south of Egremont at
Gosforth and take the minor road to Nether
Wasdale. In the village, continue straight on
at the triangle of roads, and up the west shore
of Wast Water. Take next left turn (c.1 mile
from start of lake) and park at Greendale at
NY 143 056. Follow footpath north along
stream to Greendale Tarn, and to the south
along stream to Woodhow pond. Also check
streams running into Wast Water to north.*
Over 10 species inc. Beautiful
Demoiselle, Common Hawker,
Golden-ringed Dragonfly, Keeled
Skimmer, Black Darter.

LOUGHRIGG TARN
near Ambleside
OS Map 90. NY 344 043.
Mire.
*Near the northern end of Lake Windermere.
Footpaths from Skelwith Bridge.*
Species inc. Beautiful Demoiselle,
Downy Emerald, Four-spotted Chaser,
Keeled Skimmer.
NATIONAL TRUST

PARKGATE TARN
near Egremont
OS Map 89. NY 118 006.
Wooded tarn.
*Leave the A595 south of Egremont at
Gosforth and take the minor road south-east
to Santon bridge. Then drive through the
village towards Eskdale Green to car park
after c. 1 mile. Follow forest tracks and
paths to tarn to the south.*
Species inc. Large Red, Azure,
Common Blue and Blue-tailed
Damselflies, Four-spotted Chaser,
Keeled Skimmer, Black Darter.
FOREST ENTERPRISE

WALNEY ISLAND
near Barrow-in-Furness
OS Map 96.
NORTH WALNEY NNR   SD 170 713
SOUTH WALNEY   SD 215 620
Coastal dunes, heath, marsh, ponds.
*Follow A590 through Barrow onto Walney
Island. For North Walney, car parking and
toilets at Earnse Point at SD 170 700. For
South Walney, car park at South End
Haws, beyond South End Caravan Site
along unmade road. Obtain permit (free to
CWT members) for South Walney from car
park. Nature trails.*
Over 10 species inc. Common and
Brown Hawkers, Emperor Dragonfly,
Ruddy Darter.
NATURAL ENGLAND, CUMBRIA WILDLIFE TRUST

DERBYSHIRE

Derbyshire Wildlife Trust
East Mill, Bridge Foot, Belper
DE56 1XH
TEL 01773 881188
EMAIL enquiries@derbyshirewt.co.uk
WWW.DERBYSHIREWILDLIFETRUST.ORG.UK

**The National Trust Regional Office:
East Midlands**
Clumber Park Stableyard, Worksop,
Notts S80 3BE
TEL 01909 486411

Websites
Derbyshire Dragonflies
WWW.DERBYSHIRE-DRAGONFLIES.ORG.UK

CROMFORD CANAL
near Matlock
OS Map 119. SK 333 544–SK 350 520.
Canal with adjacent marshland.
This reserve runs along the stretch of canal between Cromford and Ambergate south of Matlock. Access and parking at High Peak Junction (DCC car park and visitor centre), off the B5035 at Whatstandwell Bridge (SK 332 543), or along the footpath off the minor road (Chase Road) just north of the A610/ A6 junction at Ambergate (SK 348 519). Search from along the towpath between Cromford Wharf and Ambergate.
Over 13 species inc. Common and Brown Hawkers, Emperor Dragonfly, Ruddy Darter.
DERBYSHIRE COUNTY COUNCIL
WWW.DERBYSHIRE.GOV.UK
DERBYSHIRE WILDLIFE TRUST

HILTON GRAVEL PITS
near Burton-on-Trent
OS Map 128. SK 249 315.
See main site section page 179.
Disused gravel pits, marsh, woodland.
Hilton Gravel Pits reserve lies between Burton-on-Trent and Derby.
Over 16 species (see main site).
DERBYSHIRE WILDLIFE TRUST

THE LONGSHAW ESTATE
near Sheffield
OS Maps 110/119. SK 266 800.
Fish pond, moorland, wooded stream, oak woodland.
Situated c.3 miles south-east of Hathersage, beside the A625 Sheffield to Hathersage road. Woodcroft car park is off the B6055, 200m south of the junction with the A625. Information centre and trails. The pond is good for dragonflies.
NATIONAL TRUST

DEVON

Devon Wildlife Trust
Shirehampton House, 35–37 St David's Hill, Exeter, Devon EX4 4DA
TEL 01392 279244
EMAIL contactus@devonwildlifetrust. org
WWW.DEVONWILDLIFETRUST.ORG

The National Trust Regional Office: Devon
Killerton House, Broadclyst, Exeter EX5 3LE
TEL 01392 881691

Natural England Regional Offices
Level 2, Renslade House, Bonhay Road, Exeter EX4 3AW
TEL 01392 889770
2nd Floor, 11–15 Dix's Field, Exeter EX1 1QA
TEL 01392 477150
1st Floor, Estuary House, Peninsula Park, Rydon Lane, Exeter EX2 7XE
TEL 01392 352000
EMAIL devon@naturalengland.org.uk

Dartmoor National Park Authority
Parke, Bovey Tracey, Newton Abbot, TQ13 9JQ
TEL 01626 832093
EMAIL hq@dartmoor-npa.gov.uk
WWW.DARTMOOR-NPA.GOV.UK

ARLINGTON COURT
near Barnstaple
OS Map 180. SS 611 405.
Lake by River Yeo surrounded by woods and parkland.
This property lies c.7 miles north-east of Barnstaple. Follow signs from A39 and park (charge) at the house at SS 611 405. Nature trail. Bat cave. Leaflet.
Ten species inc. Beautiful Demoiselle, Common Hawker, Golden-ringed Dragonfly.
NATIONAL TRUST

Gazetteer

ASHCULM TURBARY
near Wellington
OS Map 181. ST 147 157.
Wet heath, peatbog, springs.
From the A38 at Wellington, take Monument Road towards Hemyock. Go over the crossroads into Simonsburrow. Park carefully here and take the track on the left past 'Flints' (ST 145 159).
Species inc. Southern Damselfly, Keeled Skimmer.
DEVON WILDLIFE TRUST

AYLESBEARE COMMON
near Exeter
OS Map 192. SY 057 898.
See main site section page 142.
Wet and dry heathland.
The reserve lies c.8 miles east of Exeter.
Species inc. Southern Damselfly, Hairy, Emperor and Golden-ringed Dragonflies, Keeled Skimmer.
RSPB

BICTON COMMON
near Exmouth
OS Map 192. SY 040 858.
Pebblebed heath, streams.
Parking along minor road around common (between Woodbury and Otterton).
Over 20 species inc. Beautiful Demoiselle, White-legged, Southern and Small Red Damselflies, Common Hawker, Hairy and Golden-ringed Dragonflies, Keeled Skimmer, Ruddy and Black Darters.
EAST DEVON DISTRICT COUNCIL

BRAUNTON BURROWS
near Barnstaple
OS Map 180. SS 450 350.
Sand dunes, grassland, scrub, pools.
Take the A361 north-west from Barnstaple. Reserve is close to the village of Braunton. Parking at SS 467 327 and SS 463 351. Some dunes have restricted access and the military area is closed when red flags are flying – check notices.
Species inc. Black-tailed Skimmer, Black and Ruddy Darters
NATURAL ENGLAND

BYSTOCK POOLS
near Exmouth
OS Map 192. SY 034 844.
See main site section page 150.
Heath, woodland, scrub, pools.
The pools lie c.6 miles south-east of Exeter and c.1 mile north of Exmouth.
Species inc. Emperor and Golden-ringed Dragonflies, Downy Emerald.
DEVON WILDLIFE TRUST

CADOVER BRIDGE
near Plymouth
OS Map 202. SX 556 647.
See main site section page 151.
Moorland pool.
On the edge of Dartmoor north of Plymouth.
Species inc. Scarce Blue-tailed Damselfly, Emperor and Golden-ringed Dragonflies.
PART OF DARTMOOR NATIONAL PARK

CHUDLEIGH KNIGHTON HEATH
near Bovey Tracey
OS Map 191. SX 837 776.
See main site section page 155.
Wet and dry heathland, scrub, pools.
Reserve lies c.12 miles south of Exeter.
Over 12 species inc. Large Red Damselfly, Common Hawker, Emperor Dragonfly, Keeled Skimmer.
DEVON WILDLIFE TRUST

COLATON RALEIGH COMMON
near Exmouth
OS Map 192. SX 050 868.
See main site section page 157.
Fast-flowing, stony-bottomed stream and bogs in heather heathland.
The area lies c.5 miles east of Exeter and is accessed via Woodbury Castle and Common.
Species inc. Large Red and Southern Damselflies, Emperor and Golden-ringed Dragonflies.
DEVON WILDLIFE TRUST

COLYFORD – RIVER AXE & UMBORNE BROOK
near Seaton
OS Map 192. SX 255 925.

Riverbanks.
Parking in Colyford. Footpath north from railway station along east side of Umborne Brook. River Axe access either at road bridge east of level crossing or along footpath north from Cowhayne along minor road to Kingsdon.
Species inc. White-legged Damselfly.

DAWLISH WARREN NNR
Dawlish
OS Map 192. SX 985 792.
Coastal grassland, scrub, pools.
Car park at SX 980 786 east of railway station.
Over 20 species recorded inc. Hairy Dragonfly, Common Hawker.
TEIGNBRIDGE DISTRICT COUNCIL
DEVON WILDLIFE TRUST
WWW.DAWLISHWARREN.CO.UK

DECOY COUNTRY PARK
Newton Abbot
OS Map 202. SX 865 702.
Lake, woodland.
The country park is on the southern side of Newton Abbot (signed) and can be reached on foot from the town centre. Toilets (inc. disabled), picnic areas.
Species inc. Downy Emerald.
TEIGNBRIDGE DISTRICT COUNCIL

DUNSFORD
near Exeter
OS Map 191. SX 798 875.
Woodland, heathland.
Park in the Dartmoor National Park car park by the Steps Bridge tearooms at SX 805 883. Reserve entrance beyond Steps Bridge on the bank opposite the tearooms. Access also from Clifford Bridge.
Species inc. Golden-ringed Dragonfly.
DEVON WILDLIFE TRUST

EXE REED BEDS
near Exeter
OS Map 192. SX 957 885.
Freshwater canal with scrub.
From the Countess Wear roundabout, take the A379 towards Dawlish, proceed over the River Exe and turn immediately left into the South West Water entrance and park on right in the university boathouse car park (SX 946 893). Walk along canal, beyond the sewage works on left, past the Old Sludge Beds reserve to motorway bridge.
DEVON WILDLIFE TRUST

EXMINSTER MARSHES
near Exeter
OS Map 192. SX 960 875.
Marshes, ditches.
Parking at SX 962 874.
Species inc. Hairy Dragonfly.
RSPB

GRAND WESTERN CANAL
near Tiverton
OS Map 181. SS 956 123–ST 074 195.
Freshwater canal.
Park in Tiverton and follow canal towpath eastwards. Other points of access near Sampford Peverell and Westleigh (see OS map or mapping websites).
Species inc. Beautiful and Banded Demoiselles, Emperor and Golden-ringed Dragonflies.
DEVON COUNTY COUNCIL
WWW.DEVON.GOV.UK

HALDON FOREST
near Exeter
OS Map 192. SX 880 840.
See main site section page 178.
Woodland, streams.
Haldon Forest is c.4 miles south-west of Exeter.
Species inc. Emperor and Golden-ringed Dragonflies, Broad-bodied Chaser.
FOREST ENTERPRISE

HALSDON
near Great Torrington
OS Map 180. SS 555 125.
River Torridge, woodland, meadows, scrub.
Leave Great Torrington along the A3124 south-east to Beaford. Just after Beaford, take the minor road south towards Dolton and then the next right turn. Follow this

Gazetteer

road for c.1.5 miles to the track on the right-hand side with a DWT sign at SS 557 133. Follow track to the car park. Keep to marked trails.
Over 10 species inc. Beautiful Demoiselle, White-legged Damselfly, Golden-ringed Dragonfly.
DEVON WILDLIFE TRUST

HALWILL JUNCTION
near Holsworthy
OS Map 190. SS 443 004.
Disused railway line.
Leave the A3072 east of Holsworthy along the A3079 (towards Okehampton) to Halwill Junction. In the village turn left (signed Hatherleigh and Black Torrington) past the Junction Inn, then left into Beeching Close. Turn immediately right into cul-de-sac and park behind the village shops. Path to reserve runs between the houses at end of cul-de-sac.
Species inc. Golden-ringed Dragonfly, Broad-bodied Chaser.
DEVON WILDLIFE TRUST

LITTLE BRADLEY PONDS
near Bovey Tracey
OS Map 191. SX 829 778.
See main site section page 184.
Ponds, scrub.
The ponds lie between Chudleigh Knighton and Bovey Tracey.
Over 20 species inc. Hairy Dragonfly, Downy Emerald, Ruddy Darter.
DEVON WILDLIFE TRUST

LYDFORD STATION
Lydford
OS Maps 191/201. SX 500 826.
Flooded disused railway line.
Roadside parking around SX 500 828, along minor road south of Lydford near old railway station.
18 species recorded inc. Small Red Damselfly, Scarce Blue-tailed Damselfly, Ruddy Darter.
PART OF DARTMOOR NATIONAL PARK

MELDON RESERVOIR
near Okehampton
OS Map 191. SX 560 911.
Moorland reservoir with willow scrub on edge of Dartmoor.
Park at dam around SX 562 916.
DARTMOOR NATIONAL PARK
WWW.DARTMOOR-NPA.GOV.UK
SOUTH WEST WATER

MOLLAND COMMON
near South Molton
OS Map 180. SS 820 304.
Moorland bog, woodland and scrub within Exmoor National Park.
East of Twitchen, park along Ridge Road at SS 835 297 or at SS 808 305 west of Twitchen.
EXMOOR NATIONAL PARK
WWW.EXMOOR-NATIONALPARK.GOV.UK

OLD SLUDGE BEDS
near Exeter
OS Map 192. SX 952 888.
Old sludge beds of sewage works.
Directions and parking as for Exe Reed Beds above. Park in the university boathouse car park (at South West Water sewage treatment works) off the A379 (SX 946 893). Walk north along canal-side to reserve and keep to footpaths.
Species inc. Large Red-eyed Damselfly, Hairy Dragonfly.
DEVON WILDLIFE TRUST

PLYM BRIDGE WOODS
near Plymouth
OS Map 201. SX 522 595.
Mixed woodland, River Plym.
The forest lies on the north-eastern edge of Plymouth. Access via a minor road between the B3432 roundabout and the B3416. Car parks including one in former quarry. Waymarked trails and cycle path.
FOREST ENTERPRISE, NATIONAL TRUST

RIVER AVON
near South Brent
OS Map 202. SX 683 647.
Park at Shipley Bridge north of South Brent (off A38) at SX 679 628. Follow footpath

north along edge of river, past Avon Dam reservoir, then left across the north of the reservoir to SX 660 660. River Avon is then immediately to the north of the footpath.
Species inc. Scarce Blue-tailed Damselfly, Keeled Skimmer.
PART OF DARTMOOR NATIONAL PARK

RIVER EXE, STAFFORD BRIDGE
near Exeter
OS Map 192. SX 921 962.
See main site section page 205.
Slow-flowing river, grassland.
Stafford Bridge is situated on the River Exe c.2 miles north of Exeter.
Species inc. Banded Demoiselle, White-legged Damselfly.

RIVER LYD
near Lydford
OS Maps 191/201. SX 521 844.
River running off moorland.
This small river (near its source) crosses under the A386 south-east of Lydford. Footpath to river just north of road bridge.
Species inc. Southern Damselfly.
PART OF DARTMOOR NATIONAL PARK

RIVER TAVY
near Mary Tavy
OS Map 201. SX 525 795 (parking).
Wooded river valley on south-west edge of Dartmoor.
Park along minor road between Horndon and Cudlipptown.
Species inc. Golden-ringed Dragonfly.
PART OF DARTMOOR NATIONAL PARK

RIVER TORRIDGE
Great Torrington
OS Map 180. SS 480 197 (parking).
River.
Park at the Puffing Billy pub along A386 on western side of Great Torrington. Follow paths along the river. The Tarka Trail (south-west from the car park) is well-surfaced suitable for wheelchairs.
Species inc. Beautiful Demoiselle.

SLAPTON LEY
near Kingsbridge
OS Map 202. SX 825 440.
See main site section page 215.
Lagoon, reedbed, scrub.
Slapton Ley lies c.22 miles east of Plymouth and c.30 miles south of Exeter.
Species inc. Southern Damselfly, Hairy Dragonfly, Downy Emerald.
FIELD STUDIES COUNCIL

SMALLHANGER, DARTMOOR
near Plymouth
OS Map 202. SX 576 595.
Abandoned clay workings.
Situated north-east of Plymouth. Access from Drakeland Corner east of B3417.
17 species recorded inc. Small Red and Scarce Blue-tailed Damselflies, Keeled Skimmer.

STOVER COUNTRY PARK
near Newton Abbot
OS Map 191. SX 834 750.
See main site section page 218.
Lake, reedbed, heath, woodland.
Stover Country Park lies c.15 miles south-west of Exeter.
Over 20 species recorded (over 15 breeding) inc. Large Red-eyed Damselfly, Hairy and Emperor Dragonflies, Downy Emerald.
DEVON COUNTY COUNCIL

STUCKEY FARM
near South Molton
OS Map 180. SS 780 140.
Grassland, river.
Take the B3137 west from Tiverton towards South Molton. Take the left turn beyond Witheridge towards Drayford and East Worthington. Park carefully in Drayford and, from the crossroads by the Little Dart bridge, take the path on right between the cottages to the reserve (SS 781 138).
DEVON WILDLIFE TRUST

Gazetteer

SWANPOOL MARSH
near Barnstaple
OS Map 180. SS 473 367.
Coastal grassland, marsh, ditches.
*Take the A361 from Barnstaple to
Braunton then the B3231 towards Croyde.
After c.0.5 mile take the first minor road
(signed Moor Lane Nursery) on the left
and the reserve entrance is c.400m on the
right. Park carefully on verge.*
DEVON WILDLIFE TRUST

VENN OTTERY
near Exeter
OS Map 192. SY 065 920.
See main site section page 228.
Wet and dry heathland, raised bog,
scrub, carr, woodland.
Venn Ottery lies c.9 miles east of Exeter.
Species inc. Emperor and Golden-
ringed Dragonflies, Keeled Skimmer.
DEVON WILDLIFE TRUST

DORSET

Dorset Wildlife Trust
Brooklands Farm, Forston, Dorchester
DT2 7AA
TEL 01305 264620
WWW.DORSETWILDLIFE.CO.UK

**The National Trust Regional Office:
Wessex**
Eastleigh Court, Bishopstrow,
Warminster, Wiltshire BA12 9HW
TEL 01985 843600

ALDER HILLS URBAN NATURE RESERVE
Poole
OS Map 195. SZ 063 931.
Wet and dry heath, carr woodland,
wildlife pond.
*Access from the end of Sharp Road,
Parkstone, or Sainsbury's car park, Alder
Hills. Keep to footpaths.*
Over 11 species recorded.
DORSET WILDLIFE TRUST

ARNE
near Wareham
OS Map 195. SY 972 878.
See main site section page 141.
Lowland heath with scattered mixed
woodland.
*Reserve lies on the southern edge of Poole
Harbour, c.3 miles east of Wareham.*
Species inc. Small Red Damselfly,
Migrant Hawker, Downy Emerald,
Keeled Skimmer, Black Darter.
RSPB

BROWNSEA ISLAND
Poole Harbour
OS Map 195. SZ 028 878.
Heathland, mixed woodland, brackish
lagoons, freshwater lakes, reedbed.
*Car parks in Poole and at Studland (at
ferry). Access via boat (charge) from
Poole Quay and Sandbanks (ferry from
Studland). Boats leave every 30 minutes.
Charge to land on the island and to enter
the DWT reserve, which is open for a
self-guided trail in April, May, June and
September. Access only by guided tour
only in July and August 2.00pm–3.45pm
(contact DWT). Café, toilets and National
Trust shop at the Quay.*
Over 20 species recorded inc. Small
Red Damselfly, Downy Emerald,
Ruddy Darter. Other wildlife includes
butterflies and Red Squirrel.
NATIONAL TRUST, DORSET WILDLIFE TRUST

GIRDLERS COPPICE
near Blandford Forum
OS Map 194. ST 798 135.
Hazel coppice, woodland, meadows.
*Parking at Fishermans' car park at ST 801
135. Girdlers Coppice accessed along
permissive footpath only.*
Species inc. White-legged Damselfly.
DORSET WILDLIFE TRUST

HARTLAND MOOR NNR
near Wareham
OS Map 195. SY 950 853.
Lowland wet and dry heathland, mire.
*From Wareham take the B3075 to
Stoborough and then the minor road east*

towards Arne (see above). Turn right towards Slepe before reaching Arne and park on the roadside opposite the entrance to Middlebere Farm. Access here to the Hartland Way (a 3-mile, marked circular walk).

Over 20 species inc. Beautiful Demoiselle, Small Red, Southern and Scarce Blue-tailed Damselflies, Common Hawker, Golden-ringed Dragonfly, Keeled Skimmer, Black Darter.

NATURAL ENGLAND, NATIONAL TRUST

HIGHER HYDE HEATH
near Wareham
OS Map 194. SY 851 902.
Heathland, bog, damp woodland.
Two miles west of Wareham, on the A352 Dorchester road, take the minor road north-west towards Puddletown. Car park and access are c.3 miles along this road on the right by the ARC buildings.
Species inc. Keeled Skimmer.
DORSET WILDLIFE TRUST

LODMOOR
Weymouth
OS Map 194. SY 686 809.
Marshland, pools.
Signed access off A353 east of Weymouth town centre. Pay & display car parks. Flat, level paths from Western Car Park. Café and disabled toilet at adjacent Lodmoor Country Park (Weymouth & Portland Borough Council) further along coastal road towards Overcombe.
Over 18 species inc. Variable Damselfly, Common Hawker, Ruddy Darter.
RSPB

POWERSTOCK COMMON
near Bridport
OS Map 194. SY 540 973.
Forestry plantations with rich native woodland, scrub, grassland, ponds.
Enter reserve from road at SY 547 973, (parking for up to six cars). Keep to footpaths. Leaflet available.

12 species inc. Beautiful Demoiselle, Common Hawker, Golden-ringed Dragonfly, Black Darter.
DORSET WILDLIFE TRUST

RADIPOLE LAKE
Weymouth
OS Map 194. SY 675 800.
Marshland, pools.
Signed off A354 in Weymouth. Pay & display car park.
Over 18 species inc. Variable Damselfly, Common Hawker, Ruddy Darter.
RSPB

RIVER STOUR
near Wimborne Minster
OS Map 195. SZ 031 989.
Riverside with weir.
Access off A341 at SZ 031 989 on outskirts of Merley. Use public footpaths only.
Species inc. White-legged Damselfly, Large Red-eyed Damselfly, Scarce Chaser, Black-tailed Skimmer.

SOPLEY COMMON
near Bournemouth
OS Map 195. SZ 129 971.
Dry and wet heathland, ponds.
Park in lay-by opposite Bosley Farm Nursery at SZ 129 971. Leaflet.
Over 20 species recorded inc. Beautiful Demoiselle, Small Red, Southern and Variable Damselflies, Common Hawker, Golden-ringed Dragonfly, Keeled Skimmer, Ruddy and Black Darters.
DORSET WILDLIFE TRUST

STOUR VALLEY LNR
Muscliff, Bournemouth
OS Map 195. SZ 095 959.
Riverside meadows, woodland.
Park in Granby Road car park, Muscliff.
NATURAL ENGLAND, BOURNEMOUTH BOROUGH COUNCIL

STUDLAND HEATH NNR
near Swanage
OS Map 195. SZ 026 842.
Sand dunes, coastal heathland, woodland, lake, ponds.
Access off B3351 Corfe Castle to Studland road and the Sandbanks/Poole ferry road (or from Poole via the toll ferry across river mouth). Parking at National Trust car park at SZ 031 835, at ferry terminal or near the Knoll House Hotel at SZ 031 832 (some roadside parking before ferry). Follow trails and paths around heath and nearby woodland. Café, visitor centre and toilets in National Trust car park.
Species inc. Ruddy Darter.
NATURAL ENGLAND, NATIONAL TRUST & PRIVATE OWNERSHIP
WWW.ISLEOFPURBECK.COM

STURMINSTER NEWTON MILL
near Sturminster Newton
OS Map 194. ST 782 135.
The mill is alongside the A357 close to the junction with the B3091 at Sturminster Newton bridge. Follow brown signs to car park. Mill open Easter–September (on Saturdays, Sundays, Mondays and Thursdays, 11am–5pm (small charge). Toilets and picnic area.
STURMINSTER NEWTON MUSEUM SOCIETY
WWW.STURMINSTERNEWTON-MUSEUM.CO.UK

WAREHAM FOREST
near Wareham
OS Map 195. SU 108 058.
A large area of dry and wet lowland heath, birch and pine woodland, bogs and pools.
The forest is situated midway between Wareham and Bere Regis. From A351 in Wareham take the minor road heading north-west past the railway station towards Bere Regis. Car park and start of Sika Trail are after c.1.25 miles on the right – some disabled access here. For Morden Heath & Bog NNR, take the B3075 off the A351 north of Wareham and park at Sherford Bridge (SY 919 926). For Gore and Decoy Heaths park at Gore Heath (SY 921 910). Do not leave paths.

The whole area is excellent and holds many species including Common Hawker and Keeled Skimmer.
FOREST ENTERPRISE, NATURAL ENGLAND

WEST BEXINGTON
near Bridport
OS Map 194. SY 525 870.
See main site section page 234.
Pool, reedbed, wet meadow, scrub.
The reserve is situated along the coastal strip between Bridport and Abbotsbury.
Species inc. Migrant, Southern and Brown Hawkers, Emperor Dragonfly, Red-veined Darter.
DORSET WILDLIFE TRUST

DURHAM

Durham Wildlife Trust
Rainton Meadows, Chilton Moor, Houghton-le-Spring, Tyne & Wear
DH4 6PU
TEL 0191 584 3112
EMAIL info@durhamwt.co.uk
WWW.DURHAMWT.CO.UK

The National Trust Regional Office: North East
Scot's Gap, Morpeth, Northumberland
NE61 4EG
TEL 01670 774691

BRINKBURN POND LNR
Darlington
OS Map 93. NZ 282 161.
Pond in urban area.
Access off Brinkburn Road by the Brinkburn public house. Public footpath runs between Faverdale and Honeypot Lane close to pond.
DARLINGTON BOROUGH COUNCIL

BURNHOPE POND
near Durham
OS Map 88. NZ 182 483.
See main site section page 149.
Pond, marsh, plantation.

Gazetteer

The site is c.6 miles north-east of Durham near Burnhope village.
Species inc. Black Darter.
DURHAM WILDLIFE TRUST

JOE'S POND
near Durham
OS Map 88. NZ 329 488.
Pond, scrub.
Take A690 north-east from Durham City and then the left turn along the B1284 just before Houghton-le-Spring. Limited parking at Chilton Moor road junction. Follow footpath to reserve. Access on foot also from East Rainton on the A690.
DURHAM WILDLIFE TRUST

LOW BARNS
near Bishop Auckland
OS Map 92. NZ 160 315.
See main site section page 191.
Lake and woodland.
The reserve lies c.3 miles west of Bishop Auckland.
Species inc. Southern Hawker.
DURHAM WILDLIFE TRUST

MALTON
near Durham
OS Map 88. NZ 182 459.
Woodland, ponds, streams, scrub.
Car park and picnic site signed off A691 east of Lanchester at NZ 177 464. Access reserve via Officials Terrace or the Lanchester Valley Walk.
DURHAM WILDLIFE TRUST, DURHAM COUNTY COUNCIL

MUGGLESWICK COMMON
near Consett
OS Map 87. NZ 020 463.
Moorland, pools, streams, reservoirs.
The common lies south of Muggleswick and is crossed by the B6278. Keep to footpaths and tracks. Parking and picnic site at NZ 031 454. Nearby Smiddy Shaw Reservoir (car park at NZ 046 461) is also worth exploring.
Species inc. Golden-ringed Dragonfly.
PART OF THE NORTH PENNINES AONB

RAISBY HILL GRASSLAND
near Durham
OS Map 93. NZ 335 354.
Limestone grassland, marsh, scrub.
From Junction 61 of the A1(M), take the B6291 into Coxhoe. Take the minor road (for Kelloe) to the right at the sharp left-hand bend. Park carefully on verge and take footpath at NZ 332 358 south across Coxhoe Beck to enter the western end of the reserve. Note – some footpaths are steep and slippery when wet.
Species inc. Emerald and Azure Damselflies, Common and Southern Hawkers, Ruddy Darter.
DURHAM WILDLIFE TRUST

SHIBDON POND LNR
Newcastle-upon-Tyne
OS Map 88. NZ 195 628.
Wetland, reedbeds.
Reserve is at Blaydon close to the A1 and the Metrocentre. Access off the B6317 Swalwell to Blaydon road. Parking at Blaydon Swimming Baths. Nature trail.
Over 10 species recorded inc. Banded Demoiselle, Emerald and Azure Damselflies, Common Hawker, Golden-ringed Dragonfly.
DURHAM WILDLIFE TRUST

THE WILDLIFE GARDEN, BOURNMOOR
near Chester-le-Street
OS Map 88. NZ 313 518.
Garden with pond.
The site is situated within the Klondyke Garden Centre, along the A183 Chester-le-Street to Sunderland road between Bournmoor and Shiney Row.
DURHAM WILDLIFE TRUST

Gazetteer

ESSEX

Essex Wildlife Trust
Abbotts Hall Farm, Gt Wigborough,
Colchester, Essex CO5 7RZ
TEL 01621 862960
EMAIL admin@essexwt.org.uk
WWW.ESSEXWT.ORG.UK

The National Trust Regional Office: East of England
Westly Bottom, Bury St Edmunds,
Suffolk IP33 3WD
TEL 01284 747500

AUBREY BUXTON RESERVE
near Stansted
OS Map 167. TL 521 264.
Parkland, woodland, grassland, pools.
*The reserve lies north of Stansted. From
the B1383 turn east onto Alsa Street and
the reserve car park is c.100m up private
road with white gateposts on the right.*
ESSEX WILDLIFE TRUST

THE BACKWARDEN
near Chelmsford
OS Map 167. TL 781 041.
Heath, marsh, woodland.
*Parking in the Danbury Common car park
at TL 781 044. Cross the road to The
Backwarden.*
ESSEX WILDLIFE TRUST

CHIGBOROUGH LAKES
Maldon
OS Map 168. TL 877 086.
Gravel pits, willow scrub, grassland.
*From Heybridge follow the B1026 north for
c.1 mile and take turn north into
Chigborough Road, past the fishery and
Chigborough Farm to the reserve entrance
c.50m past Chigborough Quarry on the left.*
ESSEX WILDLIFE TRUST

CORNMILL MEADOWS DRAGONFLY SANCTUARY
near Waltham Abbey
OS Map 166. TL 380 013.
See main site section page 161.
Meadows, woodland, slow-flowing
watercourses.
*Cornmill Meadows is on the northern
outskirts of Waltham Abbey.*
Over 20 species inc. White-legged
Damselfly, Hairy Dragonfly.
PART OF LEE VALLEY PARK, MANAGED BY LEE
VALLEY REGIONAL PARK AUTHORITY

FINGRINGHOE WICK
near Colchester
OS Map 168. TM 048 193.
Gravel pits, reedbed, ponds, heath,
scrub, woodland, grassland.
*From Colchester take the B1025 towards
Mersea for 3 miles. After crossing the
Roman River, turn left at the next sign,
then continue following the signs to the
reserve. Reserve open 9am–5pm except
Mondays (but open Bank Holiday
Mondays). Visitor centre, nature trails.*
13 species recorded.
ESSEX WILDLIFE TRUST

GREAT HOLLAND PITS
near Clacton-on-Sea
OS Map 169. TM 204 190.
Gravel pits, grassland, woodland.
*Access along minor road between Little
Clacton (A133) and Great Holland
(B1032). The entrance is c.800m west of
the Lion's Den public house north of Little
Clacton Road.*
ESSEX WILDLIFE TRUST

HATFIELD FOREST MARSH
near Bishop's Stortford
OS Map 167. TL 539 202.
Forest, lake, marsh.
*Access off minor road south of B1256 at
Takeley Street east of Bishop's Stortford.
Car park at TL 546 202.*
NATIONAL TRUST

HAWKSMERE SPRINGS
near Epping
OS Map 167. TQ 508 993.
Unimproved grassland, damp
woodland, stream.
*Access south along path off minor road
north of Stapleford Tawny at TL 509 997.*
ESSEX WILDLIFE TRUST

HUNSDON MEAD
near Harlow
OS Map 167. TL 421 114.
Grassland by River Stort.
Roadside parking at TL 420 116 north of the A414 along minor road to Hunsdonbury. On foot, cross the A414 and walk down the metalled track past Mead Lodge (on left) and then right into the Mead. Keep to paths. Alternatively, park at Roydon railway station, cross to south side of track and follow towpath.
ESSEX WILDLIFE TRUST, HERTFORDSHIRE & MIDDLESEX WILDLIFE TRUST

KNIGHTS PITS
Lee Valley Park, near Waltham Abbey
OS Map 166. TQ 378 984.
Old gravel pits.
Leave Waltham Abbey south along the A1112 and, after c.1.5 miles, turn right into Godwin Close. Park here and follow paths to L-shaped pit at TQ 379 983 (marked on OS Map).
Species inc. Large Red-eyed Damselfly, Small Red-eyed Damselfly.
LEE VALLEY PARK
WWW.LEEVALLEYPARK.ORG.UK

LITTLE WALTHAM MEADOWS
near Chelmsford
OS Map 167. TL 713 119.
Meadows, carr, river (Chelmer).
Reserve lies south of Little Waltham, east of the A130 Broomfield to Little Waltham road. Access is either from Back Lane, Little Waltham or along the bridleway to Croxtons Mill from Broomfield. A footpath runs north–south through the reserve from Little Waltham to Alder Carr and Newland Grove reserves, which adjoin the southern edge of the meadows. Cars may be parked on the wide verge at the eastern end of the bridleway.
Species inc. Emperor Dragonfly, Broad-bodied Chaser, Common and Ruddy Darters.
ESSEX WILDLIFE TRUST

LOWER RAYPITS
near Southend-on-Sea
OS Map 168. TQ 923 948.
Saltmarsh, dykes, River Crouch estuary, pasture.
The pits lie on the southern banks of the River Crouch. Access is on foot from Canewdon village. Park in the village and follow public footpath north to pits.
Species inc. Scarce Emerald Damselfly.
ESSEX WILDLIFE TRUST

ROMAN RIVER VALLEY
near Colchester
OS Map 168. TL 975 211.
Stream, marsh, woodland.
Entrance on the west of B1026 Colchester to Layer-de-la-Haye road, just north of Kingsford Bridge. Bus services from Colchester to Layer and Maldon pass the entrance.
ESSEX WILDLIFE TRUST

WATERHALL MEADOWS
near Chelmsford
OS Map 167. TL 759 072.
Flood meadows, brook and pond.
Situated along minor roads between Chelmsford and Little Baddow. At the A414/A12 roundabout, take the road signed for Boreham (Hammonds Road). After c.1 mile, turn right into Hurrells Lane. Limited parking by the entrance and across the ford on the left. Enter reserve over stile on right before ford.
17 species recorded inc. White-legged Damselfly.
ESSEX WILDLIFE TRUST

WAT TYLER COUNTRY PARK
near Basildon
OS Map 178. TQ 745 873.
See main site section page 231.
Scrub, grassland, streams, ponds, alongside saltmarsh and tidal creeks.
Country park situated on the southern outskirts of Basildon.
Species inc. Scarce Emerald Damselfly, Southern Hawker, Emperor Dragonfly, Broad-bodied Chaser, Common Darter.
BASILDON DISTRICT COUNCIL

GLOUCESTERSHIRE

Gloucestershire Wildlife Trust
Conservation Centre, Robinswood
Hill Country Park, Reservoir Road,
Gloucester GL4 6SX
TEL 01452 383333
ESSEX info@gloucestershire
wildlifetrust.co.uk
WWW.GLOUCESTERSHIREWILDLIFETRUST.CO.UK

**The National Trust Regional Office:
Wessex**
Eastleigh Court, Bishopstrow,
Warminster, Wilts BA12 9HW
TEL 01985 843600

COOMBE HILL CANAL
near Tewkesbury
OS Map 162. SO 878 271.
Disused canal, grassland.
*Leave the A38 in Coombe Hill at the
crossroads, along track opposite A4019
turn. Park in Wharf car park (SO 885
272). Access via canal towpath. Access
meadow along footpath at SO 878 271;
remain on footpath to avoid disturbing
nesting birds. Part of Severn and Avon
Vales Wetlands Partnership.*
GLOUCESTERSHIRE WILDLIFE TRUST
WWW.SEVERNWETLANDS.ORG.UK

MAY HILL COMMON
near Gloucester
OS Map 162. SO 695 215.
Grassland, scrub, heath, ponds.
*Situated north of A40 midway between
Gloucester and Ross-on-Wye. Small
parking areas. Network of paths.*
Species inc. Common, Southern and
Migrant Hawkers.
NATIONAL TRUST

NAGSHEAD
near Chepstow
OS Map 162. SO 606 080.
See main site section page 193.
Deciduous woodland along River Wye
valley.
*Nagshead lies c.10 miles north-east of
Chepstow.*

Species inc. Beautiful Demoiselle,
White-legged and Large Red-eyed
Damselflies, Southern Hawker,
Emperor, Club-tailed and Golden-
ringed Dragonflies, Common Darter.
RSPB

SEVERN HAM
Tewkesbury
OS Map 150. SO 883 323.
Riverside meadow and oxbow lake.
*Access via Mill Street opposite abbey.
Parking and picnic sites.*
Species inc. Banded Demoiselle,
White-legged and Large Red-eyed
Damselflies, Brown Hawker.
TEWKESBURY BOROUGH COUNCIL

**WETLANDS CENTRE,
SLIMBRIDGE**
near Gloucester
OS Map 162. SO 723 048.
Saltmarsh, wet grassland, seasonally
flooded areas, lakes, ponds.
*WWT HQ. Off A38 south of Gloucester.
Follow brown signs from Junctions 13 or
J14 of M5. Open daily 9.30am–5pm. Visitor
centre, toilets, disabled access, café, shop.
Part of Severn and Avon Vales Wetlands
Partnership.*
Species inc. Hairy Dragonfly, Large
Red-eyed Damselfly, Small Red-eyed
Damselfly (recorded in 2006).
WILDFOWL & WETLANDS TRUST
WWW.WWT.ORG.UK

WHELFORD POOLS
near Cirencester
OS Map 163. SU 174 205.
Flooded gravel pits.
*Part of the Cotswold Water Park.
Between Lechlade and Fairford on the
A417, take the minor road south towards
Whelford. The entrance to the reserve is
c.1 mile down this road on the left. Leaflet
available from GWT.*
11 species breed inc. Large Red-eyed
Damselfly, Emperor Dragonfly,
Downy Emerald.
GLOUCESTERSHIRE WILDLIFE TRUST

GREATER LONDON

London Wildlife Trust
Skyline House, 200 Union Street,
London SE1 0LX
TEL 020 7261 0447
EMAIL enquiries@wildlondon.org.uk
WWW.WILDLONDON.ORG.UK

The National Trust Regional Office:
Thames & Solent
Hughenden Manor, High Wycombe,
Bucks HP14 4LA
TEL 01494 528051

BEDFONT LAKES COUNTRY PARK
near Hounslow
OS Map 176. TQ 084 729.
See main site section page 143.
Old gravel works, grassland, woodland.
Bedfont Lakes Country Park lies just east of Staines within the M25 ring.
Species include Emperor Dragonfly, Four-spotted Chaser, Black-tailed Skimmer, Common Darter.
HOUNSLOW LEISURE SERVICES

BRENT RESERVOIR
(WELSH HARP)
Brent
OS Map 176. TQ 216 874.
Reservoir, shallows, reeds, scrub.
Park in nearby streets off A5. Check the shallow area north of road causeway. Walking distance from Hendon station on the Thameslink line.
Over 12 species inc. Common Hawker, Emperor Dragonfly, Ruddy Darter.
WELSH HARP CONSERVATION GROUP
WWW.BRENTRES.COM

CAMLEY STREET NATURAL PARK
St Pancras
OS Map 176. TQ 299 834.
Canal, scrub, meadow, pond.
From Pancras Road turn right under the railway bridge into Good's Way. Turn left into Camley Street after c.100m. Open 10am–5pm (or dusk if earlier) Thursday–Sunday (all week during school holidays).

Visitor centre. Disabled parking only. Nearest tube station is King's Cross.
LONDON WILDLIFE TRUST

THE CHASE
Dagenham
OS Map 177. TQ 515 860.
Mixed wetland, grassland and scrub.
Located on the Dagenham Road, Rush Green. Within walking distance of Dagenham East tube station. Take the footpath adjacent to the Rhône-Poulenc Rorer site. Alternative entrance off Upper Rainham Road, Elm Park. Nearest tube stations are Dagenham East and Elm Park.
LONDON WILDLIFE TRUST

CRANE PARK ISLAND
Twickenham
OS Map 176. TQ 128 728.
River Crane, reedbed, woodland.
Crane Park lies between Great Chertsey Road and Hanworth Road. Access via Hanworth Road or Ellerman Avenue. Follow the path to the prominent Shot Tower (houses visitor centre) and cross the bridge to the reserve. Nearest railway station is Whitton.
LONDON WILDLIFE TRUST

CROXLEY COMMON MOOR
near Rickmansworth
OS Map 176. TQ 080 948.
Meadow, marsh.
Park in Croxley Green village. Cross the Grand Union Canal and River Gade (over bridge) to common, which is c.450m south-east of station. Nearest tube station is Croxley.
Over 12 species recorded inc. Banded Demoiselle, Migrant and Brown Hawkers.
THREE RIVERS DISTRICT COUNCIL

DENHAM LOCK WOOD
near Uxbridge
OS Map 176. TQ 056 660.
Wet woodland, fen, river.
Pedestrian access via Grand Union Canal, Denham Country Park, Denham Quarry Trail or Uxbridge Golf Course. Nearest

Gazetteer

railway stations are Addlestone and
Chertsey.
Species inc. Banded Demoiselle.
LONDON WILDLIFE TRUST

FRAYS ISLAND
near West Drayton
OS Map 176. TQ 053 792.
Alder and willow woodland between
Rivers Colne and Fray.
*Access via footpath from Thorney Mill
Road, West Drayton. Cross footbridges to
the island. Nearest railway station is West
Drayton.*
Species inc. Banded Demoiselle.
LONDON WILDLIFE TRUST

GILLESPIE PARK LNR
Islington
OS Map 176. TQ 315 862.
Scrub and grassland with pond.
*Adjacent to Arsenal tube station and the
old Highbury stadium. Nearest tube
stations are Arsenal, Finsbury Park and
Drayton Park.*
Over 12 species inc. White-legged
Damselfly, Emperor Dragonfly,
Ruddy Darter.
LONDON BOROUGH OF ISLINGTON

HAMPSTEAD HEATH
near Camden
OS Map 176. TQ 270 865.
Heath, grassland, woodland, ponds.
*A large public open space with a number of
car parks (charges) serve the Heath (see
website below), or park in nearby streets.
Nearest tube station is Hampstead.*
Over 12 species inc. White-legged
Damselfly, Emperor and Golden-
ringed Dragonflies, Ruddy Darter.
CITY OF LONDON
WWW.CITYOFLONDON.GOV.UK

LONDON WETLAND CENTRE
near Barnes
OS Map 176. TQ 770 230.
Wetland created from reclaimed
reservoirs alongside River Thames.
*Take the Roehampton exit to Barnes from
the South Circular, and turn right off*

Rocks Lane by the Red Lion Pub into
Queen Elizabeth's Walk. Visitor centre,
café, WWT shop, disabled access.
Admission charges for non-WWT
members. Open 9.30am–6pm (last
admission 5pm) during the summer (tel.
020 8409 440). Nearest tube station is
Hammersmith; the Duck Bus from
Hammersmith bus station stops in the
centre.
Species inc. Emperor Dragonfly, Four-
spotted Chaser.
WILDFOWL & WETLANDS TRUST
WWW.WWT.ORG.UK

MORDEN HALL PARK
near Morden
OS Map 176. TQ 259 687.
River Wandle, grassland, woodland,
fen.
*Situated east of the A24 Morden road and
A297 Morden Hall road. Car park, NT shop
and café. Riverside walks. Nearest tube
station is Morden.*
NATIONAL TRUST

RICHMOND PARK NNR
near Richmond upon Thames
OS Map 176. TQ 200 730.
Parkland, woodland, ponds, stream.
*Café, refreshment stands, toilets, disabled
access. Numerous car parks around the
park perimeter (charges and all within the
congestion charge zone). Nearest tube
station is Richmond.*
THE ROYAL PARKS
WWW.ROYALPARKS.GOV.UK

ROWLEY GREEN COMMON LNR
near Barnet
OS Map 176. TQ 216 962.
Woodland, grassland, ponds, bog.
*Leave A1 to the east of Borehamwood and
head south-eastwards along the minor road
(Rowley Lane) towards Arkley. Park in the
lay-by on the right opposite the reserve
entrance. Nearest railway station is Elstree
& Borehamwood.*
LONDON BOROUGH COUNCIL, LONDON
WILDLIFE TRUST, HERTS & MIDDLESEX
WILDLIFE TRUST

WIMBLEDON AND PUTNEY COMMONS
near Wandsworth
OS Map 176. TQ 225 720.
Heathland, bog, woodland.
Information centre open 9am–5pm
daily next to Ranger's Office in
Windmill Road.
Park in nearby streets.
Species inc. Brown Hawker, Ruddy
and Black Darters.
WIMBLEDON & PUTNEY COMMONS
CONSERVATORS
WWW.WPCC.ORG.UK / INSECTS.HTM

GREATER MANCHESTER

**The Wildlife Trust for Lancashire,
Manchester & North Merseyside
(WTLMNM)**
The Barn, Berkeley Drive, Bamber
Bridge, Preston, Lancs PR5 6BY
TEL 01772 324129
EMAIL info@lancswt.org.uk
WWW.LANCSWT.ORG.UK

**The National Trust Regional Office:
North West**
The Hollens, Grasmere, Ambleside,
Cumbria LA22 9QZ
TEL 0870 609 5391

DAISY NOOK COUNTRY PARK
Ashton-under-Lyne
OS Map 109. SD 921 009.
Canal, river, lake.
*Car park at Crime Lake (off Cutler Hill
Road) off A627. Visitor centre, café, toilets,
disabled access.*
Species inc. Brown Hawker.
OLDHAM METROPOLITAN BOROUGH COUNCIL,
NATIONAL TRUST

HAIGH HALL COUNTRY PARK
near Wigan
OS Map 108. SD 595 085.
Canal, parkland.
Parking off B5238 (signed). Parking, toilets,
disabled access, information.
Species inc. Brown Hawker.
WIGAN LEISURE AND CULTURE TRUST
WWW.WLCT.ORG

PENNINGTON FLASH COUNTRY PARK
Leigh
OS Map 109. SJ 640 990.
Large lake (The Flash), ponds, marsh,
canal, carr, scrub and meadows.
*Well signed from all directions. Car park
(pay & display) and visitor centre off
A572. Well-maintained paths.*
WIGAN LEISURE AND CULTURE TRUST
WWW.WLCT.ORG

SANKEY VALLEY COUNTRY PARK
St Helens
OS Map 108. SJ 535 956.
Ponds, marsh, disused canal and
woodland.
*This 7-mile linear park lies north of the
A572, between Newton-le-Willows and
Carr Mill Dam, St Helens. The visitor
centre (open 12–2pm) is off Blackbrook
Road (A58), Blackbrook, St Helens, at the
side of the Ship Inn. Car park at SJ 535
956, behind the pub. Alternative parking at
Carr Mill Dam and at Waterways (off
Cromwell Avenue) – from A72, take A574
north and Waterways is east of the first
roundabout). Laffak Pond is well worth a
visit with 12 species recorded.*
Species inc. Banded Demoiselle, Ruddy
and Black Darters.
WARRINGTON BOROUGH COUNCIL
WWW.WARRINGTON.GOV.UK

WIGAN FLASHES
Wigan
OS Map 108. SD 585 030.
See main site section page 237.
Pools, canal, fen, scrub.
*These flashes are situated on the southern
outskirts of Wigan.*
Species inc. Emerald and Large Red
Damselflies, Brown Hawker, Four-
spotted and Broad-bodied Chasers.
WTLMNM

Gazetteer

HAMPSHIRE

Hampshire & Isle of Wight Wildlife Trust
Beechcroft House, Vicarage Lane,
Curdridge SO32 2DP
TEL 01489 774400
EMAIL feedback@hwt.org.uk
WWW.HWT.ORG.UK

The National Trust Regional Office: Thames & Solent
Hughenden Manor, High Wycombe,
Bucks HP14 4LA
TEL 01494 528051

County atlas/ book
The Dragonflies of Hampshire. John
Taverner, 2004, Pisces Publications.

Websites
Dragonflies of North East Hampshire
and Surrey Borders
HTTP://WEBSITE.LINEONE.NET/
~DRAGONFLIES.DELLS

ALICE HOLT WOODLAND PARK
near Farnham
OS Map 186. TQ 809 417.
Mixed woodland, ponds, lake.
Visitor centre and parking (charge) signed from A325 south of Farnham. Waymarked trails. Centre open weekends and during school holidays. Disabled access.
Species inc. Downy Emerald.
FOREST ENTERPRISE
WWW.FORESTRY.GOV.UK

ANCELLS FARM
Fleet
OS Map 186. SU 824 557.
Wet heath.
Turn north off B3014 at the roundabout into Ancells Road and reserve is on right immediately beyond Hanover Drive. Park on right on the slope down to the reserve entrance, opposite the playing fields. Boardwalk leads to platform by the pond.
Species inc. Emerald and Small Red Damselflies, Common Hawker.
HAMPSHIRE & IOW WILDLIFE TRUST

BADDESLEY COMMON & EMER BOG
near Southampton
OS Map 185. SU 395 214.
Bog, heath, grassland.
Turn north off the A27 at the traffic lights in North Baddesley. After c.0.5 mile take the left fork towards Ampfield, then the left turn at Gosport, along Green Lane towards Crampmoor. Limited parking along lane. Keep to footpaths. Boardwalk around Emer Bog.
Over 15 species recorded.
HAMPSHIRE & IOW WILDLIFE TRUST

BARTLEY HEATH
near Fleet
OS Map 186. SU 730 534.
Heath, grassland, woodland.
The area surrounds Junction 5 of the M3 immediately south of Hook. Leave the M3 at Junction 5 and take the B3349 towards Hook. The entrance and car park are on the right after c.250m.
Over 17 species recorded inc. Beautiful Demoiselle, Common Hawker, Ruddy and Black Darters.
HAMPSHIRE & IOW WILDLIFE TRUST

BASINGSTOKE CANAL FLASHES
near Fleet
OS Map 186. SU 841 526.
Canal, shallow ponds.
East of Fleet off A323. For Eelmoor Flash, park by Eelmoor Bridge and view from towpath. For Claycart Flash and Rushmoor Flash continue on the A323 and park in the sandy car park on the left. Claycart Flash is west of the car park and Rushmoor Flash is through the wooded area to the east.
Over 20 species inc. Hairy Dragonfly, Brilliant Emerald, Ruddy Darter.
HAMPSHIRE & IOW WILDLIFE TRUST

BEAULIEU ROAD STATION
New Forest, near Lyndhurst
OS Map 196. SU 346 064.
See main site section page 194.
Wet and dry heath, woodland, scrub, ponds and streams.

This site lies within the New Forest c.3 miles south-east of Lyndhurst.
Species inc. Large Red Damselfly, Keeled Skimmer.
NEW FOREST NATIONAL PARK

BLACKDAM
Basingstoke
OS Map 186. SU 654 516.
Overgrown ponds, grassland, scrub.
Adjacent to Junction 6 of M3. From the Blackdam roundabout follow signs for Blackdam and car park at SU 661 518. Access reserve via underpass.
BASINGSTOKE & DEANE BOROUGH COUNCIL,
HAMPSHIRE & IOW WILDLIFE TRUST

BLACK GUTTER BOTTOM
near Fordingbridge
OS Map 184. SU 200 160.
Boggy heathland.
Access from car parks at SU 186 157 (Stone Quarry Bottom) and SU 206 164 (Deadman Hill). Follow tracks/paths.
NEW FOREST NATIONAL PARK

BLACK WATER
near Lyndhurst
OS Map 195. SU 260 050.
See main site section page 196.
Heath, woodland, streams.
This site lies c.6 miles east of Ringwood.
NEW FOREST NATIONAL PARK

BLASHFORD LAKES
Ringwood
OS Map 195. SU 155 175.
Lakes, grassland, scrub, woodland.
From Ringwood, take the A338 for 2 miles towards Salisbury. Continue past Ivy Lane on the right and take the next right (Ellingham Drove) to Linwood. The car park and study centre are accessed via the next right turn. Access is by public footpaths.
20 species recorded inc. Beautiful Demoiselle, Large Red-eyed Damselfly, Brown Hawker, Downy Emerald.
HAMPSHIRE & IOW WILDLIFE TRUST

BRAMSHAW COMMONS
near Southampton
OS Maps 184/185. SU 297 176.
Lowland wet and dry heath.
This area of common land is situated just south of the A36 Salisbury to Southampton road, between the villages of Cadnam, Bramshaw and Plaitford. Car park with information boards at Black Hill.
Species inc. Scarce Blue-tailed Damselfly.
NATIONAL TRUST

CHILBOLTON COMMON
near Andover
OS Map 185. SU 391 402.
Wet meadow bordering River Test.
Parking in Chilbolton and Wherwell.
CHILBOLTON PARISH COUNCIL
WWW.HANTS.ORG.UK

COMMON MARSH
near Stockbridge
OS Map 185. SU 354 341.
Water meadow by River Test.
Cark park at SU 357 346 off minor road south of the A3057/B3049 roundabout south of Stockbridge.
NATIONAL TRUST

CROCKFORD BRIDGE
near Lyndhurst
OS Map 196. SZ 351 990.
See main site section page 194.
Stony-bottomed medium flowing stream fringed by boggy heathland.
The site lies c.6 miles east of the A337 Lyndhurst to Lymington road.
Species inc. Beautiful Demoiselle, Southern Damselfly, Keeled Skimmer.
PART OF THE NEW FOREST NATIONAL PARK

EYEWORTH POND
near Fordingbridge
OS Map 195. SU 229 148.
Forest pond.
Leave the M27 at Junction 1 north along the B3078 towards Fordingbridge. After c.3 miles, take the minor road south to Fritham. Pond and car park are near Eyeworth Lodge immediately north-west of

village at SU 229 145.
Species inc. Large Red-eyed Damselfly,
Downy Emerald.
<small>PART OF THE NEW FOREST NATIONAL PARK</small>

FLEET POND
near Farnborough
OS Map 186. SU 820 550.
Large lake, reedbeds, woodland,
heathland.
*Parking at Fleet station or in minor roads
around pond. Access by numerous paths.*
<small>HART DISTRICT COUNCIL</small>
<small>WWW.HART.GOV.UK</small>
<small>FLEET POND SOCIETY</small>
<small>WWW.FLEETPOND.FCCS.ORG.UK</small>

HALE PURLIEU
near Fordingbridge
OS Map 184. SU 200 180.
Heathland, ponds, streams.
*The site is c.3 miles north of Fordingbridge
and is accessed via the B3080. Car park at
Lady's Mile. Footpaths cross the site.*
Species inc. Black Darter.
<small>NATIONAL TRUST</small>

HATCHET MOOR & POND
near Lyndhurst
OS map 196. SU 365 012.
See main site section page 194.
Open lake and ponds fed by medium-
flowing stony-bottomed stream
adjacent to boggy heathland.
*This site lies within the New Forest c.4
miles south-east of Lyndhurst.*
Species inc. Large Red, Small Red,
Large Red-eyed and Scarce Blue-tailed
Damselflies, Emperor Dragonfly,
Keeled Skimmer.
<small>PART OF THE NEW FOREST NATIONAL PARK</small>

ITCHEN VALLEY COUNTRY PARK
Southampton
OS Maps 185/196. SU 446 164.
River Itchen, stream, grassland, scrub.
*From Junctions 5 or 7 of the M27, follow
the brown tourist signs to the park via the
A27 (towards West End). Parking (charge)
at country park visitor centre at SU 459*

160. *Café (closed Monday and Tuesday,
except in school holidays), waymarked
trails. The park is open 8.30am–9.30pm in
the summer.*
Species inc. Banded Demoiselle,
Southern Damselfly, Hairy and
Golden-ringed Dragonflies.
<small>EASTLEIGH BOROUGH COUNCIL</small>

LATCHMORE BOTTOM
New Forest, near Ringwood
OS Map 195. SU 185 125.
See main site section page 196.
Wet and dry heathland.
*This site lies c.4 miles north-east of
Ringwood.*
Species inc. Beautiful Demoiselle,
Small Red, Southern and Scarce Blue-
tailed Damselflies, Golden-ringed
Dragonfly, Keeled Skimmer.
<small>NEW FOREST NATIONAL PARK</small>

MILL LAWN BROOK
Burley, near Ringwood
OS Map 195. SU 223 033.
See main site section page 196.
Stream, seepages, wet and dry heath.
*This site lies c.3 miles south-east of
Ringwood.*
Species inc. Small Red, Southern and
Scarce Blue-tailed Damselflies.
<small>NEW FOREST NATIONAL PARK</small>

OBER WATER
near Lyndhurst
OS Map 195. SU 270 029.
See main site section page 196.
Stream, wet and dry heath, woodland.
This site lies c.6 miles east of Ringwood.
Species inc. White-legged Damselfly,
Keeled Skimmer.
<small>NEW FOREST NATIONAL PARK</small>

ROYDON WOODS
near Brockenhurst
OS Map 196. SU 315 009.
Woodland, scrub, grassland, heath,
adjacent to Lymington River.
*Situated c.1 mile south-east of
Brockenhurst. Several parking areas along
and just off A337 immediately south of
railway station.*

Species inc. Beautiful Demoiselle, Broad-bodied Chaser.
HAMPSHIRE & IOW WILDLIFE TRUST

SHORTHEATH COMMON
near Alton
OS Map 186. SU 775 369 (car park).
Ponds, floating bog.
From A325 take the B3004 west towards Alton, through Kingsley and turn left towards Oakhanger. Take the third entrance on the left for the car park.
Species inc. Downy Emerald.
HAMPSHIRE COUNTY COUNCIL
WWW.HANTS.GOV.UK

SWANWICK NATURE RESERVE
Southampton
OS Map 196. SU 507 099.
See main site section page 220.
Woodland, scrub, grassland, lakes.
The reserve lies between Southampton and Fareham.
Over 12 species recorded inc. Downy Emerald, Broad-bodied Chaser, Black-tailed Skimmer.
HAMPSHIRE & IOW WILDLIFE TRUST

WINNAL MOORS
Winchester
OS Map 185. SU 490 306.
Water meadows, river, reedbeds.
Within 0.5 mile of Winchester city centre. From North Walls Road, take the first left into Hyde Abbey Road and then turn right into Gordon Road. Park in car park at leisure centre. Alternative entrance on foot via Durngate Place at the end of North Walls Road. (near the police station). Open access to southern part of the reserve but permit required for northern part.
Species inc. Broad-bodied Chaser, Common Darter.
HAMPSHIRE & IOW WILDLIFE TRUST

YATELEY COMMON
near Farnborough
OS Map 175. SU 830 590.
Heath, woodland, grassland, ponds.
The common lies immediately south-east of Yateley. Several car parks in area, including at the country park. Network of bridleways and paths.
Species inc. Large Red-eyed Damselfly, Downy Emerald, Keeled Skimmer, Black Darter.
HAMPSHIRE COUNTY COUNCIL
WWW.BLACKWATER-VALLEY.ORG.UK

HEREFORDSHIRE

Herefordshire Nature Trust
Lower House Farm, Ledbury Road, Tupsley, Hereford HR1 1UT
TEL 01432 356872
EMAIL enquiries@herefordshirewt.co.uk
WWW.WILDLIFETRUST.ORG.UK / HEREFORD

The National Trust Regional Office: West Midlands
Attingham Park, Shrewsbury, Shropshire SY4 4TP
TEL 01743 708100

County atlas / book
The Dragonflies of Herefordshire. Peter Garner, 2005, Herefordshire Biological Records Centre.

CROW WOOD & MEADOW
near Hay-on-Wye
OS Map 149. SO 340 350.
Woodland, meadow, fast-flowing brook.
Leave the B4348 (between Hay-on-Wye and Hereford) between Peterchurch and Vowchurch along the minor road signed for Turnastone and Michaelchurch Escley. Park on roadside around Lower Slough (Slough Bridge and cottages) and go through the gate on the north side of the road and follow field edge to your left to the footbridge to the reserve.
HEREFORDSHIRE NATURE TRUST

LUGG MEADOW
Hereford
OS Map 149. SO 527 411.
See main site section page 192.
Riverside meadows.

Gazetteer

The reserve is situated on the eastern outskirts of Hereford.
Species inc. Banded Demoiselle, Club-tailed Dragonfly.
HEREFORDSHIRE NATURE TRUST

QUEBB CORNER MEADOW
near Kington
OS Map 148. SO 302 520.
Grassland, streams.
Leave Kington south along A4111. Park in the lay-by by the road junction with the minor road to Quebb. Walk down the lane towards Quebb for c.150m to the gate on the right. Please keep to field edges.
HEREFORDSHIRE NATURE TRUST

RIVER WYE, CAPLER WOOD
near Hereford
OS Map 149. SO 588 326.
River skirted by woodland.
Park in Fownhope and follow footpath along river towards Brockhampton. Return route to Fownhope along minor road north of wood.
Species inc. Banded Demoiselle, White-legged Damselfly, Club-tailed Dragonfly.

STOCKINGS MEADOW
Bromyard
OS Map 149. SO 633 546.
Grassland, stream.
Take the A44 west from Worcester, through Bromyard and, after c.1 mile, take the lane on your left (to The Green and Green Lane Cottages). Park along the lane beyond the gate on your right and walk back and enter meadow through gate. Please keep to field edges.
HEREFORDSHIRE NATURE TRUST

HERTFORDSHIRE

Hertfordshire & Middlesex Wildlife Trust
Grebe House, St Michael's Street, St Albans, Hertfordshire AL3 4SN
TEL 01727 858901
EMAIL info@hmwt.org
WWW.WILDLIFETRUST.ORG.UK/HERTS

The National Trust Regional Office: Thames & Solent
Hughenden Manor, High Wycombe, Bucks HP14 4LA
TEL 01494 528051

The National Trust Regional Office: East of England
Westley Bottom, Bury St Edmunds, Suffolk IP33 3WD
TEL 01284 747500

Websites
Hertfordshire Dragonfly Group
WWW.GEOCITIES.COM/HERTSDRAGONFLIES

BALLS WOOD
near Hertford
OS Map 166. TL 345 105.
Woodland.
Leave Hertford south along the B1197 to Hertford Heath. In village, turn right into Roundlings Road. Limited parking along road. Walk to the bottom of the road and turn right along the unsurfaced section of Ermine Street (Roman road). Entrance to the reserve by the Forest Enterprise sign.
HERTS & MIDDLESEX WILDLIFE TRUST

BROAD COLNEY LAKES
near St Albans
OS Map 166. TL 177 034.
Gravel pits, wet woodland, grassland.
Leave the A414 south of St Albans along the B5378 towards Shenley (Shenley Lane). Car park just south of St Annes Road by the British Legion huts.
HERTS & MIDDLESEX WILDLIFE TRUST

BROXBOURNE WOOD NNR
near Hertford
OS Map 166. TL 327 072.
Woodland, streams.
From Hertford follow signs to Brickendon. Parking at TL 329 070.
Species inc. Large Red Damselfly, Southern Hawker, Emperor Dragonfly, Broad-bodied Chaser.
COUNTRYSIDE MANAGEMENT SERVICE, HERTFORDSHIRE COUNTY COUNCIL
WWW.HERTSDIRECT.ORG

FIR WOOD AND POND WOOD
near Potters Bar
OS Map 166. TL 277 012.
Woodland, meadow, wetland.
From Potters Bar, take the B156 towards Cuffley. On the outskirts of Potters Bar, turn right down Coopers Lane Road and park in lay-by on right after c.0.75 mile opposite Oshwal Centre and reserve entrance.
HERTS & MIDDLESEX WILDLIFE TRUST

FROGMORE MEADOW
near Chorleywood
OS Map 176. TQ 022 988.
Marsh with flower-rich meadow.
Take A404 from Chorleywood north-west through Chenies and then the minor road right into Doddsmill Lane towards Flaunden. At Mill Farm park carefully along the roadside. Follow the footpath across fields to Limeshill Wood and bear right, through gate to reserve.
Species inc. Banded Demoiselle, Brown Hawker.
HERTS & MIDDLESEX WILDLIFE TRUST

HERTFORD HEATH
near Hertford
OS Map 166. TL 350 106 & TL 354 111.
Heathland, ponds, woodland.
Leave Hertford south along the B1197 to Hertford Heath. In village turn right into Roundlings Road. Limited parking along road. The other end of the reserve is at the end of Heath Lane opposite the East India College Arms pub.
Over 18 species recorded inc. Banded Demoiselle, Brown Hawker, Ruddy Darter.
HERTS & MIDDLESEX WILDLIFE TRUST

HUNSDON MEAD
Unimproved grassland by River Stort.
See entry under Essex
HERTFORDSHIRE & MIDDLESEX WILDLIFE TRUST, ESSEX WILDLIFE TRUST

OLD PARK WOOD
near Rickmansworth
OS Map 176. TQ 049 913.
Woodland and pond.

From Harefield village (south of Rickmansworth) take the Rickmansworth road, turn left into Hill End Road and left through Harefield Hospital gates. Keep to the right around the hospital to the parking area (charge). Follow the trail marks through gate and around field edge to wood.
HERTS & MIDDLESEX WILDLIFE TRUST

OUGHTON HEAD COMMON
near Hitchin
OS Map 166. TL 166 304.
River, marsh.
Park at Westmill on north-west outskirts of Hitchin and follow footpath on south bank of Oughton Head.
HERTS & MIDDLESEX WILDLIFE TRUST

PATMORE HEATH
near Bishop's Stortford
OS Map 167. TL 443 257.
Heathland.
Leave Bishop's Stortford west along the A120 to Little Hadham then head north along minor road towards Furneux Pelham. At Gravesend, turn right at Catherine Wheel public house to reserve. Parking down side of common.
HERTS & MIDDLESEX WILDLIFE TRUST

PURWELL NINESPRINGS
near Hitchin
OS Map 166. TL 206 293.
Wetland, meadow, woodland.
East of Hitchin turn south-east off A505 down Purwell Lane. Park at junction with Kingswood Avenue. Follow path along Gypsy Lane to reserve.
HERTS & MIDDLESEX WILDLIFE TRUST

RYE MEADS
near Hoddesdon
OS Map 166. TL 387 106.
Flood meadows, reedbed.
In Hoddesdon take Rye Road past Rye House railway station. Follow signs to Rye Meads Visitor Centre. Car park on left beyond bridge.
Over 20 species recorded.
HERTS & MIDDLESEX WILDLIFE TRUST

SAWBRIDGEWORTH MARSH
near Bishop's Stortford
OS Map 167. TL 493 158.
Marsh.
From Bishop's Stortford take the A1184 south to Sawbridgeworth then the minor road east towards Hatfield Heath. Just after the railway crossing, turn left towards Little Hallingbury. Park in lay-bys c.200m north of reserve entrance.
HERTS & MIDDLESEX WILDLIFE TRUST

SPRINGWELL REEDBED
near Rickmansworth
OS Map 176. TQ 041 925.
Reedbed, open water.
Leave the A412 in Rickmansworth south along Springwell Lane to car park just before Grand Union Canal. Walk south along canal towpath to view the reedbed.
HERTS & MIDDLESEX WILDLIFE TRUST

STANBOROUGH REED MARSH
near Welwyn Garden City
OS Map 166. TL 230 105.
Reedbed, pond.
From Junction 4 of the A1M take the A6129 (Stanborough Road) north to a roundabout. Take A1000 towards Welwyn Garden City, past Stanborough Lakes to next roundabout. Do a U-turn here and then turn left into Stanborough Lakes car park. Take the footpath between the river and the lake to the reserve.
HERTS & MIDDLESEX WILDLIFE TRUST

STOCKER'S LAKE
near Rickmansworth
OS Map 176. TQ 041 925.
Gravel pit, scrub, reeds.
Reserve entrance and parking via Bury Lake Aquadrome or leave the A412 in Rickmansworth south along Springwell Lane. Car park before Grand Union Canal. Second car park further south along lane.
HERTS & MIDDLESEX WILDLIFE TRUST

TARLETONS LAKE
near Ruislip
OS Map 176. TQ 065 894.
Lake, woodland.

Park at Bayhurst Wood Country Park, which is north-west of Ruislip off the A4180 and B467. Follow the edge of the wood from the car park, north-westwards to the reserve.
HERTS & MIDDLESEX WILDLIFE TRUST

TRING RESERVOIRS
near Tring
OS Map 165. SP 905 130 (Wilstone Res).
Reservoirs, canals (active and disused), meadows, scrub, woodland.
Parking at SP 903 134 (Wilstone Reservoir) or SP 919 140 (Startops, Marsworth and Tringford Reservoirs).
Over 20 species inc. Migrant Hawker, Black-tailed Skimmer.
BRITISH WATERWAYS BOARD, NATURAL ENGLAND, FRIENDS OF TRING RESERVOIRS
WWW.WATERSCAPE.COM
WWW.FOTR.ORG.UK

ISLE OF WIGHT

Hampshire & Isle of Wight Wildlife Trust
Beechcroft House, Vicarage Lane, Curdridge, Hants SO32 2DP
TEL 01489 774400
EMAIL feedback@hwt.org.uk
WWW.HWT.ORG.UK

Wight Wildlife
The Forest Office, Parkhurst Forest, Newport, Isle of Wight PO30 5UL
TEL 01983 533180

The National Trust Regional Office: Thames & Solent
Hughenden Manor, High Wycombe, Buckinghamshire HP14 4LA
TEL 01494 528051

AFTON MARSH LNR
Freshwater
OS Map 196. SZ 346 858–SZ 344 868.
Reedbeds, scrub, marsh, river.
Situated along the western edge of the A3055 between Freshwater village and Freshwater Bay. Parking in Freshwater

Bay car park at SZ 346 858. Follow footpath behind Sandpipers Hotel. Nature trail. Leaflet available from Isle of Wight Tourist Information shops.
Species inc. Southern Hawker, Emperor and Golden-ringed Dragonflies, Broad-bodied Chaser.
ISLE OF WIGHT COUNCIL
WWW.IWIGHT.COM

ALVERSTONE MEAD LNR
near Sandown
OS Map 196. SZ 577 854 (start of nature trail).
Wet meadows, river, carr and deciduous woodland.
From Alverstone village head south along the Alverstone Road. Pass over the river bridge and after c.100m take the public footpath (NC17) on the left. Nature trail leaflet available from Isle of Wight Tourist Information shops.
Species inc. Banded Demoiselle, Southern Hawker, Golden-ringed Dragonfly, Ruddy Darter.
ISLE OF WIGHT COUNCIL
WIGHT NATURE FUND
WWW.IWIGHT.COM

BRIGHSTONE MILL
Brighstone
OS Map 196. SZ 426 823.
Ponds, stream.
Park near the church in the centre of Brighstone village. Head south into New Road. Halfway down the road take the public footpath on your left. Follow the footpath until reaching Mill Lane and the millpond. Leaflet for the Brighstone Trail, which incorporates Brighstone Mill, is available from village shop.
Species inc. Banded Demoiselle, Broad-bodied Chaser.

KENT

Kent Wildlife Trust
Tyland Barn, Sandling, Maidstone
ME14 3BD
TEL 01622 662012
EMAIL info@kentwildlife.org.uk
WWW.KENTWILDLIFETRUST.ORG.UK

The National Trust Regional Office: South East
Polesden Lacey, Dorking, Surrey
RH5 6BD
TEL 01372 453401

BEDGEBURY FOREST
near Tunbridge Wells
OS Map 188. TQ 730 330.
Coniferous forest, ponds, clearings.
Access off Lady Oak Lane (B2079) north of A21. Park at Bedgebury Pinetum at TQ 715 335. Visitor centre, toilets, disabled access, trails, refreshments.
Species inc. White-legged and Large Red Damselflies, Brown Hawker, Golden-ringed Dragonfly, Downy Emerald, Four-spotted Chaser.
FOREST ENTERPRISE

BOUGH BEECH CENTRE AND NATURE RESERVE
near Sevenoaks
OS Map 188. TQ 496 489.
Pond, reservoir, woodland, farmland.
Follow the 'brown duck' signs from the B2042 south of Idle Hill or from the B2027 east of Bough Beech village. Oast House Visitor Centre north of Bough Beech Reservoir, open April to end of October, Wednesdays, weekends and Bank Holiday Mondays, 11am–4.30pm. Shop, light refreshments. Access to the main part of the reserve is by permit (charge) and for recording and study only.
KENT WILDLIFE TRUST

CLIFFE POOLS
near Rochester
OS Map 178. TQ 722 771.
Pools, dykes, marsh.
North of Rochester take the B2000 north off

the A289 to Cliffe. Park carefully in village or at bottom of Pond Hill through bollards (not on Pond Hill itself). Keep to footpaths.
Over 15 species recorded.
RSPB

DUNGENESS
near Lydd
OS Map 189. TR 088 170.
Shingle area, scrub, pools.
Take the A259 to New Romney. Parking at lighthouse, bird observatory and RSPB reserve.
Residents inc. Large Red-eyed Damselfly, Hairy and Emperor Dragonflies. Good for migrant species inc. Lesser Emperor, Yellow-winged and Red-veined Darters.
DUNGENESS BIRD OBSERVATORY, RSPB
WWW.DUNGENESSBIRDOBS.ORG.UK

EASTCOURT MEADOWS COUNTRY PARK
Gillingham
OS Map 178. TQ 808 682.
Coastal saltmarsh and mudflats with meadows, chalk pit and ponds.
Car park off B2004 (signed).
MEDWAY COUNCIL

ELMLEY MARSHES
near Sittingbourne
OS Map 178. TQ 935 675.
Marsh with dykes and scrapes.
Signed off A249 on Isle of Sheppey. Take track for c.1.5 miles and park at information centre/farm at TQ 938 679.
Over 10 species recorded.
RSPB

HOTHFIELD COMMON
near Ashford
OS Map 189. TQ 970 457.
See main site section page 180.
Boggy heathland with woodland.
Lies midway between Ashford and Charing along the side of the A20.
Species inc. Keeled Skimmer.
KENT WILDLIFE TRUST

SCOTNEY CASTLE ESTATE
near Tunbridge Wells
OS Map 188. TQ 688 353.
Ponds, River Bewl, parkland, woodland.
The estate lies c.1 mile south-east of Lamberhurst, east of the A21. Public footpaths cross the estate. Information board and map in the car park.
Species inc. Brilliant Emerald.
NATIONAL TRUST

SHORNE WOOD COUNTRY PARK
near Gravesend
OS Map 188. TQ 684 699.
Woodland, meadows, ponds.
The wood lies immediately north of the A2 Gravesend to Rochester road. Leave the A2 at the exit for Shorne. Access to the wood is on this road. Car park (charge). Visitor centre, café and toilets.
KENT DOWNS AONB
KENT COUNTY COUNCIL
WWW.KENT.GOV.UK

STODMARSH NNR
near Canterbury
OS Map 179. TR 220 609.
Lakes, dykes, reedbeds, pools and grazing marsh.
The reserve lies east of Stodmarsh village and c.500m from the A28 Canterbury to Thanet road. Natural England car park in Stodmarsh village. Leaflets available. Information boards. Nature trail.
Over 15 species recorded.
NATURAL ENGLAND

TYLAND BARN
near Maidstone
OS Map 188. TQ 754 592.
Pond, nature park.
Kent's Wildlife Conservation Centre. Café, shop and information on other places to visit. Open Monday–Friday 10am–5pm, weekends 11am–4pm. The site lies c.4 miles north of Maidstone. Follow 'brown duck' signs on the A229 Maidstone to Chatham road, between Junction 3 of the M2 and Junction 6 of the M20.
KENT WILDLIFE TRUST

LANCASHIRE
including Merseyside

The Wildlife Trust for Lancashire, Manchester & North Merseyside (WTLMNM)
The Barn, Berkeley Drive, Bamber Bridge, Preston PR5 6BY
TEL 01772 324129
EMAIL info@lancswt.org.uk
WWW.LANCSWT.ORG.UK

The National Trust Regional Office: North West
The Hollens, Grasmere, Ambleside, Cumbria LA22 9QZ
TEL 0870 609 5391

Websites
Dragonflies of Lancashire and North Merseyside
WWW.LACFS.ORG.UK/DRAGONFLIES.HTM
Wildlife of Rochdale
WWW.WILDLIFEOFROCHDALE.CO.UK/DRAGONFLIES.HTM

ARLEY LODGE, WORTHINGTON LAKES
near Wigan
OS Map 108. SD 585 112.
Lakes, streams, grassland, scrub.
Park in the Worthington Lakes car park off A5106 in Standish. Arley Lodge is the northernmost reservoir at Worthington Lakes. Keep to footpaths. Permit required from LMNMWT for some areas.
Species inc. Emerald Damselfly, Common and Brown Hawkers.
WTLMNM

BROCK VALLEY
near Garstang
OS Map 102. SD 560 440 (parking).
See main site section page 146.
Upland, river, marsh, woodland.
The Brock Valley lies c.7 miles north-east of Preston.
Species inc. Common Hawker, Golden-ringed Dragonfly.
WTLMNM

CUERDEN VALLEY COUNTRY PARK
near Preston
OS Map 102. SD 565 238.
Lake, river (Lostock), marsh, grassland, scrub.
The reserve is off the A6 north-east of Leyland (and just off Junction 29 of M6 and Junction 1 of M65). Car parks well signed. Visitor centre, trails, disabled access.
Species inc. Banded Demoiselle.
LANCASHIRE COUNTY COUNCIL, WTLMNM, THE CUERDEN VALLEY PARK TRUST
WWW.CUERDENVALLEYPARK.ORG.UK

FOXHILL BANK
Oswaldtwistle
OS Map 103. SD 740 278.
Lakes, stream, woodland, scrub.
In Oswaldtwistle limited parking and access at bottom of Mill Hill, which is off the main road (Union Road) opposite war memorial and down the side of the fire station.
WTLMNM

HEYSHAM NATURE RESERVE
near Morecambe
OS Maps 97/102. SD 407 401.
Grassland, scrub, marsh, pools.
Open 10am–6pm. At the A683/A589 junction south of Heysham, take A589 west towards Port of Heysham. After c.0.5 mile, turn left at traffic lights down Moneyclose Lane. Entrance is on the right after c.200m.
Species inc. Emerald Damselfly, Emperor Dragonfly, Ruddy Darter.
WTLMNM

LONGWORTH CLOUGH
near Bolton
OS Map 109. SD 695 102.
Wetland, woodland, grassland.
Access off Longworth Road in Egerton.
Ten species recorded.
WTLMNM

LORD'S LOT BOG
near Carnforth
OS Map 97. SD 546 705.
See main site section page 190.
Sphagnum bog, mixed woodland.

This site is c.3 miles east of Carnforth.
Species inc. Common Hawker, Black
Darter.
WTLMNM, FOREST ENTERPRISE

LUNSFIELD QUARRY
near Carnforth
OS Map 97. SD 510 680.
Pool, carr.
Park along minor road west of Nether Kellet
(east of M6). Follow public footpaths.
Species inc. Emerald, Large Red and
Azure Damselflies, Black Darter.
LANCASTER CITY COUNCIL

MERE SANDS WOOD
near Ormskirk
OS Map 108. SD 447 157.
Woodland, lakes.
Car park off B5246 c.0.5 mile west of
Rufford. Visitor centre and nature trails.
Disabled access.
Over 15 species recorded.
WTLMNM

PLEASINGTON OLD HALL
WOOD & WILDLIFE GARDEN
near Blackburn
OS Map 103. SD 646 270.
Woodland, wildlife garden, stream.
Reserve lies c.2 miles from Blackburn
centre, off the A674 Blackburn to Chorley
road, adjacent to Pleasington cemetery.
WTLMNM

WINMARLEIGH & COCKERHAM
MOSSES
near Garstang
OS Map 102. SD 445 484.
Heath, scrub.
Minor roads criss-cross the mosses but
parking is difficult. Parking in lay-by near
Cogie Hill Farm for footpath across
Winmarleigh Moss starting at Crawley's
Cross Farm at SD 436 470. Footpath across
Cockerham Moss from Gulf Lane, Moss
Edge at SD 439 492. See OS map or
Multimap.com for these and other footpaths.
Species inc. Black Darter.
DUCHY OF LANCASTER

LEICESTERSHIRE
& RUTLAND

Leicestershire & Rutland Wildlife
Trust
Brocks Hill Environment Centre,
Washbrook Lane, Oadby LE2 5JJ
TEL 0116 272 0444
EMAIL info@lrwt.org.uk
WWW.LRWT.ORG.UK

The National Trust Regional Office:
East Midlands
Clumber Park Stableyard, Worksop,
Notts S80 3BE
TEL 01909 486411

Websites
Leicestershire & Rutland Dragonfly
Group
WWW.LRDG.ORG.UK

Wild About Leicester
WWW.WILDABOUTLEICESTER.CO.UK

EYEBROOK RESERVOIR
near Corby
OS Map 141. SP 853 954.
Reservoir.
Leave Corby north on A6003. At
Caldecott, take minor road to Great Easton,
turn right in village then take next right.
Park along road.
CORBY & DISTRICT WATER COMPANY

GRAND UNION CANAL
near Leicester
OS Maps 140/141. SP 610 969–SP
731 891.
Canal.
Section of canal between Kilby Bridge and
Great Bowden Hall. Access from numerous
roads and footbridges.
Species inc. Brown Hawker, Common
Darter.
BRITISH WATERWAYS, LEICESTERSHIRE &
RUTLAND WILDLIFE TRUST

GRANTHAM CANAL
near Grantham
OS Maps 129/130. SK 743 315–SK 897 342.
Disused canal.
The canal runs from Harby east to Grantham and is accessed from many minor roads that cross the canal. One of the best sections is north-east of Barkstone Bridge. In Barkestone-le-Vale village take Jericho Lane past the church and park by the bridge at the end of the road.
17 species inc. Variable and Large Red Damselflies, Hairy Dragonfly, Brown Hawker, Ruddy Darter.
BRITISH WATERWAYS, GRANTHAM CANAL PARTNERSHIP
WWW.GRANTHAMCANAL.COM

HOLWELL MINERAL LINE
near Melton Mowbray
OS Map 129. SK 739 235.
Limestone grassland, permanent marsh, pool.
From Melton Mowbray, take the road north towards Scalford, then after c.2 miles the left turn followed by the immediate right turn (towards Holwell). Go over cattle grid to the road fork. Park on open area by the entrance to Brown's Hill Quarry reserve. Walk down the left-hand fork (towards Holwell village). Reserve entrance is to the right of the bridge over railway.
Species inc. Large Red Damselfly, Brown Hawker, Ruddy Darter.
LEICESTERSHIRE & RUTLAND WILDLIFE TRUST

HUMBERSTONE PARK LNR
Leicester
OS Map 140. SK 621 059.
Grassland, woodland.
Reserve lies to the south of Humberstone Park between Uppingham Road and Wicklow Drive, Humberstone (north-east Leicester). Park in surrounding side-streets and walk through park to reserve.
Species inc. Large Red Damselfly, Brown Hawker, Ruddy Darter.
LEICESTER CITY COUNCIL, GROUNDWORK LEICESTER & LEICESTERSHIRE
WWW.LEICESTER.GOV.UK, WWW.GWLL.ORG.UK

MERRY'S MEADOWS
near Oakham
OS Map 130. SK 938 157.
Meadows, ponds.
From Oakham, take the B668 north-west and then, at the crossroads west of Greetham, turn left and park by the T-junction opposite Great Lane. Follow the track for c.400m. Please keep to the path.
LEICESTERSHIRE & RUTLAND WILDLIFE TRUST

RUTLAND WATER
near Oakham
See main site section page 208.
Large area of open water with grassland, scrub, woodland.
Rutland Water is situated between Oakham and Stamford west of the A1.
Egleton Reserve
OS Map 141. SK 878 075.
Leave A6003 south of Oakham for Egleton and follow signs to reserve.
Lyndon Reserve
OS Map 141. SK 894 058.
Lyndon car park and information centre signed off minor road along south shore of water at Edith Weston.
Species inc. Migrant and Brown Hawkers, Black-tailed Skimmer.
ANGLIAN WATER, LEICESTERSHIRE COUNTY COUNCIL , LEICESTERSHIRE & RUTLAND WILDLIFE TRUST

SNIBSTON COUNTRY PARK & GRANGE NATURE RESERVE
near Leicester
OS Map 129. SK 417 144.
Access via Snibston off the A50 Leicester to Ashby-de-la-Zouch road at Coalville. Car park at Snibston Discovery Park – locked half an hour after museum closes.
LEICESTERSHIRE COUNTY COUNCIL
WWW.LEICS.GOV.UK

WATERMEAD ECOLOGICAL PARK
Leicester
OS Map 140. SK 602 085.
Lakes, River Soar.
Access and parking in Oakland Avenue, off Melton Road, Leicester. Cross stile by

locked field gate.
LEICESTER CITY COUNCIL, GROUNDWORK
LEICESTER & LEICESTERSHIRE
WWW.LEICESTER.GOV.UK, WWW.GWLL.ORG.UK

LINCOLNSHIRE

Lincolnshire Wildlife Trust
Banovallum House, Manor House
Street, Horncastle LN9 5HF
TEL 01507 526667
EMAIL info@lincstrust.co.uk
WWW.LINCSTRUST.ORG.UK

**The National Trust Regional Office:
East Midlands**
Clumber Park Stableyard, Worksop,
Notts S80 3BE
TEL 01909 486411

BASTON FEN
near Bourne
OS Map 130. TF 145 176.
River Glen, meres, pasture.
*Leave Bourne southwards along the A15 to
Baston. Take the left turn through the
village and out towards Tongue End.
Parking (unless indicated) over the
concrete bridge opposite Windmill Farm.
Do not obstruct gates or tracks. Follow
marked paths from parking area.*
Species inc. Hairy Dragonfly, Migrant
Hawker, Ruddy Darter.
LINCOLNSHIRE WILDLIFE TRUST

BOULTHAM MERE
Lincoln
OS Map 121. SK 957 713.
Lake, reedbeds.
*Car parks along Tritton Way, B1003 (west
side of Lincoln). Follow track down side of
drain, across gated railway crossing for
c.0.5 mile to the crossing point over the
drain by the sluice.*
Over 10 species recorded.
LINCOLNSHIRE WILDLIFE TRUST

BOURNE WOOD
near Bourne
OS Map 130. TF 080 210.
Mixed woodland, ponds.
*Car park (charge) off A151 west of Bourne.
Leaflet available on site. Tracks and rides.*
FOREST ENTERPRISE, FRIENDS OF BOURNE WOOD
WWW.FRIENDSOFBOURNEWOOD.ORG.UK

FAR INGS NNR
near Scunthorpe
OS Map 112. TA 015 234.
Open water, reedbed, saltmarsh.
*The site lies west of the Humber Bridge on
the south bank of the River Humber. Leave
the A15 south of the Humber Bridge and
head west along the A1077 and then take
the first turning on the right. Turn left at
the T-junction and the reserve is on the
right. Car park, visitor centre (manned
Saturdays and Sundays only), toilets.
Some disabled facilities.*
LINCOLNSHIRE WILDLIFE TRUST

GIBRALTAR POINT NNR
near Skegness
OS Map 122. TF 556 580.
See main site section page 173.
Coastal grassland, sand dunes, pools,
saltmarsh, freshwater marsh.
Reserve lies c.3 miles south of Skegness.
Species inc. Migrant Hawker.
LINCOLNSHIRE WILDLIFE TRUST

GREAT EAU
near Alford
OS Map 122. TF 422 812–TF 400 772.
Stream.
*Accessed from footpaths from South
Thoresby, Alby, Claythorpe and Tothill.*

**HARTSHOLME COUNTRY PARK
& SWANHOLME LAKES**
Lincoln
OS Map 121. SK 948 697.
Lakes, ornamental woodland,
grassland.
*South-west of Lincoln, on the A46 bypass,
take the B1378 signed to Birchwood.
Entrance and car park on right after c.1*

mile. Footpath through woodland leads to Swanpool Lakes. Visitor centre.
LINCOLN CITY COUNCIL
WWW.LINCOLNSHIRE.GOV.UK

KIRKBY MOOR
near Woodhall Spa
OS Map 122. TF 225 629.
Heathland, woodland, lake, ditch.
Park either along the verge of Moor Lane at the entrance to the main part of the reserve, which is c.1 mile west of Kirkby-on-Bain (along minor road to Woodhall Spa) opposite Wellsyke Lane, or in the car park at the bottom of the unsurfaced private road through the reserve. Keep gate closed and keep to waymarked paths. Check the ditch near car park for dragonflies.
Over 10 species recorded.
LINCOLNSHIRE WILDLIFE TRUST

LINWOOD WARREN
Market Rasen
OS Map 121. TF 133 877.
Heathland, woodland, pond.
Situated c.1.5 miles east of Market Rasen on the south side of the minor road to Legsby opposite the golf course. Park at the entrance or on roadside.
LINCOLNSHIRE WILDLIFE TRUST

MESSINGHAM SAND QUARRY
near Scunthorpe
OS Map 112. SK 908 032.
Lagoons, reedbeds, woodland, marsh.
Reserve lies east of B1400 south of Messingham. Entrance is opposite Scallow Grove Farm and a track leads down to the car park. Waymarked circular trail.
Species inc. Brown and Southern Hawkers.
LINCOLNSHIRE WILDLIFE TRUST

NORTHORPE SLIPE & THE CHASM
near Bourne
OS Map 130. TF 129 170 & TF 151 185.
Ditches.
Parking for Northorpe Slipe at the bottom of Thurlby Long Drove, which runs east from

Thurlby church (off A15). The Chasm is reached along the minor road east of Bourne at Tongue End.
Species inc. Emerald Damselfly, Migrant and Southern Hawkers, Ruddy Darter.
LINCOLNSHIRE WILDLIFE TRUST

RAUCEBY WARREN
near Sleaford
OS Map 130. TF 034 441.
Sandy heath, grassland, open water.
Situated c.2.5 miles south-west of Sleaford, sandwiched between the A153 and the adjacent railway. Parking at either the eastern/Sleaford end via gate at TF 033 440 or at the western end on the open space by the level crossing just south of main road at TF 024 434.
Over 20 species recorded.
LINCOLNSHIRE WILDLIFE TRUST

SALTFLEETBY– THEDDLETHORPE DUNES NNR
near Mablethorpe
OS Maps 113/122. TF 467 917 (Rimac entrance).
Sand dunes, salt and freshwater marshes with dykes and ponds.
Reserve extends for c.4.5 miles between Mabblethorpe in the south and Saltfleet Haven in the north. Several coastal car parks with access points off A1031. Leaflet available in the Rimac car park.
NATURAL ENGLAND, LINCOLNSHIRE WILDLIFE TRUST

SNIPE DALES
near Horncastle
OS Map 122. TF 330 685.
See main site section page 216.
Streams, pools, woodland, grassland.
Snipe Dales Country Park lies c.5 miles east of Horncastle off the A158.
Species inc. Emerald and Common Blue Damselflies, Southern and Migrant Hawkers, Common Darter.
LINCOLNSHIRE COUNTY COUNCIL, LINCOLNSHIRE WILDLIFE TRUST

Gazetteer

SOUTHERY WOOD
near Bardney
OS Map 121. TF 127 682.
Woodland.
*Park along B1190 in the forest track
entrance with Southery Wood sign at TF
132 684 (do not obstruct the gate).
Alternative parking along the Southery
village road. The reserve covers the north-
west corner of this woodland block at TF
129 682. Keep to forest rides.*
Species inc. Migrant Hawker,
Common Darter.
BUTTERFLY CONSERVATION NATURE RESERVE
MANAGED BY FOREST ENTERPRISE
WWW.BUTTERFLY-CONSERVATION.ORG

SWABY VALLEY
near Alford
OS Map 122. TF 390 776.
Chalk grassland and marsh.
*Park by church in South Thoresby at TF
402 770. Follow marked path across
Calceby Beck and Swaby Beck to valley.*

THURLBY FEN SLIPE
near Bourne
OS Map 130. TF 119 164.
Flooded borrow pits.
*From Thurlby church follow Thurlby Long
Drove for c.1 mile and turn right down
Baston Edge Drove and park at reserve
entrance at end.*
15 species inc. Emerald Damselfly,
Southern and Migrant Hawkers,
Ruddy Darter.
LINCOLNSHIRE WILDLIFE TRUST

WHISBY NATURE PARK
near Lincoln
OS Map 121. SK 914 661.
See main site section page 235.
Gravel pits, grassland, scrub.
*Whisby Nature Park lies on the western
outskirts of Lincoln.*
20 species inc. Migrant Hawker, Black-
tailed Skimmer.
LINCOLNSHIRE WILDLIFE TRUST,
LINCOLNSHIRE COUNTY COUNCIL

MERSEYSIDE
see Lancashire

NORFOLK

Norfolk Wildlife Trust
Bewick House, 2 Thorpe Road,
Norwich NR1 1RY
TEL 01603 625540
EMAIL admin@norfolkwildlifetrust.
org.uk
WWW.NORFOLKWILDLIFETRUST.ORG.UK

**The National Trust Regional Office:
East of England**
Westly Bottom, Bury St Edmunds,
Suffolk IP33 3WD
TEL 01284 747500

County atlas / books
The Dragonflies of Norfolk. Pete Milford
and Tony Irwin, 1990, Norfolk &
Norwich Naturalists' Society.
The Dragonflies of Norfolk. Pam Taylor,
2003, Norfolk & Norwich Naturalists'
Society.

Websites
Norfolk Dragons
WWW.NORFOLKDRAGONS.CO.UK

ALDERFEN BROAD
near Hoveton
OS Maps 133/134. TG 353 196.
Fen, open water, reedbed.
*Reserve is c.2 miles east of Hoveton, reached
along minor roads through Neatishead
(signed from Hoveton). Reserve car park
along lane from Threehammer Common.*
Species inc. Large Red-eyed Damselfly.
NORFOLK WILDLIFE TRUST

CATFIELD FEN
near Catfield
OS Maps 133/134. TG 367 215.
See main site section page 153.
Open water, reed and sedge beds,
dykes, fen, and carr woodland.
Catfield Fen lies c.10 miles north-east of

*Norwich and c.15 miles north-west of
Great Yarmouth.*
Species inc. Hairy Dragonfly,
Common, Brown and Norfolk
Hawkers.
BUTTERFLY CONSERVATION
WWW.BUTTERFLY-CONSERVATION.ORG

COCKSHOOT BROAD
near Woodbastwick
OS Maps 133/134. TG 343 163.
Fen, open water, reedbed.
*The reserve lies south of the River Bure
near Woodbastwick north of the B1140.
Park in the car park by the river and follow
footpath. Boarded walkway along River
Bure and Cockshoot dyke. Adjacent to
Ranworth Broad.*
Species inc. Large Red-eyed Damselfly,
Norfolk Hawker.
NORFOLK WILDLIFE TRUST

FOULDEN COMMON
near Swaffham
OS Map 143. TF 760 000.
Fen, pingos, open water, grassland.
15 species recorded.
*Access from minor road between Foulden
and Gooderstone north of A134.*
FOULDEN LATIMER ESTATES

HICKLING BROAD NNR
near Potter Heigham
OS Map 134. TG 428 222.
Broad with reedbeds, carr, woodland,
grazing marsh.
*Reserve signed from Hickling Green village
via Stubbs Road. Car park, visitor centre
and marked trails.*
Species inc. Large Red Damselfly,
Norfolk Hawker, Four-spotted
Chaser, Black-tailed Skimmer. Also
Swallowtail butterfly.
NORFOLK WILDLIFE TRUST

HOLKHAM MEALS
near Wells-next-the-Sea
OS Map 132. TF 870 452–TF 915 455.
Coastal woodland and dunes.
*Access either from Wells-next-the-Sea
Beach Road car park (pay & display) or from*

*Lady Anne's Drive opposite Holkham Hall
(charge) off A149.*
Species inc. Migrant Hawker.

HOW HILL NNR
near Wroxham
OS Map 134. TG 374 191.
Reedbed, carr, formal gardens.
Reserve signed from Ludham off A1062.
Species inc. Norfolk Hawker.
BROADS AUTHORITY

LENWADE WATER
near Norwich
OS Map 133. TG 100 186.
Pools, meadows, scrub, woodland.
*Lenwade is c.7 miles north-west of
Norwich on the A1067.*
Species inc. Banded Demoiselle, Large
Red-eyed Damselfly, Black-tailed
Skimmer.

NUNNERY LAKES
Thetford
OS Map 144. TL 873 822.
Pools, meadows, scrub, woodland.
*Access from Nun's Bridges via kissing gate on
the north side of the River Little Ouse, 100m
east of the bridges. Car park to the south of the
river opposite Mill Lane. Open daily.*
Species inc. Banded Demoiselle, Large
Red-eyed Damselfly, Emperor
Dragonfly, Black-tailed Skimmer.
BRITISH TRUST FOR ORNITHOLOGY

RANWORTH BROAD
near South Walsham
OS Maps 133/134. TG 357 149.
Open water, reedbed, oak woodland.
*Reserve lies north of the B1140 near South
Walsham. Park at Malthouse Staithe car
park in Ranworth village and follow signs
to reserve entrance. Nature trail.
Broadland Conservation Centre (charge).*
NORFOLK WILDLIFE TRUST

SPARHAM POOLS
near East Dereham
OS Map 133. TG 075 178.
See main site section page 217.
Pools, reedbed, scrub, woodland.

Gazetteer

Sparham Pools lie between Norwich (c.10 miles) and Fakenham (c.10 miles).
Species inc. Banded Demoiselle, Large Red-eyed Damselfly, Common Hawker.
NORFOLK WILDLIFE TRUST

STRUMPSHAW FEN
near Norwich
OS Map 134. TG 336 065.
See main site section page 219.
Fen, grazing marsh, scrub.
By the River Yare c.5 miles east of Norwich.
Over 20 species inc. Small Red-eyed Damselfy, Hairy Dragonfly, Migrant and Norfolk Hawkers, Scarce Chaser.
RSPB

THOMPSON COMMON
near Watton
OS Map 144. TL 936 956.
See main site section page 221.
Pingos, grassland, scrub.
Thompson Common lies c.10 miles north of Thetford and c.3 miles south of Watton.
Species inc. Emerald, Scarce Emerald, Large Red-eyed and Small Red-eyed Damselfies.
NORFOLK WILDLIFE TRUST

UPTON FEN
near Acle
OS Maps 133/134. TG 385 135.
See main site section page 224.
Fen, lake, reedbed, oak woodland.
Upton Fen is c.9 miles east of Norwich.
Species inc. Variable Damselfly, Norfolk Hawker.
NORFOLK WILDLIFE TRUST

WELNEY
near Ely
OS Map 143. TL 546 946.
See main site section page 232.
Grazing marsh, open water, reedbed.
Welney lies c.10 miles north of Ely and c.9 miles south-west of Downham Market.
Species inc. Large Red-eyed and Variable Damselflies, Hairy Dragonfly, Scarce Chaser.
WILDFOWL & WETLANDS TRUST

NORTHAMPTONSHIRE

The Wildlife Trust for Bedfordshire, Cambridgeshire, Northamptonshire & Peterborough (WTBCNP)
Northamptonshire Office: Lings House, Billing Lings, Northampton NN3 8BE
TEL 01604 405285
northamptonshire@wildlifebcnp.org
WWW.WILDLIFEBCNP.ORG

The National Trust Regional Office: East Midlands
Clumber Park Stableyard, Worksop, Notts S80 3BE
TEL 01909 486411

Websites
Northants Dragonfly Group
HTTP://HOMEPAGE.NTLWORLD.COM/ANGELA.TYRRELL/

BARNWELL COUNTRY PARK
near Oundle
OS Map 141. TL 034 873.
Gravel pits, grassland, scrub.
Car park and information centre south of Oundle signed off A605. Nature trail.
Species inc. Banded Demoiselle.
NORTHAMPTONSHIRE COUNTY COUNCIL
WWW.NORTHAMPTONSHIRE.GOV.UK

DAVENTRY COUNTRY PARK
Daventry
OS Map 152. SP 576 641.
Reservoir, wetland.
Car park off B4038 north of Daventry.
DAVENTRY DISTRICT COUNCIL

FARTHINGHOE LNR
near Banbury
OS Map 151. SP 518 404.
Old railway line with scrub, grassland, woodland and pond.
The reserve is just south of the A422, halfway between Middleton Cheney and Farthinghoe. Access is from the bridge on Purston Lane. Cars may be parked on the roadside verges.
NORTHAMPTONSHIRE COUNTY COUNCIL
WWW.NORTHAMPTONSHIRE.GOV.UK

FERMYN WOODS COUNTRY PARK
near Corby
OS Map 141. SP 953 849.
Woodland, grassland, scrub, pools.
Car park off A6116 south of Brigstock.
Visitor centre.
Over 15 species inc. Migrant Hawker.
NORTHAMPTONSHIRE COUNTY COUNCIL
FOREST ENTERPRISE

HIGHAM FERRERS PITS
near Wellingborough
OS Map 153. SP 949 688.
Gravel pits.
The site lies c.4 miles east of
Wellingborough. Park in Wharf Road,
Higham Ferrers (south of Market Square).
Access reserve over footbridge.
WTBCNP

PITSFORD RESERVOIR
near Northampton
OS Maps 141/152. SP 780 708.
See main site section page 198.
Reservoir, with wet margins, mixed
plantation, grassland.
The reservoir lies between the A508 and
the A43, c.5 miles north of Northampton.
Over 15 species inc. Emerald
Damselfly, Ruddy Darter.
ANGLIAN WATER, WTBCNP

SUMMER PITS
near Great Doddington
OS Map 153. SP 885 634.
Gravel pits.
The site lies c.3 miles east of
Wellingborough south of the A45. Take
B573 at Great Doddington and follow
brown reserve signs. Car park along minor
road to Wollaston.
WTBCNP

SYWELL COUNTRY PARK
near Wellingborough
OS Map 152. SP 833 651.
Reservoir, mixed woodland,
meadows.
Head north from Earls Barton along Mears
Ashby Road. Car park and information

centre off Washbrook Lane, on left after c.1
mile north of A4500.
NORTHAMPTONSHIRE COUNTY COUNCIL
WWW.NORTHAMPTONSHIRE.GOV.UK

THRAPSTON GRAVEL PITS
near Kettering
OS Map 141. TL 000 804.
Gravel pits.
Footpaths from Thrapston at SP 996 789 or
along A605 at TL 007 795.
WTBCNP

TITCHMARSH
near Thrapston
OS Map 141. TL 007 813.
Lakes, riverbanks, ponds, woodland,
scrub, grassland.
Access from car park at Aldwincle. Keep to
footpath. Stout footwear recommended.
Species inc. Banded Demoiselle, Large
Red-eyed Damselfly, Migrant,
Southern and Brown Hawkers.
WTBCNP

NORTHUMBERLAND

Northumberland Wildlife Trust
St Nicholas Park, Gosforth, Newcastle
upon Tyne NE3 3XT
TEL 0191 284 6884
EMAIL mail@northwt.org.uk
WWW.NWT.ORG.UK

The National Trust Regional Office:
North East
Scot's Gap, Morpeth NE61 4EG
TEL 01670 774691

CRAGSIDE COUNTRY PARK
near Rothbury
OS Map 81. NU 073 022.
Parkland, streams, lakes and
coniferous woodland in moorland.
Reserve is c.1 mile east of Rothbury, signed
off the B6344 Morpeth to Rothbury road.
Extensive network of paths. Car park,
visitor centre and restaurant.
PART OF NORTHUMBERLAND NATIONAL PARK,
NATIONAL TRUST

Gazetteer

HAUXLEY
near Amble-by-the-Sea
OS Map 81. NT 285 023.
Lake.
Reserve lies along the coast just south of Amble. Reach car park via track that leaves the minor road between Low and High Hauxley and also leads to caravan site. Visitor centre.
NORTHUMBERLAND WILDLIFE TRUST

NOTTINGHAMSHIRE

Nottinghamshire Wildlife Trust
The Old Ragged School, Brook Street, Nottingham NG1 1EA
TEL 0115 958 8242
EMAIL info@nottswt.co.uk
WWW.WILDLIFETRUST.ORG.UK/
NOTTINGHAMSHIRE/

The National Trust Regional Office: East Midlands
Clumber Park Stableyard, Worksop S80 3BE
TEL 01909 486411

Nottinghamshire County Council
County Hall, West Bridgford, Nottingham NG2 7QP
TEL 0115 982 3823
WWW.NOTTINGHAMSHIRE.GOV.UK

ATTENBOROUGH GRAVEL PITS
near Nottingham
OS Map 129. SK 525 346.
Flooded gravel pits, river (Trent), marsh, woodland.
Turn off the A6005 Nottingham to Long Eaton road into Barton Lane (at Chilwell Retail Park). The reserve is signed from here. Main car park at SK 516 340. Nature trail guide available.
Species inc. Migrant and Southern Hawkers.
RMC AGGREGATES (EASTERN) LTD,
NOTTINGHAMSHIRE WILDLIFE TRUST

BESTWOOD COUNTRY PARK
near Nottingham
OS Map 129. SK 548 478.
Reedbed, lakes, ponds, river, water meadows, woodland, grassland.
Bestwood village lies north of Nottingham city centre east of the A611. Park in the village in Winding House Car Park in Park Road.
NOTTINGHAMSHIRE COUNTY COUNCIL

COLWICK COUNTRY PARK
Nottingham
OS Map 129. SK 607 392.
Lakes, river, marsh, woodland.
Take the B686, which passes Nottingham Racecourse, and follow signs for 'Water User Entrance Only'. Many car parks (signed).
NOTTINGHAM CITY COUNCIL
WWW.NOTTINGHAMCITY.GOV.UK

FAIRHAM BROOK
near Nottingham
OS Map 129. SK 562 338.
Relict lowland fen bog, pond, reedbeds, meadow.
Access the reserve via Green Lane in Clifton south of Nottingham city centre.
NOTTINGHAMSHIRE WILDLIFE TRUST

MARTIN'S POND LNR
Nottingham
OS Map 129. SK 526 402.
Pool and marsh with scrub.
Leave A609 c.1.5 miles west of city ring road at Russell Avenue in Wollaton, and park at entrance to reserve. Circular walk.
Species inc. Brown Hawker.
NOTTINGHAM CITY COUNCIL
WWW.NOTTINGHAMCITY.GOV.UK

RUFFORD COUNTRY PARK
near Ollerton
OS Map 120. SK 645 650.
Parkland, lake, woodland.
Situated on the A614, c.17 miles north of Nottingham and c.2 miles south of Ollerton. Two car parks (charge). Open daily, dawn to dusk. Café.
NOTTINGHAMSHIRE COUNTY COUNCIL

OXFORDSHIRE

The Berkshire, Buckinghamshire & Oxfordshire Wildlife Trust (BBOWT)
The Lodge, 1 Armstrong Road, Littlemore, Oxford OX4 4XT
TEL 01865 775476
EMAIL info@bbowt.org.uk
WWW.BBOWT.ORG.UK

Chilterns Area of Outstanding Natural Beauty
Chilterns Conservation Board, The Lodge, Station Road, Chinnor OX39 4HA
TEL 01844 355500
EMAIL office@chilternsaonb.org
WWW.CHILTERNSAONB.ORG

The National Trust Regional Office: Thames & Solent
Hughenden Manor, High Wycombe, Bucks HP14 4LA
TEL 01494 528051

ABBEY FISHPONDS
Abingdon
OS Map 164. SU 512 980.
Wet meadow, reedbed, scrub, woodland.
Park in east Abingdon. Access off Radley Road either side of Cameron Avenue.
Species inc. Banded Demoiselle, Emerald and Azure Damselflies.
VALE OF WHITE HORSE DISTRICT COUNCIL

ASHAM MEADS
near Oxford
OS Map 164. SP 590 146.
Wet grassland, pond, plantation.
Leave Oxford north along the A43 and then take the B4027 to Islip. In Islip take the minor road towards Merton then the first right, through Oddington, Charlton-on-Otmoor and Murcott. Beyond Murcott, turn right down track past Manor and Whitecross Green Farms. Park only in car park at end of track.
Species inc. Emperor Dragonfly.
BBOWT

CHOLSEY MARSH
near Wallingford
OS Maps 174/175. SU 601 855.
See main site section page 152.
Marsh, reedbed, scrub, river.
Cholsey Marsh lies next to the River Thames c.2 miles south of Wallingford.
Species inc. Banded Demoiselle, White-legged Damselfly, Club-tailed Dragonfly.

DRY SANDFORD PIT
near Abingdon
OS Map 164. SU 467 997.
Grassland, woodland, scrub, brook, fen, pools.
Small car park situated north of Abingdon Airfield in Cothill, c.100m west of the Church Lane and Honeybottom Lane junction. Avoid fragile fen area.
BBOWT

HORNTON MEADOWS
near Banbury
OS Map 151. SP 395 465.
Grassland, scrub, hedgerows, brook.
Hornton village lies north-west of Banbury between the A422 and B4100. Park carefully in Hornton village or along minor road to north. Bridleway east of turn to Hornton village (crossroads with track to Poplars Farm).

IFFLEY MEADOWS
Oxford
OS Map 164. SP 524 038.
Wet meadow, pasture, river.
Park in Iffley village off the A423. Cross the River Thames at Iffley Lock. Reserve is just beyond The Isis public house.
20 species recorded.
BBOWT

LASHFORD LANE FEN
near Abingdon
OS Map 164. SP 468 011.
Fen, grassland, scrub, woodland.
South of A421 between Cumnor and Abingdon. Park in Dry Sandford in unsurfaced car park along Lashford Lane.
BBOWT

NETTLEBED COMMON
near Henley-on-Thames
OS Map 175. SU 704 873.
Woodland, ponds, heath, marsh.
From Henley take the A423 north-westwards to Nettlebed. Access and parking in the village. The ponds lie immediately north of the village. Network of paths. Leaflet and information on guided walks obtainable from BBOWT's Warburg Reserve at Bix Bottom.
Species inc. Southern and Brown Hawkers.
PART OF CHILTERNS AONB, NETTLEBED AND DISTRICT COMMONS CONSERVATORS, BBOWT

OTMOOR
near Oxford
OS Map 164. SP 570 125.
Wet meadow, river.
East of Oxford, leave the B4027 towards Horton-cum-Studley, then take the left turn to Beckley. In the High Street turn right at the Abingdon Arms pub and after c.180m left into Otmoor Lane to the reserve car park at the end. Note: do not enter the adjacent firing range when red flags are flying.
RSPB

RIVER THAMES
by Farmoor Reservoir
near Oxford
OS Map 164. SP 441 088–SP 434 043.
Riverside meadows and hedgerows.
Park at Farmoor Reservoir car park off B4017 between Farmoor and Cumnor. Cross causeway between reservoirs to river and follow paths north and south. three nature reserves have been created here@ Pinkhill Meadow, Shrike Meadow and Buckthorne Meadow.
Species inc. Banded Demoiselle, Club-tailed Dragonfly.
THAMES WATER, NATIONAL RIVERS AUTHORITY, ENVIRONMENTAL AGENCY
WWW.FARMOOR.IOFM.NET

RIVER THAMES
near Goring
OS Map 175. SU 616 794.
See main site section page 206.
Riverside meadows and hedgerows.
This site lies c.1 mile south of Goring.
Species inc. Banded Demoiselle, Club-tailed Dragonfly.

SYDLINGS COPSE & COLLEGE POND
near Oxford
OS Map 164. SP 559 096.
Fen, heath, grassland, scrub, woodland.
From the A40 Headington roundabout, take the Bayswater road north through Barton to the B4027. Turn left and park after c.500m on verge opposite Royal Oak farmhouse and tearoom. Walk south along bridleway and, just past the second piece of woodland Sydlings Copse is one field across on the right. Wildlife trail.
BBOWT

TUCKMILL MEADOWS LNR
near Faringdon
OS Map 174. SU 240 900.
Wet meadow, grassland, woodland.
Take the A420 from Faringdon towards Swindon and then the left turn towards Watchfield. Continue past the Military College and turn right at the sharp left bend down the track past Shrivenham Park Golf Club. Car park through gate c.100m after golf club at SU 238 897.
Over 15 species recorded.
VALE OF WHITE HORSE DISTRICT COUNCIL

WELLS FARM
near Oxford
OS Map 164. SP 620 008.
Grassland, woodland.
Leave the A4142 Oxford ring road at Cowley and head along the B480 to Stadhampton. Turn left along the A329 to Little Milton, go past the Plough Inn, up the hill, then turn sharp right (farmyard on the left) near the public telephone.
Species inc. Brown Hawker, Broad-bodied Chaser.

SHROPSHIRE

Shropshire Wildlife Trust
193 Abbey Foregate, Shrewsbury SY2 6AH
TEL 01743 284280
WWW.SHROPSHIREWILDLIFETRUST.CO.UK

Natural England Regional Office
Natural England, The Stable Block, Attingham Park, Shrewsbury SY4 4TW
TEL 01743 282000
EMAIL north.mercia@naturalengland.org.uk

The National Trust Regional Office: West Midlands
Attingham Park, Shrewsbury SY4 4TP
TEL 01743 708100

Shropshire County Council
Countryside Section, Shirehall, Abbey Foregate, Shrewsbury SY2 6ND
TEL 01743 255061

Websites
Natural Shropshire
WWW.NATURALSHROPSHIRE.ORG.UK.

BERRINGTON POOL
near Shrewsbury
OS Map 126. SJ 526 073.
See main site section page 213.
Vegetated pool.
Situated c.3 miles south of Shrewsbury.
Species inc. Large Red-eyed and Variable Damselflies, Downy Emerald.
NATIONAL TRUST

BROWN MOSS LNR
near Ellesmere
OS Map 126. SJ 563 393.
Acid heath, pools, marsh, woodland. RAMSAR site.
Take the turn for Ash off A41 at Prees Heath and follow signs. Park in designated areas.
Species inc. Large Red-eyed Damselfly, Broad-bodied Chaser.
SHROPSHIRE COUNTY COUNCIL

CRAMER GUTTER
near Kidderminster
OS Map 138. SO 647 795.
Damp grassland, bog, stream.
On the A4117 between Cleobury Mortimer and Ludlow, take the minor road north at Doddington across Catherton Common towards Oreton. After c.1.5 miles go across the crossroads (telephone box on right) and after a further c.0.25 miles turn right at the chapel. Park carefully on the verge. Access down track on right.
Species inc. Golden-ringed Dragonfly, Keeled Skimmer.
SHROPSHIRE WILDLIFE TRUST

DOLGOCH QUARRY
near Oswestry
OS Map 175. SJ 277 243.
Disused limestone quarries, woodland, ponds.
Leave Oswestry south along A483 and then head west along A495. Park in lay-by just west of Llynclys crossroads. Access opposite Turner's Lane. Walk through wood on north side of road to quarry.
SHROPSHIRE WILDLIFE TRUST

GRANVILLE PARK
Telford
OS Map 127. SJ 719 124.
Marsh, canal, grassland, woodland.
Signed from B5060 on the eastern edge of Telford. Car parks along Granville Road and along Muxton Lane. The old canal by Lodge Furnaces, in the southern half of the reserve, is good for dragonflies.
SHROPSHIRE WILDLIFE TRUST

LLYNCLYS HILL
near Oswestry
OS Map 126. SJ 273 237.
Limestone grassland and quarries, woodland, scrub, pond.
Leave Oswestry south along A483 and then head west along A495. Park in lay-by just west of Llynclys crossroads. Access on foot along Turner's Lane.
20 species recorded.
SHROPSHIRE WILDLIFE TRUST

Gazetteer

MERRINGTON GREEN
near Shrewsbury
OS Map 126. SJ 465 208.
Grassland, scrub, woodland, ponds.
Leave the A528 north of Shrewsbury through Bromere Heath to Merrington. The Green lies along the lane north of the minor road between Merrington and Walford Heath. Large car park. Disabled access.
14 species recorded.
SHROPSHIRE WILDLIFE TRUST

PREES BRANCH CANAL
near Ellesmere
OS Map 126. SJ 497 331.
Disused canal.
Limited parking at Waterloo Bridge north of Wem. Take the central towpath on the west side (no access along east bank) and walk to Dobson's Bridge.
SHROPSHIRE WILDLIFE TRUST

REA BROOK VALLEY
Shrewsbury
OS Map 126. SJ 503 108.
Flood meadow, scrub.
Park in Abbey Foregate opposite abbey.
SHREWSBURY & ATCHAM BOROUGH COUNCIL
WWW.SHREWSBURY.GOV.UK

RIVER SEVERN, ATCHAM
near Shrewsbury
OS Map 126. SJ 538 084.
See main site section page 213.
Stretch of River Severn.
Lies c.2 miles south-east of Shrewsbury.
Species inc. Banded Demoiselle, White-legged Damselfly, Club-tailed Dragonfly.

SEVERN VALLEY COUNTRY PARK
near Bridgnorth
OS Map 138. SO 755 838.
See main site section page 211.
Wood, scrub, meadow, river, ponds.
The country park lies c.5 miles south-east of Bridgnorth.
Species inc. Banded Demoiselle,

White-legged Damselfly, Club-tailed Dragonfly.
BRIDGNORTH DISTRICT COUNCIL, SHROPSHIRE COUNTY COUNCIL
WWW.BRIDGNORTH-DC.GOV.UK
WWW.SHROPSHIRE.GOV.UK

STEEL HEATH
near Ellesmere
OS Map 126. SJ 543 364.
Heathland, ponds, woodland, grassland.
Park in lay-by along B5476 c.2 miles south of Tilstock (to west of Prees Heath off A41).
SHROPSHIRE WILDLIFE TRUST

TELFORD TOWN PARK
Telford
OS Map 127. SJ 695 072.
Parkland, woods, fields, ponds.
The park is reached on foot from the Telford Town Centre complex or car parks situated along Randley Avenue (north-east corner) or by Stirchley Grange (south side).
TELFORD & WREKIN COUNCIL
WWW.TELFORD.GOV.UK
WWW.TELFORDTOWNPARK.CO.UK

WALKMILL MARSH
Market Drayton
OS Map 127. SJ 672 334.
Wetland with pool.
Turn off the A529 down Newport Road (by swimming pool). Follow signs for the golf course down Walkmill Road and then turn left into Sutton Road. Go over bridges and park carefully along lane by trees.
SHROPSHIRE WILDLIFE TRUST

WEM MOSS NNR
near Wem
OS Map 126. SJ 473 343.
Raised bog, carr.
East of Ellesmere take the B5063 Wem to Welshampton road. Park carefully in Northwood village and access along a track over a footbridge.
Over 20 species recorded.
SHROPSHIRE WILDLIFE TRUST

WHIXALL MOSS NNR
near Ellesmere
OS Map 126. SJ 493 355 (car park).
Lowland raised bog.
*The reserve lies c.5 miles south-west of
Wrexham, south of the A495 between
Whixall and Bettisfield. Several entrances
with roadside parking.*
Species inc. White-faced Darter.
NATURAL ENGLAND, COUNTRYSIDE COUNCIL
FOR WALES

SOMERSET

Somerset Wildlife Trust
Tonedale Mill, Tonedale, Wellington,
TA21 0AW
TEL 01823 652400
EMAIL enquiries@somersetwildlife.org
WWW.SOMERSETWILDLIFE.ORG

Avon Wildlife Trust
32 Jacob's Wells Road, Bristol BS8 1DR
TEL 0117 917 7270
EMAIL mail@avonwildlifetrust.org.uk
WWW.AVONWILDLIFETRUST.ORG.UK

Natural England Regional Office
Roughmoor, Bishop's Hull, Taunton,
Somerset TA1 5AA
TEL 01823 283211
EMAIL
somerset@naturalengland.org.uk

**The National Trust Regional Office:
Wessex**
Eastleigh Court, Bishopstrow,
Warminster, Wilts BA12 9HW
TEL 01985 843600

BIDDLE STREET
near Weston-super-Mare
OS Map 182. ST 423 648.
Grassland, pond.
*Footpath at end of Biddle Street on western
edge of Yatton.*
Species inc. Variable Damselfly.
PART OF THE AVON LEVELS & MOORS

BISHOPSWOOD MEADOW
near Ilminster
OS Map 193. ST 252 131.
Limestone grassland, marsh.
*From Ilminster take A303 west and leave
at right turn for Bishopswood. Access to
reserve from lane off road from west side of
village at ST 252 129.*
SOMERSET WILDLIFE TRUST

BRANDON HILL NATURE PARK
Bristol
OS Map 172. ST 578 728.
Woodland, scrub, grassland, ponds.
*Situated in Bristol city adjacent to Avon
Wildlife Trust headquarters in Jacob's
Wells Road.*
AVON WILDLIFE TRUST

BRIMLEY HILL MIRE
near Taunton
OS Map 193. ST 175 141.
Mire.
*Leave B3170, south of Taunton, west at ST
229 164 (signed for bird gardens) and then
follow signs for Churchstanton. Opposite
village church, take the minor road west to
Brimley Hill. Reserve entrance through
roadside gate just before Downlands Lane
at Brimley Hill.*
SOMERSET WILDLIFE TRUST

CATCOTT HEATH
near Bridgwater
OS Map 182. ST 407 411.
Grassland, scrub, carr, pools, ditches.
*Take the A39 between Bridgwater and
Glastonbury and then the signposted road
north to the village of Catcott. Go north
through the village and continue along
minor road towards Burtle for c.1 mile. Car
park by the hide.*
SOMERSET WILDLIFE TRUST

CHEW VALLEY LAKE
near Bristol
OS Map 172. ST 570 600.
Reservoir, reedbeds.
*Situated c.7 miles due south of Bristol.
Various access points including from car
park at Herriott's Bridge along A368 (ST*

Gazetteer

570 582) and at the visitor centre (run by Bristol Water) by the dam near Chew Stoke (ST 574 614).
Species inc. Migrant Hawker, Ruddy Darter.
AVON WILDLIFE TRUST

LAWRENCE WESTON MOOR
near Bristol
OS Map 172. ST 544 791.
Wet meadow, reedbed.
In Lawrence Weston (near Avonmouth) turn into Lawrence Weston Road (next to St Bede's School). Park just before motorway bridge and follow the track alongside the allotments to reserve.
AVON WILDLIFE TRUST

NETCOTT'S MEADOW
Nailsea
OS Map 172. ST 476 696.
Damp grassland.
Situated on the southern edge of Nailsea north of the A370. Car park along road between Backwell and Nailsea just north of railway. Follow footpath around Buckland's Pool to reserve.
AVON WILDLIFE TRUST

OTTERHEAD LAKES
near Taunton
OS Map 193. ST 225 135.
Lakes, marsh, woodland.
Reserve lies to the west of B3170 south of Taunton. Car park at ST 224 141. Keep to footpaths. Picnic area. Nature trail.
SOMERSET WILDLIFE TRUST, WESSEX WATER
WWW.WESSEXWATER.CO.UK

PILL PADDOCK
near Bristol
OS Map 172. ST 519 754.
Woodland, pond.
From A369 follow main road, The Lodway, through Easton-in-Gordano and then turn into Cross Lanes. Park here and take footpath on right, opposite Budleigh Road, to reserve.
AVON WILDLIFE TRUST

PRIDDY MINERIES
near Wells
OS Map 182. ST 547 515.
See main site section page 199.
Disused lead workings, pools.
The reserve lies c.3 miles north of Wells.
Species inc. Large Red-eyed Damselfly, Common Hawker, Downy Emerald, Black Darter.
SOMERSET WILDLIFE TRUST

REWE MEAD
near Wellington
OS Map 193. ST 105 214.
Flood-plain, meadow.
Reserve lies on south side of River Tone west of Wellington.
SOMERSET WILDLIFE TRUST

SHAPWICK HEATH
near Glastonbury
OS Map 182. ST 423 411.
See main site section page 212.
Marsh, fen, peat cuttings.
Shapwick Heath lies c.4 miles west of Glastonbury.
Over 15 species inc. Large Red-eyed Damselfly, Hairy Dragonfly, Ruddy Darter.
NATURAL ENGLAND

STOCKWOOD OPEN SPACE
near Bristol
OS Map 172. ST 625 693.
Farmland, meadow, hedgerows, woodland.
Stockwood is situated between Brislington and Keynsham on the southern edge of Bristol. Parking at bottom of Stockwood Lane in Stockwood.
AVON WILDLIFE TRUST

WESTHAY MOOR NNR
near Glastonbury
OS Map 182. ST 455 438.
Raised bog, peat cuttings, pools, fen, dykes, reedbeds, scrub.
Leave the B3151, north of Westhay, east along Westhay Moor Drove to car park at junction with Dagg's Lane Drove (ST 456

437). *Keep to marked footpaths (public and permissive).*
Species inc. Hairy Dragonfly, Common Hawker, Ruddy Darter.
SOMERSET WILDLIFE TRUST, NATURAL ENGLAND

WESTON MOOR
near Clevedon
OS Map 172. ST 443 738.
Meadow, reedbed, dykes, marsh, woodland.
Turn south off B3124 in Weston-in-Gordano down Cadbury Lane and Weston Drove. Park by reserve entrance.
Species inc. Hairy Dragonfly.
AVON WILDLIFE TRUST

WILLSBRIDGE MILL
near Bristol
OS Map 172. ST 665 708.
Woodland valley with stream, scrub, meadow and pond.
The site is on the south-east outskirts of Bristol. Leave Bristol along the A431 towards Bath. At Oldland, turn left into Long Beach Road. Park on left at ST 665 707.
AVON WILDLIFE TRUST

YARTY MOOR
near Taunton
OS Map 193. ST 235 159.
Bog and wet grassland at source of River Yarty.
Reserve lies to east of B3170. Park by road at ST 235 163.
Species inc. Keeled Skimmer.
SOMERSET WILDLIFE TRUST

STAFFORDSHIRE

Staffordshire Wildlife Trust
The Wolseley Centre, Wolseley Bridge, Stafford ST17 0WT
TEL 01889 880100
EMAIL mailto:info@staffs-wildlife.org.uk
WWW.STAFFORDSHIREWILDLIFE.ORG.UK

Natural England Regional Office
Woodthorne, Wergs Road, Wolverhampton WV6 8TQ
TEL 01902 743711

The National Trust Regional Office: West Midlands
Attingham Park, Shrewsbury SY4 4TP
TEL 01743 708100

BATESWOOD
near Newcastle-under-Lyme
OS Map 118. SJ 796 471.
Wet grassland, meadows, ponds, scrub, woodland, plantation.
From Newcastle head west on the A525. Just before Madeley Heath, take the minor road northwards towards Leycett and Alsagers Bank. After c.1 mile, at a right-hand bend on the eastern side of Leycett, turn left down a rough track alongside a house on a raised garden. Continue to the padlocked gate leading to a tarmacked road and park just before it (not block access) or obtain padlock code from SWT.
Over 12 species recorded.
STAFFORDSHIRE WILDLIFE TRUST

BICKFORD MEADOWS
near Penkridge
OS Map 127. SJ 883 140.
Wet meadows, stream, willow carr.
Access is on foot either via the Staffordshire Way from the villages of Mitton and Lapley, or from the minor road between Lapley and Whiston at a bridleway (Watery Lane) c.0.75 mile from Lapley. Please note that the 0.25-mile walk along the bridleway to the reserve is along difficult terrain. Park carefully along the roadside.
Species inc. Brown Hawker, Ruddy Darter.
STAFFORDSHIRE WILDLIFE TRUST

CHARTLEY MOSS NNR
near Uttoxeter
OS Map 128. SK 020 280.
Floating bog.
Contact Natural England for access.
Species inc. White-faced Darter.
NATURAL ENGLAND

Gazetteer

DOXEY MARSHES
Stafford
OS Map 127. SJ 915 239.
See main site section page 166.
Riverside marsh and pools.
Doxey Marshes lies alongside the River Sow on the northern outskirts of Stafford.
STAFFORDSHIRE WILDLIFE TRUST, NATURAL ENGLAND

JACKSON'S COPPICE & MARSH
near Stafford
OS Map 127. SJ 786 301.
Deciduous woodland, alder carr, marsh, river (Sow).
Take the A5013 from Stafford to Eccleshall, then follow the B5026 and at Sugnall take the road signed for Sugnall Business Park. After c.1 mile turn right before Walk Mill Pond. Jackson's Coppice is c.0.5 miles on right. Public footpath through marsh to Offleyrock. Circular walk around coppice. Species inc. Banded Demoiselle.
STAFFORDSHIRE WILDLIFE TRUST

PARROT'S DRUMBLE
near Newcastle-under-Lyme
OS Map 118. SJ 821 519.
Deciduous woodland, stream, pond.
From Newcastle-under-Lyme, head north along the A34 to the A500 roundabout. Continue along the A34 to the next roundabout and take the left exit. At the next roundabout take the third exit to Talke Pits village. Follow this road for c.0.75 miles and then turn left at the Skylark pub down Pit Lane. Park carefully on the right opposite the industrial estate – do not block any gates. The track to the reserve is on the right by a metal barrier. Visit the small pond at northern end of the reserve.
STAFFORDSHIRE WILDLIFE TRUST

SHUGBOROUGH PARK FARM
near Sheffield
OS Map 127. SJ 992 225.
River Trent, marsh, fen and carr.
The estate is on the A513, c.5.5 miles south-east of Stafford. Car park. Visitor centre and guided trails.
THE NATIONAL TRUST

SIDE FARM MEADOWS
near Cheadle
OS Map 119. SK 058 465.
Grassland, ponds, stream, scrub.
On the A52 (Stoke-on-Trent to Ashbourne road), c.0.5 mile east of Whiston, turn right into Blakeley Lane (towards Moneystone and Oakamoor). After c.0.25 mile turn left towards Cotton and then take the narrow track after c.200m on the right. Continue for c.0.75 mile to the reserve. Parking is limited and gates must not be blocked. A small pond in one of the fields is good for dragonflies. Follow footpaths.
STAFFORDSHIRE WILDLIFE TRUST

SUFFOLK

Suffolk Wildlife Trust
Brooke House, The Green,
Ashbocking, near Ipswich IP6 9JY
TEL 01473 890089
EMAIL info@suffolkwildlife.cix.co.uk
WWW.SUFFOLKWILDLIFE.CO.UK

**The National Trust Regional Office:
East of England**
Westley Bottom, Bury St Edmunds
IP33 3WD
TEL 01284 747500

Suffolk County Council
TEL 0845 606 6067
EMAIL customerservice@csduk.com
WWW.SUFFOLK.GOV.UK

County atlas/book
Suffolk Dragonflies. Howard Mendel, 1992, Suffolk Naturalists' Society.

BRANDON COUNTRY PARK
near Brandon
OS Map 144. TL 786 855.
Woodland, ponds, lake.
One mile south of Brandon on the B1106. Visitor centre and toilets.
Species inc. Migrant, Southern and Brown Hawkers.
SUFFOLK COUNTY COUNCIL, FOREST HEATH DISTRICT COUNCIL

CARLTON MARSHES
near Lowestoft
OS Map 134. TM 508 920.
See main site section page 152.
Grazing marsh, fen, ditches, pool, carr.
Carlton Marshes is situated c.2 miles
outside Lowestoft.
15 species inc. Variable Damselfly,
Hairy Dragonfly, Norfolk Hawker,
Scrace Chaser.
SUFFOLK WILDLIFE TRUST

DARSHAM MARSHES
near Saxmundham
OS Map 156. TM 420 691.
Grazing marsh, fen, dykes.
Leave the A12 north of Yoxford towards
Westleton and park on right-hand side at
reserve entrance.
SUFFOLK WILDLIFE TRUST

FLATFORD MILL
near East Bergholt
OS Map 168. TM 077 332.
River Stour, ponds, marshes.
Flatford lies c.1 mile south of East Bergholt.
Car park, information centre and café.
Riverside and circular walks.
NATIONAL TRUST

GLEMSFORD PICNIC SITE
near Sudbury
OS Map 155. TL 810 463.
River Stour, meadows.
The site is situated just south of the A1092
at Glemsford, off a minor road to Pentlow
and Foxearth. Follow riverside paths.
SUFFOLK COUNTY COUNCIL

HAZLEWOOD MARSHES
near Aldeburgh
OS Map 156. TM 435 575.
Grazing marsh, dykes.
Take the A1094 towards Aldeburgh. Just
before the golf course, turn right down
track to reserve and park here.
SUFFOLK WILDLIFE TRUST

LACKFORD WILDFOWL RESERVE
near Bury St Edmunds
OS Map 155. TL 800 708.

Gravel pits.
Reserve and car park signed off A1101
between Flempton and Lackford.
Species inc. Migrant and Brown
Hawkers, Black-tailed Skimmer.
SUFFOLK WILDLIFE TRUST

LAKENHEATH POORS FEN
Lakenheath
OS Map 143. TL 702 827.
Fen, meadow, dykes.
Park in Lakenheath and walk up the track
opposite the pond along the Undley road.
12 species recorded.
SUFFOLK WILDLIFE TRUST

MARKET WESTON FEN
near Diss
OS Map 144. TL 982 789.
Fen.
Limited parking in front of cottage at
reserve entrance along minor road to
Coney Weston from Hopton (off B1111).
SUFFOLK WILDLIFE TRUST

MINSMERE
near Saxmundham
OS Map 156. TM 470 671.
Coastal heath, marsh, sand dunes.
Follow RSPB signs off A12 at Yoxford.
Information centre, shop, café, toilets.
Over 20 species recorded.
RSPB

REDGRAVE & LOPHAM FENS
near Diss
OS Map 144. TM 046 797.
Fen, pools, dykes, carr, woodland.
From South Lopham, on the A1066 Diss to
Thetford road, take the B1113 south
towards Redgrave. After c.1 mile take the
minor road to the left. Follow this for c.0.5
mile to reach the car park. Visitor centre.
Over 20 species recorded inc. Ruddy
Darter. Also Fen Raft Spider.
SUFFOLK WILDLIFE TRUST

RIVER WAVENEY, GELDESTON
near Beccles
OS Map 134. TM 390 907.
See main site section page 207.
River, dykes, pasture, hedgerows.

Gazetteer

This site lies c.2 miles west of Beccles.
Species inc. Hairy Dragonfly, Norfolk Hawker, Scarce Chaser.

SURREY

Surrey Wildlife Trust
School Lane, Pirbright, Woking
GU24 0JN
TEL 01483 795440
EMAIL info@surreywt.org.uk
WWW.SURREYWILDLIFETRUST.CO.UK

The National Trust Regional Office: South East
Polesden Lacey, Dorking RH5 6BD
TEL 01372 453401

Websites
Dragonflies of North East Hampshire and Surrey Borders
HTTP://WEBSITE.LINEONE.NET/
~DRAGONFLIES.DELLS

BAGMOOR COMMON
near Godalming
OS Map 186. SU 926 423.
Birch woodland, stream.
On the west side of Milford, access is by footpath off the A3 through Borough Farm or off the B3001 opposite Blacklands Farm.
Species inc. Beautiful Demoiselle, Common Hawker, Golden-ringed Dragonfly, Downy and Brilliant Emeralds, Keeled Skimmer, Black Darter.
SURREY WILDLIFE TRUST

BARFOLD COPSE
near Haslemere
OS Map 186. SU 914 324.
Mixed woodland with hazel coppice.
Park along B2131 near second turning to Black Down and follow footpath to reserve.
RSPB

BASINGSTOKE CANAL
between Farnborough and Woking
OS Map 186. SU 893 550–SU 980 580.
Canal, various habitats.
Various parking places and access points, for example at SU 901 567.
Species inc. White-legged Damselfly, Southern and Brown Hawkers, Emperor Dragonfly.
WWW.BASINGSTOKE-CANAL.CO.UK

BAY POND
NEAR CATERHAM
OS MAP 187. TQ 353 516.
Hay meadow, lake, pond.
The reserve is in the village of Godstone off the A22, south of Junction 6 of the M25. In the village, park opposite the White Hart hotel and take the footpath east from the hotel past the village hall. Alternatively, access the reserve via the lane known as 'Path to Little Place' by Godstone Place.
Species inc. Blue-tailed Damselfly, Southern and Brown Hawkers.
SURREY WILDLIFE TRUST

ESHER & FAIRMILE COMMONS
near Esher
OS Map 187. TQ 130 623 & TQ 125 615.
See main site section page 168.
Woodland, grassland, ponds, scrub.
These two commons lie on the southern outskirts of Esher to the north and south of the A3.
Species inc. White-legged and Large Red-eyed Damselflies, Downy and Brilliant Emeralds.
ELMBRIDGE BOROUGH COUNCIL
WWW.ELMBRIDGE.GOV.UK

FRENSHAM COUNTRY PARK AND LITTLE POND
near Farnham
OS Map 186. SU 843 403.
Heathland, scrub, woodland, ponds.
The site lies both sides of the A287, c.10 miles south of Farnham. Car park and information centre at Great Pond.

Frensham Little Pond (not part of country park) has its own car park.
WAVERLEY BOROUGH COUNCIL, NATIONAL TRUST, SURREY HILLS AONB
WWW.SURREYHILLS.ORG

GREAT BOOKHAM COMMON
near Leatherhead
OS Map 187. TQ 130 565.
Woodland, ponds, ditches, streams.
The site lies c.3 miles west of Leatherhead and just north of Bookham station. Parking at Tunnel car park off Church Road at TQ 129 556, off Bookham Road at TQ 121 567 and off Cobham Road at TQ 133 568.
Over 20 species recorded.
NATIONAL TRUST

HEADLEY HEATH
near Leatherhead
OS Map 187. TQ 200 535.
Heathland with ponds.
The site lies c.2.5 miles south-east of Leatherhead beside the B2033, along which two car parks are situated.
Over 20 species recorded.
NATIONAL TRUST

LANGHAM'S POND, RUNNYMEDE
near Staines
OS Map 176. TQ 007 720.
Pond, fen, wet grassland, River Thames.
Runnymede is south of the A308 between Windsor and Staines. Car parks (charge). Toilets. Footpaths and Thames National Trail.
NATIONAL TRUST

LIGHTWATER COUNTRY PARK
near Camberley
OS Map 186. SU 915 620.
Heath, woodland, pond.
The park lies just off Junction 3 of the M3, between Bagshot and Lightwater. Signed from A322.
SURREY HEATH BOROUGH COUNCIL
WWW.SURREYHEATH.GOV.UK

PUTTENHAM COMMON
near Guildford
OS Map 186. SU 919 461.
Heath, woodland, ponds.
Three car parks situated off Suffield Lane south of Puttenham village.
Over 20 species recorded.
SURREY COUNTY COUNCIL, SURREY WILDLIFE TRUST

RIVER WEY
Guildford
OS Map 186. TQ 000 513.
Vegetated riverbank.
Parking in streets by river bridge. Search vegetation along towpath.
Species inc. White-legged Damselfly.
NATIONAL TRUST

THUNDRY MEADOWS
near Farnham
OS Map 186. SU 898 440.
Unimproved wet and dry meadows, river (Wey), pond.
Take the B3001 Farnham to Milford road. Access and limited roadside parking just west of Elstead. Do not damage fragile ditches and riverbanks and avoid bog areas.
Over 24 species recorded.
SURREY WILDLIFE TRUST

THURSLEY COMMON NNR
near Farnham
OS Map 186. SU 904 415.
See main site section page 222.
Heath, bog, shallow pools, runnels, streams and tree-edged lake.
Thursley Common lies c.7 miles south-west of Guildford.
Over 25 species inc. Beautiful Demoiselle, Small Red Damselfly, Emperor and Golden-ringed Dragonflies, Downy and Brilliant Emeralds, Keeled Skimmer, Black Darter.
NATURAL ENGLAND

Gazetteer

VANN LAKE
near Horsham
OS Map 187. TQ 157 394.
Ancient woodland, lake.
Contact SWT for permission to visit, access details and to arrange parking.
Over 20 species inc. Beautiful Demoiselle, Hairy Dragonfly, Downy and Brilliant Emeralds.
SURREY WILDLIFE TRUST

WARNHAM LNR
near Horsham
OS Map 187. TQ 168 323.
See main site section page 229.
Mill pond, reed fringe, meadows, scrub, woodland.
This site lies on the outskirts of Horsham.
Species inc. Banded Demoiselle, Large Red-eyed Damselfly, Downy and Brilliant Emeralds.
HORSHAM DISTRICT COUNCIL

SUSSEX

Sussex Wildlife Trust
Woods Mill, Shoreham Road, Henfield, West Sussex BN5 9SD
TEL 01273 492630
EMAIL enquiries@sussexwt.org.uk
WWW.SUSSEXWT.ORG.UK

The National Trust Regional Office: South East
Polesden Lacey, Dorking, Surrey RH5 6BD
TEL 01372 453401

County atlas/book
Dragonflies of Sussex. T.A. Belden *et al*, 2004, Sussex Wildlife Trust.

Websites
Damselflies & Dragonflies of the Adur Valley
WWW.GLAUCUS.ORG.UK/DRAGONFLY.HTM

Sussex Nature Web
WWW.SUSSEXNATUREWEB.BTINTERNET.CO.UK

AMBERLEY WILDBROOKS
near Storrington
OS Map 197. TQ 030 136.
Flood meadows with ditches.
Follow the Wey South Path either from Greatham Bridge (TQ 031 162) or from Amberley village. Keep strictly to footpath.
Species inc. Variable Damselfly, Hairy and Emperor Dragonflies, Ruddy Darter.
SUSSEX WILDLIFE TRUST

ASHDOWN FOREST
near East Grinstead
OS Map 187. TQ 435 310.
Boggy heathland with mixed woodland.
Car parks along A22 and along minor roads in area. Ashdown Forest Centre is c.1 mile along the minor road running east from Wych Cross to Coleman's Hatch.
CONSERVATORS OF ASHDOWN FOREST
WWW.ASHDOWNFOREST.ORG

BEWL WATER
near Tunbridge Wells
OS Map 188. TQ 675 330.
Open water, scrub.
Visitor centre off B2100 north-east of Wadhurst at TQ 675 337. Marsh at the southern end of Pinton Creek is good for dragonflies. Parking charge.
Species inc. Beautiful and Banded Demoiselles, Large Red-eyed Damselfly, Hairy and Emperor Dragonflies.
SOUTHERN WATER
WWW.SOUTHERNWATER.CO.UK
WWW.BEWLWATER.ORG

BUCHAN COUNTRY PARK
near Crawley
OS Map 187. TQ 245 344.
Coniferous wood, hazel coppice, parkland, lakes.
Car park along A264 at TQ 246 347. Information centre.
Over 20 species inc. Downy Emerald.
WEST SUSSEX COUNTY COUNCIL
WWW.WESTSUSSEX.GOV.UK

BURTON POND WOODLANDS & WELCHS COMMON
near Petworth
OS Map 197. SU 978 181.
Mill pond, marsh, wet heath, bog, woodland.
Two miles south of Petworth on the A285, head east on the minor road for c.1 mile. Car park by old mill.
SUSSEX WILDLIFE TRUST, WEST SUSSEX COUNTY COUNCIL

DITCHLING COMMON COUNTRY PARK
near Burgess Hill
OS Map 198. TQ 334 183.
Pond and stream surrounded by marshland and woodland.
The common lies east of Burgess Hill. Car park off B2113 at TQ 336 181. Nature trail.
Over 15 species recorded.
EAST SUSSEX COUNTY COUNCIL
WWW.EASTSUSSEX.GOV.UK

EBERNOE COMMON
near Petworth
OS Map 197. SU 976 278.
Woodland, grassland, ponds.
Head north from Petworth on the A283 for c.3 miles, then take the minor road towards Balls Cross. On reaching a red phone box, take the immediate right turn to the church and a small car park. Network of rides and paths. Beware – it is easy to get lost!
Over 15 species recorded.
SUSSEX WILDLIFE TRUST

NEWBURY POND
near Haywards Heath
OS Map 198. TQ 305 244.
Pond, marsh, woodland.
Parking along Newbury Lane off A272 on southern edge of Cuckfield.

OLD LODGE
near Crowborough
OS Map 188. TQ 460 302.
Mixed woodland, heathland, bogs.
Reserve lies west of Crowborough and is just off the B2026 to Hartfield. There is a small parking area to the west of this road

c.450m north of the junction with the B2188. Waymarked trail.
SUSSEX WILDLIFE TRUST

POWDERMILL WOOD
near Hastings
OS Map 199. TQ 735 144.
Alder woodland, pools.
Car park on north side of Powdermill Lane (B2095) south-west of Battle. Nature trail.
SUSSEX WILDLIFE TRUST, POWDERMILL TRUST
WWW.POWDERMILLTRUST.CO.UK

RIVER ARUN, NEW BRIDGE
near Billingshurst
OS Map 197. TQ 069 260.
See main site section page 203.
Disused canal and river (Arun).
New Bridge is situated along the A272 between Billingshurst and Petworth.
Over 15 species recorded inc. White-legged Damselfly, Hairy and Club-tailed Dragonflies, Downy Emerald, Scarce Chaser.

SEVEN SISTERS COUNTRY PARK
near Seaford
OS Map 199. TV 525 986.
Grazing marsh, ponds, grassland.
The country park is at Exceat between Seaford and Eastbourne. Main car park at TV 519 995. Waymarked paths. Visitor centre open daily 10.30am–4.30pm.
SUSSEX COUNTY COUNCIL
WWW.SEVENSISTERS.ORG.UK

STEDHAM COMMON
near Midhurst
OS Map 197. SU 856 218.
Heathland, scrub.
West of Midhurst, car park at Iping Common on west side of Stedham Common off A272.
SUSSEX WILDLIFE TRUST

STOPHAM BRIDGE
near Pulborough
OS Map 197. TQ 029 184.
River Arun.
Situated along A283 between Pulborough

and Fittleworth. Follow public footpaths from Stopham Bridge.
Species inc. Hairy and Club-tailed Dragonflies, Scarce Chaser.

WALTHAM BROOKS
near Pulborough
OS Map 197. TQ 129 161.
Grazing marsh, pool, dykes, river.
Park at Greatham Bridge east of Coldwaltham on the A29. Walk back towards Coldwaltham and take footpath on left after old canal bridge. No access off footpath.
Over 20 species recorded.
Sussex Wildlife Trust

WOODS MILL
near Brighton
OS Map 198. TQ 218 138.
Lake, marsh, meadow and woodland.
Entrance is just off the A2037 along a minor road c.1.5 miles south of Henfield. Reserve open 9am–5pm April to last weekend in September. Car park and information centre (open Sundays only, 11am–5pm during the same period).
Species inc. Large Red Damselfly, Emperor Dragonfly.
Sussex Wildlife Trust

TEES VALLEY
Formerly Cleveland

Tees Valley Wildlife Trust
Margrove Heritage Centre, Margrove Park, Boosbeck TS12 3BZ
Tel 01287 636382
Email info@teesvalleywt.org
WWW.TEESWILDLIFETRUST.ORG

Natural England Regional Office: North East
Quadrant, Newburn Riverside, Newcastle NE15 8NZ
Tel 0191 229 5500
Email northeast@naturalengland. org.uk

BOWESFIELD POND LNR
Stockton-on-Tees
OS Map 93. NZ 433 178.
Pond, scrub.
Leave the A135 along the A1027 at Hartburn (southern Stockton). Follow road over railway, past Ropner Park and turn left onto B6541. Path to the reserve is on left c.75m from the Bowls Club.
Tees Valley Wildlife Trust

CHARLTON'S POND LNR
Billingham
OS Map 93. NZ 461 233.
Ponds, scrub.
The pond lies behind Billingham Town FC's ground. From Billingham station take Warwick Crescent and then into Bedford Terrace to the football ground. Walk along the fenced side of the ground to the reserve.

COATHAM MARSH
near Redcar
OS Map 93. NZ 586 287.
Marsh, meadows, lakes.
Leave A1085 Redcar to Middlesbrough road west of Redcar, turning into Kirkleatham Lane and heading towards Coatham. Turn left into Tod Point Road and head towards Warrenby village to the reserve car park. Leaflet available.
Species inc. Ruddy Darter.
Tees Valley Wildlife Trust

TYNE & WEAR

Northumberland Wildlife Trust
St Nicholas Park, Newcastle upon Tyne NE3 3XT
Tel 0191 284 6884
Email mail@northwt.org.uk
WWW.NWT.ORG.UK

The National Trust Regional Office: North East
Scot's Gap, Morpeth, Northumberland NE61 4EG
Tel 01670 774691

RYTON WILLOWS LNR
Ryton
OS Map 88. NZ 152 650.
Woodland, grassland, pools.
*Park around village green and follow
footpath signed to Ryton Willows.*
GATESHEAD METROPOLITAN BORO' COUNCIL

WARWICKSHIRE

Warwickshire Wildlife Trust
Brandon Marsh Nature Centre,
Brandon Lane, Coventry CV3 3GW
TEL 024 7630 2912
EMAIL enquiries@wkwt.org.uk
WWW.WARWICKSHIRE-WILDLIFE-TRUST.ORG.UK

The National Trust Regional Office:
West Midlands
Atttingham Park, Shrewsbury,
Shropshire SY4 4TP
TEL 01743 708100

Websites
Warwickshire Dragonfly Group
WWW.REEVE60.UKLINUX.NET/WDG/

ALVECOTE POOLS
near Tamworth
OS Maps 139/140. SK 251 043.
Pools, marsh and woodland between
canal and river (Anker).
*On the B5000, c.2 miles from the centre of
Tamworth, take the minor road (Robeys
Lane) to Alvecote. Park c.0.5 mile down
this road on the right at Alvecote Priory
picnic site. Entrance gate between railway
and canal.*
Over 20 species recorded.
WARWICKSHIRE WILDLIFE TRUST

BRANDON MARSH
near Coventry
OS Map 140. SP 386 754.
See main site section page 145.
Pools, marsh, grassland, woodland.
The site is c.1 mile south-east of Coventry.
Species inc. White-legged Damselfly,
Migrant and Brown Hawkers,
Emperor Dragonfly.
WARWICKSHIRE WILDLIFE TRUST

KINGSBURY WATER PARK
near Tamworth
OS Map 139. SP 210 960.
See main site section page 185.
Gravel pits, grassland, scrub, woodland.
*The park lies c.5 miles south of Tamworth
and c.2 miles from Junction 9 of the M42.*
Species inc. Large Red-eyed Damselfly,
Migrant Hawker, Emperor Dragonfly.
WARWICKSHIRE COUNTY COUNCIL

LEAM VALLEY LNR
near Leamington Spa
OS Map 151. SP 330 658.
Woodland, grassland, marsh, ponds,
River Leam.
*The reserve lies on the eastern edge of
Leamington Spa.*
WARWICKSHIRE WILDLIFE TRUST,
WARWICKSHIRE DISTRICT COUNCIL

UFTON FIELDS
near Leamington Spa
OS Map 151. SP 378 615.
Limestone grassland, ponds, scrub.
*Leave the A425, east of Leamington, south
down the minor road at the Ufton
roundabout. Car park on the left. Disabled
access.*
Species inc. Large Red-eyed Damselfly,
Ruddy Darter.
WARWICKSHIRE WILDLIFE TRUST
WWW.GEOCITIES.COM/CROGLINUK/

WEST MIDLANDS

The Wildlife Trust for Birmingham &
The Black Country
28 Harborne Road, Edgbaston,
Birmingham B15 3AA
TEL 0121 454 1199
EMAIL info@bbcwildlife.org.uk
WWW.WILDLIFETRUST.ORG.UK/URBANWT

The National Trust Regional Office:
West Midlands
Attingham Park, Shrewsbury, Shrops
SY4 4TP
TEL 01743 708100

Gazetteer

Gazetteer

HAY HEAD WOOD LNR
Walsall
OS Map 139. SP 043 990.
Woodland, grassland, scrub, marsh, open water, stream.
Car park along Longwood Lane south off Aldridge Road (A454) between Walsall and Aldridge.
WALSALL COUNTRYSIDE SERVICES
WWW.WALSALL.GOV.UK

PARK LIME PITS
Walsall
OS Map 139. SP 029 999.
Pools, marsh, grassland, scrub.
Car park at end of Park Road south of B4154 in Rushall.
Species inc. Emperor Dragonfly.
WALSALL COUNTRYSIDE SERVICES
WWW.WALSALL.GOV.UK

SALTWELLS LNR
Dudley
OS Map 139. SO 935 868.
See main site section page 210.
Grassland, scrub, pools, streams.
Saltwells Local Nature Reserve lies within the conurbation of the Borough of Dudley.
Species inc. Emerald, Large Red and Variable Damselflies, Migrant Hawker, Emperor Dragonfly, Ruddy and Black Darters.
DUDLEY METROPOLITAN BOROUGH COUNCIL
WWW.DUDLEY.GOV.UK/

WILTSHIRE

Wiltshire Wildlife Trust
Elm Tree Court, Long Street, Devizes
SN10 1NJ
TEL 01380 725670
EMAIL admin@wiltshirewildlife.org
WWW.WILTSHIREWILDLIFE.ORG

The National Trust Regional Office:
Wessex
Eastleigh Court, Bishopstrow,
Warminster BA12 9HW
TEL 01985 843600

Websites
Wiltshire Wildlife
WWW.WILTSHIRE-WEB.CO.UK/WILDLIFE/

BLACKMOOR COPSE
near Salisbury
OS Map 184. SU 233 288.
Ancient woodland with ponds.
The reserve lies c.6 miles east of Salisbury, between the A30 and the A36, and is on the western side of the minor road from Winterslow to East Grimstead. The main entrance is at the junction with Ben Lane, the road to Farley. There is limited parking on the wide road verges around SU 231 289. Leaflet available. Information board at entrance.
Over 15 species recorded.
WILTSHIRE WILDLIFE TRUST

COATE WATER COUNTRY PARK
Swindon
OS Map 173. SU 176 826.
Lake and wetland.
Situated on the south-east side of Swindon. From Junction 15 of the M4, follow A4257 for Swindon town centre. Country park is signed from the next roundabout. Café, toilets.
SWINDON BOROUGH COUNCIL
WWW.SWINDON.GOV.UK

CONIGRE MEAD
Melksham
OS Map 173. ST 901 637.
Meadow, ponds, river (Avon).
The reserve is on the western edge of Melksham on the far side of the cemetery next to the river.
Species inc. Emperor Dragonfly.
WILTSHIRE WILDLIFE TRUST

JONES'S MILL
near Pewsey
OS Map 173. SU 169 611 (parking).
Chalk stream and wet meadows.
Park on Dursden Lane (off B3087 east of Pewsey) over the railway at SU 169 611.
WILTSHIRE WILDLIFE TRUST

KENNET & AVON CANAL
near Pewsey
OS Map 173. SU 189 623.
Canal.
Park carefully along minor roads north-east of Pewsey, around Milkhouse Water or New Mill, and access canal eastwards along towpath.

KENNET & AVON CANAL
Trowbridge
OS Map 173. ST 872 606.
Canal and meadows.
The canal lies just north-east of Trowbridge. Park carefully around Marsh Road (B3105) near Hilperton and access canal along towpath.

THE LACOCK ESTATE
Lacock
OS Map 173. ST 919 684.
River Avon.
The estate lies c.3 miles south of Chippenham, east of the A350. Park at the National Trust car park at Lacock Abbey. Footpath along riverbank. Ornamental ponds in Lacock Abbey. Entrance fee.
Species inc. White-legged Damselfly.
NATIONAL TRUST

NORTH MEADOW NNR
near Cricklade
OS Map 173. SU 099 944 (parking).
Flood-plain, hay meadow, ditches
Park in lay-by on outskirts of Cricklade at SU 099 944. Keep to rights of way.
15 species recorded.
NATURAL ENGLAND

RAMSBURY MEADOW
near Marlborough
OS Map 174. SU 273 714.
See main site section page 203.
Former water meadow with pond beside River Kennet.
Ramsbury Meadow lies c.7 miles east of Marlborough.
Many common species.
WILTSHIRE WILDLIFE TRUST

RAVENSROOST WOOD & MEADOWS
near Swindon
OS Map 173. SU 024 876.
See main site section page 201.
Woodland, ponds.
Ravensroost Wood lies c.6 miles to the west of Swindon.
Species inc. Migrant Hawker, Emperor Dragonfly, Ruddy Darter.
WILTSHIRE WILDLIFE TRUST

RED LODGE POND
near Swindon
OS Map 173. SU 054 888.
Woodland with large pond.
From Wootton Bassett, west of Swindon, take the B4042 towards Brinkworth. Just after the motorway underpass, head north on the B4696. After c.3 miles park in the gateway on the right, at SU 054 888, taking care not to block the entrance.
WILTSHIRE WILDLIFE TRUST, FOREST ENTERPRISE

RIVER AVON
near Durrington
OS Map 184. SU 155 450.
Stream and water meadows.
Park in Durrington near church and follow footpath signs.

SMALLBROOK MEADOWS LNR
Warminster
OS Map 183. ST 878 443.
Wet meadows, rivers (Were and Wylye), pond, woodland.
The reserve is just south of Warminster town centre and next to the Lake Pleasure Grounds. Park in car park on Smallbrook Road. Access either via the car park or by walking through the formal boating park from Weymouth Street. Circular walk.
WILTSHIRE WILDLIFE TRUST, WEST WILTSHIRE DISTRICT COUNCIL

STOURHEAD
near Mere
OS Map 183. ST 772 340.
Parkland with lakes and ponds.
This site is at Stourton, off the B3092, c.3

miles north-west of Mere. Garden open all year during daylight hours (charge). Car park, NT shop, Wiltshire Wildlife Trust leaflet. The upper pond is good for dragonflies.
NATIONAL TRUST

SWILLBROOK LAKES
near Swindon
OS Maps 163/173. SU 017 938.
Gravel pits, marshy edges, reedbed.
Part of Cotswold Water Park (Lakes 46 and 48). From the A419 north of Swindon, follow signposts to Cotswold Water Park. After the Keynes Country Park turning take the next left (signed to Minety). Entrance over a stile on left (Clattinger Farm is opposite). Limited parking by the road at SU 017 938.
13 species recorded inc. Emerald Damselfly, Southern and Brown Hawkers.
WILTSHIRE WILDLIFE TRUST

WORCESTERSHIRE

Worcestershire Wildlife Trust
Lower Smite Farm, Smite Hill, Hindlip, Worcester WR3 8SZ
TEL 01905 754919
EMAIL enquiries@
worcestershirewildlifetrust.org
WWW.WORCSWILDLIFETRUST.CO.UK

The National Trust Regional Office: West Midlands
Attingham Park, Shrewsbury, Shrops SY4 4TP
TEL 01743 708100

BLACKSTONE PICNIC SITE
near Kidderminster
OS Map 138. SO 797 743.
River Severn.
The site is south-west of Kidderminster and is accessed via the B4195. Parking, picnic area, trails.
Species inc. Club-tailed Dragonfly.
WORCESTERSHIRE COUNTY COUNCIL
HTTP://WORCESTERSHIRE.WHUB.ORG.UK

BROADWAY GRAVEL PIT
near Evesham
OS Map 150. SP 086 379.
Scrub, marsh, pools.
Take the A44 south-east from Evesham to Broadway. In the village, take the minor road towards Childswickham. Car park just before disused railway.
WORCESTERSHIRE WILDLIFE TRUST

THE CHRISTOPHER CADBURY RESERVE, UPTON WARREN
near Bromsgrove
OS Map 150. SO 936 677.
Pools, marsh, grassland.
From the A38 Bromsgrove to Droitwich road, turn into the lane with the AA phone box on the corner, c.200m north of the Swan Inn at Upton Warren. Car park and access at SO 936 677. Search the freshwater Moors Pools on the north side of the reserve. Non-members require a permit (charge) from Trust HQ or the Outdoor Education Centre.
WORCESTERSHIRE WILDLIFE TRUST

FECKENHAM WYLDE MOOR
near Redditch
OS Map 150. SP 012 606.
See main site section page 170.
Fen, reedbed and pools.
The reserve lies c.3 miles south of Redditch.
15 species inc. Large Red Damselfly, Brown Hawker, Emperor Dragonfly.
WORCESTERSHIRE WILDLIFE TRUST

HARTLEBURY COMMON
Stourport-on-Severn
OS Map 138. SO 820 705.
Heathland, bog and pools.
Leave Stourport south along the A4025, which crosses the common. A number of parking areas available.
Over 20 species recorded.
WORCESTERSHIRE COUNTY COUNCIL
WWW.WORCESTERSHIRE.GOV.UK

IPSLEY ALDERS MARSH
Redditch
OS Map 150. SP 076 677.
See main site section page 180.

Woodland, wet meadow, ponds.
This small nature reserve lies within the eastern outskirts of Redditch.
Species inc. Large Red-eyed Damselfly, Black Darter.
WORCESTERSHIRE WILDLIFE TRUST

THE KNAPP AND PAPERMILL
near Great Malvern
OS Map 150. SO 750 522.
Woodland, meadows, stream.
Leave the A4103 Hereford to Worcester road at Bransford and take the minor road west towards Alfrick Pound. Reserve entrance lies c.3 miles along this road. Park in lay-by before Bridge's Stone bridge (over Leigh Brook).
WORCESTERSHIRE WILDLIFE TRUST

MONKWOOD
near Worcester
OS Map 150. SO 604 806.
Deciduous woodland, pond.
Head north of Worcester on the A443 for c.3 miles, then take the Sinton Green turn on the left for c.1 mile then left towards Wichenford and Monkwood Green. After c.2 miles turn right at Monkwood Green. Follow the road through the wood to the north side where a track leads to the car park. Follow footpaths and rides.
WORCESTERSHIRE WILDLIFE TRUST, BUTTERFLY CONSERVATION
WWW.BUTTERFLY-CONSERVATION.ORG

RAVENSHILL WOOD
near Worcester
OS Map 150. SO 740 539.
Mixed woodland, pools.
Leave Worcester west along the A44 towards Bromyard and then take the minor road towards Alfrick just after the B4197 (on right). Car park on right after c.1 mile, opposite pool. Information leaflets from the Discovery Centre (Mar–Oct). Toilets.
Species inc. Brown Hawker, Emperor Dragonfly, Common and Ruddy Darters.
WORCESTERSHIRE WILDLIFE TRUST

RIVER AVON
between Pershore and Defford
OS Map 150. SO 944 448.
River Avon, tree lines, hedgerows.
Parking at Pershore Bridge at SO 952 450 south of Pershore. Follow footpath westwards along river.
Species inc. White-legged Damselfly, Club-tailed Dragonfly.

SECKLEY WOOD, WYRE FOREST
near Kidderminster
OS Map 138. SO 765 785.
Woodland alongside River Severn.
Leave Kidderminster north-west along the B4194 and park in the forest car park after c.2 miles. Follow tracks through wood to river. Picnic area, woodland trails. Other nearby woodland areas also worth searching.
Species inc. White-legged Damselfly, Club-tailed Dragonfly.
FOREST ENTERPRISE

SHRAWLEY WOOD
near Worcester
OS Map 150. SO 807 658.
Woodland, grassland, ponds, River Severn.
Entrance opposite New Inn public house in Shrawley. Keep to footpaths.
Species inc. Large Red-eyed Damselfly.
FOREST ENTERPRISE

TIDDESLEY WOOD
near Pershore
OS Map 150. SO 929 462.
Mixed woodland, coppice, rides.
Take the A44 from Evesham to Pershore. In Pershore village take the minor road signed Besford and Croome. Car park on left after c.0.75 mile. Beware – do not enter area of military firing range when red flags flying.
Species inc. White-legged Damselfly, Club-tailed Dragonfly from nearby River Avon.
WORCESTERSHIRE WILDLIFE TRUST

Gazetteer

TRENCH WOOD
near Droitwich
OS Map 150. SO 930 589.
Deciduous woodland.
Car park on the Sale Green to Dunhampstead road c.4 miles south-east of Droitwich.
WORCESTERSHIRE WILDLIFE TRUST, BUTTERFLY CONSERVATION
WWW.BUTTERFLY-CONSERVATION.ORG

YORKSHIRE

Yorkshire Wildlife Trust
1 St George's Place, York YO24 1GN
TEL 01904 659570
EMAIL info@ywt.org.uk
WWW.YORKSHIRE-WILDLIFE-TRUST.ORG.UK

Sheffield Wildlife Trust
37 Stafford Road, Sheffield S2 2SF
TEL 0114 263 4335
EMAIL mail@wildsheffield.com
WWW.WILDSHEFFIELD.COM

The National Trust Regional Office: Yorkshire
Goddards, 27 Tadcaster Road, Dringhouses, York, YO24 1GG
TEL 01904 702021

Websites
Knaresborough Wildlife
WWW.NATURE.HARROGATE.NET

Yorkshire BDS
WWW.YORKSHIREDRAGONFLIES.ORG.UK
East Riding Dragonflies
ERDRAGONFLIES.CO.UK/INDEX.HTM

AGDEN BOG
near Sheffield
OS Map 110. SK 252 929.
Bog and grassland.
Park along road at Agden Reservoir and take footpath to reserve.
YORKSHIRE WILDLIFE TRUST

BRANDESBURTON PONDS
near Kingston upon Hull
OS Map 107. TA 105 470.
Ponds.
Access off A165 south-west of Brandesburton.
Species inc. Large Red-eyed Damselfly, Migrant and Brown Hawkers, Emperor Dragonfly. Lesser Emperor Dragonfly has been recorded.

BURTON RIGGS
near Scarborough
OS Map 101. TA 032 832.
Lakes and scrub.
The reserve is east of the village of Seamer, south of Scarborough. The Scarborough to Filey railway line runs along the western edge of the reserve. Park off the roundabout on the A64, opposite supermarket and the industrial estate. Marked trail.
YORKSHIRE WILDLIFE TRUST

DENABY INGS
Doncaster
OS Map 111. SE 503 007.
Reclaimed colliery area, lakes, woodland, grassland.
Leave Doncaster south-west along the A630 and then take the A6023 north-west in Conisbrough to Mexborough. On entering Mexborough take the minor road (Pastures Lane) north-east to reserve car park at SE 498 008. Nature trail.
Species inc. Brown Hawker.
YORKSHIRE WILDLIFE TRUST

DUNDALE POND
Levisham Moor, near Pickering
OS Map 94. SE 828 918.
See main site section page 165.
Moorland, ponds, streams, seepages.
Dundale Pond lies c.8 miles north of Pickering.
Species inc. Emerald Damselfly, Golden-ringed Dragonfly, Black Darter.
PART OF NORTH YORKSHIRE MOORS NATIONAL PARK
WWW.MOORS.UK.NET

FAIRBURN INGS
near Castleford
OS Map 105. SE 451 277.
See main site section page 169.
Pools, streams, marsh.
Fairburn Ings lies on the northern outskirts of Castleford and c.4 miles from Junction 33 (Ferrybridge/A1) of the M62.
Species inc. Emerald and Azure Damselflies, Brown Hawker, Four-spotted Chaser.
RSPB

FEN BOG
near Pickering
OS Map 94. SE 853 981.
See main site section page 172.
Boggy grass moorland.
Fen Bog lies west of the A169 midway between Pickering and Whitby.
Species inc. Golden-ringed Dragonfly, Black Darter.
YORKSHIRE WILDLIFE TRUST

HARDCASTLE CRAGS
near Hebden Bridge
OS Map 103. SD 988 291.
Rock outcrops, deciduous woodland, river (Hebden Water), moorland.
The site lies 1.5 miles north-west of Hebden Bridge off the A6033. Two car parks. Marked trails through the woods and along the river.
Species inc. Common Hawker.
NATIONAL TRUST

JOHNNY BROWN'S COMMON
near Barnsley
OS Map 111. SE 460 125.
See main site section page 181.
Reclaimed coal tip. Ponds in meadows, marsh, scrub.
The area is situated c.6 miles north-east of Barnsley.
Species inc. Migrant Hawker, Emperor Dragonfly, Ruddy Darter.
WAKEFIELD METROPOLITAN DISTRICT COUNCIL
WWW.WAKEFIELD.GOV.UK

POTTERIC CARR
near Doncaster
OS Map 111. SE 593 006.
Drainage dykes and subsidence pools.
The reserve is off the A6182 just south of Doncaster. Take the turn heading east (signposted 'No Through Road') off the roundabout nearest Junction 3 of the M18. After c.50m turn right into the car park. Field centre and footpaths. Café. Entrance charge (concessions for YWT members).
Over 18 species inc. Emperor Dragonfly, Black Darter.
YORKSHIRE WILDLIFE TRUST
WWW.POTTERIC-CARR.ORG.UK

SOUTHERSCALES NATURE RESERVE
near Ingleton
OS Map 98. SD 742 769.
Limestone outcrops and grassland, peat moss with pools.
Reserve accessed from Chapel-le-Dale on the B6255, Ingleton to Hawes Road. Either start from the Ingleborough signpost at SD 744 777 on Sleights Road, above the Hill Inn, and follow the footpath across three fields to the reserve; or start from the Ingleborough signpost at SD 739 771 opposite the road to Chapel-le-Dale church and cross the fields to Souther Scales Farm. Keep to the public footpath for safety reasons and to minimise erosion. Good walking boots essential.
YORKSHIRE WILDLIFE TRUST

STAVELEY NATURE RESERVE
near Knaresborough
OS Map 99. SE 366 634.
Take the A6055, either from Knaresborough or the A1, and follow minor roads to Staveley. Park in village and follow the footpath beginning at SE 368 629.
Over 17 species recorded.
YORKSHIRE WILDLIFE TRUST

Gazetteer

WHELDRAKE INGS NNR
near York
OS Map 105. SE 702 442.
Flood meadows along River Derwent.
*Parking off Church Lane, Wheldrake at SE
690 447 and further south along Ings Lane
at SE 694 444.*
Species inc. Large Red-eyed Damselfly.
NATURAL ENGLAND, YORKSHIRE WILDLIFE
TRUST

WINTERSETT RESERVOIR
near Wakefield
OS Map 111. SE 376 147.
Reservoir.
*The reservoir lies south-east of Wakefield
and south of the A638. Parking and visitor
centre off Haw Park Lane, Wintersett.*
YORKSHIRE WATER

WALES

County/Regional Recorders
Details of recorders at
WWW.DRAGONFLYSOC.ORG.UK
WWW.ATROPOS.INFO/DRAGONFLY.HTML

Countryside Council for Wales
Maes-y-Ffynnon, Penrhosgarnedd,
Bangor, Gwynedd LL57 2DW
TEL 0845 130 6229
WWW.CCW.GOV.UK

Forestry Commission Wales
Victoria House, Victoria Terrace,
Aberystwyth, Ceredigion SY23 2DQ
TEL 0845 604 0845
WWW.FORESTRY.GOV.UK/WALES

National Trust Office for Wales
Trinity Square, Llandudno LL30 2DE
TEL 01492 860123
WWW.NATIONALTRUST.ORG.UK

RSPB Wales
Sutherland House, Castlebridge,
Cowbridge Road East, Cardiff CF11
9AB
TEL 02920 353000
WWW.RSPB.ORG.UK

Wildlife Trusts in Wales

Brecknock Wildlife Trust
Lion House, Bethel Square, Brecon,
Powys LD3 7AY
TEL 01874 625708
EMAIL brecknockwt@cix.co.uk
WWW.BRECKNOCKWILDLIFETRUST.ORG.UK

Gwent Wildlife Trust
Seddon House, Dingestow, Monmouth
NP25 4DY
TEL 01600 740358
EMAIL gwentwildlife@cix.co.uk
WWW.GWENTWILDLIFE.ORG

Montgomeryshire Wildlife Trust
Collott House, 20 Severn Street,
Welshpool, Powys SY21 7AD
TEL 01938 555654
EMAIL INFO@MONTWT.CO.UK
WWW.MONTWT.CO.UK

North Wales Wildlife Trust
376 High Street, Bangor, Gwynedd
LL57 1YE
TEL 01248 351541
EMAIL nwwt@cix.co.uk
WWW.WILDLIFETRUST.ORG.UK/NORTHWALES

Radnorshire Wildlife Trust
Warwick House, High Street,
Llandrindod Wells, Powys LD1 6AG
TEL 01597 823298
EMAIL info@radnorshirewildlifetrust.
org.uk
WWW.RADNORSHIREWILDLIFETRUST.ORG.UK

The Wildlife Trust of South and West Wales
Nature Centre, Parc Slip, Fountain
Road, Tondu, Bridgend, Mid
Glamorgan CF32 0EH
TEL 01656 724100
EMAIL info@welshwildlife.org
WWW.WELSHWILDLIFE.ORG

Websites
Dragonflies of Montgomeryshire
WWW.SUNNYMEADE.PLUS.COM

BRIDGEND

KENFIG NNR
near Porthcawl
OS Map 170. SS 800 815.
See main site section page 184.
Pools, sand dunes and dune slacks.
Kenfig lies c.2 miles north of Porthcawl.
Species inc. Hairy and Emperor
Dragonflies, Keeled Skimmer, Ruddy
Darter.
COUNTRYSIDE COUNCIL FOR WALES,
BRIDGEND COUNTY BOROUGH COUNCIL
WWW.BRIDGEND.GOV.UK

**PARC SLIP NATURE PARK &
PARK POND NATURE RESERVE**
near Bridgend
OS Map 170. SS 880 840.
Restored colliery area – grassland,
ponds, marsh, scrub, woodland.
*Leave the M4 north of Bridgend at
Junction 36 and head westwards to
Fountain village on the B4281. Turn north
along Fountain Road to visitor centre and
car park. Nature trail.*
Species inc. Scarce Blue-tailed
Damselfly, Emperor Dragonfly, Four-
spotted and Broad-bodied Chasers.
WILDLIFE TRUST OF SOUTH AND WEST WALES

CAERPHILLY

DAN-Y-GRAIG RESERVE
Risca
OS Map 171. ST 235 905.
Limestone grassland, deciduous
woodland, pond.
*On the B4591 in the centre of Risca, turn
west down Dan-y-Graig Road. Parking
available underneath the bypass. Walk
uphill to the left of Dan-y-Graig Cottages
and go through gate to reserve. Leaflet
available.*
GWENT WILDLIFE TRUST

CARMARTHENSHIRE

FFRWD FARM FEN
near Llanelli
OS Map 159. SN 420 026.
Fen, pools, ditches, reedbeds.
*From the A484 north-west of Pembury,
turn north-east onto the B4317. There are
two access points along this road, one at the
gate at SN 418 022 and the other along the
towpath of the disused Ashburnham canal.*
Species inc. Variable Damselfly, Hairy
Dragonfly.
WILDLIFE TRUST OF SOUTH AND WEST WALES

PEMBREY COUNTRY PARK
near Llanelli
OS Map 159. SN 415 007 (parking).
Woodland with rides, sand dunes,
forest pools.
*From the Kidwelly side of Pembrey village
on the A484, turn south into Factory Road.
Cross a railway bridge and continue to car
parks at SN 415 007. Entrance fee. Nature
trails, visitor centre, restaurant. Open
daily from dawn until dusk.*
CARMARTHENSHIRE COUNTY COUNCIL
WWW.CARMARTHENSHIRE.GOV.UK

CEREDIGION

CORS CARON NNR
near Lampeter
**OS Maps 135/146. SN 695 631
(parking).**
Raised peat bog and pools by Afon
Teifi.
*Car park along B4343 c.2.5 miles north of
Tregaron. Open access along disused
railway line and boardwalks. Permit
required for riverside walk (contact reserve
managers on 01974 298480). Visit the Red
Kite Centre in Tregaron for more
information on the reserve.*
Species inc. Golden-ringed Dragonfly,
Keeled Skimmer, Black Darter.
COUNTRYSIDE COUNCIL FOR WALES

Gazetteer

Gazetteer

CORS FOCHNO NNR (BORTH BOG)
near Aberystwyth
OS Map 135. SN 630 910 (centre of area).
Raised peat bog.
Permit required, however, a public footpath from Tre Taliesin runs along the southern edge of the bog, and another from Borth runs beside the Afon Leri along the western edge. Day permit and leaflets on the local area available from the visitor centre at Ynyslas dunes at SN 609 941 (at end of minor road heading north from Ynyslas village).
Species inc. Small Red Damselfly, Hairy Dragonfly.
COUNTRYSIDE COUNCIL FOR WALES

LLYN EIDDWEN
near Aberystwyth
OS Map 135. SN 607 674.
Upland lake, grassland, bog.
From Aberystwyth take the A487 and then the A485 south towards Lampeter. After c.1.5 miles turn right at Abermad onto the B4576 and follow this road until reaching Llangwyryfon. In the village head south-east along the minor road to Trefenter. Just south of Trefenter village, take the footpath which passes from north to south through the reserve and allows access to the western side of the lake. Roadside parking only. Do not walk on fragile and dangerous boggy areas. Not suitable for wheelchairs.
Species inc. Beautiful and Banded Demoiselles, Keeled Skimmer, Black Darter.
WILDLIFE TRUST OF SOUTH AND WEST WALES

LLYN FANOD
near Aberaeron
OS Map 146. SN 604 645.
Upland lake with fen.
From the B4577 between Tyncelyn and Aberarth, head north on minor road c.2.5 miles west of Tyncelyn. Roadside parking at crossroads to north-east of Llyn Fanod (SN 607 646). Follow footpath west to reserve. Keep to shores of lake.
WILDLIFE TRUST OF SOUTH AND WEST WALES

WELSH WILDLIFE CENTRE
near Cardigan
OS Map 145. SN 185 455.
See main site section page 233.
Woodland, meadow, wetland.
The Welsh Wildlife Centre is situated on the outskirts of Cardigan.
Species inc. Beautiful Demoiselle, Scarce Blue-tailed and Blue-tailed Damselflies, Southern Hawker, Emperor and Golden-ringed Dragonflies, Broad-bodied Chaser.
WILDLIFE TRUST OF SOUTH AND WEST WALES

CONWY

BLAEN-Y WEIRGLODD
near Llanrwst
OS Map 116. SH 914 633.
Peatbog, moorland.
Take the B5384 from Llansannan towards Gwytherin, take the second left, go over a cattle grid and park in the lay-by on right before a dirt track on the left and before another cattle grid. On foot, cross the field on your left and go through the kissing gate. Follow the raised bank on your left to reach the reserve. Do not walk over the fragile bog, keep to footpaths. Stout footwear/wellingtons recommended. Not suitable for wheelchairs.
NORTH WALES WILDLIFE TRUST

CORS BODGYNYDD
near Betws-y-coed
OS Map 115. SH 767 597.
See main site section page 161.
Moorland bog.
The site lies c.3 miles north-west of Betws-y-Coed.
Species inc. Four-spotted Chaser, Keeled Skimmer.
NORTH WALES WILDLIFE TRUST

DENBIGHSHIRE

GORS MAEN LLWYD
near Denbigh
OS Map 116. SH 975 580.
Heather moorland, lake, blanket bog.
Take the A543 west from Denbigh. After c.7 miles head south on B4501 to Llyn Brenig. The reserve is at the northern end of this lake. Take next left and then park at the top car park (SH 970 580) or at the bird hide (SH 983 575). Keep to footpaths. Leaflet.
NORTH WALES WILDLIFE TRUST

LLANGOLLEN CANAL
near Llangollen
OS Maps 117/125. SJ 198 433–SJ 284 378.
Canal and wood with streams next to River Dee.
Towpath to Tan-y-Cut nature trail at SJ 282 411 is accessed from Froncysyllte to the west or the B5605 to the east (the trail is also accessed from Ty Mawr Country Park in Cefn Mawr village).
Species inc. Beautiful and Banded Demoiselles.
BRITISH WATERWAYS
WWW.WATERSCAPE.COM
WREXHAM COUNTY BOROUGH COUNCIL
WWW.WREXHAM.GOV.UK

FLINTSHIRE

Y DDOL UCHAF
near Holywell
OS Map 116. SJ 142 713.OS Map 116. SJ 142 713.
Pit, ponds, woodland.
Reserve lies north of A541 near Afon-wen. Contact reserves officers on 01352 810469 for more information.
Species inc. Common, Southern and Brown Hawkers, Common and Black Darters.
NORTH WALES WILDLIFE TRUST

GWYNEDD

CADAIR IDRIS NNR
near Dolgellau
OS Map 124. SH 732 115 (car park).
Mountain with bog, heathland, grassland and scrub.
Part of the Snowdonia National Park. At Minffordd, south of Dolgellau on the A487, turn west into the B4405. Reserve car park (no charge) is immediately on the right. Visitor centre and toilets. Waymarked paths.
Species inc. Common Hawker, Golden-ringed Dragonfly, Keeled Skimmer, Black Darter.
COUNTRYSIDE COUNCIL FOR WALES

COED LLETYWALTER
near Harlech
OS Map 124. SH 602 275.
Lake, stream, woodland.
Part of the Snowdonia National Park. Accessed via minor road heading east from A496 at Llanbedr. No parking facilities at the site. Information board and waymarked walk.
Species inc. Common Hawker, Four-spotted Chaser, Keeled Skimmer.
WOODLAND TRUST
WWW.WOODLAND-TRUST.ORG.UK

MONMOUTHSHIRE

DIXTON EMBANKMENT
Monmouth
OS Map 162. SO 527 149.
Riverbank, limestone grassland.
The reserve lies between the A40 and the River Wye. Park in Dixton and follow footpath from church for c.1.5 miles. Limited parking.
Species inc. Banded Demoiselle, White-legged Damselfly.
GWENT WILDLIFE TRUST

Gazetteer

FIVE LOCKS – MONMOUTHSHIRE & BRECON CANAL
Cwmbran
OS Map 171. ST 287 968–ST 292 978.
Disused canal.
Access at Five Locks at Pontnewydd. Follow towpath.
BRITISH WATERWAYS
WWW.WATERSCAPE.COM

MAGOR MARSH
near Newport
OS Map 171. ST 427 867.
Marsh, ditches, pond, scrub.
From the village of Magor on the B4245 (reached via the A48 Newport to Chepstow road, or Junctions 23 and 23A of the M4), follow the signs south towards Redwick village. Go past the ruins of the Priory, cross the railway bridge and turn left into Whitewall Road. The reserve car park is on the right after c.0.5 mile. Information centre. Waterproof footwear essential.
Species inc. Banded Demoiselle, Hairy Dragonfly, Migrant Hawker, Common and Ruddy Darters.
GWENT WILDLIFE TRUST

NEWPORT

ALLT-YR-YN
Newport
OS Map 171. ST 299 888.
Woodland, meadows, ponds.
From Junction 27 of the M4, head east on the Newport road and, after c.0.3 mile, turn left into Ridgeway. After c.0.5 mile bear left into Allt-yr-yn View, then turn sharp left after c.0.5 mile into the reserve.
Species inc. Hairy Dragonfly.
GWENT WILDLIFE TRUST, NEWPORT COUNTY BOROUGH COUNCIL, WILDLIFE IN NEWPORT GROUP

NEWPORT WETLANDS
Newport
OS Map 171. ST 334 834.
Reedbeds, wet grassland, saltmarsh and saline lagoons.

The reserve is on West Nash Road, between Nash village and Uskmouth Power Station, south of Newport. From Junction 24 of the M4, take the A455 to Newport Retail Park and then follow the brown nature reserve signs to the reserve car park. Open 10am–5pm. Visitor centre.
RSPB, COUNTRYSIDE COUNCIL FOR WALES, NEWPORT COUNTY BOROUGH COUNCIL

PEMBROKESHIRE

AFON BRYNBERIAN
near Cardigan
OS Map 145. SN 099 347.
See main site section page 138.
Moorland, streams.
This moorland area lies c.4 miles south-east of Newport.
Species inc. Beautiful Demoiselle, Small Red, Southern and Scarce Blue-tailed Damselflies, Golden-ringed Dragonfly, Keeled Skimmer.

DOWROG COMMON
near St David's
OS Map 157. SM 770 270.
See main site section page 163.
Heathland, grassland, bog, fen, pools.
Dowrog Common lies c.2 miles north-east of St David's.
At least 13 species inc. Small Red, Southern and Scarce Blue-tailed Damselflies, Hairy Dragonfly.
WILDLIFE TRUST OF SOUTH AND WEST WALES

GOODWICK MOOR
near Fishguard
OS Map 157. SM 945 375.
Mire, ditches, reedbed, carr.
The moor is located between Goodwick and Fishguard. Public car parking in Goodwick along seafront (A40), opposite Seaview Hotel or by the ferry terminal roundabout. Walk up hill past Seaview Hotel and take public footpath/bridleway on right to reserve (SM 947 374). Boardwalk (but no wheelchair access).
WILDLIFE TRUST OF SOUTH AND WEST WALES

PENTRE IFAN WOODLAND AND COED TYCANOL NNR
near Newport
OS Map 145. SN 092 369.
Heathland, woodland, ponds.
From Felindre on the A487, head south down minor road to car park at Pentre Ifan burial chamber. Follow footpaths through the two woods. Permit required to leave footpaths at Coed Tycanol. Leaflet available.
Species inc. Scarce Blue-tailed Damselfly, Keeled Skimmer, Black Darter.
COUNTRYSIDE COUNCIL FOR WALES, PEMBROKESHIRE COAST NATIONAL PARK AUTHORITY
WWW.PCNPA.ORG.UK

STACKPOLE NNR
near Pembroke
OS Map 158. SR 976 939, SR 991 958 & SR 968 947 (car parks).
Coastal limestone grassland, sand dunes, woodland, lakes.
Access along minor roads off B4319 south of Pembroke. National Trust car parks at Broadhaven Beach (SR 976 939), Stackpole Quay (SR 991 958) and Bosherton (SR 968 947, for Lily Ponds). Tearooms at Stackpole Quay and toilets at all three car parks. Extensive network of footpaths through the property including the Pembrokeshire Coast Path and 3 miles of lakeside and woodland paths suitable for wheelchairs. Leaflet available. Open all year and free admission.
Over 20 species recorded, inc. Migrant Hawker, Black-tailed Skimmer, Common and Ruddy Darters.
COUNTRYSIDE COUNCIL FOR WALES, NATIONAL TRUST

POWYS

ABERCAMLO BOG
near Llandrindod Wells
OS Map 147. SO 074 650.
Wet pasture, small basin mires and scrub.
From Crossgates take the A44 towards

Rhayader and turn left after c.0.75 mile along the minor road towards Llanyre. Reserve is on the left after c.300m. Reserve sign and entrance stile along the track signed for Abercamlo Farm. Do not block the track. Follow trail marked by white-topped posts. Wellingtons advised.
RADNORSHIRE WILDLIFE TRUST

BAILEY EINON
near Llandrindod Wells
OS Map 147. SO 083 613.
River and deciduous woodland.
From the centre of Llandrindod Wells, follow minor roads to Cefnllys Lane at the eastern edge of the town. Follow this road for 1.5 miles until you come to Shaky Bridge. Park in the car park and access the reserve via the kissing gate next to the bridge. Boardwalk trail.
Species inc. Beautiful Demoiselle, White-legged Damselfly.
RADNORSHIRE WILDLIFE TRUST

BRECHFA POOL
near Llyswen
OS Map 161. SO 118 377.
Shallow pool, grassland.
From Llyswen head south-west on the A470. After 1.5 miles, take the minor road on the right and drive through Brechfa to the small chapel on the left. The pool is on the right. Park beside the road opposite the chapel. Wellingtons advised.
Species inc. Scarce Blue-tailed and Blue-tailed Damselflies.
BRECKNOCK WILDLIFE TRUST

DAUDRAETH ILLTUD
near Brecon
OS Map 160. SN 967 256.
Boggy heathland with pools.
Reserve lies in a triangle between the A40, A470 and A4215 to the west of Brecon. Roadside parking along minor road running north-east off A4215. Blaencamlais Pool lies along the footpath from the A4215 at SN 959 259. Danger – avoid walking over non-solid areas – deep water lies below floating vegetation.
BRECKNOCK WILDLIFE TRUST

ELAN VALLEY
near Rhayader
OS Map 147. SN 930 648.
Grassland, scree slopes, streams, peatbog, reservoirs.
Access along B4518 south-west of Rhayader. Parking at Elan Valley Visitor Centre (at SN 928 646, 3 miles south-west of Rhayader) and many other sites around reservoirs. Facilities include a café and toilets. Information available from the visitor centre (Rangers' Office: 01597 810880). Guided walks.
Species inc. Golden-ringed Dragonfly.
WELSH WATER
WWW.ELANVALLEY.ORG.UK

GILFACH FARM
near Rhayader
OS Map 147. SN 965 717.
River, deciduous woodland, meadows, moorland.
About 2 miles north of Rhayader on the A470, take the minor road to St Harmon (follow brown signs for reserve). The reserve begins at the junction and includes most of the valley to the next cattle grid. For the visitor centre (open 10am–5pm Friday to Monday from April to mid-July, and 10am–4.30pm daily from mid-July to September) drive through the reserve for c.1 mile before turning right to the farm. Restaurant area, toilets and nestbox cameras at the centre. Waymarked trails; some are suitable for wheelchairs and pushchairs.
Species inc. Beautiful Demoiselle, Emerald Damselfly, Golden-ringed Dragonfly.
RADNORSHIRE WILDLIFE TRUST

LAKE VYRNWY
near Welshpool
OS Map 125. SJ 016 190.
Large open lake, river, waterfalls, woodland, meadow, moorland.
From Welshpool, take the A470 north to Llanfyllin, then the B4393 west to Llanwyddyn and the eastern end of the reservoir. Turn left over the dam and left again to the car park and visitor centre at
SJ 016 190. Visitor centre sells drinks and snacks. Toilets. Open daily April to December 10.30am–5.30pm. Nature trails, some suitable for pushchairs and wheelchairs. Other car parks available.
Species inc. Common Hawker, Golden-ringed Dragonfly, Four-spotted Chaser.
RSPB

LLANDEILO GRABAN
near Builth Wells
OS Maps 147/148. SO 100 435.
Disused railway with meadow, woodland and marsh beside the River Wye.
This roadside reserve lies c.5 miles south-east of Builth Wells. Leave A470 at Erwood on B4594 and cross river, turn left at the junction and then next left along the minor road to Llanstephan. The reserve extends on either side of the road for about another 1.5 miles, to the railway bridge at Ciliau Dingle. Please park in lay-bys and avoid blocking this narrow road.
RADNORSHIRE WILDLIFE TRUST

LLYN COED Y DINAS
near Welshpool
OS Map 126. SJ 223 052.
Water-filled gravel pit.
The reserve lies at the south end of the Welshpool bypass, 2 miles south of the town. The entrance and car park are c.100m north of the A490/A483/A458 roundabout, along the old main road (A458) to Welshpool town centre. Footpaths suitable for wheelchairs. Leaflet available.
MONTGOMERYSHIRE WILDLIFE TRUST

LLYN MAWR
near Newtown
OS Map 136. SO 009 971.
Lake, wet heath, bog, grassland.
Take the A489 west from Newtown and then the A470 to Caersws. Pass through the village and, after 2 miles, just north-west of Pontdolgoch, turn onto the minor road to Bwlch y Garreg. Continue to the end of this road and park in the small car

park on left by the bungalow. Reserve
entrance is c.30m back down lane. Follow
footpaths around lake.
Species inc. Brown Hawker, Golden-
ringed Dragonfly, Black Darter.
MONTGOMERYSHIRE WILDLIFE TRUST

MONTGOMERY CANAL
Newtown to Llanymynech
OS Map 126. SJ 11 91–SJ 26 20.
Canal with reedbed and adjacent
grassland and woodland.
*Numerous points of access to towpath.
Good points are at Four Crosses, at Wern
Claypits nature reserve (south of Arddleen
at SJ 252 141, small car park) and at
Welshpool and Newtown.*
Species inc. White-legged and Red-
eyed Damselflies, Brown Hawker,
Common and Ruddy Darters.
BRITISH WATERWAYS BOARD
WWW.WATERSCAPE.COM

SEVERN FARM POND
Welshpool
OS Map 126. SJ 228 068.
Wetland, pond, scrub on industrial
estate.
*Reserve lies on the southern edge of
Welshpool on the Severn Farm Enterprise
Park. From the town centre take the B4381
over railway then the next right into the
enterprise park. Take the first right to the
car park and reserve entrance. Paths and
boardwalks are suitable for wheelchairs/
pushchairs. Leaflet available.*
Species inc. Banded Demoiselle, Large
Red, Red-eyed and Azure Damselflies.
MONTGOMERYSHIRE WILDLIFE TRUST

WITHYBEDS
near Presteigne
OS Map 148. SO 309 651.
River, meadows, willow scrub.
*Small car park 400m along B4355 north of
Presteigne. Picnic area. Circular path
suitable for wheelchairs.*
RADNORSHIRE WILDLIFE TRUST

YNYS-HIR
near Machynlleth
OS Map 135. SN 683 963.
Oak woodland, moorland, pools,
reedbeds, estuary.
*Ynys-hir is c.6 miles south-west of
Machynlleth. On the A487 at Eglwys-fach,
head west for 1 mile on the minor road to
the reserve (signed). Car park (SN 685
955), visitor centre and nature trails.
Reserve open 9am–9pm (or dusk if earlier).
Visitor centre open 9am–5pm April–
October (closed Monday and Tuesday); hot
drinks and snacks available and toilet
facilities. Charge for non-RSPB members.
The reserve is not suitable for wheelchairs.*
Species inc. Beautiful Demoiselle,
Golden-ringed Dragonfly.
RSPB

SWANSEA

BROAD POOL & BOG
The Gower, near Swansea
OS Map 159. SS 510 910.
See main site section page 177.
Heathland pond and bog.
This site lies c.10 miles west of Swansea.
Over 13 species recorded including
Large Red Damselfly, Emperor and
Golden-ringed Dragonflies.
WILDLIFE TRUST OF SOUTH AND WEST WALES

OXWICH NNR
The Gower, Swansea
OS Map 159. SS 502 865.
See main site section page 177.
Sand dunes, marsh, woodland.
Reserve lies c.10 miles from Swansea.
Species inc. Beautiful Demoiselle,
Hairy Dragonfly, Common, Migrant
and Southern Hawkers, Emperor
Dragonfly, Four-spotted Chaser.
COUNTRYSIDE COUNCIL FOR WALES

Gazetteer

RHOSSILI DOWN
The Gower, near Swansea
OS Map 159. SS 420 900.
Grassland, heath, marsh, mires.
The reserve lies on the western tip of the Gower Peninsula, c.15 miles west of Swansea. Car park (not NT) with toilets and information centre (at SS 414 880) in Rhossili village on the B4247.
Species inc. Southern and Scarce Blue-tailed Damselflies, Keeled Skimmer.
NATIONAL TRUST

VALE OF GLAMORGAN

COSMESTON LAKES COUNTRY PARK
near Cardiff
OS Map 171.   ST 180 692 (main entrance).
Lakes, woodland, limestone grassland.
The Country Park is signed off the A4055 between Penarth and Barry. The main entrance is off the B4267, just beyond the southern outskirts of Penarth. Free car park at entrance. Visitor centre, café, toilets (all include disabled access) and walks, including boardwalk through reedbeds. Leaflet. Other facilities include dog walk, adventure playground, Medieval Village (charge), BBQ and picnic sites.
Species inc. Hairy Dragonfly, Migrant Hawker, Emperor Dragonfly, Black-tailed Skimmer.
VALE OF GLAMORGAN BOROUGH COUNCIL
WWW.VALEOFGLAMORGAN.GOV.UK

WREXHAM

MARFORD QUARRY
near Wrexham
OS Map 117. SJ 357 560.
Disused quarry, grassland, scrub, woodland.
Reserve lies between the A483 and the B5445 immediately west of Marford, 2.5 miles north of Wrexham. From the

northern outskirts of Marford village, turn west into Springfield Lane. The reserve entrance is after 400m, just before the railway bridge. Park carefully either side of bridge. Leaflet.
Species inc. Hairy Dragonfly, Brown Hawker, Club-tailed Dragonfly, Common and Ruddy Darters.
NORTH WALES WILDLIFE TRUST

YNYS MÔN (ANGLESEY)

CORS GOCH
near Llangefni
OS Maps 114/115. SH 497 813.
Lake, heath, fen, grassland, carr.
From Menai Bridge take the A5025 northwards, then follow the minor road to Llanbedrgoch c.1.5 miles north-east of Pentraeth. At the crossroads in the middle of Llanbedrgoch, head north towards the B5108 for 1.25 miles. Park in lay-by at SH 503 817, just north of the track leading to the reserve. Footpaths are unsurfaced and unsuitable for wheelchairs. Wellingtons advised.
15 species recorded inc. Small Red and Scarce Blue-tailed Damselflies, Hairy Dragonfly, Keeled Skimmer and Black Darter.
NORTH WALES WILDLIFE TRUST

VALLEY LAKES
near Caergeiliog
OS Map 114. SH 313 765.
See main site section page 227.
Lakes, marsh.
Valley Lakes reserve lies c.5 miles east of Holyhead and c.15 miles west of Bangor.
Species inc. Variable Damselfly, Four-spotted Chaser.
RSPB

SCOTLAND

County/Regional Recorders
Details of recorders at
WWW.DRAGONFLYSOC.ORG.UK
WWW.ATROPOS.INFO/DRAGONFLY.HTML

Forestry Commission Scotland
1 Highlander Way, Inverness Business
Park, Inverness IV2 7GB
TEL 01463 232811
WWW.FORESTRY.GOV.UK/SCOTLAND

The National Trust for Scotland
Wemyss House, 28 Charlotte Square,
Edinburgh EH2 4ET
TEL 0131 243 9300
EMAIL information@nts.org.uk
WWW.NTS.ORG.UK

RSPB Scotland
Dunedin House, Ravelston Terrace,
Edinburgh EH4 3TP
TEL 0131 331 6500
EMAIL rspb.scotland@rspb.org.uk
WWW.RSPB.ORG.UK/SCOTLAND

Scottish Natural Heritage
Great Glen House, Leachkin Road,
Inverness IV3 8NW
TEL 01463 725000
EMAIL enquiries@snh.gov.uk
WWW.SNH.ORG.UK

Scottish Tourist Board
TEL 0845 22 55 121
WWW.VISITSCOTLAND.COM

Scottish Wildlife Trust
Cramond House, Kirk Cramond,
Cramond Glebe Road, Edinburgh EH4
6NS
TEL 0131 312 7765
EMAIL enquiries@swt.org.uk
WWW.SWT.ORG.UK

Websites
Dragonflies and damselflies in
Scotland

WWW.SNH.ORG.UK/PUBLICATIONS/ON-LINE/
NATURALLYSCOTTISH/DRAGONFLY/
INSCOTLAND.ASP

BORDERS

LINDEAN RESERVOIR
near Selkirk
OS Map 73. NT 500 290.
Reservoir, grassland, woodland.
*Western end of reservoir managed as a
nature reserve. Leave Selkirk east along
A699 and take next left after passing B6453
(on right). Park at NT 505 293 east of
reservoir. Footpath around reservoir;
wheelchair access to lochside. Information
board.*
Species inc. Common Hawker, Four-
spotted Chaser, Common and Black
Darters.
BORDERS REGIONAL COUNCIL
WWW.SCOTBORDERS.GOV.UK

CENTRAL

DOUNE PONDS
Doune
OS Map 57. NN 725 018 (car park).
Meadow, ponds, woodland, scrub.
*In town centre take the minor road north,
just west of church. Take second left to car
park at NN 725 018. Nature trails, some
wheelchair accessible. Reserve guide
available from box in car park. This reserve
is close to the Red Kite viewing centre at
Argaty Farm.*
STIRLING COUNCIL
WWW.STIRLING.GOV.UK

INVERSNAID
near Aberfoyle
OS Map 56. NN 337 090.
Deciduous woodland, moorland, loch,
streams.
*The reserve lies c.15 miles west of
Aberfoyle on the east shore of Loch*

Lommond. Take the B829 west from Aberfoyle and, at the end of this road, follow minor road to Inversnaid and park in hotel car park (NN 337 088). Take West Highland Way through woodland (uneven surface, steep in places and not suitable for pushchairs or wheelchairs). Insect repellent recommended. Toilets at the reserve. The hotel serves food.

Species inc. Common Hawker, Golden-ringed Dragonfly, Four-spotted Chaser, Black Darter.

RSPB

QUEEN ELIZABETH FOREST PARK
near Aberfoyle
OS Map 57. NN 517 036.

Mixed woodland, moorland, lochs, rivers and streams.

Information from the Queen Elizabeth Forest Park Visitor Centre off the A821 north of Aberfoyle at NN 520 015. Centre open 10am–6pm daily, Easter to October. Continue north along the A821 until reaching the viewpoint at Duke's Pass. On the east side of the road is the entrance to Achray Forest Drive. This drive winds for c.7 miles past Lochan Reoidhte, along the shores of Loch Drunkie, and down to Loch Achray. There are numerous stopping points from where you can walk and watch dragonflies hawking around the lochs and along forest tracks.

Species inc. Beautiful Demoiselle, Common Hawker, Golden-ringed Dragonfly, Black Darter.

Forestry Commission Scotland

DUMFRIES & GALLOWAY

BRIGTON POND
near Newton Stewart
OS Map 77. NX 359 754.

See main site section page 145.

Disused quarry, wood, scrub, rides.

Brigton Pond is situated in the Galloway

Forest Park c.8 miles north-west of Newton Stewart.

Species inc. Common Hawker, Golden-ringed Dragonfly, Black Darter.

PART OF GALLOWAY FOREST PARK, FORESTRY COMMISSION SCOTLAND, CREE VALLEY COMMUNITY WOODLAND TRUST

GALLOWAY FOREST PARK
near Newton Stewart
OS Map 77. NX 551 763 (Visitor Centre).

Loch, heathland, bog, coniferous forest, open grassland.

Signed from A712 and A714. Information from Clatteringshaws Visitor Centre along A712 at Clatteringshaws Loch (tearoom and toilets). Marked trails. The Raiders' Road Forest Drive and Loch Stroan near its southern end are both very good for dragonflies. See main site section for access to Silver Flowe NNR (p. 212).

Species inc. Common Hawker, Golden-ringed Dragonfly.

Forestry Commission Scotland

PLANTAIN LOCH
near Dalbeattie
OS Map 84. NX 841 602.

Loch.

The loch lies immediately south-east of Dalbeattie and is within Dalbeattie Forest. From Dalbeattie head south along the A710 towards Colvend. Park in Town Wood Car Park, which is the first car park you come to within the forest on the left. Follow trail from here.

Species inc. Emerald and Large Red Damselflies, Common Hawker, Four-spotted Chaser.

Forestry Commission Scotland

SILVER FLOWE NNR
near Newton Stewart
OS Map 77. NX 480 820.

See main site section page 214.

Blanket bog, forest rides, clearings.

The Silver Flowe lies c.7 miles north of the A712 between New Galloway and Newton Stewart.

Species inc. Azure and Common Hawkers, Golden-ringed Dragonfly. SCOTTISH NATURAL HERITAGE, FORESTRY COMMISSION SCOTLAND

Species inc. Northern Damselfly, Black and White-faced Darters. SCOTTISH NATURAL HERITAGE

FIFE

MORTON LOCHS
near St Andrews
OS Maps 54/59. NO 463 265.
Lochs, marsh, mixed woodland.
Take track (signed private road) east off B945 c.1.5 miles south of Tayport and continue for c.0.75 mile to car park.
Species inc. Common Hawker, Common and Black Darters.
SCOTTISH NATURAL HERITAGE

GRAMPIAN

LOCH MUICK
near Ballater
OS Map 44. NO 290 830.
Upland rock outcrops and lochs.
From the B976 south-west of Ballater, take the Glen Muick road south. At the end of this minor road, park in the car park at the Spittal of Glenmuick (NO 307 851). Visitor centre and toilets. Path leads from visitor centre to Loch Muick, from where there is a circular walk around the loch (c.8 miles). Keep to tracks.
BALMORAL ROYAL ESTATE

MUIR OF DINNET NNR
near Ballater
OS Maps 37/44. NJ 433 000 (centre of area).
Moorland, bog, lochs, woodland.
Includes Loch Davan and Loch Kinord. Burn O'Vat Visitor Centre (NO 429 997) signed from A93 between Aberdeen and Ballater and the B9119 at Milton of Logie. There are toilets here. Alternative access along the footpath from the car park in Dinnet village. Waymarked paths and information map boards. Leaflet available from SNH.

HIGHLAND

ABERNETHY FOREST
Speyside
OS Map 36. NH 960 180.
See main site section page 136.
Caledonian pine forest, bogs, pools, lochs and lochans, moorland.
The area lies c.6 miles north-east of Aviemore. There are numerous areas to search other than those covered by the main site section. Explore any accessible water body on OS map.
Species inc. Northern Damselfly, Common Hawker, Golden-ringed Dragonfly, Northern Emerald, Black and White-faced Darters.
RSPB, SCOTTISH NATURAL HERITAGE

ARIUNDLE NNR
near Strontian
OS Map 40. NM 830 634 (parking).
River Strontian bordered by woodland.
Follow signs for Forestry Commission Scotland's Airigh Fhionndail car park, c.2 miles north of Strontian. Access the reserve via a track (part of Forestry Commission Scotland's Strontian River Trail). Nature trail with information boards.
Species inc. Northern Emerald Dragonfly.
SCOTTISH NATURAL HERITAGE, FORESTRY COMMISSION SCOTLAND

BEINN EIGHE NNR
near Kinlochewe
OS Map 19. NH 001 650 (car park).
See main site section page 144.
Boggy clearings on wooded footslopes of mountains.
Beinn Eighe is a huge mountainous area flanking Loch Maree to the north-west of Kinlochewe along the A832.

Gazetteer

Species inc. Azure and Common Hawkers, Golden-ringed Dragonfly, Northern Emerald, Black and White-faced Darters.
SCOTTISH NATURAL HERITAGE

BRIDGE OF GRUDIE
near Kinlochewe
OS Map 19. NG 965 678.
See main site section page 146.
Boggy clearings, river, loch.
Area is c.9 miles north-west of Kinlochewe.
Species inc. Northern Damselfly, Azure and Common Hawkers, Golden-ringed Dragonfly, Northern Emerald, Highland, Black and White-faced Darters.

CRAIGELLACHIE NNR
near Aviemore
OS Map 36. NH 888 123.
Birch woodland, moorland, pools.
Park in Aviemore. Take the track between Youth Hostel and caravan park and access reserve via the A9 underpass by the dry ski slope. Marked trails. Tourist Information Centre in Aviemore.
Species inc. Golden-ringed Dragonfly, Highland Darter.
SCOTTISH NATURAL HERITAGE

GLEN AFFRIC
near Inverness
OS Map 25. NH 197 234.
See main site section page 174.
Lochans, bogs and pools in Caledonian pine forest.
Glen Affric lies c.30 miles south-west of Inverness.
Species inc. Azure and Common Hawkers, Golden-ringed Dragonfly, Downy, Northern and Brilliant Emeralds, Highland, Black and White-faced Darters.
FORESTRY COMMISSION SCOTLAND

INSH MARSHES
near Kingussie
OS Map 35. NH 775 998 (car park).
River Spey, pools, marsh scrub, grassland.
Leave A9 in Kingussie and follow B970 towards Feshiebridge. Car park and information centre at NH 775 998, c.0.5 mile beyond Ruthven. Picnic area. Paths not suitable for wheelchairs/pushchairs. Weekly guided wildlife walks in summer.
Species inc. Common Hawker, Golden-ringed Dragonfly.
RSPB

LOCH A'MHUILINN
near Scourie
OS Map 15. NC 166 394.
Lochans, bog, woodland.
Four miles south of Scourie on the A894, take the track south-west to Duartbeg at NC 169 399. Limited parking at entrance and along track – do not block access routes and gateways. Loch Duartbeg is particularly good for dragonflies.
Ten species inc. Common Hawker, Common, Highland and Black Darters.
SCOTTISH NATURAL HERITAGE

LOCH BRAN
near Inverness
OS Maps 34/35. NH 507 192.
See main site section page 187.
Lochans, bog, coniferous forest.
A small loch on the east shore of Loch Ness c.17 miles south of Inverness.
Species inc. Brilliant Emerald, Highland Darter.
SCOTTISH NATURAL HERITAGE

LOCH COULIN & LOCH CLAIR
near Kinlochewe
OS Map 25. NH 003 582.
See main site section page 188.
Lochs, bog, woodland.
These two lochs lie south of the A896, c.3 miles south-west of Kinlochewe.
Species inc. Azure and Common Hawkers, Golden-ringed Dragonfly, Northern Emerald, Highland Darter.
SCOTTISH NATURAL HERITAGE

LOCH GAMHNA
Loch an Eilein, near Aviemore
OS Map 36. NH 891 070.

Gazetteer

See main site section page 189.
Small loch lying in Caledonian pine forest. Stony ground with heather.
Loch Gamhna lies directly south of Loch an Eilein, c.4 miles south of Aviemore.
Species inc. Golden-ringed Dragonfly, Highland and Black Darters.
FORESTRY COMMISSION SCOTLAND, SCOTTISH NATURAL HERITAGE

LOTHIAN

BAWSINCH AND DUDDINGSTON LOCH
Edinburgh
OS Map 66. NT 284 725.
Loch, reedbeds, ponds, grassland, mixed woodland.
Public access to the northern shore of Duddingston Loch and the cavalry ground to the east. Park either by Holyrood Park gates or at NT 285 724 along Duddingston Road West. Use the latter car park for Bawsinch to the south-east of the loch. An access key must be obtained to visit this SWT reserve.
Species inc. Common Hawker, Common Darter.
SCOTTISH WILDLIFE TRUST

RED MOSS OF BALERNO
near Edinburgh
OS Maps 65/66. NT 164 636.
Raised bog, deciduous woodland.
From Edinburgh follow the A70 south-west to the village of Balerno. Head south through Balerno and, after c.1.5 miles, park in Pentland Hills Regional car park next to Little Redford Wood. Information boards. Keep to boardwalk and aqueduct as bog fragile and dangerous.
Species inc. Common Hawker, Golden-ringed Dragonfly, Common and Black Darters.
SCOTTISH WILDLIFE TRUST

STRATHCLYDE

BLACK LOCHS
near Oban
OS Map 49. NM 924 315.
Loch, marsh, deciduous woodland.
The lochs lie north-east of Oban. Park in Connel village. Circular walk of c.5.5 miles from village. Start by the bridge over Lusragan Burn and follow the burn south for 2 miles along a lane. Take track which heads east to the western side of the lochs and then walk back to village. Full details (and other walks) at www.visitscotland.com.
14 species inc. Beautiful Demoiselle, Variable Damselfly, Hairy Dragonfly, Downy Emerald.

FEOCH MEADOWS
near Girvan
OS Map 76. NX 263 822.
Upland meadows next to burn with marshy areas.
The reserve is off the A714, 1.5 miles east of Barrhill. Follow Killantringan Farm Road and take the left fork to the car park at the entrance gate (NX 263 816). Walk down to the burn.
Species inc. Common Hawker, Golden-ringed Dragonfly, Black Darter.
SCOTTISH WILDLIFE TRUST

GLEN MOSS
near Glasgow
OS Map 63. NS 368 699.
Mires, pools, grassland, heathland, scrub, woodland.
Reserve lies east of Kilmacolm and north of the golf course. Park carefully on verge along minor road from Kilmacolm to Bishopton. Public right of way runs between Glenmosston Road (eastern outskirts of village) and Kilallan Road along southern edge of the reserve.
Eight species breed inc. Azure Damselfly, Common Hawker, Common and Black Darters.
SCOTTISH WILDLIFE TRUST

Gazetteer

GLEN NANT NNR
near Taynuilt
OS Map 50. NN 013 289.
River (Nant) in oak woodland.
From the A85 at Taynuilt, head south on the B845 (signed Kilchrenan) for c.3 miles. Reserve is signed from this road. Car park at NN 020 273. Marked walks.
Species inc. Golden-ringed Dragonfly.
Scottish Natural Heritage, Forestry Commission Scotland

GOATFELL, ISLE OF ARRAN
near Brodick
OS Map 69. NR 991 416.
See main site section page 176.
Mountain heathland, dry and wet grass and heather moor.
Goatfell is situated c.4 miles north of Brodick.
Species inc. Large Red and Common Blue Damselflies, Common Hawker, Golden-ringed Dragonfly, Four-spotted Chaser, Highland Darter.
National Trust for Scotland

PARKHOUSE COMMUNITY NATURE RESERVE
Ardrossan
OS Maps 63/70. NS 236 427.
Grassland, scrub, wet meadow, ponds.
Various access points south of main A78 Parkhouse Road.
Scottish Wildlife Trust

of nearby Loch Rannoch, other lochs and burns, and forest areas (particularly sheltered tracks and rides) are worth exploring for Azure Hawker. Tearoom and toilets at Rannoch Station.
Species include Azure Hawker, Northern Emerald.
Forestry Commission Scotland

LOCH LEVEN NNR
near Kinross
OS Map 58. NT 160 989 (parking and RSPB information centre).
Loch, grassland, marsh, coniferous woodland.
Several access points including at Kirkgate Park in Kinross at NO 127 018, or at Vane Farm RSPB reserve (information centre, coffee shop and toilets) off the B9097 at NT 160 989.
Scottish Natural Heritage, RSPB

LOGIERAIT MIRES
near Pitlochry
OS Map 52. NN 967 534.
Woodland pool.
Park along the minor road signposted for Hillhead Cemetery (north from Logierait). Follow track through forest to pool.
Species inc. Northern Damselfly.
Atholl Estates
www.athollestatesrangerservice.co.uk

TAYSIDE

LOCH FINNART & LOCH MONAGHAN
near Loch Rannoch
OS Map 51. NN 522 555 (Loch Finnart
Loch, grassland, marsh, woodland.
Leave the A9 north of Pitlochry at Moulin and take the B8019 to Tummel Bridge, then the B846 for Rannoch Station. At the west end of Loch Rannoch, take the minor road on the left, through Bridge of Gaur to Finnart. Park carefully and take the path/ track south to Loch Finnart. The shoreline

ISLE OF MAN

Manx Wildlife Trust
Tynwald Mills, St Johns, Isle of Man
IM4 3AE
TEL 01624 801985
EMAIL manxwt@cix.co.uk
WWW.WILDLIFETRUST.ORG.UK/MANXWT

CLOSE SARTFIELD
near Ballaugh
OS Map 95. SC 361 956.
Fen, wet grassland, woodland.
The reserve lies c.1.5 miles north-east of
Ballaugh and is accessed via minor roads
between the B9 and the A14.
MANX WILDLIFE TRUST

NORTHERN IRELAND

County/Regional Recorders
Details of County recorders at
WWW.DRAGONFLYSOC.ORG.UK
WWW.ATROPOS.INFO/DRAGONFLY.HTML

Ulster Wildlife Trust
3 New Line, Crossgar, Downpatrick,
Co. Down BT30 9EP
TEL 028 4483 0282
EMAIL info@ulsterwildlifetrust.org
WWW.ULSTERWILDLIFETRUST.ORG

Northern Ireland Forest Service (an
executive agency within the
Department of Agriculture and Rural
Development)
Dundonald House, Upper
Newtownards Road, Belfast BT4 3SB
TEL 02890 524480
EMAIL customer.forestservice@
dardni.gov.uk
WWW.FORESTSERVICENI.GOV.UK

Department of the Environment
(Northern Ireland)/Environment &
Heritage Service
Klondyke Building, Cromac Avenue,
Gasworks Business Park, Ormeau
Road, Belfast BT7 2JA
TEL 0845 302 0008
WWW.EHSNI.GOV.UK

The National Trust for Northern
Ireland
Rowallane House, Saintfield,
Ballynahinch, Co Down BT24 7LH
TEL 02897 510721
WWW.NATIONALTRUST.ORG.UK

RSPB Northern Ireland
Belvoir Park Forest, Belfast BT8 4QT
TEL 02890 491547
EMAIL rspb.nireland@rspb.org.uk
WWW.RSPB.ORG

The Woodland Trust Northern Ireland
1 Dufferin Court, Dufferin Avenue,
Bangor, Co Down BT20 3BX
TEL 02891 275787
EMAIL wtni@woodland-trust.org.uk
WWW.WOODLAND-TRUST.ORG.UK

Book
The Natural History of Ireland's
Dragonflies. Brian Nelson & Robert
Thompson, 2004, The National
Museums and Galleries of Northern
Ireland.

Gazetteer

CO ANTRIM

BALLYCONAGAN, RATHLIN ISLAND
near Ballycastle
OS Map 5. D 146 520.

Wet and dry heathland, lakes, marsh, flower-rich grassland.
This site is reached by a ferry from Ballycastle (park at terminal). The 45-minute crossing runs four times daily in the summer – contact Caledonian MacBrayne 02820 769299. From Church Bay on Rathlin Island, walk the 0.5 mile to the site via the East Light Road. Waymarked paths. NT tearoom and toilets at Manor House Guest House.
Species include Black Darter.
NATIONAL TRUST FOR NORTHERN IRELAND

FAIR HEAD AND MURLOUGH BAY
near Ballycastle
OS Map 5. D 185 430 & D 199 419.

Coastal cliffs, dry and wet heath, grassland, lakes, deciduous woodland.
This stretch of coast lies c.3 miles east of Ballycastle and is signposted off the A2. Car parks at Coolanlough (NT) for Fair Head and above and in Murlough Bay. Footpaths, including circular path around Fair Head. Leaflet available from information centres at Causeway and Larrybane. Search springs at bases of cliffs.
Species include Common Hawker, Four-spotted Chaser.
NATIONAL TRUST FOR NORTHERN IRELAND

LAGAN MEADOWS LNR
near Belfast
OS Map 15. J 335 703.

Marsh, river (Lagan), meadow and woodland.
Lagan Meadows lies 2 miles south of Belfast city centre and within Lagan Valley Regional Park. Access and parking at Knightsbridge Park off Stranmillis Road, Belfast. Nature trail and leaflet.
Species include Banded Demoiselle, Common Darter.
ULSTER WILDLIFE TRUST

MONTIAGHS MOSS NNR
near Lurgan
OS Map 20. J 093 652.

Lowland raised bog, scrub.
The reserve lies 2 miles west of the village of Aghalee. Leave the M1 at Junction 9 (signed for Moira) and turn along the A26 towards Belfast International Airport. After c.1 mile, turn left along Soldierstown Road to Aghalee. In the village turn left along the main street, over the canal, and continue for c.0.75 mile towards Aghagallon and then turn right. Cross 'Navies Drain' to the road junction and turn right onto Montiaghs Road. Park carefully by the nature reserve sign at the corner of Montiaghs Road and Moss Road. The best time to see Irish Damselfly at this site is usually mid-May to mid-June.
Species inc. Irish and Variable Damselflies, Hairy Dragonfly, Common Hawker, Ruddy and Black Darters.
ENVIRONMENT & HERITAGE SERVICE

PORTMORE LOUGH LNR
near Glenavy
OS Map 14/20. J 105 687.

Lough, reedbeds, scrub and meadows.
Accessed off the B156 west of the lough. Take George's Island Road to the information centre (toilets) and car park. Disabled access to area around information centre only. Short trail open in summer.
Species include Variable Damselfly, Brown Hawker.
RSPB

REA'S WOOD NNR, LOUGH NEAGH
near Antrim
OS Map 14. J 142 855.

Fen, lough, wet woodland.
The wood lies c.1 mile south of Antrim. Private car park behind Deerpark Hotel. Footpaths.
ENVIRONMENT & HERITAGE SERVICE, NORTHERN IRELAND FOREST SERVICE

CO ARMAGH

The Warden, Craigavon Borough Council
Lough Neagh Discovery Centre, Oxford Island NNR, Craigavon BT66 6NJ
TEL 02838 322205

THE ARGORY
near Moy
OS Map 19. H 877 576.
River (Blackwater), raised bog, birch scrub.
Signposted from Junction 13 of the M1. The National Trust property at Argory House lies c.2.5 miles north-east of Moy on the Derrycaw road. Car park signed. Path along banks of the River Blackwater. NT shop and tearoom. The mosses are open to UWT members and are accessed via a track opposite the main entrance to The Argory. Visitors should not cross the mosses because the extensive network of overgrown drains is hazardous.
Species inc. Banded Demoiselle, Irish Damselfly, Brown Hawker, Black Darter.
ULSTER WILDLIFE TRUST, NATIONAL TRUST FOR NORTHERN IRELAND

BRACKAGH MOSS NNR
near Portadown
OS Map 20. J 019 507.
Peatbog, carr woodland.
The reserve lies c.2 miles south of Portadown. Turn left off the Portadown to Tandragee Road (B78) c.2 miles south of Portadown along Brackagh Moss Road. Park in either of the two small lay-bys on the left. Information panel and network of paths north of the road. Permission is required from the warden to visit the part of the reserve to the south of the road, owing to hazardous conditions.
Species inc. Irish and Variable Damselflies, Hairy Dragonfly, Common Hawker, Ruddy and Black Darters.
ENVIRONMENT & HERITAGE SERVICE

OXFORD ISLAND NNR
near Craigavon
OS Map 20. J 053 616.
Lough, reedswamp, grassland, scrub.
This peninsula on the south-east shore of Lough Neagh is signed from Junction 10 of the M1. Car park, Lough Neagh Discovery Centre and café. Nature trails.
CRAIGAVON BOROUGH COUNCIL, ENVIRONMENT & HERITAGE SERVICE

PEATLANDS PARK
near Moy
OS Map 19. H 904 613.
Lough, bog, woodland.
From Belfast, leave the M1 at Junction 13. Turn right over the motorway and then right along the Portadown to Dungannon Road alongside the motorway (going back towards Portadown). The entrance is on the left after c.200m. Car park, waymarked trails, visitor centre and toilets.
Species inc. Variable Damselfly, Brown and Common Hawkers, Black Darter.
ENVIRONMENT & HERITAGE SERVICE

SLIEVE GULLION FOREST
near Newry
OS Map 29. J 042 197.
Mixed woodland with nature reserve and walled garden.
The forest lies off the B113, 5 miles south-west of Newry and within the Ring of Gullion AONB. Well-signed on roads around Newry and South Armagh. Car park next to Slieve Gullion Courtyard Centre. Coffee shop in courtyard. Open daily Easter to end of summer from 10am until dusk.
Species inc. Hairy and Brown Hawkers, Keeled Skimmer.
NORTHERN IRELAND FOREST SERVICE

CO DOWN

Ulster Wildlife Centre

The Education Officer, Ulster Wildlife Centre, 3 New Line, Crossgar, Downpatrick, Co Down BT30 9EP
TEL 028 4483 0282
EMAIL INFO@ULSTERWILDLIFETRUST.ORG

BLOODY BRIDGE
near Newcastle
OS Map 29. J 383 269.

Shallow flushes in rocky heathland beside river (Bloody Bridge).
Leave Newcastle along the A2 towards Kilkeel. After c.3 miles, use the car park on the left before Bloody Bridge at J 388 271. Cross the (busy) road, go through the wooden gate and continue up the path to the north side of the river. Cross the river at the natural stepping stones to a flat, rocky open area of flushes, below a fence.
Species include Keeled Skimmer.
NATIONAL TRUST FOR NORTHERN IRELAND

CASTLE WARD
near Downpatrick
OS Map 21. J 752 494.

Lough (Strangford), parkland, woodland, ponds.
This property lies c.1.5 miles west of Strangford village on the A25. Entrance by Ballyculter Lodge. Grounds open during daylight hours. Headquarters of Strangford Lough Wildlife Scheme on estate.
Seven species of dragonfly recorded at Mallard Pond.
NATIONAL TRUST FOR NORTHERN IRELAND

GLASTRY NATURE RESERVE
near Ballyhalbert, Ard Peninsula
OS Map 21. J 640 630.

Flooded clay pits.
From the village of Ballyhalbert on the Ards Peninsula, take the A2 towards Portavogie. The clay pits are on both sides of the road after c.1 mile, just before a right-hand turn. Free entry.
Species inc. Hairy Dragonfly.
NATIONAL TRUST FOR NORTHERN IRELAND

LEITRIM LODGE
near Hilltown
OS Map 29. J 224 256.

Shallow flushes by forest and river (Shankys).
From Hilltown take the Newcastle Road (B180) and turn right towards Spega Dam (just past a bridge and before a church just outside village). After c.1.5 miles, turn right at the crossroads towards Rostrevor. After c.2 miles park in the car park on left (amongst pines). On foot, go through the gate and over bridge, turn right and ford a small stream. Cross a broken-down stone wall to the right, and head along the valley to an extensive area of boggy flushes in scattered pine woodland between the stone wall and the coniferous forest to the south.
Species inc. Scarce Blue-tailed Damselfly, Common Hawker, Keeled Skimmer, Black and Ruddy Darters.

QUOILE PONDAGE NNR
near Downpatrick
OS Map 21. J 500 478.

Lake and river with wetland margins.
The site lies between Downpatrick and the south-western corner of Strangford Lough. The Quoile Countryside Centre (open 11am–5pm daily during the summer) is just off the A25 towards Strangford. Follow brown tourist signs. Car park, toilets and footpaths.
ENVIRONMENT & HERITAGE SERVICE

ULSTER WILDLIFE CENTRE
Crossgar
OS Map 21. J 462 519.

Garden with peatbog, wet meadow and pond, wildflower meadow, woodland.
Headquarters of the UWT with visitor centre and recreated habitats. The wildlife centre lies off Killyleagh Street in Crossgar. Open during office hours (10am–4pm weekdays). Self-guided wildlife walk.
ULSTER WILDLIFE TRUST

CO FERMANAGH

CASTLE CALDWELL NNR
near Belleek
OS Map 17. H 020 601.
Swamp, fen, carr, lough, mixed woodland.
The site lies in Castle Caldwell Forest, at the western end of Lower Lough Erne. Car park and information centre in forest c.5 miles east of Belleek along A47. Access to the nature reserve is by path from the public road to the west.
ENVIRONMENT & HERITAGE SERVICE,
NORTHERN IRELAND FOREST SERVICE

CASTLE COOLE
near Enniskillen
OS Maps 17/18. H 260 430.
Parkland, damp grassland, carr, reedbed, fens and lakes.
Situated on the A4 Belfast to Enniskillen road, c.1.5 miles south-east of Enniskillen. Car park available when house is open (1pm-6pm daily except Thursday in June; 12–6pm daily in July and August. Tearoom open when house is open. Grounds accessible on foot all year during daylight hours. Visitor centre and toilets.
Species inc. Banded Demoiselle, Variable Damselfly, Hairy Dragonfly, Brown Hawker.
NATIONAL TRUST FOR NORTHERN IRELAND

CORNAGAGUE WOOD AND LOUGH
near Rosslea
OS Map 27. H 474 304.
Lake, scrub woodland.
From Lisnaskea take the A34 towards Newtownbutler. After c.3 miles (just after Moor Lough on right) turn left along the B36 towards Rosslea. After c.5 miles, turn right along a minor road just past Mill Lough (with jetty) at H 469 315. Take the next minor road on the right and follow it south through Corrardaghy to farm lane at H 478 298. Follow lane north to the lough.
Species inc. Irish and Variable Damselflies, Hairy Dragonfly.
NORTHERN IRELAND FOREST SERVICE

CROM CASTLE ESTATE
near Newtownbutler
OS Map 27. H 362 241.
Lakes, woodland, fen.
The estate lies 3 miles west of Newtownbutler. From Newtownbutler, take the road signed for Crom, then take the left turn opposite Kilturk Lough (H 380 265) and drive through the main gates. After c.1 mile, turn left at the crossroads near Lough Nalughoge (H 366 245). Continue to the visitor centre (open daily 10am–6pm in the summer; tearoom and toilets) and car park (charge per vehicle). Follow path (via Old Crom Castle) to the bridge at Inesherl Island at H 358 245. Nature trails and guided walks programme.
Species inc. Hairy Dragonfly, Brown Hawker.
NATIONAL TRUST FOR NORTHERN IRELAND

LARGALINNY LOUGH
Conagher Forest
near Derrygonnelly
OS Map 17. H 072 537.
Small lake, peatbog, scrub woodland, moorland, rocky heath.
The forest lies 4 miles north-west of Derrygonnelly. Park by the exit road from Lough Navar Forest on the Derrygonnelly to Garrison road (via Glenasheevar). Walk along the forest road for c.1.5 miles then take the track left. Continue to the end of the track and the lough lies in a hollow below some scrubby birch and oak woodland.
Species inc. Scarce Blue-tailed Damselfly, Black Darter.
NORTHERN IRELAND FOREST SERVICE

LOUGH ALABAN
Ballintempo Forest
near Belcoo
OS Map 17. H 069 437.
Lake, bog, moorland, coniferous forest.
The lough lies c.5 miles north-north-west of Belcoo. From Belcoo, take the road to Boho for c.3 miles and the left turn signed for Aghanaglack. After c.0.5 mile, turn left along a forest track along the edge of the

forest. Continue for c.2 miles and park carefully. On foot, continue along the track for c.300m and take the downhill path to the left. Take care around the lough as it is very boggy underfoot. The best time to see Irish Damselfly at this site is usually from late June to early July.

Species inc. Irish and Variable Damselflies, Hairy Dragonfly.

NORTHERN IRELAND FOREST SERVICE

CO LONDONDERRY

CREIGHTON'S WOOD
near Kilrea
OS Map 8. C 927 111.

Woodland, peatbog.

Permit and details from UWT.

Species inc. Variable Damselfly, Common Hawker, Black Darter. Irish Damselfly last recorded here in 1987.

ULSTER WILDLIFE TRUST

DRUMLAMPH WOOD
near Maghera
OS Map 8. C 841 037.

Ancient woodland, mires and meadows by River Grillagh.

At Maghera take the A29 north (Garvagh Road) for 2 miles. Drive past the Grillagh Picnic Site and take the next left turn (Gortinure Road). After 1 mile turn left onto Grillagh Road. The car park is after 0.25 miles on the right and along a short track. (You may have to open the gate.) Waymarked trail and information board.

Species inc. Large Red and Variable Damselflies, Four-spotted Chaser.

WOODLAND TRUST

CO TYRONE

BLESSINGBOURNE
near Fivemiletown
OS Map 18. H 449 484.

Parkland, woodland, lake and fen.

Situated on the outskirts of Fivemiletown off B122 Murley Road. Access at beginning of road to Blessingbourne House. Car parking in Fivemiletown. Some parts of reserve open to UWT members only.

Species inc. Hairy Dragonfly.

ULSTER WILDLIFE TRUST

BROOKEND NNR
Lough Neagh
near Cookstown
OS Map 14. H 948 727.

Fen, pools, damp grassland, carr.

From the B161 Coalisland to Ballyronan road, turn east at H 928 743 into Brookend Road (south of The Diamond and Ardboe). Continue to the end and park carefully on the roadside verge. On foot, cross the stile into the marshy area and bear left. There are no facilities at this site.

Species inc. Ruddy Darter.

NORTHERN IRELAND FOREST SERVICE

DRAGONFLY FAMILIES

GLOSSARY OF DRAGONFLY TERMINOLOGY

Abdomen The third, segmented, tail-like part of the body which consists of ten segments and contains the digestive and reproductive organs.

Anal appendages Often referred to as 'claspers', these are the appendages at the tip of the abdomen. They comprise two superior (outer) and one (true dragonflies) or two (damselflies) inferior (inner) appendage(s). Males use these to clasp the female's prothorax (damselflies) or the back of the head (true dragonflies) when in tandem and when mating.

Antehumeral stripes The stripes along the antehumeral section (upper surface) of the thorax. Referred to as shoulder stripes throughout the book.

Antennae The pair of sensory appendages (feelers) on top of the head.

Cell A section of wing membrane enclosed by veins.

Claspers Popular term for the anal appendages (see above).

Clypeus The lower (main) part of the face of a dragonfly.

Costa The main vein running along the front (leading) edge of each wing.

Exuvia (pl. exuviae) The cast-off outer skin of a dragonfly larva which remains after emergence.

Face The front of the head, consisting of the frons, clypeus and labrum.

Family A basic unit of taxonomic classification comprising a group of species considered to be closely related on account of shared characters.

Frons The uppermost part of the facial area of the head (lying between the vertex and the clypeus).

Genus A basic unit of taxonomic classification comprising a group of closely related species. Each species' genus is identified by the generic (first) name of the scientific name, e.g. *Sympetrum* is the genus of Common Darter *Sympetrum striolatum* and other related darters.

Humeral stripes Diagonal stripes on the sides of the thorax.

Immature The stage in a dragonfly's life cycle between emergence and sexual maturity.

Instar The stage of development of a dragonfly larva between two moults. Depending on the species, a dragonfly larva will pass through 6–15 instars.

In tandem Term used to describe a pair of dragonflies when the male's anal appendages are attached to the back of the female's head, during or after mating.

Invertebrate Any animal without a backbone.

Jizz The immediate, characteristic impression (feel) given by an animal.

Larva (pl. larvae) Also called nymph. The middle stage of the dragonfly life cycle, between egg and adult, which is wholly aquatic in British species.

Metamorphosis In dragonflies, the transition of the larva to the adult form.

Migration The long-distance movements made by large numbers of individuals in approximately the same direction at approximately the same time each year. In dragonflies there is not normally a return movement of individuals, migration serving as a means of dispersal to new sites.

Node The 'wrist' or notch midway along the leading edge of the wing.

Ovipositing Egg-laying.

Ovipositor A blade-like structure, lying beneath abdominal segments 8–10 in some female dragonflies, used to insert eggs into plant tissue.

Pronotum The plate covering the prothorax, the shape of the rear edge is diagnostic in some species of damselfly.

Prothorax The front section of the thorax carrying the first pair of legs.

Pruinescence A bluish powder that forms on the surface of various parts of the body in some species as they mature. Species with an obvious pruinescence include Emerald Damselfly and Scarce Chaser. This powder wears off with age.

Pterostigma The small coloured, four-sided cell along the leading edge near tip of each wing.

Range The total geographic area within which a species or subspecies occurs; distribution need not be continuous.

Segment One of the ring sections that make up the body of a dragonfly. The abdomen is made up of 10 separate segments.

Species (sp) The basic unit of classification used to describe a group of individuals which are able to breed and produce fertile offspring. Most species are visually or structurally distinguishable from other species. The species, or specific, name is the second part of the scientific name, e.g. *striolatum* is the species (specific) name of Common Darter *Sympetrum striolatum*.

Spiracles The external openings of the breathing tubes or trachea. In adult dragonflies they occur in a line along each side of the body.

Teneral A newly emerged adult dragonfly or damselfly that is not sexually mature and has not yet attained the full coloration of the mature adult insect. The teneral period is spent away from water (see immature).

Thorax The middle or second section of a dragonfly's body between the head and the abdomen.

Vein The semi-rigid tubes supporting the wing membrane.

Venation The arrangement of veins in a dragonfly's wing.

Vulvar scale The sometimes prominent structure on the underside of segment 8 of the abdomen of females of certain species which eggs are released onto the surface of the water.

GLOSSARY OF BIOLOGICAL AND OTHER TERMS

Bog An area of acid, wet, spongy ground composed largely of decayed or decaying vegetation, which eventually turns into peat.

Blanket bog An extensive area of bog formed across upland plateaux, fed directly by rain and not springs.

Calcareous Of or containing calcium carbonate or chalk.

Carr Shrub or woodland, usually of alder and/or willow, growing in waterlogged conditions.

Coniferous The term given to trees that typically bear needle-like leaves and cones, and that normally retain green leaves throughout the year.

Deciduous The term given to trees which lose their leaves in autumn as a protection against winter conditions.

Dyke A ditch or watercourse, or a bank made of earth beside a ditch.

Fen Low-lying, flat waterlogged land with a peat soil. The soil pH is generally alkaline.

Habitat The natural environment of an animal or plant, comprising the whole complex of vegetation, soil and climatic factors to which it is adapted.

Heathland An area of poor acid soil, usually sandy or gravelly, at low altitudes and dominated by small shrubs such as heather.

LNR Local Nature Reserve – LNRs are declared by a local authority.

Marsh Low-lying, waterlogged ground, of silt or clay, but not of peat.

Mere A shallow lake or pond.

Mire A general term for a wetland area, often applied to peaty areas.

Moorland An upland area of open, unenclosed ground, with acid, peaty soil, typically dominated by heather or by coarse grasses and sedges.

Moss The northern name for a bog.

NNR National Nature Reserve – NNR status is given to Britain's most important and threatened areas of wildlife habitat. These nature reserves are managed for protection and research.

RSPB Royal Society for the Protection of Birds.

Water meadow A meadow periodically flooded by a river or stream.

FURTHER READING

The following publications have been used by the authors in preparing this guide and will be of interest to readers.

Identification, behaviour and distribution
Askew, R. R. 1988. *The Dragonflies of Europe*. Harley Books, Colchester.
Atropos (journal) – various issues (see useful addresses).
British Dragonfly Society *Dig a Pond for Dragonflies*.
British Dragonfly Society *Dragonfly News* – BDS newsletter (and earlier newsletters) (see useful addresses).
British Wildlife (journal) – various issues (see useful addresses).
Brooks, S (ed.). 1997 (revised 1999). *Field Guide to the Dragonflies and Damselflies of Great Britain and Ireland*. British Wildlife Publishing, Gillingham, Dorset.
Darter (newsletter of the Dragonfly Recording Network) – various issues (see useful addresses).
Dijkstra, K-D. B. & Lewington, R. 2006. *Field Guide to the Dragonflies of Britain and Europe*. British Wildlife Publishing, Gillingham, Dorset.
Gibbons, B. 1986 (reprinted 1994). *Hamlyn Guide – Dragonflies and Damselflies of Britain and northern Europe*. Hamlyn, London.
Hammond, C. O. 1983 (2nd Edition – revised by R. Merritt). *The Dragonflies of Great Britain and Ireland*. Harley, Colchester.
Hywel-Davies, J. & Thom, V. 1986. *The Macmillan Guide to Britain's Nature Reserves in State Forests*. HMSO, London.
Jackson, N. & Eversham, B. (eds). 1989. *Nature Atlas of Great Britain, Ireland and the Channel Islands*. Pan/Ordnance Survey. Duncan Petersen Publishing Ltd, London.
Journal of the British Dragonfly Society (journal) – various issues (see useful addresses).
Kemp, R. 1981. *Dragonflies*. Worcestershire Nature Conservation Trust Ltd. Information Leaflet no. 3.
McGeeney, A. 1986. *A Complete Guide to British Dragonflies*. Jonathan Cape, London.
Merritt, R., Moore, N. W. & Eversham, B. C. 1996. *Atlas of the Dragonflies of Britain and Ireland*. HMSO, London.
Miller, P. L. 1995. *Dragonflies*. Richmond, Slough.
Powell, D. 1999. *A Guide to the Dragonflies of Great Britain and Ireland*. Arlequin Press, Chelmsford.
Smallshire, D. & Swash, A. 2004. *Britain's Dragonflies*. WildGuides, Maidenhead.

Wildlife Trust handbooks and guides
The Wildlife Trusts. *Top Wildlife Spots: The Best 200 Places to See Wildlife in the UK*. HarperCollins, London. 1999.
The Wildlife Trust for Bedfordshire and Cambridgeshire. *Your Guide to Nature Reserves in Bedfordshire and Cambridgeshire*. 1993.
Berkshire, Buckinghamshire and Oxfordshire Wildlife Trust. *Where to go for Wildlife in Berkshire, Buckinghamshire and Oxfordshire*. Fourth Edition. 1996.
Cumbria Wildlife Trusts. *Reserves Handbook*. 1993.
Glamorgan Wildlife Trust. *Where to Go for Wildlife in Glamorgan*. 1991.
Hampshire and Isle of Wight Wildlife Trust. *Wildlife & Wild Places: A Guide to Nature Reserves Managed by Hampshire and Isle of Wight Wildlife Trust*. 1996.
Herefordshire Nature Trust. *Guide to Nature Reserves*. Fourth Edition. 1994.
Lancashire Wildlife Trust. *Nature Reserves Guide*. 1991.

Leicestershire and Rutland Wildlife Trust. *Nature Reserves in Leicestershire and Rutland: A Guide*. 1994.

Lincolnshire Trust for Nature Conservation. *Your Guide to the Nature Reserves in Lincolnshire*. Fourth Edition. 1997.

The National Trust. *Countryside Handbook*. 1993.

The National Trust. *Coast & Countryside Handbook*. 2000.

Norfolk Naturalists' Trust. *Guide to the Nature Reserves of Norfolk*. 1988.

Northumberland Wildlife Trust. *Nature Reserves Guide*.

Staffordshire Wildlife Trust. *Nature Reserves Guide*. 2000.

Suffolk Wildlife Trust. *Watching Wildlife in Suffolk: A New Guide to the County's Nature Reserves*. 1994.

Surrey Wildlife Trust. *Nature Reserves*.

Sussex Wildlife Trust. *The Wild Places of Sussex*. Second Edition. 1993.

Worcestershire Wildlife Trust. *Wildlife Reserves in Worcestershire*. 1997.

In addition to the above, we consulted many leaflets produced by site managers and owners. See the *Sites Gazetteer* for postal and website addresses (where available).

Other regional guides, books and papers

Cornwall Dragonfly Group Newsletters compiled by S. Jones.

Gabb, R. & Kitching, D. 1992. *The Dragonflies and Damselflies of Cheshire*. National Museums and Galleries on Merseyside, England.

Hammond, N (ed.). 1994. *RSPB Nature Reserves Guide* (2nd Edition). RSPB, Sandy.

Hill, P. & Twist, C. 1998. *Butterflies & Dragonflies: A Site Guide* (2nd Edition). Arlequin Press, England.

Hywel-Davies, J. & Thom, V. 1984. *Guide to Britain's Nature Reserves*. Macmillan London Limited.

Jenkinson, A. 1997. *Wild Places in Mid Wales: A Guide to Protected Wildlife Sites*. Festival of the Countryside, Newtown.

Milford, P. J. & Irwin, A. G. 1990. The Dragonflies of Norfolk. *Trans. Norfolk Norwich Nat. Soc.* 28(5), 329–408.

Preddy, S. 1998. *Identifying Southern, Migrant and Common Hawkers in the Bristol Region*. Unpublished.

USEFUL ADDRESSES

The addresses of county and regional Wildlife Trusts, national organisations (such as RSPB) and nature reserve managers/owners can be found within the *Site Gazetteer* section of this book.

Atropos
A journal for active dragonfly, butterfly and moth enthusiasts.
36 Tinker Lane, Meltham, Holmfirth, West Yorkshire HD9 4EX
EMAIL atropos@atroposed.freeserve.co.uk
WEB www.atroposuk.co.uk

Biological Records Centre
The BRC provides the national focus in the UK for the recording of terrestrial and freshwater species (other than birds), working with the voluntary recording community throughout Britain and Ireland.
WEB www.brc.ac.uk

British Wildlife
A journal for those interested in all aspects of British wildlife.
The Old Dairy, Milton on Stour, Gillingham, Dorset SP8 5PX
TEL 01747 835511
EMAIL enquiries@britishwildlife.com
WEB www.britishwildlife.com

British Dragonfly Society
Members receive a newsletter and journal.
EMAIL bdssecretary@dragonflysoc.org.uk
WEB www.dragonflysoc.org.uk

Dragonfly Ireland
c/o Zoology Department, Ulster Museum, Botanic Gardens, Belfast BT9 5AB, Northern Ireland
WEB www.habitas.org.uk/dragonflyireland/

The Dragonfly Project
Formerly the National Dragonfly Museum
TEL 01733 204286   EMAIL: queries@dragonflyproject.org.uk
WEB www.dragonflyproject.org.uk

The Dragonfly Recording Network
Members receive the newsletter 'Darter'.
EMAIL SteveCham1@aol.com
WEB www.dragonflysoc.org.uk/frameset.htm?recording&recording

National Biodiversity Network
For species distribution maps and UK wildlife data
WEB www.searchnbn.net

INDEX BY SCIENTIFIC NAME

Scientific names appear only on the main species account pages, but here we provide page references for all species mentioned throughout the book.

Page numbers in **bold** refer to species accounts, those in *italics* refer to main site guide section.

INDEX BY ENGLISH NAME

Page numbers in **bold** refer to species accounts, those in *italics* refer to main site guide section.